The UK Economy
A Manual of Applied Economics

CONTRIBUTORS

Chapter 1

    M.C.Kennedy *B.Sc. (Econ.) (London)*
    Lecturer in Economics, University of Manchester

Chapter 2

    RichardHarrington *B.Sc. (Econ.) (Wales), M.Sc. (Econ.) (London)*
    Lecturer in Economics, University of Manchester

Chapter 3

    J.S.Metcalfe *B.A. (Econ.), M.Sc. (Manchester)*
    Professor of Economics, University of Manchester
             and
    C.J.Green *B.A. (Oxford), Ph.D. (Yale)*
    Sir Julian Hodge Professor of Banking and Finance,
    University of Wales Institute of Science and Technology

Chapter 4

    John R.Cable *B.A. (Nottingham), M.A. (Econ.) (Manchester)*
    Senior Lecturer in Economics, University of Warwick

Chapter 5

    David Metcalf *M.A. (Econ.) (Manchester), Ph.D. (London)*
    Professor of Economics, London School of Economics
             and
    Ray Richardson *B.Sc. (Econ.) (London), Ph.D. (Columbia)*
    Reader in Industrial Relations, London School of Economics

Prest and Coppock's
The UK Economy
A Manual of Applied Economics

Eleventh Edition

Edited by

M.J.Artis, B.A.
Professor of Economics, University of Manchester

Weidenfeld and Nicolson
London

First published 1966
Second impression 1967
Third impression 1968
Second edition 1968
Second impression 1969
Third edition 1970
Second impression 1971
Fourth edition 1972
Fifth edition 1974
Sixth edition 1976
Seventh edition 1978
Eighth edition 1980
Ninth edition 1982
Tenth edition 1984
Eleventh edition 1986

First published in Great Britain by
George Weidenfeld and Nicolson Limited
91 Clapham High St London SW4 7TA

ISBN 0 297 78995 3   cased
ISBN 0 297 78996 1   paperback

Printed in Great Britain at The Bath Press, Avon

Contents

TABLES

Chapter 1

Chapter 2

Chapter 3

Chapter 4

Chapter 5

FIGURES

Chapter 1

Chapter 3

Chapter 4

STATISTICAL APPENDIX

ABBREVIATIONS

(1) Economic Terms

BOF	Balance for Official Financing
CAP	Common Agricultural Policy
CET	Common External Tariff
c.i.f.	Cost including Insurance and Freight
DCE	Domestic Credit Expansion
ECU	European Currency Unit
FIS	Family Income Supplement
f.o.b.	Free on Board
GDP	Gross Domestic Product
GNP	Gross National Product
MCA	Monetary Compensation Amounts
MLH	Minimum List Headings
NSA	Non Sterling Area
NS	North Sea
OSA	Overseas Sterling Area
PAYE	Pay as you Earn
PDI	Personal Disposable Income
PRT	Petroleum Revenue Tax
PSBR	Public Sector Borrowing Requirement
R & D	Research and Development
RPM	Resale Price Maintenance
SDRs	Special Drawing Rights
SIC	Standard Industrial Classification
SITC	Standard Industrial Trade Classification
TFE	Total Final Expenditure at Market Prices
VAT	Value Added Tax

(2) Organizations, etc.

BTG	British Technology Group
CBI	Confederation of British Industry
CSO	Central Statistical Office (UK)
DE	Department of Employment
DTI	Department of Trade and Industry
ECE	Economic Commission for Europe
ECSC	European Coal and Steel Community
EEA	Exchange Equalization Account
EEC	European Economic Community
EFTA	European Free Trade Area
FAO	Food and Agriculture Organization
GATT	General Agreement on Tariffs and Trade

GES	Government Economic Service
IFC	International Finance Corporation
IMF	International Monetary Fund
MC	Monopolies and Mergers Commission
NEB	National Enterprise Board
NEDC(O)	National Economic Development Council (Office)
NIESR	National Institute of Economic and Social Research
NRDC	National Research and Development Corporation
OECD	Organization for Economic Cooperation and Development
OPCS	Office of Population Census and Surveys
OPEC	Organization of Petroleum Exporting Countries
TUC	Trades Union Congress
UN	United Nations
UNCTAD	United Nations Commission for Trade and Development
WB	World Bank

(3) Journals, etc.

AAS	*Annual Abstract of Statistics* (HMSO)
AER	*American Economic Review*
BB	*British Business* (formerly *Trade and Industry*)
BEQB	*Bank of England Quarterly Bulletin*
BJIR	*British Journal of Industrial Relations*
DEG	*Department of Employment Gazette* (HMSO)
EC	*Economica*
EJ	*Economic Journal*
ET(AS)	*Economic Trends (Annual Supplement)* (HMSO)
FES	*Family Expenditure Survey* (HMSO)
FS	*Financial Statistics* (HMSO)
FSBR	*Financial Statement and Budget Report* (HMSO)
GHS	*General Household Survey*
IFS	*International Financial Statistics*
JIE	*Journal of Industrial Economics*
JPE	*Journal of Political Economy*
JRSS	*Journal of Royal Statistical Society*
LBR	*Lloyds Bank Review*
LCES	*London and Cambridge Economic Service*
MBR	*Midland Bank Review*
MDS	*Monthly Digest of Statistics* (HMSO)
MS	*The Manchester School of Economic and Social Studies*
NIE	*National Income and Expenditure* (HMSO)
NIER	*National Institute Economic Review*
NWBQR	*National Westminster Bank Quarterly Review*
OEP	*Oxford Economic Papers*
QJE	*Quarterly Journal of Economics*
RES	*Review of Economic Studies*

REST	*Review of Economics and Statistics*
SJPE	*Scottish Journal of Political Economy*
ST	*Social Trends* (HMSO)
TBR	*Three Banks Review*
TER	*Treasury Economic Report* (HMSO)
TI	*Trade and Industry* (HMSO)

Foreword to the Eleventh Edition

Since the last edition of this book was published we learnt the sad news of the death of one of its editors, Professor Alan Prest; and, whilst the other editor, Professor Dennis Coppock, still leads an active life he felt the time had come to hand on the editorial torch to a newcomer. I have been flattered to accept the challenge of continuing the production of such an influential and well-known book. Reflecting the stamp of their editorial entrepreneurship, the volume is to continue to be called *Prest and Coppock's UK Economy*, and its objectives remain the same. These were summarized with great clarity in the Foreword to the first edition of the book, as follows:

> The central idea behind this book is to give an account of the main features and problems of the UK economy today. The hope is that it will fulfil two functions simultaneously, in that it will be as up to date as possible and yet will not be simply a bare catalogue of facts and figures. There are many sources of information, official and otherwise, about the structure and progress of the UK economy. There are also many authors to whom one can turn for subtle analyses of the problems before us. Our effort here is based on the belief that there is both room and need for an attempt to combine the functions of chronicler and analyst in the confines of a single book.
>
> The contributors to these pages subscribe rather firmly to the belief that economists should practise, as well as preach, the principle of the division of labour. The complexity of a modern economy is such that, whether one likes it or not, it is no longer possible for any individual to be authoritative on all its aspects; so it is inevitable that the burden of producing work of this kind should be spread among a number of people, each a specialist in his or her particular field. Such a division carries with it obvious dangers of overlap and inconsistency. It is hoped that some of the worst pitfalls of this kind have been avoided and there is reasonable unity of purpose, treatment and layout. At the same time, it is wholly undesirable to impose a monolithic structure and it is just as apparent to the authors that there are differences in outlook and emphasis among them as it will be to the reader.
>
> The general intention was to base exposition on the assumption that the reader would have some elementary knowledge of economics – say a student in the latter part of a typical first-year course in economics in a British university. At the same time, it is hoped that most of the text will be intelligible to those without this degree of expertise. We may not have succeeded in this; if not, we shall try to do better in the future.

Chapter 1, 'The Economy as a Whole', is concerned with questions of applied macroeconomics: fluctuations in output and expenditure, the

determinants and management of demand, inflation and economic growth. The chapter ends with a section on economic prospects and policies to 1990. Chapter 2, 'Money and Finance: Public Expenditure and Taxation', begins with a description of the interrelationship between fiscal and monetary policy and the background to each, which is provided on the one hand by the institutions of the financial system and on the other by the structure of the government's accounts. It contains sections dealing with the pace of financial innovation and the extent to which government policies towards public expenditure control have been successful. Chapter 3, 'Foreign Trade and the Balance of Payments', deals with the importance of foreign trade and payments to the UK economy and discusses the behaviour of, and policy towards, the exchange rate, including the prospect of entry into the European Monetary System. It then looks at current problems and policies in this field, and ends with a discussion of recent developments in the field of international economic policy co-ordination and of the world debt problem. Chapter 4, 'Industry', starts with a summary of UK industrial performance between 1960 and 1980 and then looks briefly at agriculture. Nationalized industries, privatization, competition policy and regional policy are examined at length. The final section is on industrial policy. Due regard is paid to the implications of EEC membership throughout. The last chapter, 'Labour', analyses employment and unemployment among the UK workforce, and then discusses problems of pay and income distribution. The final section is concerned with trade unions, industrial relations, wage inflation and related policy issues.

Certain themes, inevitably, crop up in more than one chapter; North Sea oil for example, is treated as it influences the balance of payments and the exchange rate in Chapter 3, as it influences the structure of production in Chapter 4, and as it affects the fiscal balance in Chapter 2. The EEC similarly makes an appearance in more than one chapter, as does the problem of inflation. The aim has been to avoid straightforward duplication of treatment of the same theme in different chapters, allowing instead for complementary treatment of different aspects of the same theme and, where appropriate, for alternative interpretations of the same theme to make their appearance (for example, readers may detect a more Keynesian treatment of policy issues in Chapter 1 than appears in some other

Each chapter is accompanied b

1

The economy as a whole

M.C.Kennedy

I INTRODUCTION
I.1 Methodological Approach

This chapter is an introduction to applied macroeconomics. It begins with a brief description of the national income accounts, and goes on to discuss the multiplier, the determination of national output and prices, and the policy problems of restoring full employment without inflation. It cannot claim to give all the answers to the questions raised, but aims to provide the reader with a basis for further and deeper study.

In principle there is no essential difference between applied economics and economic theory. The object of applied economics is to explain the way in which economic units work. It is just as much concerned with questions of causation (such as what determines total consumption or the level of prices) as the theory which is found in most elementary textbooks. The difference between theoretical and applied economics is largely one of emphasis, with theory tending to stress logical connections between assumptions and conclusions, and applied economics the connections between theories and evidence. Applied economics does not seek description for its own sake, but it needs facts for the light they shed on the applicability of economic theory.

At one time it used to be thought that scientific theories were derived from factual information by a method of inference known as *induction*.[1] Thus it was supposed that general laws about nature could be deduced from knowledge of a limited number of facts. From the logical point of view, however, induction is invalid. If ten people have been observed to save one-tenth of their income, it does not follow that the next person will do likewise. The conclusion may be true or false, but it does not rest validly on the assumptions. Inductive conclusions of this kind simply have the status of conjectures and require further empirical investigation.

More recently it has come to be accepted that scientific method is not inductive but *hypothetico-deductive*. A hypothesis may be proposed to explain a certain class of events. It will generally be of the conditional form

---

1 For an introduction to the problems of scientific method, the reader is referred to P.B.Medawar, *Induction and Intuition in Scientific Thought* (Methuen, 1969), and K.R. Popper, *The Logic of Scientific Discovery* (Hutchinson, 1959) and *Conjectures and Refutations* (Routledge and Kegan Paul, 1963). For a treatment of methodological problems in economics, see I.M.T.Stewart, *Reasoning and Method of Economics* (McGraw-Hill), 1979), M.Blaug, *The Methodology of Economics* (Cambridge University Press, 1980), and D.M.McCloskey, 'The Rhetoric of Economics', *Journal of Economic Literature*, June 1983.

'if p then q', from which the inference is that any particular instance of p must be accompanied by an instance of q. Thus the hypothesis is tested by all observations of p, and corroborated whenever p and q are observed together. It is falsified if p occurs in the absence of q.

It will be clear that this concept of scientific inference places the role of factual information in a different light from the inductive approach. Facts, instead of being the foundation on which to build economic or scientific theories, become the basis for testing them. If a theory is able to survive a determined but unsuccessful attempt to refute it by factual evidence, it is regarded as well tested. But the discovery of evidence which is inconsistent with the theory will stimulate its modification or the development of a new theory altogether. One of the purposes of studying applied economics is to acquaint the theoretically equipped economist with the limitations of the theory he has studied. Applied economics is not an attempt to bolster up existing theory or, as its name might seem to imply, to demonstrate dogmatically that all the factual evidence is a neat application of textbook theory. Its aim is to understand the workings of the economy, and this means that it will sometimes expose the shortcomings of existing theory and go on to suggest improvements.

The discovery that a theory is falsified by factual observations need not mean that it must be rejected out of hand or relegated to total oblivion. Economists, as well as natural scientists, frequently have to work with theories that are inadequate in one way or another. Theories that explain part but not all of the evidence are often retained until some new theory is found which fits a wider range of evidence. Frequently the theory will turn out to have been incomplete rather than just wrong, and when modified by the addition of some new variable (or more careful specification of the *ceteris paribus* clause), the theory may regain its status. The reader who notices inconsistencies between theory and facts need not take the line that the theory is total nonsense, for the theory may still hold enough grains of truth to become the basis for something better.

It is often argued that our ability to test economic theories by reference to evidence is sufficient to liberate economics from value judgements, i.e. to turn it into a *positive* subject. This position has more than an element of truth in it: when there is clear evidence against a theory, it stands a fair chance of being dropped even by its most bigoted adherents. Nevertheless, it would be wrong to forget that a great deal of what passes for evidence in economics is infirm in character (e.g. the statistics of gross domestic product or personal saving), so that it is often possible for evidence to be viewed more sceptically by some than by others.

The discussion of economic policy which also figures in this chapter is partly normative in scope, and partly positive. The normative content of policy discussion involves the evaluation of goals and priorities. But the means for attaining such goals derive from the positive hypotheses of economics. They involve questions of cause and effect, to which the answers are hypothetical and testable by evidence. In making recommendations for policy, howewer, the economist treads on thin ice. This is partly because his positive knowledge is not inevitably correct, but also because it is seldom possible to foresee and properly appraise all the side-effects of his recommendations, some of which have implications for other policy goals. When economists differ in their advice on policy questions it is not always clear how much the difference is due on the the one hand to diagnostic disagreements, or, on the other, to differences in value judgements. Indeed it is seldom possible for an economic adviser to reveal all the normative preferences which lie behind a policy recommendation. Policy judgements have to be scrutinized carefully for hidden normative assumptions, and the reader of this chapter must be on his guard against the author's personal value judgements.

I.2   Gross Domestic Product

Most of the topics discussed in this chapter make some use of the national accounts statistics. A complete explanation of what these are and of how they are put together is available elsewhere.[1] It will be useful, however, in the next few pages to introduce the reader to the main national accounting categories in so far as they affect this chapter.

Gross domestic product (GDP) represents the output of the whole economy, i.e. the production of all the the enterprises resident in the UK. In principle, it can be assembled from three separate sets of data – from output, from income and from expenditure. The three totals should, in principle, be equal – a point which may seem surprising when it is recalled that spending and output are seldom equal for an individual firm. But the convention in national accounting is to count all *unsold output* as part of investment in stocks, and to regard this both as expenditure and as income (profits) in kind. Thus the three estimates are made to equal each other by the device of defining expenditure and income differently from their everyday meanings.

Although there are three possible ways of estimating GDP, the output method is too slow and cumbersome to be used at frequent intervals. This leaves only two estimates of current-price GDP – the expenditure- and income-based estimates – both of which are shown in table 1.1.

The expenditure-based method classifies expenditure by four types of spending unit: persons, public authorities, firms and foreign residents.[2] Purchases by persons are described as consumers' expenditure, or, more

---

1   See, for example, W.Beckerman, *An Introduction to National Income Analysis* (3rd edition, Weidenfeld and Nicolson, 1980); S.Hays, *National Income and Expenditure in Britain and the OECD Countries* (Heinemann, 1971); R. and G.Stone, *National Income and Expenditure* (9th edition, Bowes and Bowes, 1972); H.C.Edey and others, *National Income and Social Accounting* (3rd edition, Hutchinson, 1967); or the CSO publication, *United Kingdom National Accounts, Sources and Methods* (3rd edition, HMSO, 1985).

2   The distinctions between types of spending units are not always clear-cut, e.g. expenditure by self-employed persons is partly consumers' expenditure and partly investment.

loosely, as consumption. The latter description, however, may be slightly misleading when applied to expenditure on durable goods such as motorcars and refrigerators, the services of which are consumed over several years and not solely in the year in which they are purchased. One form of personal expenditure which is not classed as such is the purchase of new houses. These are deemed to have been sold intitially to 'firms' and included under the broad heading of domestic capital formation or gross fixed investment. Fixed investment represents purchases by firms of physical assets which are additions or replacements of the nation's capital stock. The preface 'gross' warns us that a year's gross investment does not measure the change in the size of the capital stock during the year because it does not allow for the erosion of the capital stock due to scrapping and wear and tear. The concept of gross capital formation is also carried through into the definition of domestic product itself, indicating that the value of *gross* domestic product makes no allowance for capital consumption. The other category of investment is investment in stocks or, as the CSO puts it, the value of the physical increase in stocks. This makes no distinction between voluntary and involuntary stock changes.

The sum of exports, consumers' expenditure, government final consumption and gross investment is known as total final expenditure at market prices, or TFE for short. Each of the four components contains two elements which must be deducted before arriving at GDP at factor cost. The first is the import content of expenditure which must, of course, be classified as foreign rather than domestically produced output. The simplest way of removing imports is to take the global import total as given by the balance-of-payments accounts and subtract it from TFE, and this is the usual method. Estimates do exist, however, for the import content of the separate components of final expenditure in the input-output tables, but these are drawn up much less frequently than the national accounts.

The second element of total final expenditure which must be deducted to obtain the factor-cost value of GDP is the indirect tax content (net of subsidies) of the various expenditures. This is present for the simple reason that the most readily available valuation of any commodity is the price at which it sells in the market. This price, however, will overstate the factor incomes earned from producing the commodity if it contains an element of indirect tax; and it will understate factor income if the price is subsidized. The deduction of indirect taxes (less subsidies) is known as the *factor cost adjustment*, and is most conveniently made globally since it can be found from the government's records of tax proceeds and subsidy payments. Estimates of its incidence on the individual components of TFE are available annually in the National Income *Blue Book*.[1]

The income-based estimate arrives at GDP by summing up the incomes of all the residents of the UK earned in the production of goods and services in the UK during a stated period. It divides into income from employment,

---

1 *NIE*, 1985, Table 1.2.

TABLE 1.1
GDP at Current Prices, UK, 1984

FROM EXPENDITURE

	£bn	% of TFE[1]
Consumers' expenditure	194.7	47
General government final consumption	69.7	17
Gross domestic fixed investment	55.3	13
Investment in stocks	−0.2	0
Exports of goods and services	91.7	22
Total final expenditure at market prices	411.2	100
less Imports of goods and services	−91.9	
less Adjustment to factor cost	−44.8	
Gross domestic product at factor cost	274.6	

FROM INCOME

	£bn	% of domestic income[1]
Income from employment	180.3	63
Income from self-employment	26.9	9
Income from rent	18.9	7
Gross trading profits of companies	47.9	17
Gross trading surpluses of public corporations and other public enterprises	8.5	3
Imputed charge for consumption of non-trading capital	2.5	1
Total domestic income	285.1	100
less Stock appreciation	−5.2	
Gross domestic product at factor cost (from income)	279.9	
Residual error	−5.3	
Gross domestic product at factor cost (from expenditure)	274.6	

BY INDUSTRY (FROM INCOME)

	£bn	% of total[1]
Agriculture, forestry and fishing	6.0	2
Energy and water supply	31.5	11
Manufacturing	68.4	23
Construction	15.8	5
Distribution, hotels and catering, repairs	37.0	13
Banking, finance, insurance, business services and leasing	37.0	13
Education and health	26.7	9
Other services	73.6	25
Total (after providing for stock appreciation)	295.0	100
Adjustment for financial services[2]	−15.1	
Gross domestic product		
Gross domestic product at factor cost (from income)	279.9	

Source: NIE, 1985, tables 1.2, 1.3 and 1.13.
1 Details do not add to total because of rounding.
2 Deduction of net receipts of interest by financial companies.

income from self-employment and profit, and income from rent. These are factor incomes earned in the process of production and are to be distinguished from *transfer incomes*, such as pensions and sickness benefits, which are not earned from production and which, therefore, are excluded from the total. The breakdown of factor incomes for 1984 is illustrated in table 1.1.

The income breakdown of GDP contains two items which may need further explanation. The first is the imputed charge for consumption of non-trading capital, which is imputed rent from government property and private non-profit making bodies. This should not be confused with capital consumption, which is the wear and tear of capital equipment. The other item is the adjustment for stock appreciation which appears here because changes in the book value of stocks have been accredited to profits. The problem of adjustment for stock appreciation arises because the change in the book value between the beginning and end of the year may be partly due to a price change.

A firm holding stocks of wood, for example, may increase its holding from 100 tons on 1 January to 200 tons on 31 December. If the price of wood was £1.00 per ton at the beginning of the year and £1.10 at the end of the year, the increase in the monetary value of stocks will show up as (£1.10 × 200) − (£1.00 × 100), which equals £120. This figure is inflated by the amount of the price increase and fails, therefore, to give an adequate record of what the Central Statistical Office (CSO) calls 'the value of the physical increase in stocks'. In order to rectify this, the CSO attempts to value the physical change in stocks at the average price level prevailing during the period. If, in the example, the price averaged £1.05 over the period, then the value of the physical increase in stocks would be shown as £1.05 (200–100), which equals £105. The difference of £15 between this and the increase in monetary value is the adjustment for stock appreciation.

GDP by income can be rearranged in terms of the industries in which the incomes were earned. This breakdown is available annually and gives an up-to-date picture of the industrial composition of total output, showing, for example, that manufacturing production is less than one-quarter of the value of GDP. The industry breakdown is shown in table 1.1, but it is not an independent measure of GDP.

The expenditure and income estimates are derived from different and largely independent sets of data. They never add up to exactly the same total, and the difference between them is known as the *residual error*. The published residual error (which was quite large in 1984) is actually less than the real difference because of an allowance the CSO makes for the systematic under-reporting of incomes to the Inland Revenue.[1]

An output-based estimate of GDP can, in principle, be compiled by adding up the *net output* or *value added* of all the firms and productive units

1   K.M. Macafee, 'A glimpse of the hidden economy in the national accounts', *ET*, February 1980.

in the economy. To obtain such a total it would be necessary to find the *gross output* of each firm in the economy and to subtract from it the value of *intermediate input*, i.e. goods and services purchased from other firms. In practice this herculean task cannot be accomplished in the time-span of a single year. A Census of Production is, however, in a state of continuous collection, and data from the census are used to establish the weights in the volume indices which are used to measure constant-price GDP.

Gross domestic product is the most widely used of several aggregates, the others being GNP and National Income. The relationships between the various aggregates in 1984 were:

		£bn (current prices)
	GNP at market prices	322.7
less	Net property income from abroad	−3.3
equals	GDP at market prices	319.4
less	Factor-cost adjustment	−44.8
equals	GDP at factor cost (from expenditure)	274.6
plus	Net property income from abroad	+3.3
equals	GNP at factor cost	277.9
less	Capital consumption	−33.4
equals	National income	239.5

GNP, like GDP, may be valued at market prices or factor cost. It differs from GDP by including net interest, profits and dividends earned by UK residents from productive enterprises owned overseas. The other concept, National Income, differs from GNP by the amount of capital consumption, this being the CSO's estimate of depreciation. It is also the figure which must be subtracted from gross investment to find net investment. GDP and the gross concept of investment are in much more frequent use than net income and net investment because they relate directly to employment. When a machine is being produced, it makes no difference to the number of workers employed whether it is to replace one already in use or whether it adds to the capital stock.

I.3   Gross Domestic Product at Constant Prices

If we wish to compare the *volume* of goods produced in different periods, we must use the estimates of GDP at constant prices, the expenditure side of which is presented in the Statistical Appendix, table A-1. These constant-price or real estimates show the value of GDP expenditure-based for each year in terms of the prices ruling in 1980. Similar estimates are available for the output-based total, together with its main industrial components. The components of both these GDP estimates are derived almost entirely from movements in volume, the various quantities for each year being added together by means of the value weights obtaining for 1980. With the income figures, however, the only way of obtaining a constant-price estimate is to take the value of GDP by income and deflate it by the implied price index (or 'deflator') for GDP. This index is simply the result of dividing GDP at current prices by GDP at constant prices (both on the expenditure basis). This means that for GDP as a whole there are, altogether, three independent estimates of the constant-price total.

There are often sizeable discrepancies between the three estimates of GDP at constant prices. In 1984, for example, GDP in constant prices was put by the income estimate at 107.1% of the 1980 level, whereas the expenditure and output estimates made it 105.1 and 106.2 respectively. Since 1970 the largest spread between the three measures was 3.3% of GDP (in 1972) and the average difference was 1.5%. These discrepancies in the level of GDP also mean that the annual rate of change is not known unambiguously. The decline in GDP from 1979 to 1981, for example, was put at 3.4% by the expenditure-based estimate but at 4.6% by the output estimate. An inspection of the annual changes in GDP since 1970 shows that, on average, the spread between the highest and lowest estimates was 1.3%; in one year it was 2.4%; and in only five years was it less than 1.0%.

Gross domestic product is an important entity in its own right and changes in its real amount are the best estimates available of changes in total UK production. Even so, it must be remembered that it leaves a good deal out of the picture by excluding practically all productive work which is not sold for money. The national income statistics neglect, for example, the activities of the housewife, the do-it-yourself enthusiast and the so-called 'black economy', even though they must add millions of hours to UK production of goods and services. It is also important to recognize that GDP stands for the production of UK residents, not their expenditure. As an expenditure total, it measures the spending of all persons, resident or foreign, on the goods and services produced by the residents of the UK. Thus if national welfare is conceived as spending by UK residents, it is incorrect to represent it by GDP. The total appropriate for this purpose is GDP *plus* imports *minus* exports. This total is referred to as total domestic expenditure, and is equal to the UK's total use of resources, which is the sum of personal consumption, government consumption and gross investment.

II   FLUCTUATIONS IN TOTAL OUTPUT AND EXPENDITURE

II.1   Fluctuations in Output and Employment

The British economy has experienced cyclical fluctuations in output and employment since the time of the industrial revolution. During the nineteenth century these appeared to follow a fairly uniform pattern, with a peak-to-peak duration of seven to ten years and a tendency for 'full employment' (roughly defined) to reappear at each cyclical peak. After the First World War this pattern ceased, and for nearly twenty years there were well over one million unemployed. Unemployment reached nearly 10% of the labour force in the downturn of 1926 and 17% (3.4 million) in 1932.

The period after the Second World War until the early 1970s was one of continuously high employment, with only the mildest fluctuations in GDP, employment and unemployment. The unemployment rate (UK, excluding school-leavers) never exceeded an annual figure of 2.4%, and, during peak periods of activity, was as little as 1 or 1½% of the employed labour force. During this period, the decline in real GDP during cyclical downturns never exceeded 1.0%, and in most recessions GDP simply rose at a slower-than-average rate of increase. This period of high and stable employment was also characterized by a much lower average rate of inflation than has been experienced since 1970.

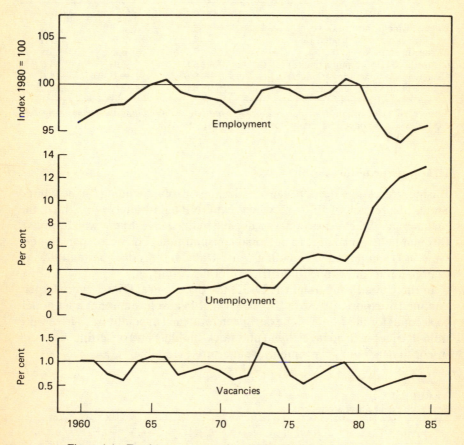

Figure 1.1   Employment, unemployment and vacancies, UK, 1960–85

Since 1970, business recessions have become much more severe. There was a sharp downturn in 1973–5, and by 1977 unemployment reached 5.3% of the labour force. A further downturn in GDP in 1979–81 brought unemployment to 10% by the end of 1981 and over 13% in 1985.

A comparison of the 1979–81 downturn with that of 1929–32 is given in table 1.2, where it can be seen that the declines in employment, manufacturing output and estimated GDP were very similar in the two depressions.

Unemployment was not as high in 1981 as in 1932, but the number rose steadily in the next 5 years, and by early 1986 the unemployment rate was only about 4% less than in 1932. A major difference between the two depressions concerned the behaviour of wages and prices, which were falling in 1929–32 but increasing rapidly in 1979–81. Inflation has posed a dilemma for policy which was not present in the 1930s.

TABLE 1.2
Output and Employment in Three Recessions (percentages)

	1929–32	1973–5	1979–81
Unemployment rate: peak year	8.0	2.7	4.8
trough year	17.0	3.9	9.5
Change in employment	3.7	0.0	−5.5
Change in GDP (output estimate)	−4.8	−3.1	−4.6
Change in manufacturing production	−10.8	−8.1	−14.6
Change in prices per annum	−6.8	+22.0	+16.0

Sources: C.H.Feinstein, *National Income, Expenditure and Output in the United Kingdom, 1855–1965* (Cambridge University Press, 1972); *ET(AS)*, 1986.

II.2   Expenditures in the Cycle

Business recessions occur because of declines in total spending. In the United States' depression of 1929–32, when real GNP fell by almost one-third, the mainspring of the recession was a decline in fixed investment which spread, through falling incomes, to personal consumption. The accompanying decline in US imports led to falling world trade and production, and thus to depression in the export industries of other countries.

In the United Kingdom in 1929–32, the decline in GDP was very largely confined to exports. These fell by 32%, which in absolute amount was enough to account for the whole of the decline in total final expenditure. There were mild declines in fixed investment and stock-building and offsetting increases in consumers' and government expenditure (see table 1.3).

TABLE 1.3
Expenditures in Three Recessions

	Level in 1929	Change 1929–32	Level in 1973	Change 1973–5	Level in 1979	Change 1979–81
	£bn at 1938 prices		£bn at 1980 prices		£bn at 1980 prices	
Consumers' expenditure	3.77	+0.07	127.7	−2.8	137.6	−1.0
Government consumption	0.44	+0.03	43.1	+3.3	48.3	+0.6
Fixed investment	0.46	−0.06	43.4	−1.8	43.9	−6.2
Investment in stocks	0.03	−0.03	5.0	−7.7	2.5	−5.2
Exports of goods and services	0.99	−0.32	49.1	+2.2	63.1	−1.1
TFE	5.69	−0.32	266.7	−6.9	295.3	−12.6

Sources: Feinstein, op. cit.; *ET(AS)*, 1986.

If 1929–32 was an export-led recession, those of 1973–5 and 1979–81 were predominantly stock recessions, with much of the decline in TFE being accounted for by large swings from stock accumulation to stock declines. Exports fell in 1979–81, partly because of the worldwide depression and partly because the exchange rate was allowed to rise: consumption fell in 1973–5 but held up in 1979–81. In both recessions there were sizeable declines in fixed investment, which by 1981 was running at its lowest level in 13 years.

Periods of recovery have usually been led by a revival of fixed investment, but in 1975–9 the main stimuli came from exports, consumption and stockbuilding. Recovery, moreover, was somewhat incomplete with unemployment in 1979 at 1.2 million, or 4.8% of total employees. It can be claimed, therefore, that the downturn of 1979–81 started from an initial level of activity which was already somewhat depressed. But this has to be seen against the background of an inflation rate in 1979 of 13%.

II.3   The Determinants of Demand

The proximity of national output to its full-employment potential is determined by the level of total expenditure on goods and services, which, in the simplest terms, can be divided into two main categories: the 'autonomous' items, which are not affected by the current level of national income, and the 'endogenous' expenditures, which depend on current or lagged income. In elementary accounts, the former category is represented as investment, and is said to be determined by the stock of unexploited technological potential, by business expectations of the rate of return, and by the rate of interest. Consumption, on the other hand, is taken as dependent on income itself, so that the line of causation runs from investment to income to consumption, with investment acting as the principal cause of movements in total output.

This simple model of income determination is of clear relevance to the way in which GDP is determined in the 'real world'. But, as we have seen, there are complications. The autonomous component of total expenditure has to include, besides fixed investment, exports, government expenditure and investment in stocks, whilst the endogenous items must include imports as well as consumption. A large area of macroeconomics and applied econometrics is devoted to the attempt to explain in some detail how these various expenditures are determined. These explanations are essential if we are to understand economic fluctuations and to be able to forecast and control them.

II.4   Consumers' Expenditure

Consumers' expenditure is the largest single element in aggregate demand. It accounts for nearly half of TFE (see table 1.1) and, after the removal of its import and indirect-tax content, for about the same fraction of GDP at factor cost. Consumption is one of the more stable elements of demand, and it held up well in the recession of 1979–81. But its total amount is so large in relation to GDP that even quite small percentage variations in its level can have important repercussions for output and employment. An understanding of consumption behaviour, therefore, as well as an ability to predict it, are important objectives for economic analysis. A great deal of attention has been given to consumption, both in theory and statistically, although this work has been more heavily concentrated upon consumption in the US where the data are more plentiful.

The starting point for the early studies of consumer behaviour was the well-known statement by Keynes:[1] 'The fundamental psychological law upon which we are entitled to depend with great confidence both *a priori* from our knowledge of human nature and from the detailed facts of experience, is that men are disposed, as a rule and on the average, to increase their consumption as their income increases, but not by as much as the increase in their income.' Keynes was suggesting that current income was the principal, although not the only, determinant of consumers' expenditure in the short run, and that the marginal propensity to consume (the ratio of additional consumption to additional income) was positive, fractional and reasonably stable.

If we focus attention upon personal savings rather than consumption, it can be seen that the ratio of savings to personal disposable income has shown a strong upward trend over the postwar period, with deviations from trend which are associated with cyclical fluctuations (see figure 1.2). The ratio was above trend in the peak years of 1961, 1965 and 1971, and below trend in the intervening recessions. In the recession of 1973–5, however, the savings ratio was on the high side.

Cyclical movements in the savings ratio can be accounted for in various ways. One possible explanation is that consumer behaviour is partly a matter of habit and convention, so that when income declines the individual attempts to maintain his expenditure at its previous level with the consequence that the average propensity to consume (APC) rises and the savings ratio declines. A related explanation can be found in the ideas of the normal-income theorists.[2] Their main proposition is that consumption depends not upon current income, but on *normal income*, which can be defined either as the expected lifetime income of the consumer or, less precisely, as his notion of average income over some future period. Thus it is changes in the level of expected income which are likely to change consumption. If current income increases, then it will raise consumption only in so far as it raises normal income, and the amount by which it does so will depend upon the expected persistence of the income change. Since cyclical changes in income are (by

1   J.M.Keynes, *General Theory*, p. 96.

2   For an examination of these theories, see M.J.Farrell, 'The New Theories of the Consumption Function', *EJ*, December 1959 (reprinted in Klein and Gordon (eds.), *Readings in Business Cycles*, Allen and Unwin, 1966). The classic reference is F.Modigliani and R.Brumberg, 'Utility Analysis and the Consumption Function', in K.Kurihara (ed.), *Post-Keynesian Economics* (Allen and Unwin, 1955).

definition) not persistent, it is to be expected that consumption will be high in relation to income whenever the economy is in depression. Conversely, the savings ratio will be low in depressions and high at peaks.

The rise in the savings ratio in the 1970s has been statistically associated with the faster inflation rate, and year-to-year movements in the two variables have also been correlated. This has led some economists to infer that changes in the inflation rate are a major influence on the savings ratio. The theory is that inflation erodes the purchasing power of liquid assets, and this leads people to step up their savings rate in an attempt to restore the real value of their assets. Although the econometric estimates of the effect of inflation on the savings ratio vary a good deal (from 0.5 to 2.5% for a 1% increase in the price level), they all point to a very strong statistical association. The lowest of these estimates, for example, implies that when the inflation rate rose by 8 percentage points in 1973–4 the induced increase in the savings ratio was 4%. Whether the effect is really as strong as the correlation estimates tell us is not clear. The evidence comes mainly from a short period, and there was no similar rise in the savings ratio in the earlier inflation of 1951. Some of the increase derives from the inclusion of the profits of unincorporated businesses in personal income. These profits include stock appreciation which is naturally high in periods of fast inflation. Thus income is raised without any induced rise in expenditure. It has also been pointed out that the main non-liquid asset is house property, and this increased in real value during the 1970s. It is not impossible, therefore, that the effect of inflation on savings has been exaggerated and that some of the correlation is not causal.[1] The increase in the saving rate could also have been precautionary, reflecting fears of unemployment and of tough anti-inflationary policies.

An important influence upon consumers' expenditure is the availability and cost of credit and particularly of credit for financing purchases of durable goods.[2] These goods, which constitute 9% of total consumption, are more in the nature of capital equipment than consumption in that they yield a flow of utility over time. It is natural where income is generally rising that such goods should be bought extensively on credit, and something like one half of their total is financed by hire-purchase. HP finance used to be regulated through government controls on the minimum percentage downpayment and the maximum repayment period. But these controls went out of use in the 1970s, and were finally abolished in 1982. It is now interest rates rather than direct controls which tend to regulate HP borrowing.

---

1 For further information and a discussion, see K.Cuthbertson, 'The Measurement and Behaviour of the UK Savings Ratio', *NIER*, February 1982. It should be noted that figures for the savings ratio are prone to substantial revision: that for 1976 was put at 14.6% in 1980, but is now (*ET(AS)*, 1986) revised down to 12.1%.

2 It should be noted that the *Blue Book* definition of durable goods includes cars, motorcycles, furniture, carpets and electrical goods, but, perhaps arbitrarily, does not include clothing, curtains, pots and pans, or books.

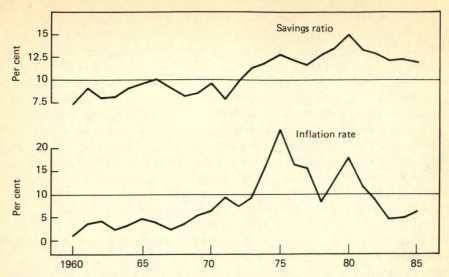

Figure 1.2   Personal savings ratio and the rate of increase in retail prices, UK, 1960–85

The marginal propensity to consume: The marginal propensity to consume (MPC) is the increase in spending which, *ceteris paribus*, an individual plans to undertake on the assumption of a unit rise in his disposable income. The aggregate MPC, likewise, is the weighted average of all individual MPCs.

An insight into the possible size of the aggregate MPC can be obtained by application of the life-cycle hypothesis, which assumes that the object of saving is to finance consumption during retirement.[1] An individual of representative age (say 38) who receives an increase in his income of £1 per year will plan to save just enough to maintain a constant annual addition to his spending. If he expects to go on receiving the extra income until he retires at age 65 and if he also expects to live for a further 12 years after retirement (the life expectation of a 65-year-old man), then his extra £1 will be earned for a further 27 years but will be needed for spending over a period of 39 years. These two periods are the key to his MPC, which will be $27/39 = 0.69$, whilst his marginal propensity to save will be 0.31. The calculation assumes that he disregards the interest on his savings, that the increase in income had not been previously anticipated, and that he expects it to be a permanent addition to his income. It also assumes that he is not interested in leaving any further bequests to his children, and that he is prepared to make calculations of the kind suggested. These are all rather stringent assumptions, but they do enable us to deduce that a 'representative' increase in aggregate income (i.e. one which is spread evenly across ages and income levels) might involve an MPC in the region of 0.7. This is lower than the average propensity to consume, which was 0.88 in 1984. It is also well below the life-cycle theory's

---

1   F. Modigliani and R. Brumberg, op. cit.

hypothetical APC, which must be unity since individuals are assumed to consume all their life-time income.

An empirical estimate of the MPC may be found either by econometric methods or by direct inspection of the data. Early econometric studies of consumption were in general agreement that the MPC deduced from short-term time series data was in the region of 0.6 to 0.8.[1] These results, which related mainly to the United States, accord with the *a priori* estimates gleaned from the life-cycle hypothesis. Data for the UK suggests that there is not a great deal of stability in the MPC when measured as the ratio of the annual change in consumption to the annual change in real disposable income. Even if 5-year periods are taken, the ratio has varied between 0.62 for 1970–4 to 1975–9 and 0.85 for 1975–9 to 1980–4. In the calculation of the multiplier in Section II.8 we shall assume that the MPC is 0.75, although some estimates have been a good deal lower.[2]

II.5   Fixed Investment

Fixed investment or gross domestic fixed capital formation consists of housebuilding in both the public and private sectors of the economy, and of business investment in plant and machinery, including investment by nationalized industries. Its breakdown by industry in shown in table 1.4, where it can be seen that investment by the service industries is much larger than in manufacturing. Nevertheless, manufacturing investment is the most

TABLE 1.4
Gross Domestic Fixed Capital Formation, UK, 1984 (£bn)

	Private sector	Public sector	Total
Dwellings	9.2	2.7	11.9
Manufacturing	6.8	0.3	7.1
Energy and water supply	3.1	3.8	7.0
Distribution, hotels, catering, repairs	4.6	0.0	4.6
Banking finance, insurance, business services, leasing	8.3	0.4	8.7
Other	9.3	6.5	15.8
Total	41.3	13.8	55.0

Source: NIE, 1985, p. 117: current prices. Detail does not add to totals because of rounding.

1   See G. Ackley, *Macroeconomic Theory* (Macmillan, New York, 1961) and R. Ferber, 'Research on Household Behaviour', *AER*, 52, 1962, for surveys of these studies.

2   For example, the estimate of the MPC implied by one version of the Treasury's model was not much above 0.3 for durable and non-durable goods spending. This seems to have been due to the introduction of a price variable which tends to lower the implied explanatory power of income. The variable was introduced in the attempt to account for the rise in the savings ratio in the 1970s, and is assumed to be a proxy for wealth. See H.M. Treasury, *Macroeconomic Model, Equation and Variable Listing* (HMSO, 1980).

volatile element in the total. In the recession of 1979–81, for example, manufacturing investment fell in real terms by 35% compared with a total decline in private fixed investment of 10%.

The explanation of investment is not without its difficulties. New capital stock is purchased and old stock replaced in the expectation of profits in the future. It is not difficult to show formally that an investment project is profitable if its marginal efficiency exceeds the rate of interest, or if its present value exceeds zero. But these calculations are based upon *forecasts* of revenues and costs which have to extend for years, even decades, into the future. When so much depends upon vulnerable and uncertain guesses about the future, it must be expected that investment expenditure will not be as readily explicable as consumption.

Two of the models which are often advanced to explain investment behaviour make their own special assumptions about expected future income. The acceleration principle is sometimes justified on the assumption that the future growth of income will be equal to the past rate of growth, and on this basis it is suggested that investment is proportional to the change in income:

$$I = a\Delta Y$$

where I is investment, ΔY the change in income and a is a constant co-efficient. A related model is the capital stock adjustment principle, which explains investment as an attempt to adjust the capital stock from its actual level to a desired level based on the expected level of output. It also assumes that there is a fixed relationship between output and the amount of capital equipment needed to produce it. The model can be expressed by the equation:

$$I = aY - K$$

where K is the actual level of the capital stock, and a is the assumed constant capital-output ratio.[1] Neither of these models say anything explicit about costs or interest rates, and although they are right to focus on income expectations, they are still extremely crude. Another theory altogether is the view that investment can be predicted by the level of business profits, the idea being that firms simply spend what they can afford.

Whatever the theoretical merits of these models it is possible to assemble data that relate to them, and this is done in figure 1.3, where the top graph is manufacturing investment in constant prices. The figure illustrates that manufacturing investment is indeed correlated with the change in income, where this is taken as the 3-year change in real GDP at factor cost up to the previous year. (The 3-year change in manufacturing output would have

---

1   Because K^*, the desired capital stock, is equal to aY^* where Y^* is expected income. Hence $I = K^* - K = aY^* - K$. And if Y^* is assumed to equal current income, Y, then $I = aY - K$. It is also possible to attach a coefficient to K on the assumption that investment demand in a single period is a constant fraction of $K^* - K$, i.e. $I = b(K^* - K) = abY^* - bK$. Replacement investment may also be allowed for on the assumption that it is proportionate to income.

given a similarly good correlation.) Figure 1.3 also shows the relationships between investment and the level of manufacturers' real profits. What we have done here is to estimate a price deflator for profits by dividing manufacturing investment in current prices by manufacturing investment in constant (1980) prices. Profits are gross profits less stock appreciation. A rather less obvious correlation exists for the capital-output ratio, where the ratio shown on the graph is the capital stock at the end of the previous year divided by manufacturing output in that year (both at 1980 prices). Finally, the graph shows the long-term interest rate on government securities, and for this there is virtually no correlation at all.

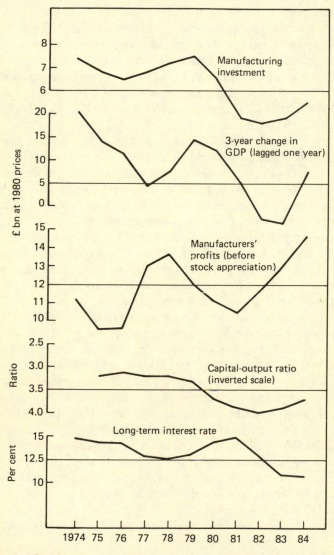

Figure 1.3   Manufacturing investment and related indicators, UK, 1974–84

The question now arises as to whether we can interpret any of these correlations as causal. The best of them is the correlation with the change in income, and this might seem to give a strong case for the acceleration principle. But the argument against this conclusion is that the fastest changes in income will be those between the trough and peak of the business cycle, whilst the slower increases will be those between years either side of the peak and trough. With a cycle of 5 years' duration, a 2 or 3-year income change will tend to reach its maximum point at the same time as income *and investment* are at their peak levels. This means that investment and the income change will both reach their peaks at about the same time. Thus the correlation shown in the figure may be simply a mechanical consequence of the business cycle.

In the case of the profits hypothesis, a similar argument applies. Profits will be high when sales are high, and this will happen when autonomous spending is at its peak. Manufacturing investment is, of course, an important element in autonomous spending, so that when it peaks income will tend to be high and so will profits. So we are now arguing that it is not profits which cause investment, but investment which causes profits. But there *could* be causation in both directions.

The correlation with the lagged capital stock is not as good as the other two, and could be simply a mechanical result of low investment leading to low economic activity and, therefore, to a high ratio of capital to output. The fact that we have incorporated a lag in the correlation does not completely remove this objection, since periods of low and high economic activity tend to occur for several years at a time. There are other objections too, namely that the stock-adjustment principle makes the naive assumptions that next year's sales will be equal to this year's and that one year's sales are the relevant consideration in plant and machinery designed to last for many years. Nevertheless, we have included the correlation, and we should also note that it performed very much better in earlier years.[1]

To the question of what actually caused manufacturing investment over the period shown, we can only give a tentative answer. We doubt whether the correlation with ΔY gives any real credence to the acceleration principle, even though it is the best of the four correlations. We think there is a bit of truth in both the profits and the capital-stock adjustment models, although it would not be surprising if the correlations overstated the importance of the variables. Finally, we believe on *a priori* grounds that interest rates are an influence even though there is virtually no correlation. The main econometric models of the UK have used both profits and interest rate variables to explain investment, besides making some use of the capital-stock adjustment and acceleration principles. But at the end of the day it is still uncertain whether anybody has a robust and reliable model for explaining and forecasting manufacturing investment.

Housing investment needs to be divided between the public and private

---

1 See, for example, *The UK Economy* (5th edition, 1974), pp. 21–3.

sectors and examined in relation to demand and supply influences in both sectors. The demand for public-sector building comes indirectly from population trends and directly from the policies of the public authorities. The demand for private-sector building depends both upon population characteristics (family formation and size) and also upon expected lifetime income, the cost of mortgage credit, the prices of new houses and of substitute accommodation. It is subject to the important and highly variable constraints set by the availability of mortgage credit, which in turn are determined partly by general credit policy and partly by the policies of the building societies. The problem of predicting housing investment is eased, however, by the statistics of new houses started, which, with an assumption about completion times, makes it possible to forecast housing for at least a short period ahead.

II.6 Stocks and Stockbuilding

Stockbuilding or investment in stocks is a change in a level – the level of all stocks held at the beginning of the period. In any one year, stock investment can be positive or negative, whilst the change in stock investment between successive years can exert an important influence upon GDP. The increase in stock investment in 1975–7, for example, and the decline in 1979–80 were both equivalent to about 3% of GDP.

At the end of 1984 the total value of stocks held in all industries was approximately £87bn, or 31% of the value of GDP in a year. Stocks held by manufacturing industry accounted for nearly £41bn, and by wholesale and retail business for £27bn.[1]

Stocks of work in progress are held because they are a technical necessity of production, whilst stocks of materials and finished goods are held mainly out of a precautionary motive. They are required as a 'buffer' between deliveries and production; or, more precisely, because firms realize that they cannot expect an exact correspondence between the amount of materials delivered each day and the amount taken into production, or between completed production and deliveries to customers.

For these reasons it seems plausible to assume that firms carry in their minds the notion of a certain optimum ratio between stocks and output. If stocks fall below the optimum ratio, they will need to be replenished; if they rise above it, they will be run down. The reasoning here is the same as that of the stock-adjustment principle which we have already mentioned in connection with fixed investment. The principle holds quite well, and is illustrated in figure 1.4, where it can be seen that peaks in stock investment generally coincided with low levels of the stock-GDP ratio.[2] This was also true in earlier years.

---

1 *NIE*, 1985, table 12.1.

2 The correlation coefficient, *r*, is 0.69 in figure 1.4 (for 1972–82).

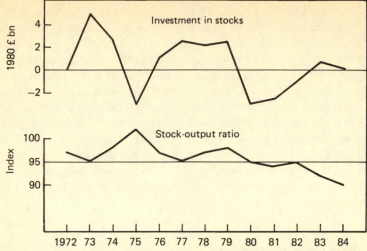

Figure 1.4   Investment in stocks and the stock–GDP ratio, UK, 1972–84

The stock-adjustment principle is only the beginning of an explanation of investment in stocks. It makes no allowance for interest rates or price expectations, both of which are relevant to the preferred stock-output ratio. Nor can it account for unplanned movements in stocks, which for finished goods will occur when sales deviate from their expected levels.

II.7   Government Consumption, Exports, Imports and Indirect Taxes

Of the two remaining components of TFE, government consumption is primarily determined by the social and political objectives of the central government and local authorities, and partly by macroeconomic and financial policy. Until 1979, it was unusual for government spending to be affected by macroeconomic policy, the preferred instrument of control being changes in tax rates. But the advent of financial targets for the PSBR, and of expenditure control by cash limits, were a change of some significance. Between 1979 and 1984 the rise in government consumption was only about 5% in real terms.

Exports of goods and services are determined by two principal factors: by the level of overseas income and by export prices, measured in terms of foreign currency. The latter, in turn, are influenced by the exchange rate for sterling. UK exports correlate quite closely with the volume of world trade in manufactures, and exports to particular countries are linked to national GNP. The influence of prices is measured by the price elasticity of demand, which according to some econometric models is not too high: the range suggested by the National Institute, Bank of England and Treasury models is −0.6 to −0.8, but other estimates vary between −0.4 and −2.8.[1] The 3% drop

---

1   See S. Brooks, 'Systematic Econometric Comparisons: Exports of Manufactured Goods', *NIER*, August 1981, p. 70, and A. P. Thirlwall, *Balance of Payments Theory and the United Kingdom Experience* (London 1980), pp. 204, 210–11, 230–1, 237–8.

in exports during 1980 was associated with a particularly sharp rise in the exchange rate and in UK export prices. Export trends are discussed in more detail in chapter 3.

TFE is the sum total of exports of goods and services, government consumption, fixed investment, stockbuilding and personal consumption. These elements are normally measured at market prices and they all contain a substantial content of imported components and materials. To proceed from TFE at market prices to GDP at factor cost it is necessary, therefore, to remove the indirect-tax and import contents of the various expenditure items. The indirect-tax content (net of subsidies) is known annually for the various expenditure items, whereas the import content is known only for TFE. Estimates of the import content for individual expenditures can be worked out by input-output methods, and are shown, together with their indirect-tax contents, in table 1.5 below.

TABLE 1.5
Domestic Output Content of Total Final Expenditure at Market Prices

	Percentages of market price totals				
	Consumers' expenditure	*Government consumption*	*Gross domestic fixed investment*	*Exports of goods and services*	*Total final expenditure*
Indirect taxes (less subsidies)	17	6	6	4	11
Imports of goods and services	21	11	30	26	22
Domestic output content	62	83	64	70	67

Sources: NIE, 1985, table 1.2; CSO, Input-Output Tables 1979.

The main determinants of imports are the level of GDP and competitive factors, such as price, quality and delivery dates. It is probably this last group which is responsible for the upward trend (see chapter 3) in the ratio of imports of goods and services (at constant 1980 prices) to TFE:

1950–54	14.0%
1955–59	14.7%
1960–64	15.6%
1965–69	16.6%
1970–74	19.0%
1975–79	19.4%
1980–84	20.5%

There is also some connection between the import ratio and investment in stocks. Some models used to assume that imports would rise by as much as £50m for every £100m of stockbuilding. But in recent years this influence has become smaller and less distinct.

II.8   Personal Income and the Multiplier

Any increase in GDP will normally give rise to a multiplier process. The initial rise in income leads to higher consumption, and thus to higher GDP. Successive rounds of higher income and consumption will lead to the eventual establishment of an 'equilibrium' level of GDP, this being the level which GDP finally settles at. The multiplier process is the succession of income changes, whilst the 'multiplier' itself is defined as the ratio of the total or cumulative increase in GDP to its initial or 'first-round' increase.

In elementary models, the multiplier may be found quite simply because no distinctions are made between GDP and personal income, and because taxation, undistributed profits and the import contents of expenditure are ignored. On these lines, it can be seen that an initial increase in GDP of 100 units, combined with a marginal propensity to consume of, say, 0.5, will lead to an eventual increase in GDP of 200 units. This is because the initial rise in GDP will cause personal incomes to rise by the same amount, so that consumption will then increase (after a time-lag) by 50 units. This, in turn, raises personal incomes in the consumer-goods industries by 50 units, so that consumption in the third round of the multiplier will increase by 25 units. Each increment of income leads to a rise in consumption half as large, so that the sequence of period-to-period additions to GDP will be:

$$100, 50, 25, 12.5, 6.25, 3.125, \ldots \text{ etc.}$$

It is not difficult to see that if all the terms are added together they sum to 200, which is the equilibrium rise in GDP. And since this is twice the original increase, the multiplier is 2. This value may also be found from the formula:

$$\frac{\Delta Y}{\Delta I} = \frac{1}{1 - \text{MPC}} = \frac{1}{1 - 0.5} = 2$$

where ΔY is the final increase in GDP and ΔI the initial increase.[1]

The multiplier for the UK follows the same principles as the simple model. But its calculation is complicated by a number of factors, one of which is the distinction which must be drawn between GDP and personal income. This may be illustrated by a direct comparison for 1984:

GDP (£279.9bn)	equals	Income from employment and self-employment (£207.2bn)	plus	Rent, total profits and trading surpluses and imputed charge for capital consumption (£77.8bn)	minus	Stock appreciation (£5.2bn)

---

1   The formula assumes that ΔI is a sustained increase in the level of investment expenditure. An unsustained or 'one shot' injection of new investment would lead only to a temporary rise in GDP.

Personal income (£279.6bn)	equals	Income from employment and self-employment (£207.2bn)	plus	Personal receipts of rent, dividends and interest (£27.8bn)	plus	Transfer incomes (£44.5bn)

The main point here is that personal income and GDP are similar in total, but different in composition. Their main common element is employment income. But personal income includes a large transfer element – mainly pensions and social security benefits – which do not figure in GDP because they are not payments for production. Personal income from rent and profit is only a small part of total domestic rent and profit.

To arrive at an estimate of the UK multiplier we may begin by assuming an initial increase in GDP of £100m. This is the domestic-output content of a larger increase in TFE at market prices, the difference being due to the import and indirect-tax contents of the expenditure. The coefficients in table 1.5, for example, suggest that £100m of GDP would typically correspond to an increase in government expenditure of £120m or fixed investment of £156m.

A series of assumptions must now be made as to the size of various 'withdrawals' or leakages between the first- and second-round increases in GDP. The first stage in the calculation concerns the likely increases in personal income. This will depend on the way in which new GDP is divided between employment incomes and profits, on how much of the latter is distributed to the personal sector as dividend income, and also on how much transfer incomes decline as a result of lower unemployment and other national social security benefits. It can be assumed that the increase in GDP is divided between employment income and profits in its usual ratio of about 4 : 1, so that £80m will go directly into personal income in the form of income from employment. To this we may add about £6m for higher dividends, since most of the £20m rise in profits will find its way into undistributed profits and corporate taxes. But we also have to allow for a reduction in transfer incomes arising from lower unemployment benefits, and this would be of the order of £4m.[1] Thus the total increase in personal income will be £80 + 6 − 4 = £82 million, which gives us the first in a series of coefficients needed to derive the multiplier (see table 1.6).

The remaining stages of the calculation involve the marginal rate of direct taxation (including higher pensions and national insurance payments) which is taken to be about 32%, the marginal propensity to consume, which we assumed in section II.4 above to be about 0.75, and the marginal import and indirect-tax contents of consumption. The latter are taken from the average contents given in table 1.5 (but note that the import content of *factor cost*

1 Derived by assuming that every 1% rise in GDP leads to a 0.5% increase in employment, and from official estimates of the cost of unemployment benefit. See *Treasury Economic Progress Report*, February 1981.

TABLE 1.6
Stages in the Multiplier Estimate

	£m	Assumed marginal relationships
1st-round increase in GDP	100	
Increase in personal income	82	$b_1 = .82$
Increase in personal disposable income	56	$b_2 = .68$
Increase (after a time-lag) in consumers' expenditure at market prices	42	$b_3 = .75$
Increase in consumers' expenditure at factor cost	34	$b_4 = .81$
Increase in domestically produced consumption at factor cost (equals 2nd-round increase in GDP)	26	$b_5 = .76$

consumption will be higher, at 0.24, than the import content of market price consumption). It is, of course, arguable that the marginal import content is higher than the average import content but we have not allowed for this possibility.

The upshot of the calculation is that the second-round increase in GDP is only £26m, or 0.26 times the initial increase. It follows that the third, fourth and later increases will all be 0.26 times the previous rise, so that the sequence of period-to-period changes in GDP can be represented as follows:

$$£100, 26, 6.8, 1.8, 0.5, 0.1 \ldots \ldots 0 \text{ million}$$

This series sums to a cumulative increase of £135m, so that the multiplier is 1.35. Its value may also be found from the expression:

$$\frac{1}{1 - 0.26} = 1.35$$

where 0.26 can be described as the marginal propensity to purchase new domestic output. It represents the five coefficients b_1, b_2, b_3, b_4 and b_5 all multiplied together.[1]

It should be noted that we have defined the multiplier as the ratio of the eventual increase in GDP to the initial increase in GDP, and not to the initial increase in market price expenditure. This is in order to keep the numerator and denominator both in terms of domestic output. The multiplier so defined applies much more directly to employment than the alternative ratio of the change in GDP to the change in market price expenditure.[2]

These calculations are based on the usual multiplier assumptions that there are unused resources of capital and labour, and that interest rates are held constant through a policy of monetary accommodation. The multiplier

---

1   Thus $0.26 = \dfrac{82}{100} \cdot \dfrac{56}{82} \cdot \dfrac{42}{56} \cdot \dfrac{34}{42} \cdot \dfrac{26}{34} = b_1 b_2 b_3 b_4 b_5$ and the multiplier is $\dfrac{1}{1 - b_1 b_2 b_3 b_4 b_5}$.

2   This discussion has followed an early estimate of the multiplier in W. A. B. Hopkin and W. A. H. Godley, 'An Analysis of Tax Changes', *NIER*, May 1965.

estimate is not meant to be precise, but is seen as indicating the right general order of magnitude. In practice, there are other effects of an increase in GDP besides the multiplier which also have to be taken into account. The most basic of these is the effect on stockbuilding, since any increase in demand will be met initially from stock, so that there will be some involuntary stock decline at the start of the process, and this will be reversed later as production is stepped up to replenish stocks and to meet the higher level of demand.[1] The National Institute's econometric model, for example, shows negative stock investment in the first quarter of an increase in total final expenditure, followed by stock accumulation in the third and fourth quarters.

Econometric models can be simulated to provide estimates of the effect of changes in expenditure on GDP quarter by quarter. According to one study, the main models show that the ratio of the 4th quarter rise in GDP to the initial increase is in the region of 1.1 to 1.3,[2] which is a bit lower than our own estimate of 1.35. But the econometric models build into the multiplier a variety of other relationships, the most important of which are the stock-adjustment effects on stockbuilding and fixed investment. The value of the multiplier is increased with variable exchange rates, because rising imports lead to a lower exchange rate and hence to higher demand for UK exports – unless, of course, interest rates are forced to rise by a policy of tight money.

III   BUDGETARY POLICY AND DEMAND MANAGEMENT
III.1   Objectives and Instruments

The period since the Second World War has been characterized by two quite different approaches to macroeconomic policy. The first of these was the demand-management approach, whereby governments sought to influence the level of demand in the economy with the intention of maintaining or restoring an acceptable level of employment. The second approach was directed more towards the restoration of price stability, with a high level of employment taking a lower priority than hitherto. This approach reached its fullest manifestation under the Conservative government elected in 1979. It is discussed in section III.5.

The demand-management approach was inaugurated by the White Paper on *Employment Policy* (Cmd. 6527) issued in 1944 by the wartime coalition government. The White Paper stated that:

> The Government believe that, once the war has been won, we can make a fresh approach, with better chances of success than ever

1   In extreme cases there may be severe oscillations in GDP or even an explosive time-path. On this the classic reference is L.A.Metzler, 'The Nature and Stability of Inventory Cycles' in R.A.Gordon and L.R.Klein (eds.), *Readings in Business Cycles* (Allen and Unwin, 1966).

2   See J.S.E.Laury, G.R.Lewis and P.A.Ormerod, 'Properties of Macroeconomic Models of the UK Economy: A Comparative Study', *NIER*, February 1978.

before, to the task of maintaining a high and stable level of employment without sacrificing the essential liberties of a free society.

The White Paper recommended that there should be a permanent staff of statisticians and economists in the Civil Service with responsibility for interpreting economic trends and advising on policy. The execution of employment policy was to be examined annually by Parliament in the debate on the Budget. The White Paper foresaw that high levels of employment were likely to endanger price stability, and it pointed out the need for 'moderation in wage matters by employers and employees' as the essential condition for the success of the policy.

For nearly thirty years the task of maintaining a high level of employment proved to be less difficult than had been expected. Employment levels were higher than the authors of the White Paper had hoped for, and inflation was remarkably moderate. The average rate of retail price inflation was 3% per year in the 1950s, and 4% in the 1960s.

As we observed in section II, however, the postwar economy passed through a series of fluctuations with the annual unemployment rate varying within a narrow range. Part of the reason for these fluctuations could be found in the different views taken by successive governments (or sometimes by the same government at different times) as to the most desirable pressure of demand. The aim of high employment was always in some measure of conflict with the balance of payments and with price stability. A conflict with the balance of payments was also present in so far as governments were unwilling to make use of instruments of policy, such as exchange-rate devaluation or import controls, for dealing with the external balance. Thus fiscal measures which act upon the level of employment were at times directed towards the required balance of payments, with the consequence that the employment objective took second place. This conflict was particularly noticeable in two periods: from 1956 to early 1959 when the Conservative government was aiming at a long-term balance-of-payments surplus, and the period of eighteen months preceding the devaluation of sterling in November 1967.

The employment objective was also in conflict with that of price stability. Here there is no independent instrument of control to parallel the variability of the exchange rate. Incomes policy, in the sense of voluntary or compulsory guidelines for the rate of increase in wages and prices, was seldom found to be particularly successful and certainly not successful enough to permit nice percentage adjustments to the permitted rate of inflation. Thus the absence of an independent instrument for controlling inflation implied a genuine conflict of aims. This, together with the balance of payments, helps to explain why the target level of employment was not wholly stable, but tended to fluctuate according to the priorities of the government of the day.

It follows that the decision on what level of employment to aim for was normally made on the basis of a compromise with the objectives of price stability and the balance of payments. But once the employment target was settled, the problem of how to attain it became a technical issue.

One of the initial difficulties in any attempt to control employment is that there are significant time-lags between the onset of a recession and the period when remedial action takes effect. The employment statistics are about a month behindhand; civil servants may take up to six months to advise the appropriate action; Parliament may take three months to enact it; and even after the policy is put into force, the full economic effects may not appear for some months afterwards. Thus a strategy based solely upon the observation of recent performance can involve a significantly long time-lag (of twelve months or longer) between the observed need for a change in policy and the effects of that change upon the level of employment.

It is partly for this reason that demand management in the UK was based upon a strategy of looking ahead rather than on response to the current economic situation. This meant that the policy-maker had to rely heavily upon the use of economic forecasts. If he could *correctly* foresee the emergence of a policy problem, then the problem of the delay between the need for intervention and its effects would be taken care of.

There is another reason, too, for relying upon forecasts. This is the need to tailor the amount of intervention to the future size of the problem rather than to what is currently observed. The mere observation of high unemployment or excessive inflation in no way guarantees that it will continue in the same degree of seriousness. The problem may get worse or it may get better. Quite clearly it is essential to form some view of what will happen in the future before deciding the degree and the direction of policy intervention required. Failure to produce a correct forecast of the course of employment over the next twelve to eighteen months could result in an *inadequate* degree of corrective policy action. Or it could be *destabilizing*,[1] in the sense that the effect of intervention is to remove the level of output still further from target than it would have been without it.

The last four decades have seen a considerable advance in the various branches of knowledge which bear upon the problems of forecasting and managing the economy. The chief of these have comprised: (i) an enormous improvement, attributable to the CSO, in economic statistics, and particularly the development of quarterly, seasonally adjusted, constant-price, national expenditure figures; (ii) the development of a conceptual framework and quantitative model for forecasting GDP and employment over a period of about eighteen months; (iii) the development of a conceptual framework and quantitative model for estimating the effects on GDP of tax changes and other instruments of demand management.

III.2 The Effects of Policy Instruments

If fiscal intervention is to achieve targets for employment and output, it is necessary for the policy-makers to make fairly precise quantitative assess-

---

1 A more accurate term would be 'perverse' since policy does not necessarily aim to stabilize anything.

ments of the effects of their policy instruments upon the level of domestic output. In this section we shall concentrate upon the effects of three such instruments: changes in government expenditure on goods and services, changes in personal income tax and changes in indirect taxation.

In the case of a change in government expenditure, the effect on GDP has to be found by, first, removing the import and indirect-tax contents of the new expenditure (see table 1.5) – since neither of these constitute domestic output. After this has been done, the cumulative effect may be found by applying the multiplier estimate of 1.35 derived from table 1.6. Thus the effects of a typical increase in government expenditure of, say, £100m, will be as follows:

	£m
increase in government expenditure at market prices	+100
increase in government expenditure at factor cost	+92
initial increase in GDP	+82
multiplied increase in GDP	+111

Some expenditures, such as the purchase of foreign missiles and military aircraft, will have a larger import content and a smaller effect on domestic output than this.

In point of fact, government expenditure was seldom used as an instrument for influencing employment during the era of demand management. This was because its level was determined by political and social objectives of a different order, and also because it was difficult to organize changes in its amount with much hope of their going precisely to schedule. The more usual instruments of demand management were changes in tax rates, particularly income and indirect taxes.[1]

The effect on GDP of a change in income tax may be illustrated by reference to a reduction of 1p in the basic and higher rates of tax. This is estimated by the Treasury to reduce revenue by £1,245m.[2] Personal disposable income would be raised by an equal amount, so that the *initial*, or multiplicand, effect upon GDP can be found using the coefficients estimated in table 1.6:

	£m
change in tax revenue	−1,245
increase in personal disposable income	+1,245
increase in consumers' expenditure at market prices	+934
increase in consumers' expenditure at factor cost	+756
initial increase in GDP	+578
multiplied increase in GDP	+780

The initial increase in GDP of £578m is simply the change in tax revenue multiplied by the marginal propensity to consume (b_3 in table 1.6), along with the coefficients b_4 and b_5 which remove the indirect-tax and import

---

1   J.C.R.Dow, *The Management of the British Economy, 1945–60* (Cambridge University Press, 1964), pp. 180–1.

2   Treasury, *Financial Statement and Budget Report*, March 1986.

contents of the increase in consumers' expenditure. The multiplier effect raises this by 1.35 to a figure which, with current-price GDP at an estimated £300bn (in 1986), is equivalent to a gain in total output of approximately 0.25%. This is the deviation in GDP from what it would have been in the absence of the tax reduction.

Changes in indirect taxation affect consumption by altering prices and the level of real personal disposable income. The effects of a change in VAT, for example, can be estimated approximately provided we know the effect on tax revenue. If taxes are reduced, the fall in revenue as a proportion of consumers' expenditure is equal to the proportionate change in prices. The latter leads to an increase in real personal disposable income, from which the effects on consumption and GDP may be estimated.[1] For a 1% fall in VAT, the Treasury estimates that revenue declines by £925 million.[2] Real personal disposable income will increase by this amount times the ratio of disposable income to consumption (i.e. the reciprocal of the APC). This leads to changes in consumption and GDP which can be found from coefficients already given for the multiplier:

	£m
change in tax revenue	−925
increase in real personal disposable income	+1,051
increase in real consumers' expenditure at market prices	+788
increase in real consumers' expenditure at factor cost	+638
initial increase in GDP	+488
multiplied increase in GDP	+659

Here the effect of a 1% cut in VAT is equivalent to about 0.2% of GDP.[3]

When discussing the effects of tax changes, it is important to remember that all changes in the budget balance have to be financed either by borrowing from the public or by increasing the money supply. Strictly speaking, the effects described above must assume that the method of financing is an expansion of the money supply. This means that we have not been describing fiscal policy *per se* but a mixed policy of fiscal changes with monetary accommodation. The name does not matter, since the Chancellor of the Exchequer is responsible both for fiscal and monetary policy, and is therefore able to ensure that budget deficits are financed in ways which do not subvert the objectives of the policy. It should be noted, however, that if fiscal changes are financed by borrowing from the public there will be consequential increases in interest rates which will tend to reduce (or 'crowd out') private-sector purchases of consumer durables and investment goods.

The alternative to fiscal policy is often taken to be monetary policy,

---

1   In terms of algebra we can denote the revenue change as ΔT, so that the change in consumer prices is $\Delta T/C$, where C is current consumption. The proportionate change in real disposable income, $\Delta Y^d/Y^d$, is equal to $-\Delta T/C$, and the absolute change, ΔY, is equal to $\dfrac{-Y^d}{C} \cdot \Delta T$.

2   Treasury, *Autumn Statement 1985*.

3   In earlier editions we have suggested an alternative procedure for estimating the effects of indirect-tax changes based on the assumption that the money value of personal savings remains unchanged despite the real change in disposable income.

although, as we have seen, fiscal expansion may be financed by an increase in the money stock. Debt management may be used to accomplish a change in interest rates without any marked alteration in the budget balance. The effects of interest changes on investment are likely to be delayed for many months and their main impact will fall outside the normal forecasting horizon of twelve to eighteen months. But the effects on consumers' expenditure through higher mortgage rates and HP payments may operate more swiftly. Monetary policy can also affect spending by altering the availability of credit.

III.3   Economic Forecasts

The Treasury's forecasts of GDP have to be published by Act of Parliament, and were originally developed as an aid to demand management. They are made to a timetable which depends on all major policy decisions, and the need, under the 1975 Industry Act, to publish at least twice a year. The published forecasts extend about 15 months ahead; that for March 1986, for example, goes forward to the first half of 1987.

One of the first problems encountered in any economic forecast is that of establishing GDP estimates for the period extending from the last known figures to the month in which the forecast is assembled. A forecast made in February, for example, has to be made with the benefit of quarterly GDP figures which do not go beyond September of the previous year. A GDP estimate has to be put together for the October-December quarter on the basis of monthly information which includes exports, imports, retail sales and industrial production. This can be difficult because of various gaps in coverage, and because different indicators frequently tell conflicting stories, as, for example, when the employment and industrial production figures move in different directions.

Once the base period is established, the forecast proper (i.e. the part relating to the future) can be started. The methods by which this is done need not be described in detail. But for six months to a year ahead the task is made easier by the presence of a number of forward indicators which provide fairly direct information on the prospects for particular sectors of demand. The CBI, for example, conducts regular inquiries into whether its members intend to invest more or less in the next twelve months than in the previous period. The Department of Industry has its own inquiry, in which business is asked to estimate the percentage change in prospective investment. There are new-order series for engineering, machine tools and shipbuilding, which provide a forward view of production (for investment or export) in these industries. There are also figures for new orders received by contractors for private construction work, whilst in the field of housing investment figures are collected for orders received by contractors, for new houses started, and Building Society commitments and advances on new dwellings.[1] Government

---

1   These figures are all published in *Economic Trends*.

since not all the election years were years of high targeted demand pressure. But it is, perhaps, disputable whether a government gets more votes from high employment than it does from tax give-aways in a year of depression. The other explanation offered is that years of high demand led to balance-of-payments difficulties and inflation, to which the various Chancellors responded with phases of demand deflation until such time as they changed their priorities once again. Whether this was really true is doubtful, but it is not established by the mere existence of fluctuations.

(ii) As regards the technical apparatus of demand management, the key question is whether, and by how much, it failed to achieve the target levels of employment and GDP which governments were aiming for. Since the target level of GDP is equivalent to the government's forecast, this question is essentially a matter of the accuracy of forecasts.[1] If the Treasury fails to forecast the increase in GDP correctly, then it will be led into taking the wrong measures. The result will be that the target level of GDP is missed by the same amount as the forecast is in error.

The question of the accuracy of Treasury forecasts can be answered most satisfactorily for those forecasts which have been published or described with sufficient clarity to permit comparisons with the outcome. For 1968 and after, the forecasts have been published as part of the *Financial Statement and Budget Report*. But before this date the information is not always as good, and must be assembled from official documents or from forecasts made by other bodies at the same time. Nevertheless, the task is worth attempting even though the results (see table 1.7) cannot be sacrosanct.[2]

The main point to emerge from an inspection of Treasury forecasts over the period since 1955 is that, whilst they have not been as accurate as might have been hoped, they have led policy seriously astray on only four or five occasions. There is not much doubt that the 1959 forecast, when the error was 4%, was one of the worst. It meant that an unforeseen recovery in total output was coupled with an expansionary Budget, and the result was a much higher level of employment at the end of the year than the government had actually intended. By contrast, the forecasting error in 1962 went the other way, with the result that there was a recession despite the policy aim of a roughly 4% rise in output. The error was put right in 1963, although the recovery went further than intended. The worst forecast of recent years appears to have been 1974, when the Treasury was much too optimistic (by 3.5% of GDP) about the economic outlook.

Taking the whole period 1955–85, the average error in Treasury forecasts (regardless of sign) was about 1.0% of GDP. This implies an average deviation of about 0.4% between the actual and desired unemployment rate, and is equivalent to an error between the appropriate rate of income tax and

---

1   Forecasting accuracy is not always simple to interpret: there may be strikes or other events of an unforeseeable nature which affect the accuracy of the forecasts without necessarily discrediting the methods by which they are derived.

2   The same qualifications carry through to the series for the Forecast Use of Potential Output.

the actual rate of about 4p in the £. The size of the forecast errors must be seen, however, against the background of conflicting and by no means accurate estimates of GDP itself. There is some evidence that the forecasts have become more accurate since 1975.[1]

(iii) A number of writers have sought to show or to deny that demand management has been destabilizing, which implies that policy intervention removed the economy further from target than it would have been if it had been left alone.[2] To do this it is necessary to make assumptions as to the target level of output and the level which output would have attained in the absence of discretionary intervention. Some of these assumptions have been questionable. Thus one writer has claimed that policy was destabilizing because it was demonstrable that 'policy-off' changes in GDP (i.e. after deducting the effects of changes in taxation and government spending) were less widely scattered round the average annual increase in GDP than policy-on (i.e. actual) changes in GDP.[3] It is arbitrary, however, to measure failures of policy in terms of dispersion around an average annual increase in GDP. There is no presumption, as we can see from table 1.7, that governments were aiming each year at a constant rise in GDP. Indeed, there is every reason to suppose that they would aim at faster-than-average increases in depressions and below-average increases in times of boom.

The stabilizing effectiveness of short-term policy was also investigated in terms of the stability of GDP around its trend. It was shown by Artis[4] that for the 1958–70 period the dispersion of quarterly levels of observed GDP from their time-trend was larger than the dispersion of estimated 'policy-off' GDP. Policy-off GDP was found by deducting the cumulative effects of all tax changes introduced after a particular base year from its own (different) time-trend. The results indicated that policy was 'destabilizing' in the sense of this particular method of measurement. But, as the author made clear, there was never any presumption that trend GDP coincided with target GDP. The ambiguity was, moreover, increased by the establishment of a different time trend for 'policy-off' than for actual GDP, so that even if one of these trends had represented target GDP the other would have failed to do so.

The main conclusion seems to be that there has not, as yet, been any convincing demonstration that demand management was destabilizing. Such a demonstration would have to make acceptable assumptions about

---

1   For an official assessment of forecasting errors since 1976, see 'Forecasting in the Treasury', op. cit.

2   For reviews of these and other studies of short-term policies, see G. D. N. Worswick, 'Fiscal Policy and Stabilization in Britain', in A. K. Cairncross (ed.), *Britain's Economic Prospects Reconsidered* (Allen and Unwin, 1971) and M. C. Kennedy, 'Employment Policy – What Went Wrong?', in Joan Robinson (ed.), *After Keynes* (Blockwell, 1973).

3   B. Hansen, *Fiscal Policy in Seven Countries, 1955–65* (OECD, Paris, 1969).

4   M. J. Artis, 'Fiscal Policy for Stabilization', in W. Beckerman (ed.), *The Labour Government's Economic Record, 1964–70* (Duckworth, 1972).

TABLE 1.7
Short-term Targets and Forecast Errors, UK, 1955–86

		Forecast use of potential output or target pressure of demand[1] %	Forecast (and/or target) change in GDP from year earlier[2] %	Actual change in GDP from year earlier[3] %	Error (forecast less actual) %
1955	(years)	100	2.9	3.5	−0.6
1956	,,	99	1.1	1.4	−0.3
1957	,,	98	1.3	1.6	−0.3
1958	,,	95	−0.4	−0.3	−0.1
1959	(4th qtr)	94	2.8	6.5	−3.7
1960	,,	98	3.1	3.4	−0.3
1961	,,	97	1.8	2.3	−0.5
1962	,,	98	3.9	1.1	2.7
1963	,,	97	4.6	6.8	−2.2
1964	,,	101	5.4	3.9	1.5
1965	,,	100	2.7	2.6	0.1
1966	,,	99	2.0	1.3	0.7
1967	,,	98	3.1	2.1	1.0
1968	(2nd half)	99	3.6	4.8	−1.2
1969	,,	100	1.9	2.1	−0.2
1970	,,	101	3.6	2.1	1.5
1971	,,	99	1.1	1.6	−0.5
1972	,,	103	5.5	3.2	2.3
1973	,,	104	6.0	5.8	0.2
1974	,,	104	2.6	−0.9	3.5
1975	,,	99	0.0	−2.1	−2.1
1976	,,	98	3.9	3.9	0.0
1977	,,	98	1.5	2.2	−0.7
1978	,,	99	3.0	3.1	−0.1
1979	,,	97	−0.5	2.8	−3.3
1980	,,	95	−3.1	−4.3	1.2
1981	,,	92	−0.2	0.4	0.6
1982	,,	91	1.5	1.7	−0.2
1983	,,	92	2.5	3.7	−1.2
1984	,,	94	3.5	2.3	1.2
1985	,,	95	3.5	2.9	0.6
1986	,,	95	3.3	–	–

Notes and sources:
1 Potential output for 1955–67 is estimated as the level of GDP which would sustain an un-employment rate of 1.0%, and for 1968–86 as the level needed to keep the vacancy rate at 0.9 to 1.0%. The rate of growth of potential output is taken as 2.9% per annum for 1955–68 and 2.1% for 1968–86.
2 M.C. Kennedy, ibid., and *Financial Statement and Budget Reports* (HMSO).
3 Average estimate of GDP: *ET(AS)*, 1986, *FSBR*, 1986.

both the objectives of economic policy and the effects of policy instruments. It is not difficult to accept that policy was destabilizing in particular years: in 1959, for example, the economy might well have remained nearer to target if an expansionary budget had not coincided with an investment boom which the Treasury had failed to predict. But this was an example of exceptionally poor economic forecasting in one particular year. The general picture was one of fairly close proximity between actual GDP and target, with an average forecast error of only 1.1%, and this implies that *on average* the degree to which policy might have been destabilizing (assuming that it was) would have been very minor.

The associated criticism that there was 'too much fine tuning' may also be discussed briefly. If this means simply that the economy would have held very nearly as close to target levels of output during the demand management period (1944–74) without the intrusion of minor alterations in tax rates, then the point must be given some weight. For there is not much doubt that the effects of these tax changes were quite small in terms of their effects on GDP. It must be borne in mind, however, that the mere ritual of changing taxes up and down in response to the declared needs of the economic situation may have engendered a degree of confidence in the economic future which was beneficial for business investment. There is no way in which this hypothesis can be satisfactorily tested, and unfortunately the fact that the era of demand management coincided with the most sustained period of high employment ever known cannot settle the issue. But it remains a point of view to be set against the complaint that there was an excess of small-scale intervention.

(iv) During the period of fast inflation in the 1970s, demand management came in for some further criticisms. One of these was that the very fast expansion of demand during 1973, together with the high pressure of demand, was responsible for the acceleration in the rate of inflation. This criticism, however, attributes to demand management an inflation which was mainly, although not entirely, due to independent factors. We discuss these factors in section IV, where the main elements in the inflation are seen as a really exceptional rise in import prices – 100% in 3 years – together with some element of wage-pushfulness.

It has also been suggested[1] that 'the whole intellectual basis of postwar "demand management" by government is undermined if the natural unemployment rate hypothesis is true'. The trouble with statements like this is that the authors seldom make it clear what they mean. The least contentious part of the natural-rate hypothesis is the view that there is some unique level of involuntary unemployment at which the rate of inflation is zero, provided also that the expected rate of inflation is zero. If this is what is meant by the natural-rate hypothesis then a government which is anxious to avoid inflation would simply set target unemployment at or above the natural rate of unemployment. It would seek to achieve its target by exactly the same combination of forecasts and instruments which we have described. Far from destroying the basis of demand management, this version of the natural-rate hypothesis simply underlines its importance.

For some economists, however, the 'natural' rate of unemployment is a full-employment situation with supply-and-demand equilibrium in all labour markets simultaneously. Unemployment is assumed and believed to

---

1 M.Friedman and D.Laidler, 'Unemployment *versus* Inflation', IEA, 1975, Occasional Paper 44, p. 45.

be voluntary. It will only fall below the natural rate if money wages are increased ahead of the perceived or expected rise in prices.[1] Eventually, however, workers realize that their real wages have fallen, withdraw their labour, and the economy returns to full employment from what was previously a state of over-full employment. On this way of thinking, an inflating economy has to be in a continuous state of full employment. There is no reason to manage demand in an expansionary direction since (a) there is no involuntary unemployment, and (b) any reduction in unemployment will be subsequently reversed as workers realize that their real wages are lower than they were expected to be. To this hypothesis the compelling objection is that the economy is obviously not at full employment all the time, and it is quite possible to have massive involuntary unemployment and inflation simultaneously. Most of the unemployed in the UK, for example, have either lost their jobs through being made redundant or have failed to find employment on leaving school because there are no vacancies for the kind of work they can do.

III.5   Demand Management and the PSBR

Demand management can, and has, been described without reference to the budget deficit or the public-sector-borrowing requirement (PSBR), which is the combined deficit of the central government, local authorities and public corporations. This was deliberate. For if tax rates are to be decided according to the government's target level of GDP, and if the government's expenditure is set according to its social or political objectives, then the government deficit will be a *consequence* of demand management and not an independent target on its own. At given tax rates, the size of the deficit will also vary with the state of the economy, since the tax base (predominantly incomes and expenditure) will vary with the level of economic activity and prices, as will certain transfer payments, notably unemployment benefits.

To disregard the size of the budget deficit, or the PSBR, may seem surprising – even irresponsible – in the present climate of opinion. But the reason for doing so is quite clear, namely that policies should be judged by their economic consequences. This is the well-known principle of 'functional finance', which was stated by its originator in the following terms:

> The central idea is that government fiscal policy, its spending and taxing, its borrowing and repayment of loans, its issue of new money and its withdrawal of money, shall all be undertaken with an eye only

---

1   The hypothesis can be summarized in the statement that the rate of unemployment can deviate from its equilibrium in the short run but will return to its natural rate level in the long run after an adjustment for inflationary expectations (H. Frisch, *Theories of Inflation*, Cambridge University Press, 1983, p. 4).

to the *results* of these actions on the economy and not to any established traditional doctrine about what is sound or unsound.[1]

During the 1950s and 1960s it was usual for budgetary policy to be appraised only by its results. But in recent years there has been much concern over the size of the budget deficit and in particular of the PSBR. The latter is held to be important, although the reasons for its importance are seldom, if ever, explained by those who take this view. If the PSBR is £7bn, as it was in 1985–6, then what this means is that the public authorities have to borrow this sum of money from the banking system, private residents or overseas lenders. If the money is borrowed from overseas, the interest paid will constitute a transfer of national income abroad. If it is borrowed from the private sector, it will lead to a competition for funds and a rise in interest rates. This will mean higher monthly payments for anyone buying his house with a mortgage; it also leads to falling security values, including those of ordinary shares. Thus the only alternative is to finance the deficit by the issue of new money, and this may be done without any undesirable effects on mortgage payments or property values. This last course, however, is resisted by many, including the present government in the belief that any increase in the money stock *necessarily* involves an increase in the level of prices. This hypothesis, which is a generalization of the quantity theory of money to circumstances where real output is not necessarily fixed, is arguably false (see section IV) but very widely held in certain quarters, particularly in the City of London. Since it implies that there is no method of financing a public-sector deficit which does not have serious economic consequences, it forms the basis of a view that the PSBR should gradually be reduced.

Since 1979 the government has made the reduction of inflation the first priority of its macroeconomic policy. To achieve this goal it introduced in March 1980 a Medium Term Financial Strategy, which set target growth rates for the money stock, along with consequential limits on the PSBR – both for several years in advance. Although the limits for *future* years have been changed in successive budgets, the PSBR figure for the current financial year has often been treated as an inflexible target (more so than the money supply). This has meant that whenever unemployment has increased by more than was allowed for in the PSBR projection, the government has felt impelled to look for cuts in expenditure, higher taxes or higher nationalized industry prices in the attempt to meet its target for the PSBR. The effect of this blind obedience to self-imposed fiscal rules has been to increase unemployment still further.

When unemployment reached alarming heights in 1980 and was predicted to rise even further in 1981 the government took no preventive action. Thus the budget forecast of 1980 pointed to a sharp decline in GDP when unemployment was already 1.4 million, and the forecast in 1981 again looked to a

1   A. P. Lerner, 'Functional Finance and the Federal Debt', *Social Research*, Vol. 10, February 1943, pp. 38–51. Reprinted in M. G. Mueller (ed.), *Readings in Macroeconomics* (Holt, Rinehart and Winston, 1966).

fall in GDP when by that time unemployment had reached 2.2 million. The government professed to believe that (a) demand management could lead to temporary jobs but not to any permanent improvement, and (b) that expansion could not be 'afforded' because the government did not have the money to finance public works schemes or tax reductions. This statement that public works could not be 'afforded' made sense only on the assumption that the government's financial targets were sacrosanct. It would, however, have been quite possible to have financed increases in government expenditure by means of a higher PSBR, and to have borrowed the money either from the public (which would have raised interest rates) or from the Bank of England (which would not). Borrowing from the Bank of England would have been tantamount to the creation of new money, and although this would have breached the government's monetary targets it would have been no more inflationary than the increase in real demand which it was being used to finance. At that time, however, the government appeared to believe that every x per cent addition to the money stock led to an x per cent rise in the price level.

The other belief that seems to have inhibited government action was the view that demand expansion leads to temporary jobs but not to any permanent improvement. Aside from the quip that even temporary jobs are better than nothing, it is not clear what was meant by this position. It is possible that ministers were being briefed by advisers who accepted the more extreme version of the natural-rate hypothesis (which assumes no involuntary unemployment) and who therefore saw the situation in terms of a temporary reduction in *voluntary* unemployment to be followed, when prices have increased and real wages have fallen, by a return to the 'natural rate'. But there are a number of ideas in modern theoretical macro-economics which might have been used inappropriately to produce the same practical conclusion.[1] The situation, however, was one of idle resources in which a permanently higher level of demand would undoubtedly have increased permanent employment – although not without some risks of additional inflation.

IV   INFLATION
IV.1   Meaning and Measurement

Inflation is defined variously as *any* increase in the general level of prices, or as any *sustained* increase. In this chapter we shall use the wider definition since it enables us to include short-lived increases in the general price level, such as those of 1920, 1940 and 1951–2, within the sphere of discussion without raising the further definitional question of whether they were sufficiently sustained to be classed as inflations.

---

1 For a critique of these ideas, see Gavyn Davies, *Governments Can Affect Employment* (Employment Institute, London, 1985).

In measuring the rate of inflation we have a choice of index numbers. The appropriate index of the prices charged for all goods produced in the UK economy is the implied deflator for total final expenditure, so called because it is obtained by dividing the value of TFE at current prices by TFE at constant (1980) prices. The TFE deflator includes export prices. If an index is required to measure the prices of goods purchased by UK residents, the best general measure is the implied deflator for total domestic expenditure, since this is an average of the prices paid for consumption and investment goods, both privately and publicly purchased. If we are chiefly interested in the prices paid for consumer goods and services, we have a choice between the implied deflator for consumers' expenditure and the index of retail prices. The former, like all implicit indices, is not compiled directly from price data but is found by dividing the current value of consumers' expenditure by the volume estimate as measured at constant prices.[1] By contrast, the index of retail prices (the cost-of-living index) is compiled directly from price data. It registers the prices of a collection of goods and services entering a typical shopping basket. The composition of the basket has been revised from time to time so as to keep up with changes in the pattern of expenditure. Being a base-weighted index it gradually becomes outdated in coverage. In periods of inflation, it will tend to exaggerate the increase in the cost of living because consumers will switch their expenditure patterns towards those goods which are rising less rapidly in price. Nevertheless, it is accurate enough for most purposes.

There is nothing new about inflation. The retail price index in 1980 was approximately 25 times its level at the beginning of the century. Prices fell in only 13 out of the last 80 years (notably in 1920–23 and 1925–33). During the rest of the period they generally rose, with a particularly fast inflation during and immediately after the First World War (13% per annum during 1914–20). The rate of price increase was much lower in the Second World War because of widespread price controls. In the period after the war the average rate of increase was still quite low – 3% per annum in the 1950s and 4% in the 1960s – despite the high level of employment. It was not until the 1970s that inflation became really serious, with a record 24% increase in 1975 and an average rate for the whole decade of 13%.[2] In the early 1980s the rate of inflation was falling, and in the three years from 1983 to 1986 the year-on-year rates of increase had fallen to 5 or 6% – the lowest since 1970.

IV.2   A Model of Inflation

To explain inflation in an open economy like the UK it is necessary to take account of at least three independent types of impulse. These are (i) increases in world prices and UK import prices, (ii) excess demand in the home economy, and (iii) the independent influence of 'wage pushfulness'.

---

1   The volume or constant-price estimates are derived from base-weighted quantity indices.

2   This is the average of annual increases. The compound rate for 1970-80 was 14%.

The influence of import prices is important because imports of goods and services account for 20% of TFE. Some imports are in competition with home production, so that if their prices are raised home buyers may switch to domestic substitutes. But the major part of UK imports cannot be made at home at all. Imports of some foods, most raw materials and many of the semi-manufactures are in this category, and as the demand for them is also highly inelastic, increases in world prices for such commodities are followed by increases in the level of UK costs and prices. UK prices will also rise if there is an increase in the world price of oil, which is the one major primary commodity it produces at home. Many of the most violent inflations in the UK can be traced to changes in the world prices of primary commodities.

The second main element in our model of inflation is the degree of excess demand (i.e. demand less supply at going prices) in the various markets for goods and labour. Wages and prices in individual markets may be expected to increase whenever demand runs ahead of supply. The rate at which they increase, moreover, will probably be related to the degree of excess demand in the market. In markets where there is excess supply, there will be a tendency for prices to fall. In the case of wages, they may increase less rapidly than the general price level, with a consequential fall in the real wage. The balance of excess supply and excess demand in the labour market used to be measurable by the rate of unemployment or the vacancy percentage. But in the last decade or so, these two series have lost their old relationship to each other, so that there is now some uncertainty about comparisons of the pressure of demand over long periods of time. (See section IV.4 below.)

The third ingredient in our model of inflation is more controversial, and is the potentially independent force of wage-pushfulness. It seems necessary to include it as a separate force because wages are widely fixed by bargaining between the representatives of powerful groups, the union and the firm or employers' federation, each of which has the ability to influence the bargain by threatening to interrupt production and employment. Whilst there are reasons to expect that the pressure of demand for labour will normally be an influence in the bargaining process, we cannot exclude the possibility that alterations in the strength of the union, in the loyalty of its members and in its readiness to strike may act as an independent force (i.e. independent of market forces) in determining wage increases.

We can combine these three main causes of inflation into a more complete model by relating them to expected price increases and the exchange rate in the manner illustrated in figure 1.5. The model assumes that the *process* by which excess demand leads to price inflation is through the rate of increase in wages. Higher wages mean higher average costs of production and these lead, after a time-lag, to higher prices. This will happen either because business firms tend to set prices by a constant mark-up over variable costs or because they seek to maximize profits. Higher prices lead, again after a time-lag, to higher wages, since trade unions will tend to claim compensation for increases in the cost of living, or in other words to restore the real wages of their members. Thus the central ingredient of our model is a wage–price spiral which is superimposed upon the excess demand for labour. But besides excess demand, the spiral may also be set in motion by exogenous increases in wages coming from wage-push, by increases in import prices as a consequence of movements in world commodity prices, or by exchange-rate changes induced by movements in the balance of payments.

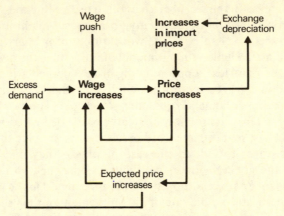

Figure 1.5   Inflationary processes

The model as it stands makes no allowance for a direct influence of excess demand upon price increases. This omission is justified for the 1960s where various investigations found no evidence for such a relationship.[1] In the 1970s, however, some correlation was observed between profit margins and output. The margins of industrial and commercial companies fell by about 7 percentage points in the downturn between 1973 and 1975, and they rose by 7% when demand recovered in 1975–8.[2] These are fairly small changes, and the main influence of demand pressure still seems to run through the labour market.

A second objection to the model might be that there is no reference to the quantity of money. This lack of an explicit reference, however, does not rule out monetary causation of inflation, since additions to the quantity of money will lead to increases in wages through the medium of excess demand, and excess demand has a prominent place in the model. This amounts to saying that monetary inflation is a branch of demand-pull inflation. An increase in the money supply will act through interest-rate reductions or more directly through credit availability to increase the demand for goods and services,

---

1 For example, L. A. Dicks-Mireaux, 'The Inter-Relationship between Cost and Price Changes, 1945–1959', *OEP* (NS), Vol. 13(3), reprinted in R. J. Ball and P. Doyle (eds.), *Inflation* (Penguin, 1969). The model of figure 1.5 is an extension of the relationships investigated by Dicks-Mireaux.

2   See the discussion in *NIER*, November 1982, pp. 21–2.

and hence create excess demand. There is no place, in our model, for an influence of money upon prices which is not transmitted through the medium of excess demand.

Besides excess demand and the wage-price spiral, figure 1.5 allows for two other possible interactions between wages and prices, both of them operating through the effect of rising prices upon expected future prices. The first of these is the possibility that expectations of future price changes, rather than compensation for past increases, may be a major factor in wage bargaining. It has been suggested by some writers[1] that the expectation of a price increase of, say, 10% in the next twelve months will induce trade unions and employers to settle for increases in nominal wages of as much as 10% more than would have occurred if prices had been expected to be stable. This hypothesis assumes a degree of sophistication in the process of wage bargaining which may not be characteristic of many trade unions. It is certainly arguable that wage claims are more likely to be based on the actual than on the expected rise in the cost of living. But the employers' side must not be neglected, and here there may be something in the idea that the propensity of firms to grant wage increases is influenced by their expectations of price increases on the part of their competitors. Price expectations, therefore, cannot be ignored in a model of the inflationary process, and they become increasingly important as people learn to live with inflation.

The second additional link between wages and prices runs from expectations of higher prices to the level of excess demand. As consumers become aware that prices are going to rise rapidly in the future, they may seek to protect themselves from an erosion of the value of their money by switching out of money and financial assets into goods. The effects of this form of behaviour will be manifested in a tendency for the savings ratio to decline (which has not happened in the UK) and for the velocity of circulation of money to rise (which has also not happened). We have included it in the figure, along with the link between price expectations and wage bargaining, because it is a mode of behaviour which has been observed in other countries in periods of hyperinflation.[2] It is a form of behaviour which, along with expectational wage bargaining, is likely to develop as inflation gathers pace and as people learn from experience how money can lose its value. The fact that such behaviour can become general adds to the danger of inflation getting out of hand and provides a powerful case for stopping it as early as possible.

A third linkage in the system is that running from domestic prices to the exchange rate and back to import prices. As domestic costs and prices rise, exporters have to increase their prices too. If the foreign demand for exports

---

1　For example, M. Friedman, 'The Role of Monetary Policy', *AER*, Vol. 58(1), pp. 1–17, and *Unemployment versus Inflation*, op. cit.

2　See, for example, A. J. Brown, *The Great Inflation* (London, 1955) and P. Cagan, 'The Monetary Dynamics of Hyperinflation' in M. Friedman (ed.), *Studies in the Quantity Theory of Money* (Chicago, 1956).

(or the home demand for imports) is elastic, this leads to a deterioration in the balance of payments which leads, in turn, to a decline in the exchange rate. When this happens, the sterling price of imports increases, and domestic costs and prices go up further.

One further point which will not be clear from the scheme in figure 1.5 is that increases in the price level always tend to raise the demand for money. If the quantity of money is kept unchanged, the effect will be to raise interest rates, thus lowering the levels of real output and employment, reducing excess demand and dampening the rate of inflation. These effects will not occur, however, if the central bank is aiming to hold interest rates constant. It will then have to *increase* the money supply as the demand for money rises. Thus although inflationary processes may be initiated by excess demand, by wage-push or by increased import prices, they may be supported through permissive increases in the supply of money.

IV.3   Imported Inflation

Nearly every major increase or decrease in the UK price level has been associated with a major change in import prices (see table 1.8). Import prices were very volatile in the early 1920s; they rose rapidly in 1940 at the beginning of the Second World War; and again in 1951 with the Korean War. Between 1972 and 1974 they rose by 87% as a result of a very fast rise in fuel prices (260% in two years), together with price increases for basic materials (up 100%) and food, beverages and tobacco (70%). There are strong grounds for believing that this was the main factor responsible for the protracted spiral of price and wage increases in the 1970s.

The main effect of a rise in import prices is to increase costs of production which, in turn, means higher final prices. With imports comprising some 20% of TFE, it can be expected that each rise of 1% in import prices will

TABLE 1.8
Major Changes in UK Import Prices since 1920

	Change in import prices (%)	Change in retail prices (%)
1920	19	16
1921	−33	−9
1922	−20	−19
1940	39	17
1951	33	9
1973	28	9
1974	46	16
1975	14	24
1976	22	17
1977	16	16

Sources: retail prices: *BLS, DEG*; import prices 1920–40: *LCES* (average index for merchandise imports); 1951–77: *ET(AS), AAS* (unit value index).

lead to an initial rise in final prices of 0.2% ; and these will be raised further by the response of wages. An additional effect occurs in the case of imports in inelastic demand such as foodstuffs and materials. Here the difficulty of substituting domestic output for imports means that the import bill rises and the exchange rate, assuming this to be flexible, declines. When this happen the sterling price of imports rises further and there are further increases in final prices.

Imported inflation is not readily curable because, unless the exchange rate can be raised, there is not much prospect of offsetting the effect on final prices other than by inducing large reductions in total demand and employment. Between 1972 and 1974 the dollar prices of primary commodities in world trade rose by 130%, and this was accompanied by rapid increases in prices in all the main industrial countries: 39% in Japan and Italy, 27% in France and 13% in Germany. The UK increase, at 44%, was higher than elsewhere, but this was because of high internal demand pressure and the indexation of wages under stage III of Mr Heath's incomes policy. The much lower inflation in Germany was partly attributable to an 18% appreciation of the Deutschmark which went some way to offset higher import prices.[1]

IV.4   Excess Demand, Unemployment and Vacancies

Whilst external influences have been responsible for most, if not all, the major inflationary episodes in UK economic history, there is not much doubt that the pressure of demand on internal resources has been an important influence too. The measurement of this pressure is not without difficulties. For many years it was taken for granted that a reasonably reliable measure of demand pressure was given by the unemployment percentage. Involuntary unemployment in a particular labour market is equal by definition to the excess of supply over demand at the going rate of pay. The degree of excess supply is measured by unemployment as a percentage of the labour force.

It might be thought that a more direct index of excess demand is given by the number of unfilled vacant jobs. But the figures here are much less complete than those for unemployment. The unemployed have an incentive to register because, as a rule, they are entitled to unemployment benefit. Unfilled vacancies, however, are recorded by employers only if they believe it worth their while to notify them. They may prefer to recruit through the local newspapers rather than through job centres. And an employer who has already notified the job centre of vacancies for a particular kind of worker will not need to register new vacancies because the original notice will be sufficient to attract applicants. Thus the vacancy statistics are bound to be incomplete, and it is officially recognized that only about one-third of all new vacancies are notified to the Department of Employment.

---

1   These statistics are taken from the *National Institute Economic Review*.

For many years the unemployment and vacancy statistics moved in a close and consistent relationship to each other. The same unemployment percentage was always observed against the same given vacancy rate, and changes in the two percentages were the same in absolute magnitude. It was possible, therefore, to regard either measure as an index of excess demand, whilst the unemployment percentage also served as an indication of the degree of personal and social distress caused by lack of work.

Since the 1960s, however, the measurement of excess demand has become problematical because of a gradual change in the relationship between the unemployment and vacancy statistics. A given level of vacancies is now associated with a much higher level of unemployment than it used to be. The extent of the change can be seen from the following comparisons:

	Unfilled vacancies, UK		*Unemployment, UK*	
	(000s, percentages in brackets)			
1965–6 (average)	262	(1.1)	346	(1.5)
1973–4 (average)	302	(1.3)	557	(2.4)
1979	241	(1.3)	1,173	(4.8)
1962–3 (average)	147	(0.6)	497	(2.2)
1971–2 (average)	139	(0.6)	748	(3.3)
1975–6 (average)	138	(0.6)	1,032	(4.3)
1982–4 (average)	145	(0.6)	2,876	(12.0)

The figures illustrate a continuing tendency for unemployment to increase relative to a given vacancy percentage. Thus the unemployment rate associated with a vacancy rate of 0.6% (as experienced in the recession period of 1982–4) has increased from 2% in the early 1960s to 12% in the 1980s. The increase in the 1980s has been particularly rapid.

The reasons for this change in the $U–V$ relationship are various. There have, first of all, been increases in the ratios of recorded to actual unemployment and also of recorded to actual vacancies. But the net effect has been to increase recorded unemployment in relationship to recorded vacancies. The evidence for this comes mainly from a comparison of registered unemployment with the Census counts taken in 1966, 1971 and 1981. The population census includes the unregistered unemployed, and when these are compared with the unemployment register, it is clear that the ratio of registered to Census unemployment has increased. It rose from 56% for male unemployment in 1966, to 71% in 1971 and around 100% in 1981. Between 1971 and 1981 the unemployment register rose by 1.7 million whilst Census unemployment rose by 1.4 million. As for vacancies, improvements in the government employment service are believed to have led to a rise in the ratio of recorded to actual vacancies.

A second reason for the change may be that unemployment has become less involuntary because of a rise in unemployment compensation relative to earnings. The point here is not that workers have surrendered their jobs in order to prosper on the dole, but rather that once they have been made redundant they have chosen to remain longer on the register whilst looking for the right job. They have turned down more job vacancies than in earlier years. This explanation cannot extend much beyond the early 1970s, however, since the benefit earnings ratio has been level or falling since then. But supporters of this view can point to the fact that the *U-V* shift was much more noticeable for male workers, who most generally qualify for benefit, than for female workers, who are frequently not entitled to it.

A third hypothesis is the shake-out theory, which rests on the supposition that during the 1960s employers were in the habit of holding on to labour during periods of business recession in the expectation of a quick return of boom conditions. This expectation, it is argued, has been gradually removed by the withdrawal of interest in demand management since the 1960s, so that hoarding labour has been seen as increasingly wasteful. This explanation, which originated in connection with a sharp rise in productivity in 1968, was put in question by the absence of any 'shake-in' during the boom of 1973. Unemployment declined in 1973, but not by enough to restore its previous relationship to vacancies. A further shake-out may have occurred in the 1980s.

A fourth hypothesis, which seems plausible but is again not too well supported by independent evidence, is that there has been a growing mismatch in terms of skill, occupation and locality, between the demand and supply of labour.

Finally, it is maintained by some labour economists that workers who have been unemployed for long periods lose interest in applying for jobs, and cease, therefore, to be part of the effective supply of labour. The unemployment rate becomes increasingly unrepresentative of the true excess supply of labour as the duration of unemployment increases. This explanation seems particularly pertinent to the last seven years, when the numbers unemployed for over 1 year have increased from 300,000 (in 1979) to 1.3 million (in early 1986).

It is not easy to make sense of what has happened. But the main statistical conclusion is that neither the unemployment rate nor the vacancy rate can be taken as consistent indicators of excess demand over long periods of years. If a single indicator has to be used, then the vacancy percentage is preferable.[1]

IV.5   Demand-pull Inflation

Whilst there is some doubt about how to measure the intensity of excess demand in recent years, there is ample evidence from earlier periods of its influence upon the rate of inflation. Numerous studies in the 1950s and 1960s

---

1   A recent discussion of this problem is in *NIER*, November 1983, pp. 39–41. But see also A. Evans, 'Notes on the Changing Relationship between Registered Unemployment and Notified Vacancies: 1961–1966 and 1966–1971', *Economica*, May 1977; S.J. Nickell, 'The Effect of Unemployment and Related Benefits on the Duration of Unemployment', *EJ*, March 1979; A.B. Atkinson and J.S. Flemming, 'Unemployment and Social Security and Incentives', *MBR*, 1978, and R. Layard and S. Nickell, 'The Causes of British Unemployment', *NIER*, February 1985.

showed a strong negative relationship between the level of unemployment (which is inversely related to excess demand) and the rate of change of money wage rates. One of the earlier studies of this kind, and certainly the most influential, was published in 1958 by Professor A.W.Phillips.[1] This examined the relationship between unemployment rates and wage increases for nearly a century, and on the basis of data for 1861–1913 suggested that the wage increases to be associated with different rates of unemployment were as follows:

Unemployment rate	1.0	2.0	3.0	4.0	5.0
% change in wage rates	8.7	2.8	1.2	0.5	0.1

The relationship became known as the *Phillips Curve*.[2] It implies a non-linear, marginal 'trade-off' between the rate of wage increase and unemployment. Thus the rate of wage increase declines by nearly 6% when the unemployment rate goes up from 1.0% to 2.0%, but by only 1.6% when it goes up from 2.0% to 3.0%. The trade-off suggested was a modest one at all but the highest pressures of demand for labour.

One of the more remarkable features of the Phillips Curve, and one which distinguishes it from most similar studies, was that it was found to be highly reliable in predicting increases in wages during much later periods of time than the years 1861–1913 which had been used to derive the equation. Thus Phillips was able to show a very close correspondence for 1948–57 between the wage changes implied by his relationship and those that actually took place. The Phillips Curve was also accurate in predicting wage increases over the period 1958–66, which was after the study had been published. During these eight years there was not a single error in excess of 2.5%, and the mean error (regardless of sign) was only 1.1%; furthermore, the positive and negative errors tended to offset each other. These predictive successes, however, have to be seen in the light of what was an exceedingly stable level of unemployment compared with the experience from which Phillips had started. In 1861–1913 unemployment rates ranged from 1 to 11%, whereas in 1948–66 they were between 1 and 2.3%. Thus one could argue that postwar experience up to 1966 tested only a small part of the Phillips relation. Nevertheless, it passed this test fairly well.

---

1   A.W.Phillips, 'The Relation between Unemployment and the Rate of Change of Money Wage Rates, 1861–1957', *Economica*, November 1958, although A.J.Brown, op. cit., had illustrated the same relationship.

2   The equation for the schedule was:

$$\frac{\Delta W}{W} = -0.900 + 9.638U^{-1.394}$$

It can also be expressed in logarithmic terms as

$$\log \frac{\Delta W}{W} + 0.9 = 0.984 - 1.394 \log U$$

where $\frac{\Delta W}{W}$ is the percentage rate of wage change and U is the unemployment rate (Phillips, op. cit.).

After the mid-1960s, however, the pure Phillips Curve became increasingly unreliable as a guide to the rate of wage inflation. It under-predicted by about 4.5% per annum in 1967–9, by 10–12% in 1970–3, and by more than 20% in 1974 and 1975. For several years there was no recognizable relationship between statistics of the unemployment percentage and the rate of wage increase. It is important, therefore, to ask whether the breakdown of the Phillips relationship can be explained, and here several factors come to mind:

(i)   Easily the most important factor is the omission from the pure Phillips equation of the causal influence of price changes. This would not have mattered so much in the early 1960s when inflation was moderate. But the omission is serious with inflation at the rate experienced in the 1970s.

(ii) A connected factor is the probability that wage increases have become much more sensitive to price increases as a result of learning to live with inflation. This is not an easy matter to establish empirically, but it is nonetheless probable that a growing number of trade-union negotiators have insisted on full compensation for price changes whilst others have sought wage negotiations at more frequent intervals. There may also have been some tendency to follow the 'expectations-augmented Phillips curve', with expected rather than actual price changes being taken as the basis for wage awards.

(iii) A third factor is the influence of 'wage-pushfulness', which, as we discuss below, appears to have been more prevalent in the period after 1970.

(iv) A fourth factor was the change in the relationship between unemployment and vacancies. With given rates of unemployment signalling a higher pressure of demand than previously, there was bound to be some movement in the Phillips relation.

(v)   Finally, the Phillips relationship may have been partly obscured by a number of attempts, notably in 1972–3 and 1975–8, to control wage increases by incomes policy.

These considerations are sufficient to explain why the link between wage increases and the pressure of demand became obscured after the end of the 1960s. The theoretical linkage has remained unimpaired, and since 1980 has been corroborated by the expected combination of falling rates of wage inflation and rising unemployment (see table 1.9).

IV.6   Wage-push Inflation

The questions of whether wages have increased as a result of unions pushing up wages independently of market forces is controversial chiefly because of the volume of historical evidence in favour of a demand-pull explanation.

This evidence, however, need not preclude the possibility of sporadic out-bursts of wage-push inflation. Nor is there any reason in principle why wage-bargaining procedures should respond precisely and consistently to the pressure of demand in the labour market.

The first real evidence in favour of a wage-push contribution to recent inflation came with the 'pay explosion' of 1970, when the rate of wage increase was about 12% faster than could be predicted by the pure Phillips Curve. It was also about 7% higher than could have been predicted from a relationship estimated by Artis in which price changes were included as an additional causal variable and excess demand was measured by the number of vacancies.[1] It can be argued that this was a consequence either of the relax-ation of incomes policy in late 1969 or of direct wage-push on the part of the trade unions. The two types of explanation are not unconnected because the government was under strong pressure from the unions to bring incomes policy to an end.

In the next few years there was further evidence of wage-push inflation in terms of a tendency for money wage rates to press ahead of prices. This was certainly true of the old wage-rate index for manual workers. If this index is deflated by the retail price index to arrive at an index of real wage rates, then a very conspicuous rise in real wages appears in the early 1970s – as is shown by the following comparison of 5-year periods:

1960–65	3%
1965–70	7%
1970–75	23%
1975–80	1%

This, however, is not the story told by other indicators. The index of average weekly earnings (again deflated by the RPI) shows much the same real gain in 1970–75 as in 1965–70, and if the national accounts data of wages and salaries are deflated by prices they also fail to show a significant jump in real wages in 1970–75. This is a case of conflicting evidence. There was, however, a history of confrontation and industrial unrest in the 1970–75 period (and also in 1979) and the very sharp rise in the number of industrial disputes was at least suggestive of wage-pushfulness.

IV.7   Inflation since 1970: a Summary

Since 1970 the annual rate of inflation has been consistently higher than in the earlier postwar period. It rose sharply in the 1970–72 period and accelerated violently in 1973–5, when it reached 24%. In the next three years the inflation rate declined, reaching 8% in 1978. But the rate rose in 1979 and 1980, when it was 18%, before falling to around 5 or 6% a year in

---

1   M.J.Artis, 'Some Aspects of the Present Inflation', *NIER*, February 1971, reprinted in H.G.Johnson and A.R.Nobay (eds.), *The Current Inflation* (Macmillan, 1971).

TABLE 1.9
Inflation and inflationary pressures 1960–85

	(1) Change in retail prices (%)	(2) Change in average weekly earnings (%)	(3) Unemployment percentage	(4) Unfilled vacancies percentage	(5) Days lost in industrial disputes (m)	(6) Change in import prices (%)	(7) Change in exchange rate (%)	(8) Change in money stock (£M3) (%)
1960	1	6	1.7	0.9	3	0		
1961	4	7	1.5	0.9	3	-2		
1962	4	3	2.0	0.6	6	-1		
1963	2	4	2.3	0.6	2	4		
1964	3	9	1.7	0.9	2	3		5
1965	5	8	1.4	1.0	3	1		8
1966	4	7	1.5	1.1	2	1		3
1967	2	4	2.3	0.8	3	0		10
1968	5	8	2.4	0.8	5	12	-14	7
1969	5	8	2.4	0.9	7	4		2
1970	6	12	2.6	0.8	11	4	-1	9
1971	9	11	3.1	0.6	14	5	0	14
1972	7	13	3.5	0.6	24	5	-4	27
1973	9	14	2.4	1.4	7	28	-9	27
1974	16	18	2.4	1.3	15	46	-3	11
1975	24	27	3.7	0.6	6	14	-8	6
1976	17	16	5.0	0.6	3	22	-14	10
1977	16	9	5.3	0.7	10	16	-5	9
1978	8	13	5.2	0.9	9	4	0	16
1979	13	15	4.8	1.0	29	7	7	13
1980	18	21	6.1	0.6	12	10	10	19
1981	12	13	9.5	0.4	4	8	-1	14
1982	9	9	11.0	0.5	5	8	-5	9
1983	5	8	12.1	0.6	4	9	-8	11
1984	5	6	12.6	0.6	27	10	-5	10
1985	6	8	13.1	0.7	6	4	0	13

Sources: *ETAS*, 1986; *DEG*, February 1986 and earlier; *NIER*, February 1986.
Notes: Col. (2) earnings in GB production industries linked to earlier indices. Col. (3) UK unemployed excluding school-leavers as percentage of employees plus *total* unemployed. Col. (6) unit value of merchandise imports on balance-of-payments basis. Col. (7) sterling exchange rate index 1969–85, parity rate 1967–8. Col. (8) end-year, seasonally adjusted.

1983–5. These movements, together with the main factors which have been suggested as the causes or contributory factors, are set out in table 1.9.

The inflation of the 1970–72 period is difficult to associate with either the pressure of demand or with increases in import prices. In each of these years, as table 1.9 shows, the unfilled vacancy rate was well below normal, and unemployment exceptionally high. Since import prices were rising by only 4 or 5% a year, it seems clear that the main factors responsible were the 'rebound effect' of the ending of incomes policy in 1970, and, as evidenced by the figures for industrial disputes, an element of trade-union pushfulness. We have seen already that on some evidence, but not all, there was a strong tendency for wages to push ahead of price increases during this period.

The next question is why did inflation rise even further in the period 1973–7? One candidate here is the pressure of demand for labour which, on the evidence of unfilled vacancies, was for two years higher than it had been in any year since 1955. Combined with an exceptionally fast *increase* in demand, it was clearly one element in the rapid inflation of 1973 and 1974. Nevertheless, it could hardly have been responsible for inflation rates of 16 and 24%. The main factor in this period was the huge rise in oil and other import prices. The index of import prices rose by 87% between 1972 and 1974, and with imports accounting for one-fifth of TFE, must have added 20–25% to the internal price level during these two years. An additional factor during 1974–5 was the influence of indexed incomes policies under Stage III of the Mr Heath's statutory policy and the 'Social Contract'. The effect of indexing wages against the cost of living was almost certain to increase the responsiveness of wages to prices above what it would have been in the absence of such policies.

In all of these explanations, we have to bear in mind the wage-price spiral which serves to continue and prolong the effects of inflationary impulses well beyond the period of their first impact.

After 1975 there was a particularly sharp decline in the inflation rate for three years, and by 1978 the rate had fallen 16 points to 8%. This decline may be partly attributable to the lower pressure of demand in 1976 and 1977, but the main factor responsible was the introduction in July 1975 of an incomes policy which won the consent of the trade-union movement. Phase I of the policy set a limit of £6 a week on wage increases, whilst Phase II, which began in July 1976, imposed a limit of 5%. Thus the rise in average weekly earnings fell from 27% in 1975 to 9% in 1977.

The rise in the inflation rate between 1978 and 1980 can be traced to a number of influences, of which the first was the revival of demand pressure in 1978 and 1979. Oil prices rose sharply between 1978 and 1980, with the OPEC price more than doubling between these two years. Possibly the most serious factor, however, was the withdrawal of union co-operation with incomes policy and the wage increases associated with the 1978/9 'winter of discontent'. But a further 4 percentage points were added to retail prices by the budget decision of June 1979 to raise VAT from 8 to

15%. Without this increase, the task of reducing inflation in the next three years might well have proved easier.

Between 1980 and 1985 the inflation rate fell by 13 percentage points, although the decline would have been much less without the VAT increase. Although world primary product prices were falling at this time (in terms of dollars), UK import prices (in sterling) were rising each year at a fairly steady 8–10%. Thus the cause of the reduced rate of inflation in this period was primarily internal and can probably be traced either to the Phillips Curve effect of very high unemployment or to declining trade-union militancy. The figures for industrial disputes in table 1.9 show a marked reduction after the late 1970s, apart, that is, from the 1984 figure which is swollen as a result of the unsuccessful miners' strike. In this period, however, it must be doubted whether the apparent decline in militancy was an independent force of its own, rather than a symptom of the depressed state of the labour market.

The main contrast with the late 1970s was the series of declines between 1980 and 1982 in the rate of increase in hourly earnings, and the absence in those years of much increase in real earnings. It might be claimed by supporters of the government's monetary policies that the declines were attributable to the effects of monetary targets on price expectations of wage negotiators. But direct evidence of such effects is lacking, and many would argue that it is singularly naive to imagine that trade-union officials believe that the quantity of money determines the price level. The status of price expectations, however formed, in wage bargaining is also open to dispute. Thus the main cause of the decline in the inflation rate has probably to be seen as the massive increase in unemployment: from 6% in 1980 to 11% by 1982 – and its Phillips Curve effect in reducing the increase in earnings. This explanation must not be taken, however, to exclude the possibility that once unemployment reaches a high enough level, the Phillips Curve becomes horizontal, so that wage increases are insensitive to increases in unemployment beyond that point.[1]

IV.8   Monetary Explanations of Inflation

The increased rate of inflation in the 1970s was accompanied by markedly faster increases in the stock of money. The money supply had been rising at about 6% a year in 1964–9, whereas in 1972 and 1973 the rate of increase was 27%. A number of economists, journalists and stockbrokers interpreted the connection between the rise in the rate of monetary expansion and the faster

---

1 For further discussions of recent inflation see W. Beckerman and T. Jenkinson, 'What stopped inflation? Unemployment or Commodity Prices?', *EJ*, March 1986, and M. J. Artis and M. K. Lewis, 'Inflation in the United Kingdom', in V. Argy and J. Nevile (eds.), *Inflation and Unemployment: Theory, Experience and Policy-Making* (Allen and Unwin, 1985).

inflation rate as cause and effect. Some have attributed to money the sole blame for the inflation.[1]

It is generally accepted in economic theory that increases in the supply of money *can* lead to higher real output or to higher prices. But they do so by raising the aggregate demand for goods and services, thus adding to the pressure of demand. This means that if the inflation of the 1970s had been caused by the rise in the money supply, it would have been accompanied by a rise in vacancies and lower unemployment. These changes, moreover, would need to have been substantial to account for such a sharp rise in the inflation rate. However, as we have already explained above, there was no general or sustained increase in the pressure of demand in the 1970s. Unemployment was higher than it had been, and the vacancy rate, although high in 1973 and 1974, was lower on average in the 1970s than it had been earlier. This absence of any increase, let alone any marked increase, in the pressure of demand is fairly compelling evidence against the monetarist point of view.

This conclusion, however, does not prevent us from agreeing that *if* the money supply had not been allowed to increase so fast, then inflation in the 1970s would have been less severe. If, for example, the money stock had increased in the 1970s at its 1964–69 rate of increase of 6% a year instead of the recorded 14%, then it is reasonable to conjecture that interest rates would have been very much higher than they were, and the pressure of demand would have been lower. This would have had some effect on the rate of wage increase and the exchange rate. It is difficult to believe, however, that tighter money could have cancelled out the effect of the rise in oil and other import prices.

IV.9   Inflation and Economic Policy

In the period when inflation was merely creeping, it was possible to regard it as a small price to pay for the benefit of high employment. A gently sloping trade-off between inflation and unemployment made the problem of political compromise minimal compared with the situation in the 1970s and 1980s. The advocacy of an incomes policy in the 1960s was associated either with those who hoped to be able to run the economy at a pressure of demand which now seems unthinkable, or else with those who sought to use it as an instrument of income redistribution.

The arrival of fast inflation in the 1970s transformed the policy problem. It meant that real incomes were rapidly eroded between wage settlements, with effects that were socially divisive and disruptive. It also transformed

1   For example, M.Parkin, 'Where is Britain's Inflation Rate Going?', *LBR*, July 1975, W.Rees-Mogg, *The Times*, 13 July 1976, and, for an American example, M.Friedman, *Money and Economic Development* (Praeger, 1973). The monetarist case against the Keynesians is put in D.Laidler, *Monetarist Perspectives* (Philip Allan, 1982), and the Keynesian case against the monetarists in N.Kaldor, *The Scourge of Monetarism*, (Oxford University Press, 1982), E.H. Phelps Brown, 'A Non-Monetarist View of the Pay Explosion', *TBR*, March 1975, and M.C.Kennedy, 'Recent Inflation and the Monetarists', *Applied Economics*, June 1976.

economic behaviour. Economic units learned how to live with inflation and sought to defend their real wages either by insisting on full compensation for past increases in the cost of living or possibly, in a few cases, by bargaining on the basis of price forecasts. This meant that there were two main methods of bringing inflation under control. One was to deflate domestic demand to such a low pressure that the effect of unemployment upon the rate of wage increase was large enough to offset that of cost-of-living compensation and/or price expectations. Given that prices in some years were increasing at rates of over 15%, this would have necessitated either intolerably high unemployment or what was thought to be an intolerably long period of correction. The other alternative was an incomes policy under which the rate of wage increase was subjected to statutory or firm quasi-statutory control.

A statutory incomes policy was tried by the Conservative government in 1972–4 after its attempt to secure a voluntary policy had failed. The policy coincided with a major rise in import prices, and the provision in stage III of the policy for the effective indexation of wages to the cost of living had the unfortunate further effect of indexing them to the international terms of trade. But the policy collapsed, despite its statutory powers, because one strong trade union, the National Union of Mineworkers, was prepared to 'go slow' and finally strike rather than accept the terms of the policy. It was this which led to the early election of February 1974, and, it is argued, to the defeat of the Conservative Party.[1]

The incoming Labour government continued the indexation provisions under a 'Social Contract' but did little further to prevent inflation until July 1975, when a voluntary incomes policy was introduced in three stages, starting with a maximum increase of £6 per week.

This was certainly the first time that an incomes policy can be said to have made a significant impact upon the rate of wage inflation. But the government was not able to obtain union agreement to a continuation of incomes policy in 1978, and it was unwilling to enforce a statutory policy.

The Conservative government which was returned in May 1979 was strongly opposed to incomes policy, and strove to contain inflation by a progressive reduction in the rate of increase in the money stock. This approach, which was formalized as a Medium Term Financial Strategy in the Budget of 1980 and reiterated in subsequent budgets, was discussed at greater length in section III of this chapter.

V   ECONOMIC GROWTH
V.1   The Growth of Productive Potential

In ordinary language one usually speaks of any increase in GDP, however it comes about, as economic growth. In economic theory and applied economics it is best to reserve the term for increases in a country's productive

---

1   For an account of this period see M.J.Stewart, *Politics and Economic Policy in the UK since 1964* (Pergamon, 1978).

TABLE 1.10
Economic Growth, UK, 1900–79 (percentage increases per annum)

	GDP (average estimate)	GDP per person employed	Employed labour force	Capital excluding dwelling
1900–13	1.5	0.6	0.9	1.7
1922–38	2.3	1.2	1.1	1.7
1950–60	2.6	2.2	0.4	2.8
1960–70	2.9	2.5	0.3	4.3
1970–79	2.1	1.8	0.2	3.2

Sources: 1950–79: *NIE*, 1983; *ET(AS)*, 1986; 1900–38: C.H. Feinstein, op. cit.

potential. This means that demand-induced spurts of economic expansion, such as those occurring in cyclical recoveries, do not qualify as economic growth in the sense we have in mind. Table 1.10 shows that both the growth rates of productive potential and the underlying trend in productivity increased between the beginning of the century and the 1960s, but fell back somewhat in the 1970s.

The growth rate of productive potential can only be measured satisfactorily over very long intervals of time or between periods when the utilization of resources was closely similar. Thus the periods indicated in table 1.10 have been chosen because they begin and end with similar rates of unemployment. The exception is 1970–79, where unemployment was considerably higher at the end of the period, so that a full use of the labour force (assuming that this would have been possible) might have added about 0.3% to the growth rate of GDP.

The concept of the growth rate of productive potential is not without its limitations. In the first place it says little or nothing about the causes of growth, but simply describes a time-trend. An extrapolation of the growth rate for any period into the future could easily turn out wrong if the forces that determine full-employment output are going to be present in different amounts or combinations from those of the past.

A second reservation concerns the interpretation of growth *rates* generally and their relation to *levels*. In calculating growth from 1960 to 1970, for example, one takes the compound rate of increase which will transform the level of GDP in 1960 into that of 1970. This does not tell us anything about the intervening years, during which the level of GDP could have been above or below the implied time-path. Thus the average *rate* of growth is, in general, no guide to the average *level* of output over the period. An allied point is that the *level of potential output* is arbitrarily defined by the unemployment or vacancy rate at which it is measured. This does not necessarily represent the most desirable level.

One of the questions which the economics of growth must try to answer is why some countries have grown so much faster than others and why, in particular, the underlying growth rate of the UK economy has been slower in the postwar period than that of most other industrial countries (see table

1.11). The answer must be sought under the more general heading of the causes of economic growth – a question which has been debated since the time of Adam Smith. Growth must depend, in the first instance, upon the increase in the quantity and quality of the factors of production and the efficiency with which they are combined. These increases may be influenced, however, by factors on the side of demand such as the pressure of demand on resources and the degree to which it fluctuates.

The supply of labour depends primarily on the evolution of the population of working age, including net migration, the secular decline in hours worked, and the increase in the length of annual and national holidays. Changes in the pressure of demand, however, affect the size of the labour force and the number of hours worked, and, over the longer period, may influence migration.

The quality of labour must in large degree depend upon the facilities available for education and training, the opportunities taken of them, and the degree to which they match the changing demands for skills arising out of changes in technology and the structure of aggregate demand. Measurement of these influences, however, is difficult and there is little evidence to show which way, if at all, they have affected the international comparison in table 1.11. The mobility of labour from job to job and from area to area is probably an important factor in economic growth in so far as it reflects the degree to which the labour force can adjust to economic change. It has been argued, not without evidence, that much of the relatively fast growth of the German, Italian and French economies can be attributed to the movement of labour from the agricultural to the industrial sectors.[1] But it is still not clear how much of this mobility has been a cause and how much a consequence of the disparity in growth rates between the agricultural and industrial sectors.

One obvious influence on the growth of labour productivity is the rate of increase in the nation's stock of capital, both in quantity and in quality. Some indications of the growth of the UK capital stock are given in table 1.10, where it can be seen that the rate of increase, like that of productivity, has tended to rise during the course of this century – although it, too, fell back in the 1970s. The stock of capital, however, is extremely difficult to measure. This is because the figures of depreciation in the national accounts are based on data collected for tax purposes and cannot serve as very precise indications of the rates of scrapping and deterioration of existing capital. Moreover, the economic value of a piece of capital equipment is a subjective concept, depending on expectations of future returns and modified by problems of evaluating risk. Estimates of the capital stock, therefore, must be treated with a good deal of reserve.

The quality of the capital stock is, perhaps, even more important and even more difficult to measure. According to one widely accepted view, the quality of capital depends, by and large, upon its age structure. This view looks

1 A. Maddison, *Economic Growth in the West* (Allen and Unwin, 1964).

TABLE 1.11
Rates of Growth, 1970–79 (annual percentage rates)

	GDP	GDP per capita
Belgium	3.3	3.0
Denmark	2.5	2.1
France	3.9	3.3
Germany	2.9	2.8
Italy	3.0	2.4
Japan	4.9	3.6
Netherlands	3.1	2.3
Norway	4.7	4.2
Sweden	2.1	1.8
United Kingdom	2.2	2.2
Canada	4.5	3.2
United States	3.4	2.3

Source: National Accounts of OECD Countries, 1982.

upon the capital stock as a series of vintages of gross investment, each new vintage containing machines of higher quality than the previous one. Scientific and technical progress are embodied in new machines, not old ones, so that the most recent capital equipment is likely to be the most efficient. This view is the basis of the 'catching-up hypothesis' which has been advanced to explain the faster growth of some countries in the early postwar period. The argument is that those countries in which the capital stock was seriously depleted by the war were in a position to replenish it with brand-new equipment, and were thus enabled to grow faster than those countries where the bombing and destruction had been less severe. The embodied view of technical progress, together with the difficulties of measuring the quantity of capital, has led a number of economists[1] to emphasize gross rather than net capital formation as the better indicator of the extent to which capital resources have been enhanced. A high rate of gross investment, even if it is entirely for replacement purposes, will reduce the age of the capital stock and increase its quality.

Turning to influences on the side of demand, two aspects of the question need to be distinguished: the average pressure of demand and the size of fluctuations around the average. It can certainly be argued that a very low average pressure of demand, such as we had during the 1930s and are experiencing again today, is inimical to innovation and investment. It hinders investment because capital equipment is under-utilized and because its continuation for any length of time is likely to set an unfavourable climate for expectations. High demand, on the other hand, will generally have the opposite effect. It has also been argued that high demand encourages managers and workers to devise new and better ways of working with existing equipment, thereby making technical progress of a variety which is not embodied in new types of machine. This effect has sometimes been

---

1 For example, A. Maddison, *ibid.*

described as 'learning by doing', and it fits in with the view that the scale of production problems that have to be solved is itself a stimulus to their solution. Evidence has been produced, for example, to show how the time taken to assemble a prototype airframe has progressively diminished as the workforce has gained experience of repeating the same jobs over and over again. On the other hand, it has also to be borne in mind that high demand pressure may work the other way. The presence of a sellers' market with easy profits could diminish the incentive to innovate and even lead to lazy attitudes to production. An extreme pressure of work can promote mental and physical exhaustion.

Another question is whether the amplitude of fluctuations tends to impede economic growth. It seems probable that the expectation of fluctuations will retard capital formation because profitability will be held down in periods of recession. It may also be the case that expectations of cycles leads to the installation of machinery which can be adapted to use in periods of both high and low output, whereas the prospect of steady growth could enable the introduction of machinery which would be specially designed to produce a steadier level of sales. In this case it is likely that the extra adaptability will be achieved at some cost to the efficiency of capital, and growth will be slowed down. It may be no coincidence, there-fore, that three countries with some of the lowest growth rates in the 1950s – the UK, US and Belgium – suffered sharper fluctuations in unem-ployment than the others (Japan was the exception to this rule).

V.2   Economic Growth and Policy

Governments prefer a fast rate of growth to a slow rate because it results in greater tax revenues from a given structure of tax rates, and thus permits tax reductions at full employment or a larger provision of public services (hospitals, schools and so forth) than would otherwise be possible. Fast growth may also render a policy of income redistribution less painful to the better-off than would be so if the growth of income was slow or non-existent. Thus it is not surprising that governments have sometimes announced a faster growth rate as a goal of economic policy.

What is not so clear, however, is whether the means of attaining faster growth are sufficiently well known and understood. There is considerable controversy among economists as to the effects on economic growth to be had from, say, a faster growth of the capital stock and from technical progress. Many would argue that neither are quantifiable, and that the attempts which have been made to quantify them are suspect in a number of ways. Thus it does not seem that growth policy is in the same category as, for example, demand-management policies, in which moderately fine calculations can be made as to the effects of changing the instruments of policy by known amounts. At one time it was believed by many that investment and the growth rate could be stepped up together merely by the announcement of a high growth target. This was tried in the National Plan of 1964–70, when the target growth rate was put at 4% per annum. But in the event the growth rate turned out to be only 2.6% (average estimate), and much of the public investment which had been based on the 4% assumption proved to be excessive. Probably all that can be hoped for from growth policy is the creation of an environment which is favourable to investment, innovation and enterprise. This, broadly speaking, is what the present government is trying to do with its 'supply side' policies. But whether these can succeed in a period of deep depression is, perhaps, doubtful.

VI   ECONOMIC PROSPECTS AND POLICIES 1986–90
VI.1   The Economic Situation in 1986

By 1986 the UK economy had been in a deep depression for six years. There is no conflict between this observation and the fact that the level of real GDP, as estimated for 1985, was some 8% higher than it had been in the peak employment year of 1979. Real consumption per capita was also 8% higher than in 1979, and total fixed investment nearly 5% higher. This impression of prosperity – for most people – was enhanced in early 1986 by record share prices and falling rates of interest.

The appearance of a prosperous economy was qualified, however, by the fact that manufacturing output was still below its 1979 level, and, more generally, by the depressed state of the labour market. Employment had recovered some way from the low point reached in 1983, but much of its increase had been part-time, and even by early 1986 its level was still more than 1 million below that of 1979. Unemployment, which was 1.2 million in 1979 had reached 3.2 million in March 1986 (UK, seasonally adjusted, excluding school-leavers). This total was probably affected by exceptionally bad weather, which is not allowed for in the seasonal adjustment. The underlying level, however, was still well above 3 million, and there was no prospect of any substantial decline.[1] The total included 1.4m who had been out of work for more than 12 months and 1.2m who were below the age of 25. The overall unemployment rate was 13.2%, whilst for those aged 20–24 it was 23%. Unemployment was above 15% in the West Midlands, Yorkshire and Humberside, the North, North West and Scotland and 21% in Northern Ireland. In some inner cities, male unemployment was as high as 50%.

This situation, besides being tragic and socially disruptive, was wasteful of national resources. The 8% gap between the unemployment rates of 1985 and 1979 represented a loss of potential output of £25–30bn (at 1986 prices) – a figure which was substantially in excess of the amount spent annually on

---

1   Since 1979 a number of statistical adjustments had been made to the unemployment count, so that the March 1986 figure was nearer 3.8 million (15.7%) on the 1979 basis of recording. This figure excluded about 670,000 workers on special employment and training schemes.

education (£14bn), health (£18bn), or defence (£19bn). It is this figure, rather than the Exchequer's outlay on unemployment benefits (£12½bn), which represents the opportunity cost of unemployment.

VI.2 Economic Prospects to 1990

The economic outlook in early 1986 was for a continuation of high unemployment and a decline in the rate of inflation. Helped by falling oil prices, the official forecast was that the RPI would rise by 3½% in the annual period ending in the 4th quarter of 1986, and by a similar rate in the first six months of 1987.

The Treasury was forecasting in March a moderate expansion of demand during 1986 and early 1987. The increase in GDP was put at 3.3% from the second half of 1985 to the second half of 1986, and 2.4% from the first half of 1986 to the first half of 1987. The main contributors to the increase were expected to be fixed investment, exports and personal consumption.

The prospective increases in GDP (which allow for budget changes) were not enough to make any significant impact on the level of unemployment. Similar rates of increase over the previous three years had been accompanied by a slight rise in unemployment. Looking further ahead, the assumptions behind the government's budget projections were not encouraging for unemployment. The assumed increases in real GDP in the 3 financial years 1987–8 to 1989–90 were all put at 2½% (see table 1.12). Thus the short- and medium-term outlook was for no significant change in the numbers unemployed, or the degree of economic waste.

VI.3 Economic Policy and the MTFS

The budget of March 1986 did nothing significant to alleviate unemployment. Whilst income tax was reduced by 1p in the £ to a standard rate of 29p,

TABLE 1.12
Official Projections, Assumptions and Targets to 1989–90[1]

	1985–6	1986–7	1987–8	1988–9	1989–90
Percentage changes in:					
Money GDP	9½	6¾	6½	6	5½
MO[2]	3½	2–6	2–6	1–5	1–5
£M3[2]	14¾	11–15			
Real GDP	3½	3	2½	2½	2½
GDP deflator	6	3¾	3¾	3½	3
PSBR as percentage of					
GDP at market prices	2	1¾	1¾	1½	1½
Money GDP at market					
prices (£bn)	358	382	407	431	455

Source: Treasury, *Financial Statement and Budget Report 1986–87*, March 1986.
Notes: 1 Financial years.
    2 1985–6 percentage change from mid-February to mid-February. 1986–7: target ranges. 1987–8 onwards: illustrative ranges for MO.

the reduction was supported on the grounds that it would encourage enterprise and hard work. Its effect on GDP would, according to the calculations in section III, be to raise it by something of the order of 0.25% after a period of 12 months (an effect which was incorporated in the budget forecasts). The government was hoping to reduce income tax further in 1987, but even a possible fall to 25p in the £ would stimulate GDP by no more than about 1.0%.

The government's principal aim and achievement had been the reduction of the inflation rate. The avowed instrument for lowering inflation had been the quantity of money, which in the early days of the MTFS had been regarded as crucial. The Chancellor repeated this position in the 1986 budget speech, saying that downwards pressure on inflation 'means, above all, controlling the growth of money in the economy'.[1] Nevertheless, the thinking behind policy and the Medium Term Financial Strategy had been changed significantly since 1980. Whereas the 1980 MTFS had targeted the growth rate of £M3 for 4 financial years, and appeared to be built upon the crude 'monetarist' idea that the growth rate of the money supply was a forward predictor of the inflation rate, the MTFS of 1986 targeted £M3 only one year forward. Experience since 1980 had shown not only that it was difficult to hold down the growth of the money supply to its target level, but also that inflation could be brought down to low single figures whilst the money stock was increasing at more than 10% per annum.

The 1986 MTFS put the main emphasis on the narrow money stock, MO, which excludes all bank deposits and in terms of magnitude is a mere fraction – only one-eighth – of £M3. The replacement of £M3 by MO was supported on the grounds that the latter bore a more stable velocity relationship to income, but this could simply reflect the dependence of the transactions demand for cash on nominal expenditure. Thus the 'illustrative ranges' for MO in the 1986 MTFS can probably be regarded as medium-term forecasts based on tentative projections of real GDP and prices. Critics of government policy were arguing that the substance of the MTFS had been abandoned, and that the name was being retained merely as a pretence of consistency with earlier policies.[2] In support of this view was the fact that government forecasts of the rate of inflation are dependent upon the factors mentioned in section IV – demand pressure, wage costs, import prices and, of course, oil prices – rather than on the money supply.

Both in 1985 and 1986 the budget speech made overtures to the 'new Keynesian' position under which it is thought helpful to announce target growth rates for nominal GDP. The 1986 speech stated the objective of 'reducing the growth of total spending power in the economy, as measured by GDP in cash terms'. It did not explain, however, how the growth of GDP

---

1   *Financial Times*, 19 March 1986.

2   See W. Keegan, 'Newspeak, doublethink, money and employment', *Observer*, 20 April 1986, and H. McRae, 'Nigel didn't say anything new, but he did a good PR job on monetary policy', *Guardian*, 17 April 1986.

in cash terms could or should be regarded as an additional objective when its two dimensions, a reduced inflation rate and a faster growth of real GDP, are objectives in their own right. Thus the suspicion remained that the new interest in nominal GDP had little more than novelty value.

VI.4   Alternative Strategies

Any attempt to lower the level of unemployment was likely to 'cost money' to the Exchequer and to run some risk of increasing inflation. Various schemes and packages for the relief of long-term unemployment were studied by a House of Commons committee, where one of the principal criteria discussed was the exchequer cost per job created.[1] As a matter of logic, however, the exchequer cost is immaterial. There are no costs, only benefits, in moving people out of unemployment into useful or marketable work. Public works programmes inevitably involve increases in public expenditure, but there is no question of their being financed out of higher taxation. With under-utilized resources they should not, and do not, 'cost the taxpayer money'. The finance for higher public spending (or for lower taxes) can be raised from credit creation, and it costs virtually nothing to put more money into circulation. Thus 'cost-effectiveness' is misleading and mis-placed as a criterion for choosing between alternative methods of job creation.

The criteria which should be applied are those of usefulness and inflation-avoidance. Quite clearly it is better to spend money on projects that are genuinely needed, such as roads, urban renewal, hospitals and educational facilities rather than 'digging holes and filling them in again'. But the main problem with all attempts to lower the level of unemployment is that they are likely to run some risk of adding to inflation. Here the first factor to be reckoned with was the Phillips Curve effect of lower unemployment on the rate of wage increase. The original Phillips Curve was flat for unemployment levels in excess of 4%. But with the experience of the 1970s and early 1980s it was probably optimistic to expect no response of wages to a recovery of demand.

A second factor was the effect of higher GDP on imports, the exchange rate, and hence on import prices. Each 1% addition to GDP could be expected to add 1 to $1\frac{1}{2}$% to the import volume. But the fall in the exchange rate (and consequent rise in import prices) needed to hold the balance of payments in equilibrium is easily exaggerated. It depends mainly upon the price elasticities of demand for exports and imports. If these are -1.5 and -0.5 respectively, the exchange-rate decline would have to be about

1 House of Commons, *Special Employment Measures and the Long-Term Unemployment*, First Report from the Employment Committee, Session 1985–86 (HMSO, 1986), and Charter for Jobs, *Economic Report*, February 1986.

1–1.5% for each 1% rise in GDP.[1] Even a 10% addition to GDP would, on these assumptions, add only 10 or 15% to import prices, and, in the first instance, 2 or 3% to final prices. Subsequent rounds of the wage-price spiral would, of course, raise this amount, but the main point is that the pure adjustment effects are not serious.

There was, however, the further danger that anything that looked like a 'retreat from sound finance' would affect the exchange rate more dramatically through its effects upon the prejudices of foreign-exchange dealers. It seems possible that these dealers are still influenced by monetarist ideas, and even if they are not they may believe that others are.[2] Thus it might be feared that an expansion of the economy with a step-up in the monetary growth rate would trigger off a run on sterling, with serious effects on import costs. It seems that this is what happened during M. Mitterand's brief excursion into Keynesianism in 1981–2, and the same thing could happen to Britain.

These effects through the exchange rate, however, might be neutralized if all industrial countries could be persuaded to expand together. A concerted recovery would, of course, drive up the prices of primary commodities – to the advantage of Third World countries – but it would probably be less inflationary for the UK than going it alone.

Some rise in import prices and some upwards pressure on wages must be expected from most attempts to expand domestic demand. The question, however, is whether these effects can be alleviated by a judicious choice of instruments for demand expansion. The instruments should be chosen not to minimize Exchequer costs – since these are not real costs at all – but rather on the criterion of the extent to which they minimize inflation. The Charter for Jobs, the Labour Party and the SDP–Liberal Alliance have all supported the idea of concentrating demand expansion in those areas where there is unemployed labour in plentiful supply.[3] This would minimize the risk of wage increases, whilst the low import content of such investment would mean only a slight rise in the exchange rate. Another idea is to reduce VAT. A reduction from 15 to 5% would, for example, reduce domestic prices by a bit less than 6% whilst at the same time adding 3% to GDP. A reduction in employers' contributions to national insurance would be another way of increasing demand and reducing costs simultaneously. Such policies, moreover, might pave the way for wage restraint.

The central dilemma of current economic policy is that 3 million are

---

1 The reasoning is as follows: a 1% fall in the exchange rate leads to a 1% fall in UK export prices in terms of foreign currency and a 1.5% rise in their volume. The value of exports in terms of £s rises by 1.5%. At the same time, import prices (in £s) rise by 1%, whilst the import volume falls by 0.5%. The value of imports must rise, therefore, by 0.5%. Thus, a 1% exchange-rate reduction improves the foreign balance by 1.5% on exports *less* 0.5% on imports, making a net improvement of approximately 1% of the value of imports.

2 On this and the need for international co-operation, see Michael Stewart, *Controlling the Economic Future* (Wheatsheaf, 1983).

3 See *Medium Term Employment Strategies: A Discussion Paper*, Charter for Jobs, *Economic Report*, March 1986.

denied employment in order to protect society from the ill effects of inflation. Whilst the objective is understandable, the costs are very serious. It must be asked, therefore, whether there are not better ways of stopping inflation – or curing its consequences – than the policies which have been pursued for the past six years. If, as seems probable, the most serious result of inflation is the impoverishment of retired people on fixed money incomes from private sources, then it would seem sensible for the government to consider some form of indexation for these incomes. The state pension scheme is already indexed to the cost of living. The extension of indexation to private pensions and retirement incomes would *not* be inflationary because it would simply maintain real demand at existing levels. It would, however, enable the government to help the unemployed without side-effects on a defenceless social group.

REFERENCES AND FURTHER READING

F.T.Blackaby (ed.), *British Economic Policy 1960–74* (NIESR and Cambridge University Press, 1979).

Charter for Jobs, *We Can Cut Unemployment* (London, 1985).

Charter for Jobs, *Economic Report* (monthly), from Southbank House, Black Prince Road, London, SE1 7SJ.

Economic Policy Review, Department of Applied Economics, University of Cambridge.

C.H.Feinstein, *National Income, Expenditure and Output of the United Kingdom 1855–1965* (Cambridge University Press, 1972).

Sir Bryan Hopkin, M.Miller and B.Reddaway, 'An Alternative Economic Strategy – A Message of Hope', *Cambridge Journal of Economics*, March 1982.

W. Keegan, *Mrs Thatcher's Economic Experiment* (Penguin Books, 1984).

A.P.Lerner, 'Functional Finance and the Federal Debt', *Social Research*, 1943, reprinted in M.G.Mueller (ed.), *Readings in Macroeconomics* (Holt, Rinehart and Winston, 1966).

R.C.O.Matthews, C.H.Feinstein and J.C.Odling-Smee, *British Economic Growth 1856–1973* (Stanford University Press, 1982).

Midland Bank Review.

National Institute Economic Review.

C.Pratten, *Applied Macroeconomics* (Oxford University Press, 1985).

P.Riddell, *The Thatcher Government* (Martin Robertson, 1983).

D.Savage, 'Fiscal Policy 1974/5 – 1980/81: Description and Appraisal', *NIER*, February 1982.

M.Stewart, *Politics and Economic Policy in the UK Since 1964* (Pergamon, 1978).

M.Stewart, *Controlling the Economic Future – Policy Dilemmas in a Shrinking World* (Wheatsheaf, 1983).

Treasury, *Economic Progress Report*.

Treasury, *Financial Statement and Budget Report 1986–87*.

2

Money and finance: public expenditure and taxation

Richard Harrington

I INTRODUCTION

Chapter 1 considered the UK economy from the macroeconomic point of view. As well as examining the main categories of expenditure and considering some of the main macroeconomic problems, the chapter also dealt with government policies for managing aggregate demand. Such policies involve adjusting the levels of public expenditure and of taxation (budgetary policy), and varying the cost of funds in the financial markets, so as to increase or decrease the amounts of money and credit available to the economy (monetary policy).

These policies are likely to have many repercussions on the economy over and above their effects on aggregate demand. Further, how well any particular policy works is likely to depend on the structure of the economy at any one time. That is to say, macroeconomic policy, like other policies, does not operate in a vacuum. In planning and in assessing policy, governments must take into account potential side-effects of policy actions; equally they have to consider the influence of changes in the structure of the economy on the effectiveness of policy.

Consider first budgetary policy. The prime purpose of public expenditure is not as a means of regulating aggregate demand. We have public expenditure because we want the things it buys: hospitals and people to work in them, schools and school-teachers, fighter aeroplanes and pilots, etc. The many services provided collectively and paid for out of taxation are of importance in their own right. Demand management should, therefore, be conducted in ways which do not adversely affect the efficiency of publicly provided services. One way that budgetary policy can work adversely in this manner is when policies are changed too frequently. If, in attempts to adjust finely the level of demand in the economy, governments continually alter their expenditure plans, it becomes difficult for those responsible for providing public services to plan ahead and efficiency is likely to suffer.

So attempts to use public expenditure as a means of influencing the level of aggregate demand are constrained by the need not to chop and change spending plans too frequently. For this reason, budgetary policy has tended to rely more on tax changes. But here also, policy is constrained by concerns other than demand management. Taxes have many side-effects. Changes in the taxation of company profits may affect the ability or willingness of firms to undertake new investment. High marginal rates of taxation on persons may diminish productive effort and increase the amount of time and resources devoted to tax avoidance. And frequent changes of tax regime will be justly unpopular with companies trying to predict their cash flow and with the Inland Revenue, responsible for collecting direct taxes such as income tax and corporation tax.

The effectiveness of taxes can vary over time as economic circumstances change. An example is the stamp duty imposed on transactions in ordinary shares. For many years this tax produced modest sums of revenue and there was little scope for it to be avoided. But in recent years, there has been a rapid internationalisation of finance, and many transactions in shares, including shares of large UK companies, can now be carried out equally well outside the United Kingdom as within it. There is increasing scope for the tax to be avoided by switching share-dealing abroad. To lessen the incentive for this, the government first reduced the tax from 2% to 1% in 1984 and then announced a further reduction to $\frac{1}{2}$% in 1986.

Consider now monetary policy. The problems are the same in principle, but in practice they have become more acute. During the 1950s and 1960s the authorities could think in terms of a national financial system and could impose a variety of constraints on financial intermediaries in order to influence the availability and/or the cost of finance. But the process of internationalisation of finance has gone so far, that by the mid-1980s, it makes more sense to view the British financial system as part of a world financial system. And it is a world financial system in which much business is mobile and in which different centres, e.g. London, New York, Tokyo, Zurich, are in competition with each other. The UK authorities, not unnaturally, wish to see London maintain its position as a key financial centre, with all the earnings and the jobs that go with it, and so they have had to adjust policy accordingly. Constraints imposed on financial institutions which reduce their ability to compete with foreign institutions, or which create incentives for business to be done abroad, have been dropped. The authorities have had to completely rethink their methods of implementing monetary policy.

Enough has been said to show that one cannot properly understand macroeconomic policy unless one understands the context and the institutional environment in which it takes place. This requires both an understanding of the working of the financial system and of that important subset of it which is the monetary system, and also an understanding of the size and composition of public expenditure and of how it is financed. Of course, knowledge of private finance and of public finance is not only necessary in order to comprehend policy. Both are crucial for all aspects of economic life. It is the purpose of the rest of this chapter to explain first private finance, then public finance in the UK. We look first at the financial system and then, since the system is now in the throes of revolutionary changes, we consider these changes and some of their implications. Finally, we look at the composition of government spending and at the sources of government revenue.

II   THE FINANCIAL SYSTEM
II.1   Introduction

A financial system is composed of institutions and markets which fulfil a variety of economic functions. Central to all is arranging or facilitating the lending of funds from one economic agent to another. Most other financial services are ancillary to, or derived from, this one. The lending of funds from one economic agent to another – from lender to borrower – can be accomplished in many different ways; but all of these can be classified into just two distinct approaches.

Firstly, the lender can lend direct to the borrower, albeit perhaps with the assistance of brokers who act in an agency capacity. This is what happens when a person subscribes to a new issue of government stock, deposits money with a local authority or buys a share in a public company. In each case, the person is lending direct to the borrower and is incurring all the risks that such lending involves. This may be called direct finance.

The second approach, which may be called indirect finance, involves a financial intermediary standing between borrower and lender. The lender lends his funds to the intermediary, e.g. a bank or a building society. The intermediary collects funds from many lenders and decides to whom it will lend. Borrowers approach the intermediary and, if credit-worthy, they receive loans. There is no direct contact between lender and borrower. Each deals with the intermediary, each has his contract with the intermediary; instead of one direct transaction, there are two.

This form of finance seems at first sight to be more roundabout, and to involve the use of more real resources of capital and labour than direct finance. But financial intermediaries are numerous and indirect finance more common than direct finance. What, then, are its advantages? They are many, and they derive from the ability of financial institutions to use their size and their expertise to transform financial claims, so that they can offer to savers a wider choice of assets than ultimate borrowers are able to do. At the same time, they can offer to borrowers a more varied choice of credit terms than ultimate lenders are able to do. To fully appreciate this, consider the most important financial intermediary: the general-purpose bank.

Such a bank accepts deposits of all sizes and on a variety of terms. In the United Kingdom, the largest banks each have many millions of individual deposits, which in the aggregate sum to more than £20 billion. Such banks know that, every day, many depositors will withdraw money, but that many others will make new deposits. The law of averages will, in normal circumstances, ensure that the total sum of money deposited with them does not vary greatly. In consequence, they can allow each individual lender of money the freedom to withdraw his funds with little or no notice, whilst at the same time making loans to borrowers which last for many years. The banks are said to engage in *maturity transformation*, that is, they borrow short and lend long. It is not only banks that do this. Building Societies lend money on mortgages for periods up to thirty years, whilst still allowing most depositors freedom to withdraw their money on demand.

Financial intermediaries not only transform maturities, they also transform risk. With direct finance, the ultimate lender bears the risk of default by the borrower, e.g. a person who buys a share in company X is likely to lose money if company X goes into liquidation. The retail banks, who between them have millions of loans outstanding, also stand to lose when borrowers default. But because they are large institutions and employ trained staff who are able to judge to whom it is safe to lend and to whom it is not, they are usually able to keep loan losses to a small proportion of total sums advanced. And as past experience enables them to estimate the likely amount of bad debts, they can allow for this by adding a risk premium to the interest they charge borrowers. In this way banks, like other intermediaries, can bear risks and absorb losses, whilst their depositors, in normal times, can know that their deposits are virtually riskless.

Financial intermediaries provide other services. Retail banks not only offer deposits withdrawable on demand, they also provide facilities for deposits to be transferred from one account to another, and thereby provide a money-transfer system. Sight deposits in banks have become a superior form of money to notes and coin for most purposes, other than small day-to-day transactions. Life assurance companies, whose main business nowadays is accepting regular payments from lenders of funds, over a number of years, and then providing either a lump-sum payment or an annuity, combine this business with insurance against death. Thus, while the lender expects to receive a certain sum of money in, say, 20 years' time, he knows that should he die prematurely, the same or another guaranteed sum will be paid to his dependants.

So financial intermediaries perform many functions. And for this reason, many lenders and borrowers find it preferable to deal with intermediaries, rather than dealing direct with each other. This is especially true of small lenders and borrowers, for whom the time-and-trouble costs of direct dealing would normally far outweigh any gain in terms of a more favourable interest rate. But there is still need for direct finance. Many wealthy persons are prepared to incur risk by lending direct to private enterprises in the hope of earning extra returns. If the enterprises fail, they lose money, but if the enterprises prosper, they will receive increased returns in the form both of higher dividends and of capital gains. Further, many persons, rich and poor alike, are happy to lend direct to the government as, here, the risk of default is considered negligible. Those with large sums to lend can buy gilt-edged stock (marketable government bonds) but small savers can also lend direct to the government by purchasing such assets as savings certificates and premium bonds.

II.2   The Bank of England

The Bank of England was established as a joint-stock company by Act of Parliament in 1694. In return for a large loan to the then government, it was granted important monopoly rights. Over the years, while still a privately-owned institution, it came to exercise a number of important public functions, notably holding the nation's stock of gold and (later) foreign-currency reserves. The Bank (as it is known in financial circles) was nationalized in 1946 and made subject to the authority of the Chancellor of the Exchequer. It is now unambiguously an arm of government and its main purpose is to carry out a number of important public functions; although it continues to provide banking services for a number of private clients, comprised chiefly of members of its staff, a number of banks, and a small number of old-established clients who have had accounts with the Bank from the days when it was still a joint-stock company.

Of the many functions of the Bank of England, the following are the most important:

(a) banker to the government;
(b) banker to the clearing banks;
(c) holder of the nation's stock of gold and foreign-exchange reserves;
(d) manager of the issue of notes and coins;
(e) implementation of government monetary policy;
(f) supervision of banks and of certain other financial institutions.

The Bank of England is banker to Her Majesty's Government; that is to say, it keeps all the main government accounts, receives tax revenues and makes payments in respect of government expenditures. The Bank also arranges borrowing for the government through the issue of new gilt-edged stock. Outstanding government stock, which constitutes the greater part of the national debt, is actively traded on the Stock Exchange. The Bank of England is in a position to exert an influence over this trading, in that it is regularly selling newly issued bonds. By varying its terms, the Bank can have an influence upon market expectations about future interest rates. However, in recent years, the Bank has tended to issue new stock at rates in line with prevailing market interest rates, and has chosen to exert its main influence on interest rates through the short-term bill markets.

The Bank of England is also banker to the clearing banks, i.e. those retail banks which operate the system through which cheques are cleared and monies transferred from one bank account to another. Although the gross sums transferred through clearing, each day, are very large, payments due from one bank to another are normally offset, to a great extent, by payments due in the reverse direction, and it is only necessary to settle a relatively small net balance. This is done, each working day, by transfers between bankers' accounts at the Bank of England.

The Bank of England holds, on behalf of Her Majesty's Government, the nation's stock of gold and foreign-exchange reserves. It can use this stock to intervene on the foreign-exchange market. If it is government policy to support the international value of the pound, the Bank will sell dollars and maybe other foreign currencies in exchange for sterling. If it is government policy to prevent the pound from rising in value, the bank will sell pounds and buy dollars and other foreign currencies.

The Bank of England acts as the note-issuing authority and (on behalf of the government) manages the minting and the issue of new coins. This is a large task: notes wear out and old notes have to be continually withdrawn from circulation and new ones printed and distributed to the banks. Also, as the economy expands and as inflation erodes the value of money, there is a need for more notes and coins, so the Bank has to see that the supply is continually augmented. There are also seasonal fluctuations, with demands for extra notes and coin at Christmas and over bank-holiday weekends.

The Bank implements government monetary policy. In some accounts of monetary policy, there has been confusion about the division of responsibility between the Bank and the Treasury; but the position is, in principle, quite clear. It is the government, acting through the Treasury, which is responsible for monetary policy, and it is the Chancellor of the Exchequer who has to defend to Parliament the government's exercise of policy. The Bank can give advice, and given its knowledge and experience of financial markets, its advice will often be influential, but ultimate responsibility lies with the government.

Once the broad outlines of policy have been decided, it is the task of the Bank of England to implement policy. In order to do this, the Bank is allowed a considerable degree of autonomy. This is quite usual; central banks in other developed countries are also granted autonomy in their day-to-day operations. The reason is readily apparent. Monetary policy is conducted largely through operations in financial markets where conditions change from hour to hour, or even minute to minute. Thus, while the objectives of policy may be clear, the Bank must still use discretion in how best to pursue these objectives. For instance, if it were policy to support the international value of the pound, the Bank still has to decide when, and by how much, to intervene on the foreign-exchange market. If there were heavy selling of sterling, the Bank might judge that immediate intervention would be futile. On the other hand, if there were signs that market traders were hesitating and were unsure of official intentions, even modest intervention by the Bank might be effective in halting a decline. Similarly, in dealing in the domestic markets in government bonds and in short-term bills, the Bank has to exercise discretion in the timing of its actions and in the amount which it buys or sells.

The supervision of the financial system has become of increasing importance. Many modern financial institutions are of such size that were they to fail there would be serious consequences for thousands, or even millions, of persons and firms, with obvious secondary effects on the economy as a whole. Further, many institutions, especially the banks, borrow and lend amongst themselves, so there is a degree of inter-dependence between institutions. The failure of one could provoke the failure of others and, in the worst case, there could be a chain reaction with a succession of financial institutions becoming insolvent. One only has to imagine what would be the consequences of the failure of even one large bank, let alone several, to see that there is a clear public interest in ensuring the efficient and prudent management of banks, as well as of other financial intermediaries.

The 1979 Banking Act gave legal backing to the role of the Bank of England as supervisor of the banking system. In order to carry on a banking business, any institution, apart from a limited number of specific exceptions, now requires to be recognised or licensed by the Bank of England. The distinction between a recognised bank and a licensed deposit-taker, is that the former status is only granted to long-established banks undertaking a wide range of banking functions; newly-established banks or specialist institutions offering only a narrow range of services are given the status of licensed deposit-taker. However, in 1985, a committee set up to examine banking supervision, proposed that the distinction be dropped and replaced by one category of authorised bank. This proposal has been accepted by the government but not yet (April 1986) implemented.[1]

All banks are expected to supply the Bank of England with information about their business on a regular basis, and they have to respond to directives given to them by the Bank. For instance, the Bank has laid down criteria for the capital adequacy of banks, and how these should apply to each bank is one of the matters discussed at the regular meetings that officials of the Bank hold with senior staff at each bank. Whilst at present the Bank can, if it its dissatisfied with the management of a bank, withdraw its recognition or licence – and thereby effectively prevent it from operating as a bank – this is seen as an extreme weapon, only to be used as a last resort. The White Paper on banking supervision, issued by the Treasury in December 1985, envisages a strengthening of the powers of the Bank of England to monitor and, where necessary, to give directions to banks, short of actually forcing them to cease business.[2]

II.3   The Retail Banks

The retail banks, as their name suggests, are banks which offer retail banking services to business and personal clients, both small and large, through a network of branches. Such services traditionally cover the taking of deposits at sight and at short notice, the provision of cheque books and the

---

1 See the *Report of the Committee Set up to Consider Banking Supervision*, Cmnd. 9550 (HMSO, June 1985) and *Banking Supervision*, Cmnd. 9695 (H.M. Treasury, December 1985).

2 *Banking Supervision, op. cit.*

clearing of cheques, the making of short- and medium-term loans, sale and purchase of foreign currency and travellers' cheques, dealing with international remittances, safe-deposit facilities, financial advice and maybe insurance broking. In recent years, banks have been actively seeking to increase business and a number of other services have been introduced, of which the most notable are cheque-guarantee cards, networks of automated teller machines, eurocheques (cheques which may be written in any one of a number of foreign currencies), long-term mortgage lending for house purchase, and opportunities for investment in equity shares and other securities through bank-managed unit trusts.

Retail banking is nowadays contrasted with wholesale banking which involves dealing in large sums of money (one million dollars and over) at fixed term, in sterling and in foreign currencies. A large part of such business is undertaken in organised short-term financial markets and it is concentrated in a limited number of international centres such as London, New York, Luxembourg and Paris. The distinction is conceptual rather than legal and most of the banks classified as retail banks are, in reality, mixed banks which undertake both retail and wholesale banking. Other banks specialise largely or entirely in wholesale banking.

The published balance sheets of the different groups of banks are drawn up in the same way, so it will only be necessary to discuss these once. Accordingly, we shall discuss in detail the combined balance sheet of the retail banks, and will then confine ourselves to noting the main differences when we look at the other groups of banks.

The banks classified by the Bank of England as retail banks are (at 19 February 1986) as follows:

> Allied Irish Banks plc
> Bank of England, Banking Department
> Bank or Ireland
> Bank of Scotland
> Barclays Bank plc
> Central Trustee Savings Bank Ltd
> Clydesdale Bank plc
> Co-operative Bank plc
> Coutts & Co.
> Girobank plc
> Lloyds Bank plc
> Midland Bank plc
> National Westminster Bank plc
> Northern Bank Ltd
> The Royal Bank of Scotland plc
> Trustee Savings Banks
> Ulster Bank Ltd
> Yorkshire Bank plc

Of these banks, Barclays, Lloyds, Midland and National Westminster are the main retail banks of England and Wales; Bank of Scotland, Clydesdale Bank and Royal Bank of Scotland are the main retail banks in Scotland, although the last named also has a number of branches in England and

Wales; and Allied Irish Banks, Bank of Ireland, Northern Bank and Ulster Bank are the main retail banks in Northern Ireland.

The combined balance sheet of the retail banks as at 19 February 1986 is given in table 2.1. This table covers all business of the retail banks (including wholesale business) on the books of their UK offices on that date.

Both liabilities and assets are classified according to whether they are denominated in sterling or in foreign currencies. In recent years, foreign-currency business has grown rapidly as a share of total business. On the liabilities side of the balance sheet, it will be noticed that most sterling deposits are from the UK private sector, although significant amounts are also received from other banks and from abroad. Most foreign-currency deposits come from abroad, although again there are large deposits that have been made by other banks. The items labelled 'certificates of deposit' refer to term deposits taken against the issue of a certificate. Such certificates of deposit (CDs) are negotiable and hence allow lenders of money to make a deposit for a fixed period of, say, three or six months, whilst having the option of selling the CD, should they wish to get their money back before the end of the fixed period. Since CD prices fluctuate in value, an early sale may involve a capital gain or loss.

The small item 'notes issued' refers to private banknotes issued by Scottish and by Northern Ireland banks. These banks alone retain the historic right to issue their own notes, although apart from a small fiduciary issue, they have to be backed by holdings of Bank of England notes. The last item within the balance sheet proper, covers items held in suspense for whatever reason (e.g. uncertainty as to who is the rightful owner of a deposit); items in transmission between accounts; and banks' long-term liabilities to shareholders and to bondholders.

Acceptances outstanding and eligible liabilities do not constitute additional actual liabilities. Acceptances relate to bank acceptances of commercial bills. A bank accepts a commercial bill when it puts its own name on the bill as a guarantee that, if the company due to redeem the bill should default, the bank itself will pay all monies due. For this service the bank is paid a fee. As it is only in the case of a prior default by another party that the bank becomes liable, acceptances outstanding represent contingent liabilities rather than actual liabilities.

Eligible liabilities are a subset of all bank liabilities and are defined, broadly speaking, so as to represent, for each bank, its total sterling resources. More formally, eligible liabilities comprise the following:

(1) all sterling deposits from non-bank sources with an original maturity of two years or less;
(2) net sterling interbank borrowing;
(3) sterling CDs issued, less sterling CDs held;
(4) any net deposit liabilities in sterling to overseas offices;

TABLE 2.1

Retail Banks: Balance Sheet, 19 February 1986 (£m)

Sterling Liabilities	
Notes issued	946
Deposits: UK monetary sector	10,319
UK public sector	2,375
UK private sector	81,599
overseas	10,249
certificates of deposit	7,177
Other Currency Liabilities	
Deposits: UK monetary sector	8,148
other United Kingdom	4,349
overseas	31,676
certificates of deposit	3,876
Items in suspense and transmission, capital and	
other funds (sterling and other currencies)	29,778
Total Liabilities	190,493

Acceptances outstanding	4,187	
Eligible liabilities	87,207	

Sterling Assets	
Notes and coins	2,112
Balances with Bank of England: cash-ratio deposits	375
other	127
Market loans: secured money with the discount market	4,176
other UK monetary sector	15,564
UK monetary sector CDs	3,148
UK local authorities	1,661
overseas	1,462
Bills: Treasury bills	139
eligible local authority bills	509
eligible bank bills	7,374
other	95
Advances: UK public sector	400
UK private sector	74,850
overseas	3,450
Investments: UK government stocks	5,570
others	2,872
Banking Department lending to central government (net)	−4,270
Other Currency Assets	
Market loans and advances: UK monetary sector	11,758
UK monetary sector CDs	310
UK public sector	193
UK private sector	4,605
overseas	33,651
Bills	687
Investments	5,045
Miscellaneous (sterling and other currencies)	14,630
Total Assets	190,493

Source: BEQB, March 1986.

(5) any net liabilities in currencies other than sterling
   less
(6) 60% of the net value of transit items.[11]

This magnitude is of importance, as it is the volume of its eligible liabilities that determines for each bank the amount of 'cash ratio deposits' that it must make with the Bank of England. Since August 1981, all banks with eligible liabilities in excess of £10 million have been required to deposit a sum equal to 0.5% of eligible liabilities in a non-interest-bearing account with the Bank. Cash-ratio deposits are not, at present, of significance for monetary policy, but are used as a means of providing resources and income to the Bank of England to enable it to carry out its general central-banking functions.

Retail bank assets have become very diverse, as table 2.1 shows. Of the sterling assets, firstly there are holdings of notes and coin (till money), together with balances at the Bank of England. The former are necessary for retail banks on account of their large volume of sight deposits, and the need to be able to convert these into currency, on demand. It will be seen below that the other banks, whose main business is wholesale banking and who have few deposits subject to cheque, keep only negligible amounts of notes and coin in their tills. Balances with the Bank of England are composed of obligatory cash-ratio deposits and of other deposits, which are those deposits that banks choose to keep with the Bank for their own convenience.

Sterling market loans are sums of money lent in one of several short-term money markets. Secured money with the discount market represents loans against the security of bills or bonds made to the nine discount houses which comprise the London Discount Market Association. Loans to 'other UK monetary sector' represent short-term interbank lending. The sterling interbank market is a very active over-the-telephone market in which banks borrow and lend large sums of money of £1 million and above. It is used for many purposes. Banks temporarily short of funds can borrow there; banks temporarily with excess funds can lend there; those who wish to, can improve liquidity by, say, borrowing for two months and lending for two weeks; and those prepared to take risks, in the hope of earning extra profit, can anticipate future interest-rate movements by borrowing short and lending long (if rates are expected to fall) or by lending short and borrowing long (if rates are expected to rise).

Holdings of UK monetary sector CDs represent another form of interbank lending: lending to another bank by purchasing its certificate of deposit. This has the same advantage to a bank as it does to a non-bank purchaser of a CD; the loan is more liquid in that the CD can always be sold prior to maturity.

---

1   These components of eligible liabilities are described in detail in 'Reserve Ratios: Further Definitions', *BEQB*, December 1971.

Loans to UK local authorities are short-term loans of periods ranging from a few days up to one year. Loans made to overseas residents include many loans to banks abroad. Banks also make many loans by discounting bills. Bills are short-term IOUs which may be issued by the government (Treasury bills), local authorities (local-authority bills) or private companies (commercial bills). They are usually issued for three months, although other terms are possible, and are sold to banks, discount houses or other purchasers, at a discount on their value on redemption. The discount is calculated so as to give the purchaser a rate of interest in line with current market rates of interest for similar types of lending. For instance, if a bank buys a 91-day commercial bill worth £1,000,000 at a 2% discount, it pays £980,000. That is to say, it is lending, for 91 days, a sum of £980,000 in the expectation of earning interest of £20,000. It is easy to calculate that this represents a rate of interest of 2.04% over the 91 days, or 8.16% when expressed at an annual rate.

Bills are highly marketable, and a bank having made a loan in exchange for a bill is free to rediscount it (i.e. sell it) if it wishes to do so. The Bank of England uses the bill market as a means of influencing the liquidity of the banking system. When it wishes to take money out of the system (and hence raise interest rates), it sells bills. When it wishes to put money into the system (and hence lower interest rates), it buys bills. All Treasury bills are eligible for rediscount with the Bank of England, but only certain 'eligible' local authority bills and only those commercial bills which bear the acceptance of a bank which has fulfilled certain conditions laid down by the Bank of England are. Such commercial bills are described as eligible bank bills.

Advances represent the main form of sterling lending to non-bank customers. It will be seen that the greater part of such lending is to the UK private sector – persons and firms – with a relatively small amount being lent to customers abroad, and an even smaller amount being lent to the UK public sector. But this does not, of course, represent total bank lending to the public sector. We have already seen that banks lend to local authorities via money market loans and by discounting their bills. And banks lend to central government in a number of ways, including discounting Treasury bills and buying government bonds.

For statistical purposes, the Banking Department of the Bank of England is included within the retail-banking sector. This may seem anomalous, but it will be recalled that the Bank of England as well as being banker to the government and to the banks also has a number of private accounts. Lending by the Banking Department to central government is shown net, and it can be either positive or negative. In February 1986 it was negative, reflecting the large sums that central government then had on deposit.

Sterling investments cover bank holdings of securities, chiefly British government bonds, but also a number of other securities, including sterling-denominated bonds issued by foreign borrowers.

Assets denominated in currencies other than sterling are dominated by interbank lending (within the UK) and by lending overseas, much of which is to banks abroad. Significant sums have also been used for lending to the UK private sector and for the purchase of securities.

II.4   Accepting Houses and Other British Banks

In Bank of England statistics, the British-owned banks which are not retail banks are divided into two groups: accepting houses and other British banks. The distinction, as far as banking business is concerned, is less one of function than of status. The accepting houses are mostly long-established City institutions and are members of the Accepting Houses Committee. Currently there are 16 members, although a number of houses operate subsidiary banking firms whose business is included within the official statistics for accepting houses. The houses take their name from their traditional business of accepting commercial bills.

The banking business of the accepting houses is composed largely of wholesale banking – dealing in large sums of money in the short-term money markets. Their retail business is small and only a minority of accepting houses have offices in mainland Britain outside London. An abridged balance sheet for the accepting houses is given in table 2.2. It can be seen that over half of deposits are in currencies other than sterling. Nearly one-third of all deposits originate abroad and a further 22% of all deposits is derived from the interbank markets. Correspondingly, on the assets side of the balance sheet, much lending is through the various money markets. Large sums are lent on the domestic interbank market and a large amount is lent abroad, much of it to banks abroad. Direct advances to non-bank customers represent a much smaller proportion of total assets than in the case of the retail banks. Eligible liabilities are relatively low.

Accepting houses also undertake a number of other financial activities. They act as issuing houses; that is to say, they act for companies wishing to offer shares to the public and make all arrangements necessary including drawing up the prospectus, receiving applications for shares and making the initial allotment. They also act as fund managers and manage the investments of wealthy individuals, companies, pension funds, etc. Many run unit trusts. And a number are prominent as financial advisers, notably in the field of corporate mergers and take-overs.

The category of other British banks comprises a large number of banks of varying origins. Some are specialized subsidiaries of large retail banks, a few are long-established institutions with historical connections with particular areas abroad, but many are relatively small institutions providing only a limited range of financial services. A number regard themselves as merchant banks and, as well as undertaking wholesale banking activities, compete with the accepting houses for the business of arranging new issues, fund management, and advising on mergers and take-overs. But for many of

TABLE 2.2

Accepting Houses: Balance Sheet, 19 February 1986 (£m)

Sterling Liabilities		
Deposits: UK monetary sector		2,327
other United Kingdom		7,166
overseas		1,307
certificates of deposit		1,336
Other Currency Liabilities		
Deposits: UK monetary sector		3,252
other United Kingdom		1,831
overseas		6,471
certificates of deposit		298
Items in suspense and transmission, capital and other funds (sterling and other currencies)		3,634
Total Liabilities		27,622
Acceptances outstanding	3,925	
Eligible liabilities	5,572	
Sterling Assets		
Notes and coins		2
Balances with Bank of England: cash-ratio deposits		26
other		2
Market loans: UK monetary sector		5,403
UK monetary sector CDs		1,177
UK local authorities		337
overseas		619
Bills		136
Advances: United Kingdom		3,407
overseas		1,021
Investments		1,497
Other Currency Assets		
Market loans and advances: UK monetary sector		2,736
UK monetary sector CDs		510
other United Kingdom		1,084
overseas		6,460
Bills		61
Investments		1,299
Miscellaneous (sterling and other currencies)		1,844
Total Assets		27,622

Source: *BEQB*, March 1986.

these banks, the main business is that of a finance house: raising money in the wholesale markets and lending both to industry, for the purchase of capital equipment, and to persons, for the purchase of consumer durables.

An abridged balance sheet of the other British banks is given in table 2.3. It can be seen that, as with the accepting houses, foreign-currency deposits exceed sterling deposits and that a large amount of business is accounted for by transactions on the interbank market and with overseas clients. But there is also a large amount of sterling lending to domestic borrowers, of which all bar a small amount is to the private sector. Eligible liabilities account for nearly 30% of total liabilities.

TABLE 2.3

Other British Banks: Balance Sheet, 19 February 1986 (£m)

Sterling Liabilities		
Deposits: UK monetary sector		17,025
other United Kingdom		9,704
overseas		4,515
certificates of deposit		1,052
Other Currency Liabilities		
Deposits: UK monetary sector		8,024
other United Kingdom		1,619
overseas		15,086
certificates of deposit		1,884
Items in suspense and transmission, capital and other funds (sterling and other currencies)		7,659
Total Liabilities		66,567
Acceptances outstanding	1,227	
Eligible liabilities	19,298	
Sterling Assets		
Notes and coins		3
Balances with Bank of England: cash-ratio deposits		90
other		3
Market loans: UK monetary sector		9,896
UK monetary sector CDs		1,314
UK local authorities		449
overseas		1,064
Bills		127
Advances: United Kingdom		19,277
overseas		1,187
Investments		1,889
Other Currency Assets		
Market loans and advances: UK monetary sector		6,359
UK monetary sector CDs		186
other United Kingdom		3,166
overseas		18,916
Bills		14
Investments		1,203
Miscellaneous (sterling and other currencies)		1,424
Total Assets		66,567

Source: *BEQB*, March 1986.

II.5   Foreign Banks and Consortium Banks

On 19 February 1986 there were 348 different foreign banks operating in the UK, of which 62 were American and 25 were Japanese. Most had only the one office in, or close to, the City of London. A small number of North American and Western European banks have had a London office since the days before World War II, in some cases since the nineteenth century, but for the most part these foreign banks are comparative newcomers. Most arrived during the 1960s and 1970s.

It was during these decades that a new international banking system was developing. This system, often referred to as the eurodollar market or, more accurately, the euro-currency markets, proved a magnet to banks worldwide. All large banks, as well as many medium-sized banks, wished to become involved. And while the euro-currency markets were truly international, with active dealing in many centres in Western Europe and elsewhere, London was, and still remains, the most important single centre. So it was to London that most foreign banks went, when they decided to compete for a share of the new international banking business; although, naturally, the larger banks also established offices in the other important centres of the market as well.

The growth and the functioning of the euro-currency markets are discussed below. For present purposes it is sufficient to note that virtually all of the foreign banks have as their main business wholesale banking in foreign currencies, notably the US dollar, and that much of this business is conducted with companies, persons and banks outside the UK. This is evident from inspection of the abridged balance sheet for foreign banks in table 2.4.

In the Bank of England statistics, a separate balance sheet is given for the American banks, the Japanese banks, and for all other overseas banks. So as not to overburden the reader with statistics, we give here just one combined balance sheet for all foreign banks. Those readers who require more detail are referred to the *Bank of England Quarterly Bulletin*.

Table 2.4 shows all assets and liabilities on the books of UK offices of foreign-owned banks on 19 February 1986. It will be seen that the total of assets and liabilities is far greater than the total of domestic assets and liabilities held by all British-owned banks. The business of the foreign-owned banks is primarily in dollars and other non-sterling currencies, and sterling deposits account for only about 12% of total deposits. Of the foreign-currency deposits, two-thirds come from abroad (much of it from banks abroad) and approximately a further 17% is accounted for by borrowing in the London interbank market. On the assets side of the balance sheet it will be seen that much lending is to foreign residents, of which a large proportion goes to banks abroad. There is also substantial domestic interbank lending.

Although sterling business of the foreign banks only represents a small proportion of total business, it is far from negligible. Eligible liabilities, which give a good indication of sterling business with the domestic sector after netting out interbank transactions, amounted to £36,518 million, or nearly 42% of the eligible liabilities of the UK retail banks. Having come to London primarily to do international banking, many of the foreign banks have, nonetheless, been very ready to compete for domestic business as well. In a small number of cases, foreign banks have opened offices in provincial centres, such as Birmingham or Manchester.

In February 1986, there were 23 consortium banks active in London. These are banks jointly owned by a number of other banks or financial

TABLE 2.4

Foreign Banks: Balance Sheet, 19 February 1986 (£m)

Sterling Liabilities		
Deposits: UK monetary sector		22,027
other United Kingdom		11,930
overseas		17,349
certificates of deposit		4,928
Other Currency Liabilities		
Deposits: UK monetary sector		68,504
other United Kingdom		11,400
overseas		271,809
certificates of deposit		54,589
Items in suspense and transmission, capital and other funds (sterling and other currencies)		11,764
Total Liabilities		474,301
Acceptances outstanding	12,751	
Eligible liabilities	36,518	
Sterling Assets		
Notes and coins		22
Balances with Bank of England: cash-ratio deposits		170
other		14
Market loans: UK monetary sector		18,256
UK monetary sector CDs		1,546
UK local authorities		875
overseas		6,423
Bills		345
Advances: United Kingdom		22,815
overseas		4,769
Investments		3,435
Other Currency Assets		
Market loans and advances: UK monetary sector		64,880
UK monetary sector CDs		9,413
other United Kingdom		27,850
overseas		279,329
Bills		1,329
Investments		25,943
Miscellaneous (sterling and other currencies)		6,882
Total Assets		474,301

Source: BEQB, March 1986.

institutions. There are many reasons why such consortia are formed. They may serve as a means for a number of small banks to establish a presence in London which they could not afford individually. Consortia can also be formed to deal with special types of business or to provide finance for certain geographical areas such as the Middle East or Latin America. Their business is primarily with non-residents, and most of it is in currencies other than sterling. In February 1986, total assets and liabilities of all consortium banks amounted to £16,825m. Eligible liabilities were £1,210m.

II.6   The Discount Market

The discount market is composed primarily of the nine discount houses that are members of the London Discount Market Association, although additionally a small number of banks run special money-trading departments which operate in ways similar to the discount houses. This market plays a central role within the monetary system. Discount houses borrow money from banks and, to a limited extent, from other sources, and invest this in short-term financial assets, chiefly bills, short-term government bonds and certificates of deposit. The funds they borrow are almost wholly short-term, either overnight or at call (i.e. can be recalled without notice) and are secured against the financial assets they hold. Thus, the discount houses provide the banks with a convenient form of liquidity which can be added to, or subtracted from, on a day-to-day basis. Banks finding themselves with temporarily surplus funds can add to their deposits with the discount market; banks with a shortage of funds can call back monies already lent to the market. Deposits with discount houses earn a competitive rate of interest and, as they are fully secured, any risk is slight.

The discount market's role in providing liquidity does not end here, for the discount houses also act as market makers in Treasury bills, local authority bills, commercial bills and in certificates of deposit. The role of market maker is an important one. For financial assets to be negotiable (i.e. readily tradeable), there have to be dealers who stand ready to buy and sell on a regular basis. Assets that are not negotiable are not liquid. And efficient financial markets need liquid assets in order that market participants can quickly respond to changes in cash flow by buying or selling assets. The discount houses stand ready to buy or sell bills and certificates of deposit and in so doing, they guarantee the negotiability of these instruments, thus making them that much more useful as liquid assets, both for banks and for other market participants.

It is not only the commercial banks who benefit from an active market in bills. The Bank of England uses the bill market for purposes of monetary policy, in order to put money into, or take money out of, the banking system. The operations of the Bank can be summarised as follows. Each day, there are very large flows of funds between the commercial banks and the Bank of England. Since the Bank acts as banker to the government, all payments to the government involve money flowing out of the commercial banks into the Bank. Similarly, all payments by the government involve money flowing from the Bank toward the commercial banks. And the Bank of England will also be making and receiving other payments as well, e.g. on account of foreign-exchange transactions, or due to payments by banking clients of the Bank other than the government. These movements of money both ways will only exactly cancel out by accident; usually there will be a net balance either way. This will normally mean that the banking system will find itself with either a surplus or a shortage of cash. Whichever is the position, it will quickly be communicated to the discount market, as banks either offer new deposits or call for the repayment of existing ones. When the market is in surplus, the Bank of England will sell bills in order to absorb the surplus. When the market is short of funds, the Bank will announce its willingness to buy eligible bills, but will leave the discount houses individually to decide at what price to offer these. If the Bank is happy with the level of short-term interest rates implied by the offers from the discount houses, it will then buy the bills, thereby relieving the shortage of cash. On the other hand, if the Bank is not happy with the interest rates implied by the offers of any discount houses, it can reject those offers. The discount houses will then have to seek a 'lender-of-last-resort' loan from the Bank and will pay a penal rate for it.

In this way, the Bank of England uses the bill market and the discount houses to smooth out shortages or surpluses of cash in the banking system. Its tactics are designed so as to avoid imposing a pattern of interest rates on the market, whilst still leaving itself free to resist those interest-rate movements it judges undesirable.[1]

Given that the Bank of England has chosen to operate in the bill market in the way and for the purposes described, it is important that the market should remain a large and active one. In an effort to ensure that it does so, the Bank has stipulated that only those banks which have an acceptance business of sufficient size, and which regularly make deposits with the discount market, shall have their acceptances deemed as eligible for rediscount by the Bank. That is to say, only commercial bills accepted by approved banks are eligible bills. Two important conditions for being an approved bank are to maintain deposits of a minimum of $2\frac{1}{2}\%$ of eligible liabilities with members of the London Discount Market Association; and to maintain deposits of an average (over a period of six or twelve months) of 5% of eligible liabilities with members of the London Discount Market Association, or with money brokers, or jobbers in government stock. These conditions give an assurance of adequate funding for the discount houses which will enable them to continue to hold substantial bill portfolios.

Although the Bank of England does, at times, make loans direct to a number of financial institutions, e.g. stock jobbers, money brokers, it is traditionally through the discount market that the Bank deals with the banking system. And whilst, on occasions, the bank will deal direct with one or more clearing banks, it is still the case that only the discount houses are formally entitled to request loans from the Bank of England as lender of last resort.

II.7   Building Societies

The Building Societies began as part of the self-help movement among skilled workers during the Industrial Revolution. Early societies pooled the savings of members to build houses for them. Often, lotteries were used to decide in

---

1 This description of Bank of England operations in the money market is, necessarily, a brief one. For a detailed account, the reader should refer to the article, 'The Role of the Bank of England in the Money Market' in the *Bank of England Quarterly Bulletin*, March 1982.

what order members had access to the houses as they were finished. When all members were housed, the society was wound up. But, over time, the societies ceased to do their own building and evolved into purely financial institutions. They also largely ceased to be terminating societies and the word 'permanent' entered the name of many societies.

The building societies have grown rapidly in the period since World War II, playing the dominant role in the finance of the great growth of owner-occupancy. Their traditional business is simple to describe. They are mutual societies which collect money from many millions of savers in the form of shares and deposits. The word 'share' is a misnomer, and shareholders do not participate in profits. The difference between shares and deposits is that shareholders are members of the society and are entitled to vote at annual general meetings. They receive a slightly higher rate of interest but rank below depositors, as creditors, in the event of a dissolution of the society. But since the risks of investing with building societies are low, most investors opt for the higher interest offered by shares and the amount of money held as deposits has dwindled.

The societies devote approximately 80% of their funds to making loans on the security of first mortgages on residential property. The remaining 20% serves as a reserve of liquidity and is invested chiefly in British Government bonds, local authority debt and such money-market assets as term deposits with banks and certificates of deposit.

In recent years, the building societies have begun to diversify their sources of funding and have raised large sums of money from the wholesale financial markets in the form of syndicated bank loans, negotiable bonds, certificates of deposit and large time deposits. Such wholesale liabilities had grown to approximately 4% of total liabilities by the end of 1985.

Other changes are in prospect. A Green Paper, published in 1984,[1] proposed legislation to widen the existing powers of the building societies. It is proposed they be allowed to make up to 10% of their commercial lending other than by way of first mortgages on property. Within this limit, all societies would be able to lend on second mortgages, and those with commercial assets in excess of £100 million would be able to lend unsecured, or on security other than property. This proposal, if enacted, will represent a modest extension of the societies' lending ability. It is expected that most new lending will be housing-related: loans for carpets and curtains, etc. However, it may well prove to be the thin end of the wedge. As societies get used to making loans other than against first mortgages on property, and as borrowers adjust to the idea of borrowing from building societies for furniture and other large purchases, it is likely that pressure will grow to relax the 10% limit.

The societies are also to be allowed to hold and develop land intended to be used primarily for residential purposes, and to undertake mortgage credit business elsewhere in the EEC through the medium of subsidiaries. But

---

1   *Building Societies: A New Framework*, Cmnd. 9316 (H.M. Treasury, 1984).

such higher-risk assets will be limited to not more than 5% of all assets. In addition, building societies will be enabled to develop a money transmission service and provide foreign exchange (something they have already begun to do in partnership with other institutions) and to provide a number of services including estate agency, insurance broking and some forms of property management.

These proposals are expected to become law in 1986 or 1987. They represent a significant extension of building society activities and reflect a cautious step towards further despecialisation of building societies, something which has already begun with the development by some societies of automatic cash dispensers and cheque books. There is a general trend to less specialisation in most areas of finance and already the building societies find themselves in direct competition with the banks both in attracting funds and in making loans. If present trends continue, the societies will in time evolve into all-purpose financial institutions similar to retail banks.

TABLE 2.5

Building Societies: Balance Sheet, 30 September 1985 (£m)

Liabilities	
Shares and deposits	100,211
Interest accrued but not credited	2,426
Other borrowing	4,520
Reserves and other liabilities	7,419
Assets	
Mortgages	92,905
Land, building, equipment, etc.	1,808
British government securities	10,457
Local-authority debt	2,526
Other investments	6,879
Total assets = total liabilities	114,575

Source: Building Societies Association, *Bulletin No. 45*, January 1986.

Notes: 'Other borrowing' comprises negotiable bonds, time deposits, certificates of deposit issued *less* building society CDs held by other Societies, and bank loans. 'Other investments' comprise cash, bank deposits, CDs issued by banks, tax instruments, Treasury bills, and a small amount of overseas government securities.

The number of societies has declined steadily during recent decades. Prior to World War II, most societies were local or regional societies and very few had a national network of branches. But since the 1950s, building societies have opened many new branches and large national societies have emerged. Inevitably, this has meant overlapping branch networks, and the gains from merger have increased. In 1960 there were 726 societies but, by end-1985, this number was down to 167. Of these 167 societies, the largest five account for over 55% of the total assets of all societies and the largest 20 account for nearly 90% of total assets.

Due to their origins and to their present mutual status, the building societies do not come under the direct authority of the Bank of England, but are subject to supervision by the Chief Registrar of Friendly Societies. However, it is intended that the forthcoming legislation to widen building society powers will also create a new Building Societies Commission which will take over the task of supervising the societies.

Table 2.5 shows the assets and liabilities of building societies at 30 September 1985.

II.8   Life Assurance Companies and Superannuation Funds

Both life assurance companies and pension funds must be classed as financial intermediaries in terms of the description given of financial intermediaries in the introduction to this section. Both take funds from savers and lend these to borrowers. The big difference between them and the institutions previously considered is that they do not provide liquid financial assets. Both offer savers long-term investment possibilities.

The most popular form of life assurance contract nowadays is the endowment policy, although this can come in a number of forms. The essential feature of an endowment policy is that the assured agrees to pay, to the insurance company, regular premiums over a fixed number of years, e.g. 20 or 25. At the end of this time, the insurance company guarantees to pay a lump sum. If the policy is without profits, this will be a known amount (the sum assured) agreed at the outset. If the policy is with profits, it will be a basic sum assured plus bonuses, as with-profits policies share in the profits of the assurer and earn regular bonuses.

Should the policyholder die before expiry of the policy, his dependants will receive the sum assured plus bonuses (if any). Thus, an endowment policy is a mixed financial instrument. It is largely a straightforward long-term financial contract, in which what is returned reflects what has been paid-in plus accrued interest and, maybe, a share in profits, but it also includes insurance cover against death within the currency of the policy.

There are a number of other forms of life assurance contract, but almost all involve regular payments by the assured over a number of years, or possibly a single large payment, in exchange for a guarantee of an eventual lump-sum payment to the assured, or to his dependents.

Life assurance has been a popular form of saving in the United Kingdom and was, until the 1985 Budget, encouraged by tax relief on premiums paid. The life assurance companies comprise a number of specialist life companies as well as the large general insurance companies who also offer marine, fire and accident insurance. The latter categories of insurance do not represent financial contracts, as we are here using the term, as there is no lending or borrowing involved. The person who insures his house or his car buys a service (indemnity in the event of loss) for which he pays a price. His payment represents consumption expenditure, not saving. The law recognises the fundamental difference between the two forms of insurance by requiring all general insurance companies to keep separate the funds accumulated to pay for claims under marine, fire, and accident policies and the funds accumulated in order to meet liabilities to holders of life policies.

Total accumulated funds held by all life assurers (specialist and general insurance companies) amounted, at end-1984, to £112,851 million. Apart from a number of short-term assets, this money was largely invested in three different ways: in ordinary shares of UK companies, in British government securities, and in land, property and ground rents in the United Kingdom. Although it should be added that since the abolition of exchange control in 1980, life companies have begun to build up their foreign assets.

Superannuation funds are set up to provide pensions for members of a particular occupational group, or for employees of a particular firm or public-sector body. The principle is simple: those covered by the fund make regular contributions over a number of years and, upon retirement, are entitled to an annual pension until death. This pension may be of a fixed amount or it may allow for adjustments to compensate for inflation.

The number and size of pension funds have grown rapidly during recent decades as more and more firms have set up funds to cover their employees. In some cases of large firms or public corporations, the pension funds now administer considerable sums of money and are numbered among the largest discretionary managers of funds in the country. At end-1984 total net assets of superannuation funds amounted to £130,291 million, of which nearly £18,000m was accounted for by local authority pension funds, over £35,000m by other public-sector pension funds and just over £77,000m by private-sector pension funds.

Nearly one-half of total assets is invested in the ordinary shares of UK companies, and most of the rest is spread over British government securities, ordinary shares of foreign companies, land, property and ground rents in the UK and short-term assets.

Life assurance companies also provide pensions both for individuals (notably the self-employed) and for groups. For many small firms, it is easier to make pension provision for staff through a life assurance company, than to set up one's own fund. All pension funds, whether administered by independent superannuation funds or by life assurance companies, have a favourable tax status and do not pay tax on interest and dividends received on their investments.

II.9   Other Financial Intermediaries

Unit trusts and investment trusts: There are two forms of mutual investment that are common in the United Kingdom: unit trusts and investment trusts. The intention of mutual investment is to enable small investors to pool resources in order to gain the benefits of diversification which would not be available to each one individually. There are high fixed costs of dealing in negotiable securities and a small investor with, say, £5,000 to invest would not be able to spread this over a number of different companies. He would, most likely, have to put all his eggs in one basket and invest all the money in one company. That would be a risky strategy. But if 1,000 investors, each with £5,000 to invest, were to come together and put their money in a common pool, they would have £5 million to invest. This could be diversified over many companies, so reducing risk. This is the principle of mutual investment.

Unit trusts are legally constituted as trusts with a trust deed and a trustee. The trustee, which is usually a bank or an insurance company, holds all the assets of the unit trust on behalf of the beneficial owners – the unitholders. The trust is managed by a professional manager who is responsible for decisions about investment policy, subject to the provisions of his trust deed. Units can be sold at any time and the sums raised added to the pool of investible resources. Similarly, units can be sold back to the manager, who is then obliged to sell some investments to repay the unitholder. Unitholders are each entitled to a *pro-rata* share of the value of the invested funds of the trust, and the Department of Trade and Industry lays down precise rules for calculating the value of individual units.

Investment trusts are not, in fact, trusts in the legal sense. They are limited companies which issue their own shares and which use the proceeds to invest in other companies. Thus, anyone who buys shares in an investment trust automatically buys a diversified investment. Investment trusts have their shares listed on the Stock Exchange and they are bought and sold like other equity shares.

At end-1984, funds managed by unit trusts amounted to just over £15 billion of which the greater part was invested in ordinary shares of companies, both in the United Kingdom and abroad. At the same date, the total assets of investment trusts also amounted to something over £15 billion and again most was invested in ordinary shares. A larger number of investment trusts specialise in investment overseas and this is reflected in foreign assets accounting for more than half of all assets.

Finance houses: There are a number of finance houses and consumer credit companies active in the UK. They tend to be small as most of the larger institutions have now taken the status of bank and are included within the category 'other British banks', discussed above. Many are specialised institutions set up to finance the products of particular manufacturers or retailers. Funds are raised largely by issuing bills and by borrowing from banks. At end-1985, such companies had assets outstanding of £4,648m, of which nearly £3,900m was accounted for by loans to persons and to industrial and commercial companies, and a further £500m was accounted for by physical assets owned, but which had been leased, hired or rented out.

II.10   The Capital Market

The capital market is a general term which covers the markets in which securities – equity shares, preference shares and bonds – are bought and sold. Essentially, there are two related markets: the new-issue market, where new securities are offered to the public by borrowers wishing to raise new funds; and the secondary market, where existing securities are bought and sold. In principle, the capital market is an example of what we earlier termed direct finance: lenders of funds lending direct to the ultimate borrower, without the intervention of a financial intermediary. In some cases this is so, as for instance when many individuals subscribed to the issue of shares by British Telecom. But, it is by no means always the case. The majority of the securities listed on the Stock Exchange are now held by institutional investors such as insurance companies, superannuation funds, unit trusts and investment trusts. Over the years, many personal holders of securities have chosen to sell out and to entrust their financial wealth to intermediaries; so indirect finance has increased. This has been encouraged by a tax system which has favoured saving via superannuation funds and (until 1984) life assurance. The Conservative government of the 1980s has tried to reverse the trend and to encourage more personal share-owning. It has met with some initial success, but it is too early to say whether this will be durable.

The new-issue market is the market where private companies, the government, local authorities and some foreign borrowers seek money from the general public against the issue of securities. Not all securities are offered to the general public. There are many small companies, termed private companies, which have shares held by a limited number of owners (sometimes all from the same family) and where there is no formal means of trading these. But the new-issue market is concerned with securities that are offered to the general public. Such offers are governed by legislation designed to prevent fraud and, if it is proposed to have the securities listed on the Stock Exchange, by the rules of that institution also. The two most frequent types of issue of new securities are issues of equity shares by firms going public (i.e. a hitherto private company offering its shares to the public) and issues of bonds on behalf of the government.

In the case of equity shares, the issue will normally be managed by a merchant bank – usually an accepting house or a subsidiary of one of the retail banks – or by a stockholder, or both. Much legal and administrative work has to be done and a detailed prospectus has to be prepared giving full information on the existing owners and managers of the firm, on its history, its past and present trading performance and giving audited profit figures for a number of years. This prospectus will be distributed to stockbrokers, banks, investment managers and financial advisers in the United Kingdom and (for large issues) abroad as well. It must also be advertised in a number of national newspapers. The issue will probably be underwritten, that is to say, a number of institutional investors will, for a fee, agree to take up any shares which remain unsold. The managers of the issue have to arrange for applications for shares to be received and checked and shares allocated among would-be purchasers. If applications for shares exceed the quantity offered for sale, some form of rationing becomes necessary: all investors may be allotted the same proportion of the shares for which they applied, or a preference may be given to certain types of applicant, e.g. those applying for small amounts.

In the case of an issue of government bonds, the procedure is somewhat simpler. The issue is managed by the Bank of England. A prospectus is issued and published but it is much shorter than a company prospectus because (a) the government is a regular borrower and (b) the affairs of the government are already public knowledge in a way that those of a company are not. But, it may be noted that, if a foreign government wishes to raise money in Britain, it does have to produce a lengthy prospectus including information on the recent political and economic history of its country. For UK government bonds, issues are usually made in large amounts – anything from £100m to £1,000m – and applications are invited at a minimum price. In most cases, total applications fall short of the amount of stock on offer so applicants receive the amount applied for. The unsold stock is taken on to the books of the Bank of England and is sold on the Stock Exchange over a period of time, as demand materializes. The Bank normally expects to have at least one such stock on its books at any time, so that it can always make new sales of stock, whenever the demand is there.

There is no legal requirement on issuers of new shares or bonds to seek a listing on the Stock Exchange, but they almost invariably do. Those that do not, make other arrangements to ensure the securities offered for sale will be easily negotiable. People are more likely to buy securities if they know they can sell them again. Neither persons nor corporate bodies can reliably predict their financial circumstances far into the future and know what needs for money may arise. They will not wish to be locked into investments for many years ahead; so assets that can easily be resold will be more attractive than those which cannot. This is the importance of secondary financial markets.

Complying with the requirements for a full listing on the Stock Exchange is expensive. But, so as not to discourage smaller companies from making a public offering of shares, the Exchange permits trading in what are called unlisted securities, i.e. securities not admitted to the official list. The conditions to be fulfilled before a company can have its shares traded on the unlisted securities market are not negligible, but they are less onerous and less costly than for a full listing. A number of companies have gone public through this route.

It should also be noted that a small over-the-counter market in securities exists outside of the Stock Exchange. But there are few regular dealers and only a limited number of shares are quoted.

The Stock Exchange is the dominant secondary market where securities issued in the British Isles and sold to domestic investors are traded. It was formed in 1973 by the merger of a number of hitherto independent exchanges in London, in a number of UK provincial cities, and in the Republic of Ireland. There is now active trading only in London and Dublin, and London has much the greater share of total business.

Trading on the Stock Exchange has traditionally involved two parties – stockbrokers and stockjobbers – but a radical change is due to take place on 27 October 1986. The traditional method of dealing has made a sharp distinction between those who trade on their own behalf (the jobbers) and those who trade as agents of others (the brokers). It works as follows. The broker is the person in contact with the public. Persons wishing to buy or sell shares must approach a stockbroker who will act on their behalf. The broker's is an agency function and for this he charges a commission. In order to execute his client's instructions, the broker has to deal with a stockjobber. Jobbers are market makers who hold portfolios of securities and who stand ready to buy and sell for their own account. There are a number of jobbers, each specialising in a range of securities. There is competition between them and brokers are free to shop around and do business with whoever quotes the most favourable price. Stockjobbers are restricted to dealing only with stockbrokers and do not deal direct with the public. All trading is conducted on the floors of the Exchange, apart from some after-hours business conducted over the telephone.

This system imposes what is called 'single capacity', that is to say a firm that is a member of the Stock Exchange either deals as agent for non-members or it deals for its own account, in which case it does not deal directly with non-members. The system has a number of advantages. There is no problem of conflict of interest, and investors in securities get a disinterested service from their broker. Trading in all securities is continuous during the hours the Exchange is open, unlike the position in some overseas exchanges where dealing is direct between brokers and where each security is only 'called' once or twice each day.

But whether it is a good system or not, it is not the way the rest of the world operates. In national markets abroad and in international security dealing, there is dual capacity. Large firms combine the roles of broker and jobber and hold portfolios of securities in their own name, while still dealing direct with investors. And trading in securities, like other financial activity, is becoming increasingly international. By the early 1980s, member firms of the Stock Exchange faced a stark choice: to continue in their traditional ways and thereby, in large measure, lose the chance of becoming involved in the expanding international business in securities, and, maybe, also see the shares of leading UK companies increasingly traded abroad, or to change their practices and bring these more into line with what happens elsewhere. They chose the latter. A series of changes was set in motion culminating in the 'big bang' due to take place on 27 October 1986 when the function of broker and jobber is to be merged. After that date, firms will have dual capacity and will operate along the lines of American and Japanese security houses: making a market in securities, acting as principals but also dealing direct with the public. This sea change in the Stock Exchange and in its members' firms is discussed further in section III below.

Some indication of the importance of the capital market can be gained by looking at the sums of money raised on the new-issue market, and also by looking at turnover of securities on the secondary market. During the three years 1983–5, new issues of all securities, excluding UK government bonds, averaged £4,825m a year. Of this total, approximately one-half was accounted for by rights issues, i.e. issues of additional shares by existing public companies and offered, in priority, to existing shareholders. A certain amount of outstanding fixed-interest stock was redeemed each year, both by public companies and by local authorities, so the net amount of new money raised was less than the gross figure given above. For public companies and all overseas borrowers, total net new money raised, in 1983–5, averaged £3,925m a year.

Whilst quite substantial, this sum is not large relative to net new lending by banks or by building societies. But it should be borne in mind that equity capital is a strategic form of fund-raising in that it is risk-bearing. All firms require risk-bearing capital in order that small or temporary losses can be sustained without the existence of the firm being called into question. This is as true of banks as it is of industrial and commercial companies, and many banks have figured among the companies raising new capital in recent years. The capital market is not the largest source of funds to domestic enterprises, but it remains a crucial one.

Long-term funds raised by the government usually exceed those raised for the private sector and for foreign borrowers. This was true during the years 1983–5, when the Bank of England made net sales of government bonds averaging £9,207m a year.

Turnover on the Stock Exchange during the same three years averaged nearly £350bn a year, or nearly £1,400m per working day. Of the annual average, nearly £247bn was accounted for by transactions in UK government stock and over £78bn was accounted for by transactions in ordinary shares.

III CHANGES IN THE FINANCIAL SYSTEM
III.1 Introduction

During the last 20 years, the financial system, both in the United Kingdom and elsewhere, has been changing rapidly. Banks have introduced new financial instruments; they have developed new techniques of raising funds and of making loans; new financial markets have been created. This process – known as financial innovation – is already having an important impact on government policy and on the wider economy. The impact on policy is easy to see.

In a number of countries, including the UK, monetary policy has, in recent times, been directed towards controlling the supply of money. The adoption of this variable as a proximate target of policy, instead of, say, the level of interest rates, stems from the view that there is a correlation between the money supply and price inflation. We are not concerned here to pass judgement on this policy, but it is important to note that what matters is not the absolute growth of the money supply (however defined) it is growth relative to demand. If the money supply grows slowly, but there is no increase in demand for money, this is likely to result in inflation; on the other hand, if the money supply grows rapidly, but, at the same time, there is a corresponding rise in the demand for money, this will not result in inflation. When governments first specified annual targets for the growth of the money supply, this was in the belief that the public's demand for money was stable and well understood. But financial innovation has called this into question. When new financial assets appear or when existing assets change their characteristics, it is to be expected that demands for all financial assets will be affected.

In consequence, due to the continuing changes in financial assets and in financial behaviour, the demand for monetary assets has become more variable and harder to predict, both in the UK and elsewhere. New definitions of 'money' have been proposed and governments have accorded varying degrees of attention to measures of narrow money and broad money. In the UK, official targets for the broad measure, £M3 (defined as all sterling deposits of the private sector plus holdings of notes and coins), were exceeded by large margins in financial years 1980–1 and 1981–2. The targets were then raised for subsequent years and were met during the next three financial years. But in 1985–6, £M3 was again substantially above target and the government reacted with a further easing of the target range for the following year. At different times, targets for other monetary aggregates have been specified in addition. For financial year 1986–7, there are target ranges for £M3 and for a narrow definition of money, MO, defined as notes and coins with the public plus banks' till money and non-obligatory balances with the Bank of England. So targets are still set, but it is now accepted that financial innovation can influence all monetary series in unpredictable ways. Monetary targets may still have some use but they cannot, in present circumstances, be a precise guide to policy.

Financial innovation is also having other consequences. It is affecting the ways in which financial services are provided, what costs are involved, and where financial services are provided. For all these reasons, it is important to understand what is going on and why.

III.2   Internationalization

The world is shrinking rapidly. Advances in technology have made communications of all sorts easier and faster. People can travel rapidly by air between different parts of the globe and they can communicate easily and cheaply by telephone and telex between different parts of the globe. Computer networks can be operated on a worldwide basis and information made instantly available to people in many different countries. For many economic purposes, national frontiers are of less and less significance, and it is now possible for large firms to run their operations on a global basis. Of course, multinational firms are not new in themselves. But, in earlier times, such firms could not easily integrate their worldwide operations, as communications between head office and foreign subsidiaries were slow and costly. Subsidiaries tended to operate with a considerable degree of autonomy. Now, it is possible for head office to be in almost continuous contact with foreign subsidiaries and branches and to co-ordinate operations in one worldwide strategy.

These changes have been particularly in evidence in banking and in other areas of finance. Large banks have established networks of offices around the world. These offices can deal actively in the financial markets where they are situated and still report, promptly to head office, full details of all business done. In consequence, senior officials in head office can monitor closely the worldwide position of the bank in many different financial markets. And if they wish, they can undertake new business, designed to offset or to complement the activities of offices abroad, so as to keep the bank's global balance-sheet in line with what is desired.

At the same time, new international markets have grown in short-term financial assets, in bank loans and in securities. These markets are worldwide, although they tend to be dominated by trading in a limited number of major financial centres. London, with over 700 banks, is the largest, but other centres are important as well; and since much business is potentially mobile, international financial centres are, inevitably, in competition with each other. International bank loans arranged in New York could be arranged in Paris or Amsterdam: international securities issued in London could be issued in Brussels or Zurich. Success in this competition depends upon things such as good telecommunications facilities, the availability of skilled labour, the tax regime, reserve requirements imposed on banks, the time zone in which a centre finds itself, and many others. This, in turn, means that governments and central banks, if they are concerned about the size of their financial industry (and most of them are) now have to consider carefully how policy actions may affect their national share of what has become an international business.

III.3   Technology

Developments in micro-electronic technology have been a crucial factor in the internationalization of banking, but they have also had other effects on banking, as well as on other areas of finance. This is a complex topic, about which books have been written, so what follows should only be seen as a brief summary.[1]

---

1   A recent authoritative survey of developments in this area is provided by J.R.S.Revell, *Banking and Electronic Fund Transfers* (OECD, 1983).

The initial uses of computers in financial institutions were in keeping records and in automating labour-intensive activities such as cheque clearing. As computers became more sophisticated and computing power cheaper, it became possible for records to be updated with increasing frequency and for the information to be accessed more easily. This was of great importance: decisions in banking depend on information. Decisions about new business depend on what existing loans are outstanding, to which industrial sectors, in which geographical areas, to which large firms; what is the banks' position in the short-term financial markets; what are the maturity structures of assets and liabilities; what is the currency-composition of assets and liabilities, and on many other aspects of the existing portfolio. Banks which have such information readily available will be able to take quicker decisions about new transactions than banks which do not. In modern banking, keeping track of one's position is not just for purposes of record, it is a key input into new business decisions.

Computers have also made it possible for financial institutions to cope with a much wider range of business. This is one reason for the fading of traditional demarcations between different types of financial institutions. When calculations were done manually, it was cost-efficient for intermediaries to keep operations simple and this meant undertaking only a restricted range of business. But now that all sorts of complex calculations can be performed instantaneously, banks and other intermediaries can introduce a more varied range of assets and liabilities, they can deal easily in assets and liabilities denominated in many different currencies (including composite currencies such as the ECU) and they can more readily envisage competing for new types of business. And however complex the balance sheet, however variegated are assets and liabilities, if a bank has access to appropriate computer hardware and software, its managers can still keep track of credit exposures to firms or to industries, of maturity mismatches, interest-rate exposures, etc.

New technology has changed dealing rooms out of all recognition. Dealers, whether in foreign exchange, in short-term financial assets or in securities, now use the latest micro-electronic equipment. They have access to video screens on which any one of a number of pages of information on interest rates, exchange rates, etc., can be displayed at the touch of a button. Telephone contact with money brokers, with foreign-exchange brokers and with other leading banks is also instantaneous and deals once struck can be automatically recorded in seconds. This considerable mechanization of dealing has both permitted and encouraged the surge in money-market activity that has occurred during the last two decades, both in London and elsewhere.

The foregoing can be described as back-office technology; it is not seen by most bank clients. But the use of new technology has spread to the front office, to the point of direct contact between banks and clients. The most obvious manifestation to date is the growth in usage of automatic teller machines (ATMs) which permit depositors to withdraw cash or carry out other simple transactions automatically and outside normal banking hours. But experiments are taking place, both in the UK and abroad, on what is known as electronic funds transfer at point of sale (EFT/POS). This is a system, already technologically feasible, which is expected, in time, to re-place many payments in cash or by cheque. It requires retailers to have specially designed computer terminals at check-outs or cash desks, and it requires bank customers to have their own personal debit card. When the card is inserted in the retailer's terminal and when, at the same time, the card-holder registers his personal identification number, then payment for purchases is made automatically by the instantaneous debit to the buyer's account and credit to the retailer's account of the sum due.

It is common for newspaper accounts of EFT/POS to claim that it heralds the advent of the cashless society. This is clearly a gross exaggeration. For inter-personal transactions and for many small purchases, e.g. bus fares, newspapers or packets of chewing gum, cash is likely to remain the cheapest and most efficient means of payment. But EFT/POS may, in time, substan-tially reduce the number of payments by cash and by cheque, with conse-quent savings in cost for both banks and retailers. It will also mean further changes in the demand for different types of media of exchange and further difficulties in interpreting movements in statistics of the money supply.

Another way in which new technology is directly affecting relations between banks and their customers is through what is called office banking. In essence, what this means is that corporate clients, provided they have basic computing facilities, can communicate directly with their bank's computer to obtain details of their accounts or to initiate any of a number of transactions. Thus, the finance director can send instructions to the bank to make payments, to move money between accounts, to buy or sell foreign exchange or to buy any of a number of short-term financial assets, simply by tapping at a keyboard in his own office. For important clients, banks guaran-tee fulfilment of the instructions within agreed limits as to amount. In some cases, involving large clients and large banks, such direct computer links can be international.

A number of banks and one building society are offering analogous facil-ities to personal clients under the name of home banking. This enables anyone with a home computer and a telephone to call up details of his bank account and to initiate a number of transactions.

III.4   The Growth of Short-Term Markets

One of the great changes in banking has been the growth of active markets in short-term bank deposits, in bank loans, and in a number of other financial instruments. Rates of interest determined in these markets are now widely used as determinants of, or as guides to, other bank interest rates. There has been, what may be termed, a marketization of banking. It is a development that has occurred in virtually all developed countries.

In London, the main short-term markets are the interbank market, the market in short-term time deposits from non-bank sources, the market in certificates of deposit (all in sterling, dollars and in a number of other currencies), the markets in Treasury bills, commercial bills and local authority bills and the market for discount-house deposits (all primarily or wholly in sterling). There are also markets for deposits with local authorities and with finance houses (in sterling), and recently new markets have started in deposits denominated in European Currency Units (ECUs) and Special Drawing Rights (SDRs). Transactions in these markets are made over the telephone, often through specialist money brokers, but also, on occasions, direct between the contracting parties.

The existence of active markets in a number of different currencies means that banks and other dealers will frequently wish to buy or sell particular currencies, so a foreign-exchange market is a necessary complement to these short-term markets. In London, a large and active market exists in both spot and forward foreign exchange. Dealing is usually conducted through specialist foreign-exchange brokers.

There are also a growing number of markets in financial futures and in traded options. A financial future is a financial asset, e.g. a three-month bank deposit or a long-term government bond, which is traded today for delivery in the future. A traded option contract is a saleable right to buy or sell a standard quantity of a given financial asset at a fixed price within a given period of time. Both futures and options markets include contracts to buy or sell currencies, as well as contracts to buy or sell a number of financial assets denominated in sterling or in dollars. It may seem surprising that people should wish to deal, now, in contracts that only come into force (or may be exercised) in the future. But such contracts can be used to manage risk. For instance, a bank makes a six-month, fixed-interest loan on the basis of a three-month deposit. It runs the risk that in three months' time, when it replaces the maturing deposit, rates of interest will have risen and it will lose money on the deal. It can hedge the risk by negotiating, now, a three-month deposit, at an agreed rate of interest, for delivery three months hence.

The growth of short-term money markets where rates of interest are determined by supply and demand for funds is something new. Traditionally, most banks in the UK had their interest rates tied to the Bank of England's discount rate (Bank rate), which meant that rates were administered rather than being competitively determined. It also meant there was little scope for price competition between banks and, apart from some elements of non-price competition, most banks were in the position of just accepting passively such deposits as were offered. Lending was restricted in accordance with funds available as well as by frequent official credit-control measures. Credit rationing was an entrenched feature of the UK financial system.

All this started to change when banks began to compete with each other on price and to bid for new deposits. It started with the growth, in the 1960s, of the market in dollar deposits. The market was international and not subject to the many traditional restraints on domestic sterling business. It was a new development and there was no established customer loyalty among depositors. It involved sufficient numbers of banks from many different countries that agreements on rates of interest were unlikely. The market began as a highly competitive market and has remained so.

The growth of an international market in dollar deposits, centred in London, precipitated an influx of foreign banks, which banks, being new-comers to the United Kingdom, were outside all traditional agreements on interest rates. In addition, they had no existing stock of sterling deposits. If they were to do any business in sterling they would have to compete for deposits by offering a competitive rate of interest. And since they were already competing actively for dollar deposits, this was not a difficult step to take. The process snowballed as domestic banks sought, where possible, to match the rates being offered elsewhere. In 1971, the Bank of England introduced new monetary measures, known as Competition and Credit Control which, significantly, abolished all the old controls and agreements on rates of interest. Thenceforth, all banks were free to set their own rates of interest and to compete for funds.

For many banks, it soon became the case that virtually all deposits were taken at market-determined or market-influenced rates of interest. And even for the large retail banks, who had long had large volumes of modestly remunerated deposits, the position was changing as competition spread downwards with better terms being offered, even on comparatively small deposits. This, inevitably, meant a higher average cost of funds and, in turn, greater pressure on banks to maximize the return on assets. Non-obligatory reserve assets and especially unproductive cash holdings were cut to a minimum. This could be done without increasing the risk of illiquidity, as banks were able to use the new markets, and especially the interbank market, as a means of lending funds short-term. In this way, they could maintain liquidity at little sacrifice of interest.

So, the short-term financial markets served the dual function of providing funds for those banks that needed them and providing remunerative short-term assets for banks with surplus funds. Both functions were a source of liquidity. Banks can regard their short-term assets as being a source of liquidity, in the traditional manner, but they can also, quite legitimately, regard their ability to borrow new funds at short notice as an additional source of liquidity.

As markets grew, both in number and in depth, so banks became more confident of being able to borrow and lend as they wished. 'Liability man-agement' – the continual adjusting of short-term liabilities – became accepted as a part of modern banking and as a necessary complement to the more traditional asset management. Non-bank borrowers and lenders also adjusted their behaviour. Cash management became the order of the day, with finance departments of large companies devoting considerable re-sources to monitoring market trends and ensuring that their own borrowing and lending were on the best terms.

By 1986, the process of marketization of banking appears irreversible. The short-term markets have become an integral part of the financial system, and much business is premised on their continued existence. And for many banks, their standing in the short-term markets and their ability to deal quickly and in large amounts is an important weapon in the competitive struggle for business. We saw above that many banks, as part of their office-banking packages, were ready to guarantee, within limits, the fulfilment of clients' orders for foreign exchange or for the purchase or sale of short-term assets. Such guarantees can only be given by banks confident of their own ability to deal instantly in the relevant financial markets.

III.5   Euro-Currency Markets

Of the short-term markets, the largest are the Euro-currency markets. In broad terms, these markets can be defined as international markets for short-term time deposits and for bank loans (not necessarily short-term) in currencies other than that of the country where the transaction takes place. That is to say, the Euro-dollar market is a market in dollar deposits and loans outside of the United States of America; the Euro-Deutschmark market is a market in Deutschmark deposits and loans outside of Federal Germany, etc. And for completeness, it should be added that, in addition to loans and deposits, the markets now trade certificates of deposit and other short-term financial instruments.

This raises the obvious question: what is so important about location? Why is a dollar deposit held at a bank in London different from a dollar deposit held with a bank in Chicago? After all, apart from location, there is no difference whatsoever in the actual dollars themselves; the holder of either deposit could use it to acquire goods and services in America in the normal way. The answer, essentially, is that dollar deposits held in the USA are subject to all the rules and regulations of the Federal Reserve Board and the other American regulatory agencies; dollar deposits held outside the USA are not. It is a question of jurisdiction. The position of other monies is analogous, but to explain this point more fully we shall remain with the US dollar and with the Euro-dollar market.

Dollar deposits held outside the USA are not normally subject to reserve requirements. This is so with dollar deposits in most European countries, including the UK. Since reserve requirements in the USA, as in most other countries, earn no interest, they are a significant cost to banks. In their absence, banks can operate on narrower margins and hence can offer better interest rates to both lenders and borrowers of money. Other costs are lower too. The Euro-dollar market is a wholesale market dealing almost entirely in sums equal to or in excess of $1 million. Deposits and loans are for a fixed term and there are virtually no retail deposits. So the first advantage of the non-resident dollar market is low costs which enable banks to offer more favourable rates of interest.

A second advantage is freedom from exchange controls. This was illustrated in the 1960s when the American authorities introduced a range of measures designed to curb the high level of capital exports from the USA. These included restraints on resident US banks lending dollars abroad. But the demand for dollars in the rest of the world remained high and this demand was channelled into the Euro-dollar market, where rates of interest rose above the level of rates in the USA. This led non-American residents, who were not subject to US regulations, to switch holdings of dollars from American to European banks, including European branches of American-owned banks. Also, those who received dollars in the normal way of business (e.g. exporters to the USA) and wished to hold on to them, rather than sell them for another money, naturally chose to keep the dollar in Europe rather than in America. Even central banks switched some of their dollar holdings to commercial banks in Europe. In general, the American measures were a failure and were abolished in January 1974, but not before most of the internationally-mobile dollar funds had shifted to Europe.

The Euro-dollar market is not subject to national restrictions on interest rates. This was also an important influence on developments in the 1960s. Twice during that decade, the US authorities put an effective ceiling on the interest rates that resident American banks could pay on time deposits. The ceiling did not apply outside the USA, so again there was scope and reason for higher rates of interest to be paid on dollar deposits in Europe than in the USA. Analogous situations have occurred with other monies. On occasions, the German authorities, in attempts to curb speculative buying of Deutschmarks, have ordered domestic banks to pay zero or very low rates of interest on new mark deposits by non-residents. But the chief result was not to discourage non-residents from holding mark deposits, but to ensure that they held them with banks in Luxembourg or Zurich not subject to the German controls.

During the 1960s and 1970s, the Euro-dollar market and the parallel markets in other currencies grew rapidly. During the 1980s, due, *inter alia*, to the international debt problem, growth has been more subdued. But the markets remain large, unfettered, competitive markets for both time deposits and for term loans. Their very size is an attraction in itself, as loans can be arranged of much larger amounts than would be possible in the domestic markets of many European countries. Large loans are usually syndicated, i.e. shared by a group of banks.

A key element in Euro-dollar trading is the active interbank market. This market fulfils the functions described in section III.4 above, and in the process, effectively knits together the many hundreds of different and disparate banks into one coherent market. General shortages or surpluses of funds are quickly reflected in demands for borrowing or in offers of funds in the interbank market and have prompt effects on interest rates there.

Such rates are a barometer of market conditions and are widely used as a basis for determining the rates charged on loans to non-bank customers. The most important rate is the London interbank offered rate for dollar deposits, or LIBOR. It is the rate at which the larger banks are prepared to lend dollars. The key term is for three-month loans, although there are also LIBORs for six-month dollar loans, for one-month loans, etc. There are also LIBORs for a number of other currencies widely traded in London. But since the dollar remains the dominant currency in international banking, it is LIBOR for dollar deposits which is of most significance.

Most Euro-currency deposits are short-term, but lending to non-bank borrowers is often for a period of years. In order to make such medium-term (1–5 years) and long-term (over 5 years) loans, banks have to regularly replace or renegotiate maturing short-term deposits. But they cannot know in advance what interest rates they will have to pay in the future. It follows that it would be highly risky to offer loans stretching over a number of years at fixed rates of interest. The solution adopted has been to make loans on a variable-rate basis, where the interest rate is expressed as LIBOR plus a percentage and is recalculated every three or six months. The percentage depends on the borrowers' credit standing. In this way, banks avoid a direct interest-rate risk, although they only do so by passing the risk to the borrower, which is not always a satisfactory solution.

III.6   The Eurobond Market

The Eurobond market is an international capital market in which securities – predominantly fixed-interest securities and floating-rate notes (FRNs) – are issued and sold worldwide. The market is dominated by a number of international security houses and international banks which act both as issuing houses and as market makers. The main borrowers of funds are international organisations, public corporations and large internationally-known companies. Securities are issued in a range of currencies, but again the dollar is the dominant one. There is no physical market-place and the market functions as a worldwide over-the-telephone market. London is the single most important centre.

The issue of new securities involves a lead manager or managers and a syndicate of subscribing banks and security houses. The lead managers arrange the details of the issue: size, currency, duration, interest terms, etc. and then assemble the syndicate of subscribers. Members of the syndicate will intend to place the securities with clients and will subscribe for that amount of securities they feel they can re-sell. The syndicate will normally be international, and in this way, the securities will end up spread among a wide range of investors in a number of different countries.

The securities are not normally traded on a recognised Stock Exchange. Instead, for each security, a number of banks and security houses act as market maker and stand ready to buy or sell. They will usually be comprised of the original lead managers and a number of the original syndicate members. Competition between them ensures that the prices quoted to would-be buyers or sellers of the security remain in line with prevailing market conditions.

Several features of the market are noteworthy. Firstly, it is a largely unregulated market; for while dealers are subject to laws against fraud and malpractice in the countries where they operate, they are not subject to rules such as apply to those wishing to have securities listed on the London or New York Stock Exchanges. No lengthy prospectus is prepared for a new issue and there is no requirement to advertise a proposed new issue in national newspapers. This is justified by market practitioners on the grounds that Eurobonds are not offered for sale to the general public; they are traded by professional dealers and only sold to a relatively narrow range of professional investors. The result is that issue costs are low and considerably less than for a public offering of securities in most domestic markets. But, at the same time, the scope for worldwide distribution of Eurobonds means that large sums of money – often in excess of $100 million – can be raised.

The market represents an internationalization of security dealing in the same way that the Euro-currency markets represent an internationalization of banking. It also represents a diversification of business for a number of banks who through this market have become actively involved in the issuing and trading of securities. In many cases, banks are doing business in the international capital market that they would not be allowed to do in their own domestic market. In Canada, Japan and the USA, national laws impose a separation of banking and security trading.

In the Eurobond market, there is no separation of stockbrokers and stockjobbers as on the UK Stock Exchange. The dealers are the security houses and the banks who buy and sell shares on their own behalf and who combine the functions of jobber and broker. For this reason, British stockbrokers and stockjobbers have been unable to participate in what has been a fast-growing market; the jobbers because the regulations of the Stock Exchange prevented them from dealing direct with the general public; the brokers because the regulations prevented them from dealing in securities as principals. And the newer market has taken away business from the Stock Exchange: a number of large UK firms have chosen to issue international bonds rather than raise new funds on the domestic market. This exclusion of its member firms from such a large and growing market is the main reason why the Stock Exchange is about to change fundamentally its traditional practices. After 27 October 1986, member firms will be able to compete for international business in the Eurobond market.

III.7   The International Debt Problem

During the 1970s, banks active in the Euro-currency markets increased substantially their lending to a number of developing countries. These loans were directed towards a number of actual or future oil producers (Indonesia, Mexico, Nigeria, Venezuela) and to a number of middle-income oil importers (Argentina, Brazil, and other Latin American countries). The loans were of varying terms, but all or virtually all were at rates of interest pegged to LIBOR, or other reference rates, and adjustable regularly.

In the early 1980s, a sharp recession in the developed world coincided with a period of exceptionally high rates of interest. Developing countries found their exports stagnating and their debt-service charges rising. For the oil importers, this was on top of the jump in import bills after the 1979 oil-price rise. The result was that in 1982 and 1983 a succession of countries announced they were unable to meet their obligations to the banks as well as to other official creditors. Thus began what has become known as the international debt problem.

A discussion of this episode and of the subsequent negotiations between the IMF, the banks and the debtor nations, which resulted in the widespread rescheduling of bank debts, can be found in section III of Chapter 3 below. It need not be repeated here. What we are concerned with are the consequences of this problem for banks and for the wider financial system.

Many banks found themselves faced with a sudden and, to all intents and purposes, forced conversion of short-term loans into what were long-term and effectively frozen assets. This was preferable to having the debtor countries default outright, but it was, nevertheless, undesirable in itself. Firstly, there was the obvious question mark over the value of the rescheduled assets – whether all interest payments and amortization would, in practice, be forthcoming. Secondly, there was a substantial increase in the gap between maturities of assets and of liabilities. While banks operating in the Euro-currency markets have always granted loans of terms longer than those of deposits, they have been careful to control the extent of the maturity mismatch between assets and liabilities. Some mismatching was seen as acceptable, even inevitable; too much was seen as dangerous. Now, all of a sudden, many banks found themselves with a greater maturity mismatch than could be considered prudent.

There have been two main responses to this situation. Firstly, the banks, under pressure from national supervisory authorities (the Bank of England, in the UK) have built up their capital resources by issuing new equity shares, in some cases new long-term bonds, and by diverting large amounts of annual profits into reserve funds against possible future losses. This was an obviously sensible measure to take and will enable banks to withstand greater loan losses, should they occur, without their solvency being called into question.

The second response has been to try to compensate for the large volumes of frozen loans by increasing the liquidity of other bank assets. One way to do this is for banks to make new international loans against the security of marketable assets. Previously, although large Euro-currency loans were syndicated among a number of banks, each bank retained its portion of the loan. Loans and participations in loans were not normally re-saleable. Now, in the wake of the international debt problem, large loans are often arranged in ways which involve the borrower issuing a succession of short-term negotiable notes. For instance, a five-year loan may involve the borrower in issuing a succession of three-month notes at three-monthly intervals throughout the five years. Individual banks bid for the notes, at each time of issue, as they choose. If they wish to make a long-term loan, they can do so, by purchasing and repurchasing the borrower's notes. If they wish to curtail their involvement in the loan, they can decline to bid for new notes at the next issue date. In this way, banks have more flexibility in managing their assets.

It should be noted, however, that many borrowers, sensitive to the risk of not being able to sell notes at some time in the future, ask for guarantees of stand-by funds in such an eventuality. Certain banks choose to provide such guarantees in exchange for a fee, thereby incurring long-term contingent (and off-balance-sheet) liabilities, instead of long-term actual (and on-balance-sheet) liabilities. Not all banks choose to avoid all long-term commitments, but the system of loans via renewable notes does allow many banks scope to adjust their loan portfolio more quickly than was hitherto possible.

This development is likely to prove of considerable significance for the whole financial industry. For, once bank loans are commonly made against the issue of negotiable paper, the gap between direct and indirect finance is diminished. The same issue of paper can be sold partly to banks (indirect finance) and partly to final investors (direct finance). This already happens with international issues of notes. Along with the banks who bid for notes to hold in their own name, are international security houses (usually of American or Japanese origin) who purchase notes with the intention of re-selling them to their clients. And a number of banks have created, or are creating, their own security-dealing capacity and are seeking to expand their client base among mutual funds and wealthy personal investors, with whom they can place notes and other securities. In the end, the economic difference between an institution that first borrows funds from lenders and then subscribes, in its own name, for the notes of borrowers, and an institution that arranges for lenders to subscribe direct, may not be very great.

III.8   Towards the Financial Supermarket?

At several points in this chapter, we have remarked on the fading of demarcations between different methods of finance and between different types of financial intermediary. We noted early on that the banks and the building societies are increasingly in direct competition for the business of the personal sector, both in taking deposits and in making loans. This competition can only increase when the proposed measures to widen the lending powers of the societies are introduced. There is also increasing competition between banks and security houses for the business of large companies and of public-sector agencies, both in the investing of funds and in the provision of loans. This has led many banks to develop their own security-trading capacity and has led security houses to add a number of banking functions to the list of financial services offered. Where the law and the regulations of the domestic Stock Exchange permit, there have been a number of outright mergers.

These changes are part of a general trend for financial intermediaries to offer a wider range of services, not always from the same office, but from within the same company or group of companies. Diversification continues to take place, both in terms of products and in terms of geography. For many years this was most evident in the international markets, where many banks have long been active both as bankers and as security dealers. At first, the overlap between the different roles was limited, as the Euro-currency market provided loans at short and medium term, whereas the Eurobond market provided mainly long-term finance. But, in the 1970s, the terms of bank loans lengthened, and, more recently, there has been the growth of Euro-notes. Now the overlap is complete and competition between traditional banking and security dealing direct.

Recently, quite fundamental changes have become evident in the British domestic market. These are associated with the forthcoming 'big bang' on the Stock Exchange. We have already seen that, in October 1986, the separation between broker and jobber is to end and that, thereafter, Stock Exchange member firms will function as do foreign security houses: dealing for their own account, acting as market maker, and dealing directly with the public. Such firms inevitably hold large blocks of securities. They thus stand to make losses when security prices are falling. In the long term, such losses should be counter-balanced by gains when prices are rising. But it is essential for security dealers to be well capitalized (i.e. to have large amounts of equity capital plus reserves) so that they can absorb short-term losses without difficulty. And the more business they wish to undertake, the more capital they need.

Due to the traditional method of dealing, Stock Exchange firms were only lightly capitalized. Stockjobbers did need adequate capital but brokers, acting only as agents, needed very little. Therefore, any move by Stock Exchange members to establish general security houses, dealing in a wide range of domestic securities – let alone foreign and international securities – meant that they would need new capital. New capital was most likely to be forthcoming from other financial institutions. This meant there was a unique opportunity for those banks who wished to create, or to expand, their own security-trading capacity. The council of the Stock Exchange relaxed the rules on outside ownership of member firms and this resulted in a succession of takeovers of both broking and jobbing firms by British and foreign banks. The new security houses got the capital backing they needed, and, in the process, the traditional separation between banking and security dealing in the United Kingdom was swept away.

The large UK banks have, in effect, become financial conglomerates offering a broad range of financial services. They join the banks in Federal Germany and in Switzerland which have traditionally been issuers of and dealers in securities. A number of banks active in the international markets can also be said to be congomerates in that they provide a wide range of services but, on the other hand, many only cater to a restricted clientele and do not engage in retail banking. Will the growth of all-purpose conglomerates be repeated in other countries? It would be rash to make forecasts for the whole world, but it can be said that, at present, the trend and the pressures are towards large international financial companies offering a wide range of services. Of course, many specialists will remain, but it seems probable that it will be large diversified financial companies which will increasingly dominate national and international markets. Size, diversity and geographical reach will all become more important as weapons in the competitive struggle.

IV   GOVERNMENT SPENDING AND TAXATION
IV.1   The Volume and Composition of Government Spending

Government expenditure accounts for a large part of national income. In the financial year to end-March 1985, total expenditure of general government (i.e. central and local government combined) amounted to £150 bn, or 46% of gross domestic product. But not all of this represented purchases of goods and services by the public sector; nearly one-half was accounted for by transfer payments such as pensions, unemployment benefits and sickness payments. For many purposes, it is important to distinguish these two categories of expenditure. General government expenditure on goods and services represents a claim on the resources of the country: government hires the services of school-teachers, policemen, etc., it purchases warships from shipbuilders, ambulances from car manufacturers, etc. Transfer payments, on the other hand, involve no direct claim on resources. Government collects the money in the form of taxes and national insurance contributions and promptly redistributes it as cash payments to pensioners, social-security claimants and others. Transfer payments represent a redistribution of income and it is only when the recipients of the pensions, benefits, etc., spend the money that there is an actual claim on resources.

Government expenditure has been growing over time. This is equally true of expenditure on goods and services and of total expenditure inclusive of transfer payments, both of which have risen in absolute amount and as a share of national income. These trends, which are of long standing and date back to the nineteenth century, have continued for much of the period since World War II. This is illustrated in table 2.6, which shows general government expenditure on goods and services and total government expenditure, both expressed as percentages of GDP, over the period 1946–84.

It can be seen that both series, after dropping back from high wartime levels, have shown a tendency to rise subsequently. Expenditure on goods and services, which accounted for approximately 20% of GNP in the years prior to 1965, rose thereafter to an average of 24% in the years 1975–84. Total expenditure, which had amounted to 30–35% of GDP prior to 1965, rose to an average of 44% in the years 1975–84.

TABLE 2.6

General Government Expenditure as a Percentage of GDP, 1946–84

	Expenditure on goods and services	All expenditure including transfer payments
1946	23.9	45.6
1950	19.8	34.4
1955	20.3	32.3
1960	19.7	32.4
1965	20.9	34.5
1970	22.3	38.2
1975	26.5	45.0
1976	25.7	44.4
1977	23.6	42.2
1978	22.7	42.0
1979	22.4	41.8
1980	23.7	43.7
1981	23.6	45.0
1982	23.4	45.4
1983	23.9	45.7
1984	23.8	46.4

Source: *Economic Trends*, annual supplement, 1986.

Note: GDP is GDP at market prices.

During the 1970s, the size of public expenditure and the level of taxation became major political issues. But it is interesting to see that the Conservative government elected in 1979, which was expected to cut government spending, and which is now widely believed to have done so, has not, in fact, reduced public expenditure. Both in absolute terms, and as a share of national income, public expenditure rose in the years to 1984. Subsequently, expenditure has gone on rising in absolute terms, but has fallen somewhat as a share of GDP. Preliminary estimates for the financial year 1985–6 show general government expenditure equal to 44% of GDP,[1] still significantly in excess of what it was in 1979.

British experience with public expenditure is not out of line with what has happened abroad. This is evident from table 2.7 which shows, for seven industrial countries, the average share of total government expenditure in GDP, in three different time-periods between the years 1960 and 1981. The figures have been standardized, as far as possible, to make them comparable. It will be seen that the increase in the share of government expenditure is common to all seven nations. The share of government expenditure in the UK is very close to that in France, West Germany and Italy in all three periods. The relative size of the public sector is larger in the European countries than in the USA and Japan.

The composition of government spending is shown in table 2.8. This table gives a breakdown of all expenditure by general government into fourteen separate categories. It covers the years 1979, 1982, 1983 and 1984. In

---

1   *Financial Statement and Budget Report 1986–87* (H.M. Treasury, March 1986).

TABLE 2.7

Total Government Expenditure: Seven Industrial Countries (% of GDP, average figures)

	1960–67	*1968–73*	*1974–81*
United States	28.9	31.7	34.0
Japan	19.1	20.5	29.8
West Germany	35.8	39.9	47.9
France	37.4	39.0	44.7
United Kingdom	35.0	40.0	45.3
Italy	31.9	36.0	44.3
Canada	29.8	35.3	40.2

Source: OECD, *Historical Statistics 1960–1981*, Table 6.5.

addition to the three latest years for which comprehensive data were available, 1979 has been included as this was the year in which the present Conservative government came into office. In view of the considerable public discussion about cuts in government expenditure, it seems of interest to show what has happened to spending in all the different spheres of government activity under Mrs Thatcher's administration. The percentage change in nominal spending, over the years 1979–84, is shown, for each category, in the last column of the table. During this five-year period, prices rose by an estimated 58% ; therefore, increases greater than this can be seen as a rise in real expenditure, increases of less than this can be seen as a decline in real expenditure.

But comparisons of this sort involve a number of difficulties, so it is important to be clear what is involved. The stated increase in prices of 58% is an approximation, but it is the best indicator available of the movement of all prices within the economy. It is derived from the so-called GDP deflator, which in turn is derived from a comparison of index numbers of nominal output and real output across the whole economy. As such, it is an attempt to capture the change in all prices, including those of exports, capital goods and publicly-provided services, not just those of consumer goods. It shows that expenditure on a representative basket of goods and services produced in the UK would have had to rise by 58% over the years in question in order to purchase the same volume of output. In this sense we can talk about a constant level of real expenditure.

But not all expenditure is on a representative basket of goods and services. Some prices rose more than average, some less. Constant real expenditure on goods whose prices were in the former category would be insufficient to maintain a constant volume of output; constant real expenditure on goods whose prices were in the latter category would be more than sufficient to do so. The cost of providing government services is normally estimated to rise faster than prices generally, although there are severe problems in making any estimate at all due to the near-impossibility of deriving measures of real output for much of government activity. For instance, due to technological development, the cost of military equipment tends to rise faster than the average level of prices: as new equipment is purchased, should we view this as an increase in the efficiency of the military services and, therefore, an increase in output of defence provision, or should we view it as an increase in the cost of providing the same level of output? There is no space to discuss this issue here, but the point to bear in mind is that constant real expenditure does not mean a constant volume of any particular type of output. This is as true at the national level as it is at the personal level. In what follows, we are concerned with expenditure.

TABLE 2.8

General Government Expenditure by Category (£m)

	1979	1982	1983	1984	% change 1979–84
General public services	4,636	5,564	5,850	6,242	34.6
Defence	8,990	14,557	15,878	17,046	89.6
Public order and safety	2,894	4,839	5,294	5,893	103.6
Education	10,316	15,187	16,210	17,064	65.4
Health	9,074	14,075	15,904	16,822	85.3
Social security	20,922	36,164	39,256	42,414	102.7
Housing & Community Amenities	7,264	6,468	7,254	7.239	0
Recreational & Cultural Affairs	1,133	1,685	1,952	2,042	80.2
Fuel & Energy	1,193	1,097	843	1,379	15.6
Agricultural, Forestry & Fishing	1,168	2,000	2,468	2,218	90.0
Mining & Mineral Resources, Manufacturing & Construction	2,547	2,808	2,684	2,474	−2.9
Transport & Communication	3,266	4,923	4,899	3,448	5.6
Other Economic Affairs & Services	1,673	2,746	3,227	3,822	128.5
Other expenditure	10,203	16,287	16,668	18,239	78.8
Total	85,279	128,400	138,387	146,342	71.6

Source: *NIE, 1985.*

Memorandum item: Increase in prices (GDP deflator) 1979–1984 = 58.0%.

It is clear from table 2.8 that the largest categories of spending are social security, education, defence, health and the final 'other expenditure' category. Social security expenditure, which in the years 1982–4 accounted for over 28% of all government expenditure, is largely composed of transfer payments: grants and allowances paid direct to beneficiaries. Expenditure has been increasing steadily for many years. The largest single item is the retirement pension and as the number of pensioners has risen steadily, so, inevitably, has the cost of pensions. This cost, at £15.6bn in 1984, was nearly double the real cost of pensions twenty years earlier. Other large items of expenditure are supplementary benefits (£6.5bn in 1984) and family benefits (£4.7bn in 1984). The cost of unemployment benefit has risen in line with the rise in unemployment, but it is not large relative to other social security expenditures, and amounted to £1.5bn in 1984. Real expenditure on education (which includes expenditure on the research councils) has changed little in real terms since the early 1970s. This lack of growth is, perhaps, unsurprising when it is recalled that the number of children of school age has declined for much of this period. Expenditure on primary and secondary schools accounts for nearly 60% of this item. Defence expenditure, on the other hand, has grown in real terms, in most periods since 1950. But, for much of the time, growth has been slow, and until 1979, defence represented a declining share of total public expenditure. Subsequently, this trend has been reversed with a sharp rise in real expenditure in the years 1979–84. Expenditure on health, most of which is accounted for by the cost of the National Health Service, has tended to rise rapidly since 1950 and has accounted for a steadily increasing share of public expenditure. The category of 'other expenditure' represents mainly interest payments on the national debt. Growth in expenditure, in recent years, is chiefly due to high levels of interest rates.

The category 'housing and community amenities' includes, as well as housing, water, sanitation, street lighting and other community services. Expenditure on housing, which usually accounts for over two-thirds of the total, is a mixture of capital expenditure, subsidies and grants. This category has been cut heavily since 1979. The figures shown are for expenditure net of receipts from sales of council houses. If we count such receipts as income, and not as negative expenditure, then the reduction in expenditure is some-what less, but it is still substantial. Even on this basis, real expenditure on housing has fallen, in the five years, by approximately one-third.

General public services include the costs of running the apparatus of government, i.e. expenditure on the home and foreign civil service, local government administration, Parliament and tax collection, as well as the UK contribution to the EEC and foreign aid. In real terms, expenditure on this heading has been reduced, since 1979, by nearly 15%. About half of this is accounted for by a reduction in civil service manpower of over 100,000.[1] Public order and safety covers expenditure on police and fire services, law courts and prisons. Here, real expenditure has increased by nearly 30%, since 1979, and this increase has been spread evenly over all four sub-categories.

Expenditure on transport and communication covers government expenditure on road, rail, air and water transport, pipelines and communications. It appears to have been cut drastically in 1984, but this is not so. The figures are misleading. The government figures show expenditure net of receipts from sales of public assets (privatization). In 1984, such receipts were large, due mainly to the privatization of British Telecom. Without this deduction, total expenditure in 1984 was £5,175m and growth over the years 1979–84 was approximately 58%, equal to the rate of inflation. Hence, there was no real decline in expenditure over the period.

There is a similar problem with the category 'fuel and energy'. This covers government expenditure on coal mining, petroleum and natural gas, nuclear fuel and electricity. While there were receipts from sales of assets in all years covered by table 2.8, these were particularly large in 1983 and 1984. Without

---

1 See *Economic Progress Report* (H.M.Treasury, June 1984).

this negative item, total expenditure in 1984 totalled £2,085m and growth in expenditure over the years 1979–84 was of the order of 60%. Again, there was no real decline in spending over the period.

The heading 'mining and mineral resources, manufacturing and construction' is self-explanatory, except to add that it excludes expenditure on fuel resources, dealt with elsewhere, and that it includes expenditure on consumer protection. The bulk of expenditure is accounted for by transfer payments, notably capital grants to the private sector and the provision of capital for public corporations. There has been a reduction in expenditure on the latter of these items since 1980 and this more than accounts for the fall in total spending.

The remaining two specific categories of expenditure – 'agriculture, forestry and fishing' and 'recreational and cultural affairs' – are largely self-explanatory. Expenditure under both headings has increased, in real terms, since 1979. The final category – 'other economic affairs and services' – covers government expenditure on the distributive trades, hotels and restaurants, tourism, multipurpose development projects, other economic and commercial affairs and general labour services. About 60% of expenditure is accounted for by subsidies and by grants to the personal sector. Total expenditure, in real terms, has increased considerably since 1979.

This discussion of public spending has been in terms of aggregate expenditure by general government, i.e. central and local government combined. The share of local government is slightly less than 30%. In 1984, total expenditure by all local authorities was nearly £41bn, of which education alone accounted for over £13bn. Other large claims on local authority resources are social security, housing, public order and safety, and debt interest.

IV.2   The Budget

The Budget is presented by the Chancellor of the Exchequer to the House of Commons each Spring, in March or April. It is the most public of the several occasions on which the government sets before Parliament its economic forecasts and its policy proposals. The Budget serves several purposes. Firstly, it is the normal occasion for the government to propose changes in taxation. These changes may include the introduction of new taxes or the abolition of existing taxes, they may include changes in tax rates, and they almost certainly will include changes in the law concerning what persons or what activities are liable to tax. Proposed changes in the law include both substantive changes, i.e. where the government is introducing a new policy, and changes designed to block loop-holes in existing laws that are being exploited to avoid paying tax. The government's proposals become effective either on Budget Day itself, or on an announced date shortly thereafter; but they still require the subsequent approval of the House of Commons. After debate and possible modification, the Budget proposals are presented to the House of Commons in the form of a Finance Bill. When passed by the

House, this becomes the Finance Act and is the definitive legal statement of the changes in taxation.

A summary statement of the proposed tax changes and of their effect on Exchequer revenues is given in the *Financial Statement and Budget Report* (*FSBR*), published immediately after the Chancellor's statement to the House of Commons. This document also gives details of estimated tax receipts for the past financial year and forecasts of tax receipts for the forthcoming one. Table 2.9 reproduces the figures given in the *FSBR*, 1986–7.

TABLE 2.9
Consolidated Fund Revenue (£m)

	1985–6 Latest Estimate	1986–7 Forecast
Inland Revenue		
Income tax	35,100	38,500
Corporation tax	10,700	11,700
Petroleum revenue tax	6,400	2,400
Capital gains tax	930	1,050
Development land tax	60	35
Capital transfer tax	890	910
Stamp duties	1,230	1,430
Total Inland Revenue	55,300	56,000
Customs & Excise		
Value Added Tax	19,300	20,700
Petrol, derv, etc. duties	6,500	7,300
Cigarettes and other tobacco	4,300	4,700
Spirits, beer, wine, cider and perry	4,200	4,400
Betting and gaming	730	800
Car tax	880	980
Other excise duties	20	20
EEC own resources		
customs duties, etc.	1,200	1,300
agricultural levies	160	160
Total Customs & Excise	37,300	40,400
Vehicle excise duties	2,400	2,500
National insurance surcharge	30	–
Gas levy	520	500
Broadcasting receiving licences	990	1,000
Interest and dividends	910	840
Other	8,400	7,400
Total Consolidated Fund Revenue	105,800	108,600

Source: Financial Statement and Budget Report, 1986–7.

The figures given in table 2.9 are for tax revenue of central government. They do not include national insurance payments, nor do they include revenues collected directly by local government. It can be seen that the greater part of tax receipts is accounted for by the collections of the Inland Revenue (broadly speaking, direct taxes) and the Customs & Excise (broadly speaking, indirect taxes). In addition, there are a number of other receipts of which the most important is provided by vehicle excise duties. The final 'other' category includes receipts from the EEC, oil royalties and privatization proceeds. Tax receipts of central government are traditionally known as consolidated fund revenue because all such receipts are consolidated in the Exchequer No. 1 account at the Bank of England.

The Budget is frequently the occasion for announcing some changes in government expenditures. It is also the time when the Supply Estimates, i.e. the estimates for the coming year of tax-financed public expenditure, are presented to the House of Commons. But the expenditure changes announced in the Budget are usually small in size and the Estimates only repeat what has already been made public. The main discussion of public expenditure is when the government produces its annual Public Expenditure White Paper, usually well before the Budget, either in late Autumn or early in the New Year. This White Paper gives firm projections of government expenditure for the financial year ahead and more tentative projections for the two following years. The figures are broken down into the main categories of expenditure and within each category there is a further breakdown, giving a detailed picture, item-by-item, of public expenditure.

Until recently, it was a frequent criticism of the annual Budget procedures that tax changes were presented separately from public expenditure changes. In addition, there was the problem that the Budget only concentrates on the tax revenue of central government and does not consider national insurance contributions and local authority revenues. Similarly, the annual Supply Estimates presented with the Budget proposals cover only expenditures financed by these tax revenues. For many years, there was no attempt to give an overall picture of total public spending and total public receipts.

But in 1980 the Conservative government introduced, as part of its economic policy, a medium-term financial strategy (MTFS) in which total public expenditure and total public resources are central elements. This strategy has been reconfirmed in subsequent years, and it is now the case that considerable attention is paid to the total spending and the total receipts of general government, both in the Chancellor's Budget speech and in the *FSBR*. The medium-term financial strategy emphasizes the linkages between the authorities' need to borrow money, the growth of the money supply and the level of rates of interest. It is the need to borrow which is seen as the crucial policy variable.

IV.3   The Public Sector Borrowing Requirement (PSBR)

The PSBR is the combined borrowing requirement of central government, local government and the public corporations. It is calculated as a net requirement and is, therefore, unaffected by the considerable amount of borrowing

TABLE 2.10

Public-Sector Borrowing Requirement 1984/85–1986/87 (£m)

	1984/5 *Actual*	*1985/6* *Estimated*	*1986/7* *Forecast*
Central government	6.7	4.9	⎫
Local authorities	2.4	2.1	} 7.0
Public corporations	1.2	−0.2	⎭ 0
PSBR	10.2	6.8	7.0
PSBR as per cent of GDP	3.1	2.0	1.75

Source: 1984/5, *ET(AS), 1986;* 1985/6 and 1986/7, *FSBR 1986/7.*

and lending within the public sector. Table 2.10 gives figures – actual, estimated or forecast – for the PSBR for the three financial years ending March 1987. The figures in this table show the contribution of the three different sectors to the total borrowing requirement. They do not indicate which sectors actually undertake the necessary financing. In recent years, central government has provided loans to meet most or all the borrowing needs of the other two sectors, and accordingly it is central government which has managed the financing of most or all of the total PSBR.

The importance of the PSBR lies in how it is financed. The authorities have a basic choice: they can borrow from the banking system (including, for this purpose, the Bank of England), in which case the money supply rises; or they can borrow from the non-bank private sector, in which case there is no effect on the money supply. As it is a central objective of the MTFS to limit the growth of the money supply, there is a clear preference for the latter. But, other things being equal, the more the authorities borrow from the non-bank private sector, the more they will bid up rates of interest. And high rates of interest are not desirable either, as they are likely to act as a disincentive to capital investment. So we have the situation that the government wishes to control the money supply, and wishes to do this without pushing up rates of interest any more than necessary. The implication is that the government should limit its own borrowing; hence the importance of the PSBR.

The MTFS is controversial and has many critics. There are two main lines of argument against it. Firstly, that the total amount of saving is not independent of the PSBR; higher government spending would generate, through the multiplier, higher income and higher saving. Secondly, that UK interest rates have, in recent years, been kept high due to a high level of world interest rates, determined largely by American economic policies. Given this, it is argued, a more relaxed fiscal policy and a higher PSBR would have been possible without appreciable effect on UK interest rates.

The PSBR may be financed in a number of ways. The government can borrow from the banking system, but for the reasons given, it prefers not to do so. The main forms of finance are sales of gilt-edged stock (marketable bonds) to large investors and sales of national savings instruments to small investors.

IV.4   Income Tax

Income tax is the single most important tax in terms of revenue produced. It can be seen from table 2.9 that income tax receipts in financial year 1985/6 amounted to over £35 bn, or one-third of total tax receipts. It is also one of the oldest of taxes, having been first introduced by William Pitt in 1799. Income tax is straightforward in principle, but is complex in practice. All personal incomes are assessable to tax, but each tax payer is allowed to earn up to a certain amount before starting to pay tax. This amount is known as the personal allowance. There are a number of other possible allowances. For instance, expenses necessarily incurred in earning income are not taxable and constitute an additional tax allowance. The sum of all allowances is deducted from total income and what is left is taxable income. It is this that is subject to tax.

There are different personal allowances for the single and for the married. The single person's allowance in financial year 1986/7 is £2,335, which means that a single man or woman, without other allowances, can earn £195 a month or £45 a week before starting to pay tax. For married couples, one spouse can claim a higher married allowance, which in 1986/7 amounts to £3,655. Therefore, a married man, claiming the higher allowance, but with no other allowances, can earn up to £305 a month or £73 a week before starting to pay tax.

Income tax in Britain, as in most other countries, is a progressive tax, that is to say, the share of income that is taken in tax rises as income rises. Those with higher taxable incomes pay a larger proportion of their income in tax. This is justifiable on the principle of ability to pay: those with higher taxable incomes are presumed to be able to afford to contribute a larger proportion of their income in tax. It is also justifiable if one accepts that the taxation system should serve as a means of income redistribution. Progressivity is achieved by having different tax rates apply to different levels of taxable income. The relevant rates and levels of taxable income for financial year 1986/7 are as follows (source: *FSBR 1986/7*):

Tax rate (%)	Taxable income (£)
29	0–17,200
40	17,201–20,200
45	20,201–25,400
50	25,401–33,300
55	33,301–41,200
60	over 41,200

Personal allowances, rates of tax and the tax bands to which they apply are announced each year in the Budget speech. The Chancellor is free to vary these, although he is now under a requirement to state what upward variation would be required to compensate for inflation. This means that proposed tax changes can be promptly judged by their real, not just their monetary, effects. Clearly, if annual inflation were 10% and personal allowances were only raised by 5%, then people would start to pay tax at lower levels of real income than before. Similarly, if higher tax-rate thresholds were raised by less than 10%, people would find themselves moving into higher tax bands at lower real levels of income than before. If such changes are deliberately sought, the Chancellor can alter allowances and thresholds accordingly, but he now has to do so openly and compare the changes he is making with neutral (i.e. inflation-adjusted) changes.

There are a number of problems with the present system of income tax. It must be accepted that some problems are inevitable, and one should not look for perfection in a system which involves several hundred tax offices assessing the income of over 20 million people, all of whom have their own unique circumstances. However, it is desirable to improve equity and efficiency as far as is possible. One source of general dissatis-faction is the taxation of husbands and wives. A Green Paper on this subject, proposing possible reforms, was issued by the government in March 1986.[1]

The issues is primarily one of equity, although other considerations are also involved. The present system of personal allowances provides for a single allowance and for a married allowance. This latter was introduced as the married man's allowance at a time when relatively few married women took paid employment. It was reasoned that the married man's income was supporting two people (at least) and therefore, on the prin-ciple of ability to pay, he should be required to pay less tax than a single person. So a married man's allowance was set at approximately $1\frac{1}{2}$ times that of a single person. But the allowance is still there, even when both spouses are working; and as a working wife has an earned-income allow-ance equal to that of a single person, it means that a married couple, when both work, receive tax allowances equal to $2\frac{1}{2}$ times that of a single person. This, in itself, does not seem equitable, but there are further complications. A wife's earned-income allowance is not transferable, so a married couple, where only the husband works, receives the married allowance equal to $1\frac{1}{2}$ times the single person's allowance. But the hus-band's allowance is transferable, so a married couple, where only the wife works, receives both the married allowance and one single allowance, and hence has total allowances equal to $2\frac{1}{2}$ times that of a single person. This is obviously not equitable either.

Some of the anomalies can be illustrated best by means of a simple example. Below, we show the position of three families, each of which has a joint income of £16,000 a year. We assume personal allowances at the rates set for financial year 1986–7. In Case 1, both spouses are working and they earn £8,000 each. The combined tax allowances are £6,000; taxable income is £10,000. In Case 2, only the husband is working and he earns £16,000. Tax allowances are £3,665; taxable income is £12,335. In Case 3, only the wife is working and she earns £16,000 a year. Tax allowances are £6,000; taxable income is £10,000.

---

1 *The Reform of Personal Taxation*, Cmnd. 9756 (HMSO, March 1986).

		Personal Tax Allowances: Three Families		
		Income £	*Personal allowances* £	*Joint taxable income* £
	Husband	8,000	3,665	
Case 1	Wife	8,000	2,335	
	Total	16,000	6,000	10,000
	Husband	16,000	3,665	
Case 2	Wife	0	0	
	Total	16,000	3,665	12,335
	Husband	0	0	
Case 3	Wife	16,000	6,000	
	Total	16,000	6,000	10,000

On the criterion of equity, there is no reason why the family in Case 2 should pay more tax than the family in Case 3. But, equally, there is no reason why they should pay more tax than the family in Case 1, given that family incomes are the same. In all three cases, on the information given, ability to pay is the same. Each family ought to incur the same tax liability.

Consider another example. Many families start in the position of Case 1 above: both husband and wife are earning. If the wife stops working in order to have a child, the joint family income will drop, and so too will tax allowances. Just when income falls, so does the level at which the family (jointly) starts to pay tax.

One solution, suggested in the Green Paper, would be to abolish the married allowance and give everybody a single transferable allowance. Then all married couples could claim two allowances regardless of whether husband or wife or both were working. This would seem to offer greater equity between married families. But it could be seen to be unfair to the single. It is usually assumed that the cost of living of a single person is more than half that of a couple. So on grounds of ability to pay, the tax allowance of a single person should be more than half that of a two-person family. But, as was said earlier, it is idle to look for perfection in a tax system.

IV.5   Corporation Tax and Oil Taxation

Corporation tax is levied on company profits. As with persons, companies can take advantage of a number of allowances against earnings, and it is the total of profits less allowances which is subject to tax. For many years, the rate of tax was relatively high at 52% but, at the same time, there were generous provisions whereby much capital expenditure constituted an allowance against income and served to reduce taxable profits. The result was that the yield from corporation tax was low: many companies, in spite of earning substantial profits, paid little in tax.[1] In 1984, the government initiated a major reform of the tax which involved the progressive reduction of

---

1   See J.A.Kay and M.A.King, *The British Tax System* (third edition, Oxford University Press, 1983).

the rate of tax and the simultaneous phasing out of some of the more generous tax allowances. From March 1986, the standard rate of corporation tax is 35%. For companies with profits below £100,000, a reduced rate of 29% applies.

The tax payable by a company depends directly on the size of taxable profits and is unaffected by whether profits are distributed to shareholders or are retained in the business. But the tax is paid in two parts: advanced corporation tax (ACT) and mainstream corporation tax, and the division between these two parts does depend on how much is paid to shareholders in the form of dividends. For when dividends are paid, these are treated as net-of-tax payments and the company has to pay tax on behalf of the shareholders at the basic rate of income tax. It is these payments which constitute ACT. The system is best explained by an example.

Assume a company with taxable profits of £100m. Its total liability for corporation tax is £35m. That is fixed. Now, suppose the company pays to shareholders, dividends of £20m. Since these payments are regarded as being net-of-tax, they have to be grossed-up in order to determine the shareholders' gross income and the company's liability to ACT. The principle of grossing up is straightforward. If a taxpayer with a marginal tax rate of 50% receives a net-of-tax payment of £500, it can easily be seen that the gross payment must have been £1,000: the taxpayer needed to earn £1,000 in order to be left with a net £500 after tax. If the marginal rate of tax had been 29% (the basic rate in 1986/7), a net-of-tax payment of £500 would have corresponded to a gross payment of $100/71 \times £500 = £704.2$. On the same basis, shareholders who have received £20m net of tax are deemed to have received a gross income of $100/71 \times £20m = £28.17m$, of which £8.17m is tax due. And this is the amount that the company has to pay in ACT. Subsequently, it will pay mainstream corporation tax of £35m less the £8.17m already paid.

For shareholders liable to tax at the basic rate of income tax, there is no further tax liability. They are deemed to have received a gross income equal to $100/71$ of dividends received and to have had tax paid on their behalf by the company. For shareholders whose marginal tax rate exceeds 29%, additional tax is due on the deemed gross payment. Conversely, shareholders such as pensions funds, who do not pay tax, can claim a refund of the tax paid on their behalf.

Of the allowances which companies can set against income, the most important are in respect of depreciation. In order to produce, and to generate, profits, all companies require some capital. But capital depreciates in value due to use and due to age. If a company is to remain in business, it has to set aside sufficient funds to be able to replace worn-out plant and machinery. So not all corporate earnings can be viewed as profit, in the sense that they could be distributed and spent by shareholders: some earnings have to be set aside in order to maintain intact the capital stock. This is recognised by the tax authorities and corporation tax is levied on profits after provision for depreciation. To avoid the trouble and expense of trying to assess physical depreciation for each company separately, general rules are laid down. Physical depreciation is translated into accounting depreciation and standard percentage allowances are granted in respect of plant and equipment and in respect of industrial holdings.

There are two common methods that accountants use to calculate depreciation. These can be explained by the following example. Assume a depreciation allowance of 20% a year applied to a machine costing £1,000. We could assume that, each year, the machine loses 20% of its existing value. So, in year 1, it loses £200 in value and is then worth £800. In year 2, it loses 20% of £800, i.e. £160 and is then worth £640. In year 3, it loses 20% of £640, i.e. £128 and so on. This is the declining-balance method and it results in depreciation allowances being greater in the early period of life of capital equipment. Alternatively, we could assume that, each year, the machine loses 20% of its initial value. This would mean that depreciation was a constant £200 a year, and that the machine was fully depreciated after five years. This is the straight-line method. Both methods are used at times by the Inland Revenue.

Depreciation allowances have been widely used in the years since World War II as a means to try to stimulate investment. Governments have increased the permitted rate of depreciation so that firms installing new equipment could get the tax relief earlier, and they have also granted initial allowances or first-year allowances whereby a large part of new investment became tax deductible in the year in which it was installed, regardless of any actual physical depreciation. This was carried to its logical conclusion in 1972, when all capital expenditure on plant and machinery, excluding passenger cars, was made subject to a first-year allowance of 100%. This meant that a company purchasing a machine worth £10,000 could immediately reduce taxable income by this amount and, at the then rate of corporation tax, save £5,200 in tax. Subsequently the initial allowance in respect of industrial buildings was raised to 75%.

These first-year and initial allowances were phased out between 1984 and 1986. After 1st April 1986, allowances are limited to 25% (on a reducing-balance basis) in respect of plant and machinery and to 4% (on a straight-line basis) in respect of industrial buildings, agricultural buildings and hotels. These are the standard allowances, but additional allowances, as part of regional policy, are given on certain categories of expenditure in development areas, special development areas and in Northern Ireland. (There is a discussion of regional policy in section V of Chapter 4 below.)

Oil taxation involves three separate elements: royalties, petroleum revenue tax (PRT), and corporation tax. Royalties, which are now charged only on certain oil and gas fields, are a direct levy on the value of all production. PRT is a tax levied on the receipts from the sale of oil and gas –

---

1   For a discussion of investment allowances in general and of the specific changes introduced in the 1984 Budget, see J.R.Sargent and M.F.G.Scott, 'Investment and the Tax System in the UK', *MBR*, Spring 1986.

above an exempt initial amount – less operating costs and royalties. Both royalties and PRT are imposed on oil and gas fields individually. Corporation tax is applied normally to the profits of oil and gas producers, but after deduction of royalties and PRT.

This range of taxes, which, at first sight, appears unduly complicated, was designed to ensure a high yield to the Exchequer from the profitable large fields whilst, at the same time, not overtaxing smaller or more costly fields. To further ensure that taxation should not deter the extraction of oil and gas from marginal fields, the Secretary of State for Energy is given the power to refund royalties and to cancel PRT in cases where the profitability of a field is low.

In the early 1980s, there was concern that the most promising geological areas had already been exploited and that companies were increasingly unwilling to look for oil in other offshore areas, many of which were in less congenial situations and involved drilling at great depths below sea level. To provide additional incentive, the government announced, in the 1982 Budget, the abolition of royalties on newly-developed oil and gas fields, apart from onshore fields and those in the relatively shallow waters of the Southern Basin of the North Sea (between 52°N and 55°N). In 1984, it was officially estimated that this change and the subsequent changes in corporation tax and in investment allowances would have the result of reducing the marginal rate of taxation of new offshore oil fields, outside the Southern Basin, from 88% to 83.75%.

Total revenues from all royalties and taxes on oil and gas production depend closely on the sterling price of oil and gas. These depend on changes in world prices expressed in dollars, and on the pound-dollar exchange rate. Receipts were at a peak during financial years 1984–5 and 1985–6 but are forecast to fall sharply thereafter, due to the drop in world oil prices. Table 2.11 shows past revenue and forecasts for the future for financial years 1983–4 to 1989–90.

TABLE 2.11

Revenue from the taxation of oil and gas production (£bn)

1983–84 (actual)	9
1984–85 (actual)	12
1985–86 (estimate)	11½
1986–87 (forecast)	6
1987–88 (forecast)	4
1988–89 (forecast)	4
1989–90 (forecast)	4

Source: *FSBR*, 1985–6 and 1986–7.

IV.6   Capital Gains Tax

Tax is levied on capital gains at the rate of 30% for persons and at the corporation-tax rate for companies. The case for such a tax is partly one of equity: why should a person who receives £1,000, in the form of a capital gain, pay no tax, when a person who receives the same sum, in the form of income, does have to pay tax. But there is also a case for such a tax on the grounds of efficiency: without it, much energy will be spent on seeking ways to convert income into capital gains, in order to avoid tax. The case for capital gains tax (CGT) is strong.

But there are inherent difficulties in implementing fairly such a tax and, in consequence, the present tax represents something of a compromise between what is desirable in theory, and what is convenient in practice. Many assets are exempt entirely from the tax. These include a person's principal private residence, agricultural property, motorcars, most life assurance policies, assets donated to charities, winnings from gambling, National Savings instruments and, if held for more than twelve months, gilt-edged stock and most corporate fixed-interest securities. There are provisions for allowing losses on assets subject to CGT to be offset against gains; and to avoid the high cost of collecting many small amounts of tax, there is an annual personal allowance, whereby gains below a certain amount are exempt from taxation. Since 1982, this allowance has been raised, each year, in line with inflation and in financial year 1986–7 it stands at £6,300.

A complication of capital gains tax is that gains usually accrue over time and hence it is desirable to distinguish between real and monetary gains. A person who bought a share in company X in 1979 for £1,000 and sold it in 1986 for £1,700 has made a gain on paper; but since the general level of prices has risen over the same period by approximately 70%, it is clear that has been no real gain. Since March 1982, CGT has been on an indexed basis and only real gains have been subject to tax.

IV.7   Capital Transfer Tax (Inheritance Tax)

There is a good case on grounds of equity for a tax on wealth. If two people earn the same income, but one also owns a large personal fortune whereas the other has no capital, it would normally be presumed that the former had a greater ability to pay than the latter. But there are a number of severe practical problems that arise in attempts to tax wealth directly. While income usually accrues in the form of money, which means there is no special problem in making a money payment of taxes, much wealth is in illiquid form and may be indivisible. Thus, a person who owns a stately home, but who has little other wealth, may find himself unable to pay even a modest rate of wealth tax, without selling the home. Similarly many farmers and many small businessmen (who often have more debt than liquid assets) would find themselves unable to pay a wealth tax without selling part of the farm or the business. But governments usually wish to encourage both an efficient agriculture and a productive small business sector, and this is one main reason why they have shied away from direct wealth taxes which would make difficult the accumulation and productive use of wealth.

A common fall-back position has been to tax wealth when it changes hands at death. This was the approach in Britain between 1894 and 1974. But, in practice, estate duty, as it was known, yielded only modest amounts of revenue. There were a number of exemptions from and reductions in duty in respect of certain assets (e.g. agricultural land), and, in any case, those with large estates could transfer them to their heirs during their lifetime. Provisions were introduced to levy estate duty on property disposed of within a specified period prior to death, and this period was progressively extended to seven years. But, in spite of this, it was still commonly alleged that estate duty was an avoidable tax.

In 1974, the new Labour government replaced estate duty by a capital transfer tax (CTT), under which disposals of property were made subject to tax, whether made during life or at death. Tax was levied, at a progressive rate, on the cumulative value of all gifts over a period of ten years. That is to say, in calculating tax due, gifts in any one year were aggregated with the cumulative total of gifts in the preceding nine years. It was the total of all gifts over the ten-year period which determined which rate of tax should apply.

There were a number of exemptions. Transfers of property between husbands and wives, in life and at death, were free of all tax, as were outright gifts and bequests to charities. Gifts, during any one year, to one individual, up to the value of £250 were exempt from duty, and so also were total gifts, during any one year, up to the value of £3,000. After allowing for exemptions, all transfers of property were cumulated. Of the cumulative total, an initial amount (£67,000 in 1985–6) was free of duty and then tax rates increased as total transfers increased. In financial year 1985–6, the maximum rate was 30% for lifetime gifts and 60% for bequests, and was reached when cumulative transfers of property reached £300,000.

In 1986, the government abolished the tax on lifetime gifts between persons. Gifts into, or out of, trusts and gifts involving companies remain subject to tax. Gifts, at death, are taxed as before and provisions to tax gifts made within seven years of death have been re-introduced. The reason given for this change was that CTT deterred lifetime giving, had the effect of freezing the ownership of assets, especially the ownership of family businesses and that this was often detrimental to such businesses. The tax now applies mainly to transfers of property at death and has been renamed the inheritance tax. Rates of duty payable in 1986–7 are shown in table 2.12.

IV.8   Value Added Tax

Value added tax (VAT) is, after income tax, the largest producer of revenue to the Exchequer. It is intended as a broadly based expenditure tax and was introduced, in 1973, following the accession of the United Kingdom to the

TABLE 2.12

Inheritance Tax: Rates of Duty, 1986–7

Value of estate (£000)	Rate of duty (%)
0–71	0
71–95	30
95–129	35
129–164	40
164–206	45
206–257	50
257–317	55
over 317	60

Source: FSBR, 1986–7.

EEC; the tax, by then, having, become part of the process of fiscal harmonization within the Community. Although, since there has been no attempt to harmonize rates of tax, it remains more a harmonization of form than of substance. The tax is intended to be non-discriminatory and is levied on producers of intermediate goods as well as on producers of final goods. This raises considerably the costs of collection which fall both on the revenue authorities – the Customs & Excise – and on the taxpayers themselves. But since complete non-discrimination would have undesirable redistributive effects, there are different rates of VAT, so the objective is not achieved in practice.

The tax is levied at all stages of production and is imposed on the value added by each producer. How it works in practice can be illustrated by the following simple example. We assume a VAT of 15%, which is the standard rate in force in the United Kingdom since 1979. A manufacturer purchases raw materials at a price of 115 inclusive of VAT, i.e. the cost of the raw materials is 100 and tax is 15. This is known as the input tax. The manufacturer then uses capital and labour to produce a finished article which he sells to a retailer for 230 including VAT. 30 is the output tax, and the manufacturer has to pay to the Customs & Excise the difference between output and input taxes, namely 15. So the cost of the product, net of tax, is 200 and tax, at the rate of 15%, has been paid. The initial suppliers of raw materials added value of 100 and so paid 15 in tax; the manufacturer also added value of 100 and so paid the same amount in tax. If we, now, assume that the retailer will earn 20 net on each product he sells, then this sum is the value added at the retail stage, and tax is due thereon. The retailer will sell the product at a price of 253; his output tax will be 33, his input tax was 30, so he is liable to pay VAT of 3. The total amount of tax paid (33) is equal to 15% of the total net-of-tax sale value of the product. It has been collected, at each stage of the production process, by taxing each producer according to his value added.

It may be asked at this stage, why not levy the 15% tax at the retail stage and save bothering all manufacturers and suppliers with calculations of input and output taxes? This was essentially the procedure adopted with the purchase tax in force prior to 1973. The only answer to this question would appear to be that we have VAT because it is an EEC requirement. It is not obviously superior to alternatives and it is costly to collect for the authorities and complex, and therefore costly, for many of those who pay it. Large firms with sophisticated accounting systems cope without difficulty but, for many small businesses, the costs of calculating VAT are high. It may be noted that the change from purchase tax to VAT raised the number of taxpayers from 74,000 to 1.2 million and the number of collectors from 2,000 to 13,000.[1]

If the standard rate of VAT of 15% were levied on all items, it would bear heavily on the poor: unlike income tax, where no tax is payable on very low incomes, the full tax would be levied on very low expenditures. To prevent this and to introduce some progressivity into the tax, certain items, which form a large proportion of the expenditure of those on low incomes, are zero-rated. Not only is no VAT levied on the production and sale of these commodities, but producers can also reclaim VAT paid by suppliers of intermediate goods. Such items include food, fuel and power, transport and children's clothing. There is a third category of goods, those that are exempt for VAT. Exemption is not the same as zero-rating: producers of exempt goods pay no VAT themselves, but cannot reclaim what has already been paid on inputs supplied to them. Exempt goods and services include health care, education, insurance and financial services, postal services and land. Very small firms with a turnover less than a prescribed amount are also exempt from VAT. In financial year 1986–7, this amount is £20,500 per annum or £7,000 per quarter.

IV.9 Excise Duties and Customs Duties

Excise duties are duties levied on goods, whether produced domestically or imported, and which have as their prime objective the raising of revenue. Customs duties are duties levied specifically on imported goods and where the objective may be to protect domestic producers, to raise revenue, or both. Following the entry of the United Kingdom into the EEC, and after an initial transitional phase, customs duties have no longer been levied on imports from other member states of the EEC; and those that are levied on imports from non-member countries are now determined jointly for all EEC members in order to maintain a common external tariff. Receipts of customs duties are regarded as part of the own resources of the Community and are paid over to Brussels.

The most significant excise duties, in terms of revenue raised, are clearly those on oil, tobacco and alcohol. As can be seen from table 2.9 these three duties raised, in financial year 1985–6, a total of £15bn. It could be asked why one should single out for tax, in what is a highly discriminatory way, these three commodities? The first answer is that all three have inelastic demands,

---

1 See Parr and Day, 'Value Added Tax in the United Kingdom', *NWBQR*, 1977, and the discussion in Kay and King, *op.cit.*

i.e. increases in price have only a small effect on demand, so they are eminently suitable as a means of raising revenue. This, and the fact that the duties are all of long standing and have become accepted (albeit grudgingly), are probably sufficient reasons for most Chancellors of the Exchequer. But other good economic reasons can be advanced. The consumption of tobacco, as a widely accepted cause of cancer, has a very high human cost in terms of suffering and premature death. Alcohol abuse, which is widespread, has both a high human cost and a high social cost. Motoring has high social costs in terms of congestion, pollution and the expense of policing, and the large numbers of accidents, to which it gives rise, have both high human and social costs.

The duties on oil, tobacco and alcohol are all stated as fixed monetary amounts. So, unlike VAT – defined as a percentage rate – they are not automatically indexed for inflation. Increases in the duties are regularly made at the time of the Budget, but for many years during the 1960s and 1970s there was a tendency for increases to fall short of the rate of inflation, with the result that the real value of the duties fell. Increases in excise taxes inevitably raise prices, and so themselves contribute to measured inflation, and this may, on occasions, have dissuaded Chancellors from making sizeable increases. But in recent years, duties have been raised more systematically and have tended to maintain or even to increase their real value. The tax on cigarettes has been raised considerably.

IV.10   Local Taxation

Local authorities levy rates on immovable property: residential houses, industrial and commercial properties, but not farms, which remain exempt from rating. The rates charged depend both upon the value of the property and upon the levy imposed. The value of property is defined as its rental value and rates are then levied on the basis of so many pence per pound; i.e. if the assessed rental value (termed the rateable value) of a property is £400 and the local authority rate set at 80p in the pound, then the sum payable is £320.

Rates are an exceedingly unpopular form of taxation. Partly, this is because they are a tax on wealth and have the practical disadvantages associated with such a tax that were mentioned earlier, in the discussion of CTT. Many people, and especially the elderly, live in houses which reflect past income more than present income. They resent paying high rate demands, but equally, and not unnaturally, they do not wish to sell a home that they spent many years saving to buy. And this problem is not limited to domestic rates. In the early 1980s, there were substantial increases in rates at a time when the economy was experiencing its worst depression since the 1930s. Many firms found their rate demands rising steeply, precisely at a time when revenues and profits were falling.

There is an additional reason for the general dislike of domestic rates: they are widely believed to be inequitable between one property-owner and another. There is some justice in this complaint. The problem stems from the valuation of properties in terms of their rental value; something which was justifiable when most private residences were rented from landlords, but which is no longer so in an age when the vast majority of all houses and flats are either in owner-occupancy or are in the council-housing sector. Nowadays, there is no broadly-based free market for rented accommodation and so rental values have to be estimated and periodically re-estimated. Revaluations of domestic properties were carried out in 1963 and in 1973, and both led to much discontent. Such a response seems inevitable, as the resentment (usually directed against the government of the day) of those who see their rateable value increased will invariably outweigh any gratitude of those who see their rateable value reduced. In consequence, rating re-valuations are not an attractive prospect for any government; the one due in 1983 was cancelled. The idea of basing rates on sale values rather than rental values has been widely canvassed and has much to commend it. But, the initial effect of such a change would, almost certainly, be large shifts in liability to tax, and so, again, it is a politically unattractive measure for any government. So rates continue to be levied on out-of-date assessments of rental values which become increasingly arbitrary as time passes.

Resentment against rates is one reason why so much of the expenditure of local government is financed by grants from central government. For many years, such grants were regularly increased in order to avoid significant rises in rates and by the mid-1970s they accounted for over 60% of all local authority expenditure. Subsequently, the percentage has been reduced, and in consequence both domestic and non-domestic rates have risen appreciably; but, in the mid-1980s, the contribution of central government to local authority finance is still in excess of 50%. And since non-domestic rates and other sources of income account for well over half of what remains, it means that domestic ratepayers contribute, directly, less than one-fifth of local authority revenues. This contribution has been declining over a number of years, as can be seen from table 2.13. This raises the obvious problem of accountability: local electors have every incentive to vote for more and more services if they know they will only pay a small part of the cost of providing them. In principle, such a situation can be avoided – if central government grants are for a known amount, fixed in advance, then local ratepayers will know that marginal additions to expenditure will be largely reflected in their own rate bills. But prior to the mid-1970s, there were frequent changes in central government support for local authorities and this tended to respond to the size of local government expenditure and to political pressure and lobbying on behalf of ratepayers. So local government expenditure continued to rise rapidly and those voting for it paid only a fraction of its cost. But, after 1976, central government support has been less readily forthcoming and has not increased in real terms. And, not altogether by coincidence, local government expenditure has also ceased to grow.

However, the situation is still unsatisfactory. Domestic rates are highly unpopular and business rates are increasingly contested. Yet they remain

TABLE 2.13

**Proportion of Local Authority
Revenue Expenditure Financed by
Domestic Ratepayers (%)**

1948–49	31*
1958–59	28*
1968–69	15.1
1978–79	14.2
1982–83	13.8
1983–84	12*

Source: Hepworth[1]

* Approximate percentages.

the only source of finance under local government control. Many commentators and an official committee of enquiry (the Layfield Committee[2]) have argued the case for the supplementation of rates by a local income tax. Moreover, the Conservative Party has stated its intention to abolish domestic rates. But, to date, nothing has been done. The case for an additional form of tax, raised directly by local authorities and paid for by local electors, is a strong one. But a tax to replace rates entirely seems unlikely and also undesirable. Rates are predicted to yield £15.6bn in financial year 1986–7 and such a sum will not easily be shifted to a wholly new tax. It would, in any case, be undesirable. Existing rate liabilities will have been, to a large extent, capitalized in property values. The abolition of rates would lead to a once-and-for-all rise in these values, to the benefit of existing owners, but to the detriment of future generations of house-buyers who would have to pay higher capital values. Higher mortgage payments would largely nullify the absence of rate bills, while there would still be other taxes to pay to finance local government.

IV.11   Taxation and the EEC

Membership of the European Economic Community impinges on taxation within the UK in two main ways: some tax revenue has to be paid to the Community, and the structure and rates of certain taxes are influenced by Community requirements.

Tax paid to the EEC is comprised of all customs duties, certain agricultural levies, and a proportion of the proceeds of a flat rate of VAT imposed on a standardized range of goods and services. The amount actually paid depends upon the size of the EEC budget but is subject to a maximum, due to payments of VAT being limited to 1.4% of total proceeds. This limit is an

1   N. Hepworth, *The Reform of Local Government Finance*, Transactions of the Manchester Statistical Society, 1985–86.

2   *Local Government Finance*, Report of the Committee of Enquiry (Chairman F. Layfield), Cmnd. 6543 (HMSO, 1976).

increase on the 1% in force prior to 1984. For various reasons, these rules, which apply to all member countries, result in the UK making a net contribution to the EEC far in excess of its relative resources. To offset this, a rebate is paid annually to the UK amounting to 66% of the difference, in the previous year, between its share in the Community's VAT receipts and its share in expenditures from the 'allocated' Community budget. The allocated budget accounts for over 90% of Community expenditure, the main 'unallocated' item being foreign aid. (This issue is discussed further in section III.7 of Chapter 3 below.)

The EEC is concerned to harmonize certain indirect taxes levied by member states. We have already seen that VAT is now the required form of general expenditure and tax throughout the Community, albeit with wide variations between countries in the number of different rates and in the level of rates. There is also a requirement that member countries should not use excise duties so as to discriminate in favour of domestic produce and against the produce of other member states. In 1983, the European Court of Justice decided that British excise duties on alcoholic beverages were discriminatory in that beer, largely home-produced, was less heavily taxed than wine, most of which was imported from other EEC countries. As a result, in the 1984 UK Budget, tax on beer was raised more than was necessary to keep pace with inflation, while tax on wine was reduced.

SUGGESTIONS FOR FURTHER READING

A.D.Bain, *The Economics of the Financial System* (Martin Robertson, 1981).

Bank of England, *The Development and Operation of Monetary Policy 1960–83* (Oxford University Press, 1984).

Bank of England Quarterly Bulletin.

J.A.Kay and M.A.King, *The British Tax System* (3rd edition, Oxford University Press, 1984).

B.Kettell, *Monetary Economics* (Graham & Trotman, 1985).

T.M.Podolski, *Financial Innovation and the Money Supply* (Basil Blackwell, 1986).

A.R.Prest and N.A.Barr, *Public Finance in Theory and Practice* (7th edition, Weidenfeld & Nicolson, 1985).

3

Foreign trade and the balance of payments

C.J.Green and J.S.Metcalfe

I THE UK BALANCE OF PAYMENTS
I.1 Introduction

The importance to the UK of foreign trade, foreign investment and the balance of international payments will be obvious to anyone who has followed the course of events since 1960. The growth of the UK economy, the level of employment, real wages and the standard of living have been, and will continue to be, greatly influenced by external economic events. It is the purpose of this chapter to outline the main features of the external relationships of the UK and to discuss economic policies adopted to manipulate these external relationships, with the primary focus of attention being on the years since 1960.[1]

To begin with, it is often said that the UK is a highly 'open' economy, and some indication of the meaning of this is given by the fact that in 1985, exports of goods and services were 29.1% of GDP and imports of goods and services were 27.6% of GDP, both figures being greater than the corresponding figures for the mid-1960s and substantially greater than those for 1938.[2] A high degree of openness implies that the structure of production and employment is greatly influenced by international specialization. For the UK it also means that about 36% of the foodstuffs and the bulk of raw materials necessary to maintain inputs for industry have to be imported. In the sense defined, the UK is a more open economy than some industrial nations, e.g. West Germany and France, but less open than others such as Belgium.

I.2 The Concept of the Balance of Payments

The concept of the balance of payments is central to a study of the external monetary relationships of a country but, as with any unifying concept, it is not free from ambiguities of definition and of interpretation. Such ambiguities stem from at least two sources, *viz.* the different uses to which the concept may be put – either as a tool for economic analysis or as a guide to the

---

1 Earlier editions of this volume contain a discussion of external developments between 1945 and 1960. See, e.g., the 5th edition (1974).

2 In 1938 the export:GNP ratio stood at 14%, and the import:GNP ratio at 18.9%.

need for and effectiveness of external policy changes; and the different ways in which we may approach the concept – either as a system of accounts or as a measure of transactions in the foreign-exchange market.

From an accounting viewpoint, we may define the balance of payments as a systematic record, over a given period of time, of all transactions between domestic residents and residents of foreign nations. In this context, residents are defined as those individuals living in the UK for one year or more, together with corporate bodies located in the UK, and UK government agencies and military forces located abroad. Ideally, the transactions involved should be recorded at the time of the change of ownership of commodities and assets, or at the time specific services are performed. In practice, trade flows are recorded on a shipments basis, at the time when the exports documents are lodged with the Customs and Excise, and at the time when imports are cleared through Customs. The problem with this method is that the time of shipment need bear no close or stable relationship to the time of payment for the goods concerned and it is this latter which is relevant to the state of the foreign-exchange market, although over a year the discrepancies between the two methods are likely to be small. All transactions are recorded as sterling money flows, and when transactions are invoiced in foreign currencies, their values are converted into sterling at the appropriate exchange rate. Because sterling is a 'key' or 'vehicle' currency, and is used as an international medium of exchange, it transpires that 76% of UK exports and roughly 38% of UK imports are invoiced directly in sterling.[3]

Like all systems of income and expenditure accounts, the balance-of-payments accounts are an *ex post* record, constructed on the principle of double-entry bookkeeping. Thus, each external transaction is effectively entered twice, once to indicate the original transaction, say the import of a given commodity, and again to indicate the manner in which that transaction was financed. The convention is that credit items, which increase net money claims on foreign residents, e.g. exports of goods and services and foreign investment in the UK, are entered with a positive sign, and that debit items, which increase net money liabilities of domestic residents, e.g. imports of goods and services and profits earned by foreign-owned firms operating in the UK, are entered with a minus sign. It follows that, in sum, the balance-of-payments accounts always balance and that the interpretation to be read into the accounts depends on the prior selection of a particular sub-set of transactions. It will be clear, therefore, that there can be no unique picture of a country's external relationships which may be drawn from the accounts.

When analysing the balance of payments, it can be useful to make a distinction between autonomous external transactions, transactions undertaken for private gain or international political obligation, and accommodating external transactions, transactions undertaken or induced specifically to finance a gap between autonomous credits and autonomous debits. This

---

1 Cf. the article by S.A.Page, 'The Choice of Invoicing Currency in Merchandise Trade', *NIER*, No. 98, 1981.

distinction is by no means watertight, as we shall see subsequently, but it provides a useful starting point when structuring the accounts and when trying to formulate notions of balance-of-payments equilibrium.

The structure of the external accounts of the UK: It is current practice to divide the external accounts of the UK into three sets of items: (i) current-account items; (ii) capital-account items; (iii) official financing items. Current-account items and all, or part (depending on taste), of capital-account items can as a first approximation be treated as if they correspond to autonomous external transactions, while official financing items may be treated as corresponding to accommodating transactions. The structure of the external accounts and figures for the period 1981–85 are shown in table 3.1.[1]

Current-account items consist of exports and imports of commodities (visibles) and services (invisibles, e.g. insurance, shipping, tourist and banking transactions), profit and interest payments received from abroad less similar payments made abroad, certain government transactions, e.g. maintenance of armed forces overseas, and specified transfer payments, e.g. immigrants' remittances, payments to and from the EEC budget and foreign aid granted by the UK government. The rationale for collecting these items together is that the majority of them are directly related to flows of national income and expenditure, whether public or private. In particular, visible and invisible trade flows are closely related to movements in foreign and domestic incomes, the division of these incomes between expenditure and saving, and the division of expenditure between outlays on foreign goods and services and outlays on domestic goods and services. It should be remembered, however, that trade flows may change not because of changes in incomes, but because of spending out of past savings (dishoarding) or because of the need to build up inventories of means of production, changes which correspond to variations in holdings of assets. Profit and interest flows are classified in the current account because they correspond directly to international flows of income.

Capital-account items can be arranged in several ways. One may distinguish official capital flows (line 3) from private capital flows (e.g. lines 4, 5 and 6). Alternatively, one may classify by the maturity date of the assets involved and distinguish long-term capital flows (e.g. lines 3–6 inclusive) from short-term capital flows (e.g. lines 7–14 inclusive). Equally one could, in principle, distinguish capital flows according to the implicit time-horizon of the investor undertaking the appropriate decisions. The inevitable limitations of alternative classificatory schemes should not be allowed to hide one basic point, that all capital flows correspond to changes in the stocks of foreign assets and liabilities of the UK, although not necessarily to changes

1 For further details the reader may consult the *UK Balance of Payments 1985* (HMSO, 1985). This annual publication is known as the *Pink Book*.

TABLE 3.1
UK Summary Balance of Payments 1981–1985 (£m)

		1981	*1982*	*1983*	*1984*	*1985*
Current account (credit+/ debit−)						
Exports (fob) (+)		50,977	55,565	60,776	70,367	78,072
Imports (cif) (−)		47,617	53,234	61,611	74,758	80,140
Visible-trade balance		+3,360	+2,331	−835	−4,391	−2,068
Government services and transfers (net)		−2,193	−2,647	−804	−3,418	−4,776
Other invisibles and transfers (net)		+5,361	+4,979	+6,807	+4,297	+9,796
Invisible-trade balance		+3,168	+2,332	+4,003	+5,270	+5,020
Current balance	1	+6,528	+4,663	+3,168	+879	+2,952
Capital transfers	2	—	—	—	—	—
Investment and other capital flows:						
Official long-term capital	3	−336	−337	−389	−327	−310
Overseas investment in UK public sector[1]	4	+195	−393	+700	+323	+1,351
Overseas investment in UK private sector	5	+3,252	+3,094	+4,463	+3,271	+6,129
UK private investment overseas	6	−10,179	−10,428	−11,241	−15,377	−22,247
Overseas currency borrowing (net) by UK banks	7	+1,462	+4,274	+1,413	+9,075	+5,055
Exchange reserves in sterling:						
British Government stocks	8	+207	−212	+227	+188	+1,646
Banking and money market liabilities	9	−118	+438	+785	+1,089	+95
Other external banking and money market liabilitites in sterling	10	+2,607	+4,134	+3,167	+5,160	+4,107
External sterling lending by UK banks	11	−2,854	−3,299	−1,339	−4,718	−1,666
Import credit	12	+133	−205	+12	+172	+50
Export credit	13	−970	−1,211	−1,563	−673	−189
Other short-term flows[2]	14	+67	+196	−520	−576	−431
Total investment and other capital flows	15	−6,972	−3,199	−4,865	−5,713	−2,860
Balancing item	16	−401	−2,748	+877	+3,518	+835
Balance for Official Financing	17	−845	−1,284	−820	−1,316	+927
Allocation of SDRs and gold subscriptions to IMF	18	+158	—	—	—	—
Total lines 17–18	19	−687	−1,284	−820	−1,316	+927
Official financing						
Net transactions with IMF	20	−145	−163	−36	—	—
Net transactions with overseas monetary authorities plus foreign borrowing by HM government[3]	21	−353	+26	+249	+408	+831
Drawing on (+)/additions to (−) official reserves	22	+2,419	+1,421	+607	+908	−1,758
Total Official Financing	23	+687	+1,284	+820	+1,316	−927

Source: *ET*, March 1984.
Notes: 1 Excludes foreign-currency borrowing by the public sector under the exchange cover scheme.
2 Includes other external borrowing and lending.
3 Includes foreign-currency borrowing by the public sector under the exchange cover scheme.

in the net external wealth of the UK. As such, these capital flows are motivated primarily by the relative rates of return on domestic and foreign assets after due allowance is made for the effects of risk and taxation. Flows of direct and portfolio investment in productive capital assets (lines 5 and 6) thus depend on prospective rates of profit in the UK compared to those abroad, and changes in holdings of financial assets depend on relative domestic and foreign interest-rate structures. A relative increase in UK profit and interest rates will normally stimulate a larger net capital inflow or a smaller net capital outflow, and vice versa for a relative fall in UK profit and interest rates. One important factor which should not be overlooked here, is the influence of anticipated exchange-rate changes upon the capital gains and losses accruing to holdings of assets denominated in different currencies. If a sterling depreciation is anticipated, for example, this will provide a powerful incentive for wealth holders to switch any sterling-denominated assets they hold into foreign-currency-denominated assets, in order to avoid the expected capital losses on holdings of sterling assets.[1] The 'capital value' effect is particularly important in inducing changes in the flow of short-term capital.

It is worth commenting at this stage upon lines 8, 9 and 10, which correspond to changes in sterling balances. Sterling balances arose out of the key currency role of sterling, which led to private traders and foreign banks holding working balances in sterling, and which also led governments to hold part of their official exchange reserves in sterling. This latter aspect was particularly important for the overseas sterling area (OSA), countries who traditionally maintained their domestic currencies rigidly tied to sterling, maintained the bulk of their foreign-exchange reserves in sterling, and pooled any earnings of gold and non-sterling currencies in London in exchange for sterling balances. Furthermore, between 1940 and 1958, OSA countries were linked to the UK through a tightly knit system of exchange controls which discriminated against transactions with non-sterling area (NSA) countries, and especially those in the dollar area. The sterling area was effectively a currency union which allowed members to economize on their total holdings of gold and non-sterling currency reserves. One important consequence of this was that the sterling area system created substantial holdings of UK liabilities to foreigners which had no maturity date and which could be liquidated at a moment's notice, so forming a permanent fund of contingent claims on the UK gold and foreign currency reserves. OSA countries could acquire sterling balances in the following three ways: by having a current-account surplus with the UK; as the result of a net inflow of foreign investment from the UK; and from pooling in the UK any gold and foreign currency earned from transactions with NSA countries.

At the beginning of World War II, the total of sterling balances stood at approximately £500m; by the end of the war they had risen to £3.7bn, around which figure they fluctuated between 1945 and 1966. In contrast to the

---

1   Subject to the possibility that forward exchange cover may have been taken.

stability in the total quantity of sterling balances, there were marked changes in the country composition – some countries, e.g. India and Pakistan, ran down their wartime accumulation of balances, while other countries, e.g. some Middle East countries, acquired new holdings of sterling balances.[1] The continued existence of the sterling area financial arrangements depended upon two conditions being satisfied. Firstly, the OSA countries had to have a high proportion of their transactions with each other and with the UK. Secondly, there had to be a continued confidence in the ability of the UK, in its role of banker to the OSA, to match short-term sterling liabilities with an equivalent volume of official reserves or other short-term assets. From 1958 onwards, neither of these conditions was satisfied. The OSA countries began to transact more intensively with NSA countries and the UK moved into a position of seemingly permanent deficit on her basic balance, so increasing short-term liabilities relative to official reserves and other short-term assets and creating the conditions for the sterling crises which became frequent in the 1960s.[2] It was not unexpected, therefore, when the sterling area effectively ceased to exist in June 1972.[3]

We come next to the balancing item (line 16), which is a statistical item to compensate for the total of measurement errors and omissions in the accounts, arising from, for example, the under-recording of exports and the reliance upon survey data for certain items such as foreign investment and tourist expenditure. A positive balancing item can reflect an unrecorded net export, an unrecorded net capital inflow, or some combination of the two. The major source of changes in the balancing item is likely to be unrecorded changes in net trade credit, reflecting discrepancies between the time goods are shipped and the time when the associated payments are made across the exchanges. As can be seen from table 3.1, the balancing item is very volatile and can on occasions, e.g. in 1984, be of a magnitude comparable to the surplus or deficit on visible trade. The total of investment and other capital transactions together with the balancing item is known as the balance for official financing (BOF, line 17), which can, in principle, be treated as the net balance of autonomous transactions.[4] Before we come to accommodating transactions, two adjustments to the BOF have to be made in line 18, both of which relate to the UK's membership of the IMF. First, we have the

1   Detailed information on this may be found in Susan Strange, *Sterling and British Policy* (Oxford, 1971), Chs. 2 and 3.

2   If official short-term and medium-term foreign borrowing by the UK government is subtracted from the official exchange reserves, this gives a measure of 'cover' for the sterling liabilities. In 1962 the ratio of 'cover' to total sterling liabilities was 51%. By end 1967, the 'cover' had disappeared entirely, and outstanding official borrowing exceeded the official reserves by £3.8bn.

3   Prior to 1972, the OSA consisted of the Commonwealth, except Canada, South Africa, Iceland, Ireland, Kuwait, Jordan and some others. Before June 1972, these countries were known as the scheduled territories but after June 1972 only Ireland and Gibraltar remained in this category. The demise of exchange control in October 1979 formally ended the OSA, NSA distinction.

4   Prior to 1976, this measure of external transactions was known as the total currency flow.

allocation of special drawing rights, which is treated as a credit item since it effectively adds to the official reserves of the UK (line 22). Secondly, we have the UK's reserve tranche subscription to the IMF. When the UK's IMF general quota is increased, the UK is obliged to subscribe 25% of the increase to the IMF in the form of SDRs or other convertible foreign exchange (up to April 1978 this subscription was paid in gold and the reserve tranche was known as the gold tranche) and the official reserves fall by the corresponding amount. The corresponding entry in line 18 is the requisite double entry to balance the accounts, and may be treated as the acquisition of assets at the IMF.

The total of lines 17–18, the *adjusted balance for official financing* (line 19), has to be matched by an equal amount of official financing. If, for any one year, line 19 has a negative sign, then the authorities must reduce the official external assets or increase the official external liabilities of the UK, undertaking the reverse operations if line 19 is positive in sign. There are three ways in which the necessary adjustments can be made. First, the UK may draw upon or add to the official gold and currency reserves (line 22). Over the period 1970–6, the average annual value of the UK's gross reserves was $5.41bn, but since then they have increased almost fourfold with an average value for 1979–85 of $18.1bn. During the period since 1970, the composition of the reserves has also altered considerably, through policy decisions and changes in the market values of the various assets. At end-1970 the reserves consisted of 48% gold, 43% convertible currencies and 9% SDRs. However, by December 1985, the gold portion had fallen to 27% and the convertible currency portion had risen to 55%. During 1979, the basis on which the gold and SDR portions of the reserves are to be valued was changed to a market-price-related basis. Since then, the gold reserves have been revalued annually according to a formula based on the average London fixing price in the three months prior to March. The first revaluation of March 1979 increased the gold component of the reserves from 5% to 19%. Similarly, SDRs are now valued at their average dollar exchange rate in the three months to end-March or at their actual dollar values at this date, whichever is the lower. Both these valuation rules are subject to annual revision. At end-1985, SDRs accounted for only 6% of UK reserves. Over the period 1979–85, the UK reserves averaged 20% of total imports. As a second line of defence, the UK can borrow foreign currencies from the IMF. An amount equal to 25% of the UK's quota may be borrowed automatically, the so-called reserve tranche position which is classed as part of the official reserves.[1] The UK has further access to four credit tranches, each of which corresponds to 25% of quota, but access is dependent upon the UK government adopting economic policies which meet with the approval of the IMF, this being particularly so for drawings beyond the first credit tranche. The maximum amount the UK could borrow

1 Automatic borrowing can exceed the reserve tranche position to the extent that the total IMF holding of sterling falls below 75% of the UK quota.

at year-end 1985, including the reserve tranche position, stood at SDR 8.8bn. The points to remember about IMF finance are that it is temporary (borrowings have to be repaid within 3–5 years), conditional, and cheap, relative to current commercial rates of interest. Finally, the UK has access to a considerable network of borrowing facilities built up with foreign central banks in the 1960s, primarily as a short-term defence against speculative capital flows. These have proved to be of considerable value to the UK, and have been supplemented since 1973 by direct government borrowing, mostly from the Euro-dollar market.

It may already be apparent that the distinction between autonomous and accommodating transactions upon which this discussion is based, is not entirely satisfactory. For example, by manipulating UK interest rates the government can create an inflow of short-term capital to accommodate a given current-account deficit, even though from the point of view of individuals or banks buying and selling the assets, the transactions are autonomous. Similarly, autonomous government items such as foreign aid may be deliberately adjusted to accommodate a deficit elsewhere in the accounts. At a more general level, whenever the government adopts policies to change the balance of payments, the effects of these policies will influence the totals of autonomous transactions so that they cease to be independent of the underlying state of the balance of payments. Despite these difficulties, the autonomous/accommodating distinction provides a useful starting point for any arrangement of the external accounts.

So far we have examined the external accounts in isolation, but they may equally be examined as an integral part of the national income and expenditure accounts.

From this viewpoint, the balance-of-payments deficit (surplus) on current account is identically equal to the excess (shortfall) of national expenditure over national income and hence to the reduction (increase) in the net external assets owned by UK residents. It follows that the UK can only add to its external net assets to the extent that it has an equivalent current-account surplus.

Finally, we should note that, although the accounts separate current-account items from capital-account items, there are several important links between the two sub-sets of transactions. We have already pointed out that a non-zero current account results in changes in the net external assets of the UK. As these assets and liabilities have profit and interest flows attached to them, any change in the total of external net assets will feed back into changes in the interest, profit and dividend flows which appear in the current account. Furthermore, because they also result in equivalent changes in national income, they will affect the current account indirectly through any effects on national expenditure and the demand for imports. Similarly, within the context of a given current-account position, capital flows which change the composition of external net assets will change the average rate of return on these assets and so react back on the current account. These are perhaps the more straightforward links, but others exist, for example between trade flows and the balance of export and import credit and between trade and investment flows and changes in total sterling balances. As has often been said, the balance of payments is akin to a seamless web and it can be grossly misleading to treat individual items in isolation from the rest of the accounts.

I.3   Equilibrium and Disequilibrium in the Balance of Payments

It is obviously important, both for purposes of economic policy and historical analysis, to have clear notions of balance-of-payments equilibrium and disequilibrium. However, the formulation of such concepts is not easy and depends upon the exchange-rate regime which is in operation. It is tempting to begin by defining balance-of-payments equilibrium as a situation in which, at the existing exchange rate, autonomous credits are equal to autonomous debits and no official financing transactions are required. Unfortunately, this definition raises more questions than it answers. The time-span over which equilibrium is defined is obviously important. A daily or even monthly span of time would be of little value and it is generally accepted that a sufficient span of years should be allowed so that the effects of cyclical fluctuations in income will have no appreciable net impact on external transactions. However, if the exchange rate is allowed to fluctuate freely to equate the demand with the supply of foreign exchange, then equilibrium is always attained automatically, and any notion of payments disequilibrium based on a discrepancy between demand and supply of foreign exchange becomes redundant. By contrast, if the exchange rate is managed in some way to make it partially or completely independent of market forces, we must then accept that policies can be adopted to manipulate autonomous transactions in such a way as to make them balance over an extended period of time. The problem which this raises is that the attainment of external equilibrium, at a given exchange rate, may involve unacceptable levels of employment or inflation, an interest-rate structure which is counter to economic growth objectives and a trade policy inconsistent with international obligations.

Since 1972, successive UK governments have allowed sterling to float but subject to a variable degree of exchange-market intervention. The problems of balance-of-payments disequilibrium which troubled governments in the 1960s have been avoided. Nonetheless, it is still of some interest to focus attention on particular groups of transactions within the accounts which provide particularly important economic information. Of central interest is the balance on current account, since the UK is adding to its net external wealth whenever this is positive. Within the current account, the balance of trade in goods and in services provide an important indication of trends in the UK's position in international competition. If attention is directed to other items in the accounts, we find additional clues to the changes in the external capital structure of the UK.

The basic balance, defined as the sum of the current account and the net flow of long-term capital, attracts attention on several grounds, not least as one indicator of secular trends in external transactions. If the basic balance is zero, any net outflow (inflow) of long-term capital corresponds to an equivalent increase in the stock of external assets (liabilities) of the UK. Furthermore, all net flows of short-term capital must be matched by equivalent offsetting changes in official financing. Thus, the basic balance puts below the line all capital flows essentially related to the role of the UK as an international banking and financial centre; capital flows which may be particularly sensitive to accommodating monetary manipulation, and speculation on short-run movements in the exchange rate.

Although sterling has floated against all currencies since June 1972, this does not mean that at each moment in time the net balance of autonomous transactions has been zero, as table 3.1 illustrates. In these circumstances, the BOF is an appropriate indicator of the balance of autonomous pressures on the exchange rate. In contrast to the basic balance, this places all short-term capital flows above the line, so that a zero BOF corresponds to a situation of constancy in the total of officially held external net assets. These are several arguments in favour of the BOF, *viz.* (i) many short-term capital flows are linked to items in the trade balance, e.g. trade credit, or to the financing of long-term investment, and cannot sensibly be separated from items in the basic balance; (ii) short-term private capital flows are inherently volatile and, therefore, they provide poor accommodation; and (iii) the BOF avoids the problem of separating the balancing item from the basic balance, with the attendant danger of a misleading treatment of any errors and omissions. In the short term, of course, the BOF is more volatile than the basic balance, but over the longer run, the two measures should coincide, provided that short-term flows net out to zero. A further advantage of the BOF is that it shows the potential increase (decrease) in the UK money supply as a result of a surplus (deficit) in the aggregate of autonomous balance-of-payments transactions.

I.4   The Balance of Payments 1961–85

We now turn to assess the balance-of-payments performance of the UK since 1961. To assist in this, table 3.2 contains average annual figures for selected items in the balance of payments in the periods 1961–4, 1965–7, 1968–71, 1972–8 and 1979–84, with 1985 entered separately for comparative purposes. The first sub-period covers a complete short cycle ending in a boom year, while the remaining four are somewhat aribtrary and may be separated in the reader's mind by the 1967 devaluation, the floating of sterling in June 1972, and the second oil-price increase in 1979. The averages, of course, hide substantial annual variations but they will suffice for present purposes.

In the *Brookings Report*, R.Cooper suggested that the UK balance-of-payments position, at least up to 1966, could be summarized in terms of four propositions: (i) the UK is normally a net exporter of long-term capital, with a surplus on the current account; (ii) the visible trade balance is normally in deficit, but the invisible balance shows a surplus more than sufficient to offset this; (iii) the role of the UK as a banker to the OSA and to the world financial community in general gives volatile short-term capital flows an important position in the balance of payments; and finally, (iv) the trading, investing and international financial activities of the UK are carried out with a very inadequate underpinning of foreign-exchange reserves.[1]

Certainly, the years 1956–60 discussed by Professor Cooper fit into this pattern, with an average annual long-term capital outflow of £189m offset by a current-account surplus of £149m per annum and a net short-term capital inflow of £53m per annum. After taking account of the balancing item and other factors, the UK was able to add to its reserves at an annual rate of £79m. Some of these characteristics have also extended into the period to 1985, as table 3.2 indicates. The visible balance is generally in deficit and the total invisible balance in surplus, despite a growing deficit on government services and transfers to which a substantial contribution is made by EEC transfers. The chief source of the strength of the invisible balance has been the growing surplus on trade in services, rather than a surplus on interest profits and dividends, though this does make a positive but declining contribution to the invisible balance. From line 7 we see that the UK has maintained its position as a long-term capital exporter, while line 8, and its differences from line 7, indicates the volatility and magnitude of short-term capital flows. The surplus on the visible balance between 1979 and 1984 is clearly a reflection of North Sea oil exploitation and to this extent it is a temporary phenomenon, as the figure for 1985 perhaps illustrates.

In other dimensions the traditional picture has ceased to be applicable. The first two columns of table 3.2 indicate an unmistakeable slide into fundamental disequilibrium at the prevailing exchange rate, in terms of the current-account deficit and the basic balance. The chief proximate source of this deterioration was the worsening balance of visible trade which occurred despite the rapid growth in the volume of world trade in manufactures. A reduction in the net long-term capital outflow, relative to that of the late 1950s, helped cushion the basic balance, but the improvement here was more than offset by the short-term capital outflows during the sterling crises of 1961, 1964 and each of the three subsequent years. The deficit in the BOF is reflected in reserve losses, the incurring of substantial foreign debts and the liquidation (in 1967) of the government's portfolio of dollar securities.

The inevitable devaluation, which took place in November 1967, was followed by a remarkable turn-around in the external payments position,

---

1 R.Caves (ed.), *Britain's Economic Prospects* (Allen and Unwin, 1968), Chapter 3.

TABLE 3.2
Trends in the UK Balance of Payments, Annual Average for Selected Periods (£m)

	1961–4	1965–7	1968–71	1972–8	1979–84	1985
1 Visible balance	−226	−322	−191	−2,825	−270	−2,068
Balance on NS oil	—	—	—	−2,676	+3,681	+8,163
2 Govt. services and transfers net	−377	−459	−485	−1,251	−3,653	−6,190
Net transfers to EEC	—	—	—	−282	−781	−2,039
3 Private invisibles, transfers, IPD	+595	+725	+1,228	+3,337	+6,702	+11,210
4 Invisible balance	+218	+266	+743	+2,086	+3,049	+5,020
5 Current balance	−8	−56	+552	−739	+2,779	+2,952
6 Balancing item	−35	+35	+25	+654	+581	+835
7 Balance of long-term capital	−139	−161	−223	−345	−6,665	−15,077
8 Balance of total capital flows	−183	−506	+350	+412	−3,676	−2,860
9 Basic balance (5+7)	−147	−217	+329	−1,084	−3,305	−12,125
10 Basic balance + balancing item (9+6)	−182	−182	+354	−430	−2,724	−11,290
11 Balance for official financing (5+6+8)	−226	−527	+927	+327	−316	+927
12 Gold subs to IMF and SDRs	—	−15	+65	+18	+89	—
13 Total (11+12)	−226	−538	+992	+345	−227	+927
Official Financing						
14 Net foreign-currency borrowing by HMG	+144	+420	−594	+425	−387	+825
15 Transfer from $ portfolio	—	+173	—	—	—	—
16 Drawing on (+) additions to (−) official reserves	+82	−55	−398	−770	+614	−1,758
17 Total (14–16)	+226	+538	−992	−345	+227	−927

Sources: ET, March 1985, and *AAS* various.

although it is not completely clear to what extent this is attributable to the devaluation alone, to the contemporaneous acceleration in the growth of world trade or, indeed, to measures to restrict demand growth and money-supply growth after 1968 (between 1969 and 1971 the average rate of growth of real GDP fell to 1.7%). During this period of severe domestic restraint, the visible deficit was almost halved which, when combined with the continuing increase in the invisible surplus, resulted in the current account moving back into substantial surplus. Though the net outflow of long-term capital also increased during this period, this was not sufficient to prevent a very strong position emerging in the basic balance, especially when account is taken of the balancing item. Furthermore, confidence in sterling returned after 1968, no doubt helped by the Basle Arrangements of that year, and short-term capital flowed back into the UK at an identified annual average rate of £573m. So strong was the improvement in the payments position, that the UK was able to repay a substantial part of the debts raised in defence of sterling in the previous two periods and, at the same time, add to the official reserves. It cannot be claimed that this period saw a return to equilibrium in the external accounts, simply because of the severe restraint on domestic growth which took place. However, it can at least be argued that the foundations were laid for a return to equilbrium once the foreign debts had been repaid.

With the benefit of hindsight, it is clear that the years 1968–71 marked a watershed in the balance-of-payments performance of the UK. The subsequent decade is played out within an entirely different international economic environment from that which formed the postwar framework. With the adoption of a floating exchange rate in 1972, the rules of balance-of-payments management changed drastically, while the increases in the real price of oil in 1973 and 1979 resulted in major disruption to the postwar system of international trade and investment. Indeed, the world recession which followed the 1979 oil-price increase was associated with a decline in world trade volumes of 2.8% between 1981 and 1985. The resulting sharp deterioration which occurred in the UK visible balance during the years 1972–8 is clearly illustrated in table 3.2, with average deficits of quite unprecedented magnitude. Even the record invisible surpluses of this period could not prevent the average current-account deficit reaching £0.74bn. Capital outflows added to the basic-balance deficit, despite the growth in private imports of long-term capital (primarily to exploit North Sea oil and gas resources). To accommodate the negative balance of official financing, the governments of the period quite sensibly drew on the reserves and engaged in substantial foreign borrowing, effectively mortgaging a portion of anticipated future North Sea oil revenues. The current-account and basic-balance deficits were thus absorbed without an immediate cutback in output levels and the standard of living in the UK. This policy was not without its moments of difficulty, as the events of 1976 and 1977 demonstrated. With overseas confidence weakened by the basic-balance position and the rapid rate of UK inflation, short-term capital flowed out of the UK on an unprecedented scale in 1976, placing substantial downward pressure on the exchange rate and resulting in heavy reserve losses. The official UK reserves fell from $7.20bn in February 1976 to $4.13bn at the end of that year, only to be replenished even more rapidly in 1977, following the successful negotiation of support from the IMF. By the end of 1977, the reserves had increased to a total of $20.5bn. The policy of official borrowing to finance the oil-related deficits resulted in total official foreign debts of $14.2bn at the end of 1976, of which $11.2bn was due for repayment by the end of 1984.[1]

By comparison, the period after the second oil-price shock indicates a remarkable turnround in the external situation. The chief element here is, of course, the growth of production from the North Sea oil and gas fields and

---

1   Cf. *BEQB*, March 1982, Appendix Table 17, and the article 'UK Official Short Term and Medium Term Borrowing from Abroad', *BEQB*, March 1976, pp. 76–81. Approximately $10.4bn represented public-sector borrowing under the exchange cover scheme introduced in 1973. The IMF standby arrangements and oil facility borrowings of early 1977 added a further $4.2bn to official debts.

the effect on the visible trade balance. When combined with the ever-strengthening private invisible balances – and despite, we may note, the growth of net government transfers to the EEC amounting to £781m per annum in 1979–84 and £2,039m in 1985 – we find a surplus on the current account of quite unprecedented magnitude. A second, but important, element from 1979 onwards was the rapid decline in UK industrial output and the associated reduction in inventory holdings. With respect to capital flows, the relaxation of exchange controls in 1979 clearly contributed to the tremendous and accelerating outflow of long-term capital, while the petrocurrency status of sterling encouraged short-term inflows which offset some 40% of the longer-term outflows. Taking account of the balancing item, we can see that the basic balance has moved into a position of substantial deficit despite the surplus on current account. In a period of fixed exchange rates, this would indeed be a crisis situation. The negative balance of official financing in this period is reflected in a decline in the level of official reserves from a peak of $27.5bn at end-1980 to $17.8bn at end-1985. Part of the reserve loss reflects a reduction in official external debt of $5.5bn over the same period. The period since 1971 is clearly *sui generis* as far as the balance of payments is concerned. Even though the exchange rate has been nominally free to float, it is clear that it has been actively managed since 1972 and that the fixed-rate system could not have coped with the strains of this period.

Looking forward, the picture does not appear promising. The continuing competitive weakness of UK industry (discussed in section II) is reflected in the fact that the balance of trade in non-oil visibles became negative for the first time ever in 1982, this deficit reaching £10.2bn in 1985. Any substantial expansion of the UK economy, in the absence of a concomitant growth in overseas markets, would be likely to further worsen this deficit. Moreover, the marginal costs of oil extraction are rising sharply as less productive strata are exploited. Combined with the collapse of the oil price in the first quarter of 1986, this would suggest an important decline in UK production from the North Sea and a consequent deterioration of the oil account. Once the underpinning of North Sea oil disappears, one may reasonably conjecture that the familiar questions of trade performance and an excessive propensity to export long-term capital will emerge again to dominate discussion of balance-of-payments policy, as they did in the 1960s.

I.5   North Sea Oil and Gas

Much recent economic policy discussion in the UK has been concerned with the economic effects of the exploitation of oil and gas resources in the North Sea. Although exploration began in 1960, the production of North Sea oil first became substantial in 1975 and self-sufficiency was reached during 1981. It was generally argued that the net effect on GDP would be relatively small, effectively offsetting the loss of real income imposed on the UK by the increase in the relative price of oil since 1973, and the direct effects on employment negligible.[1] However, the effects on the balance of payments and public-sector revenue have been substantial. The major effect was, therefore, to alter the environment in which economic policy was formulated and to open up prospects of substantial real growth, unimpeded by trade-balance constraints. Section III.5 discusses some of the policy implications of North Sea oil. In this section, we briefly outline some calculations of the likely effects of North Sea oil upon the balance of payments and the difficulties surrounding such calculations.

The major difficulties relate to important areas of uncertainty, e.g. with respect to oil yields, trends in exploitation and development costs, the share of extractive equipment provided by UK firms and, most importantly, in the sterling price of oil. This latter element depends jointly on the ability of the OPEC cartel to determine the future real increase in the dollar price of oil, itself dependent on the balance of world oil demand and production, and upon the policies which the UK government adopts with respect to the exchange rate. Certainly the power of OPEC has been greatly weakened during 1985; whether it will remain so weak in the longer term is more uncertain. The more sterling appreciates relative to the dollar, the smaller will be government tax revenue from the North Sea. Other aspects of government policy, as yet uncertain, will be of equal importance – in particular, the production and depletion policy adopted, whether it matches production to domestic demand or allows net exports of crude oil, and the levels of royalty and petroleum revenue tax charged, which will determine the proportion of profits left to the oil producers for potential remission overseas. One further obvious difficulty is that the total benefits from North Sea oil to the balance of payments will not be independent of how the government feels able to exploit these benefits for domestic purposes.[2]

When calculating the direct impact of North Sea oil and gas on the UK balance of payments, account has to be taken of the following items. First, the net effect on the balance of trade in oil and gas as home output is exported or substituted for imports. Second, the net trade in equipment and technical services to discover and extract the oil and gas. Third, the inflows of foreign capital to finance extraction and development, and finally, the net inflows of interest, profits and dividends, remitted overseas by the foreign-owned firms operating in the North Sea. It is worth remembering that the balance-of-payments effects of these operations began well before the flow of North Sea oil commenced. Thus, in the years 1973–6, total net imports of equipment and services to exploit North Sea resources amounted to

---

1   At 1978 prices, North Sea oil and gas contributed some 7.3% extra to GDP in 1980, perhaps rising to 9.6% in 1985. *TER*, No. 112, August 1979.

2   In particular, the exchange-rate policy adopted to accommodate North Sea oil is an important determinant of the total economic effect on government revenue and the balance of payments. For a useful account of the effect of different exchange-rate assumptions, see S.A.B. Page, 'The Value and Distribution of the Benefits of North Sea Oil and Gas, 1970–1985', *NIER*, No. 82, 1977, pp. 41–58.

£2.49bn, an amount which was almost covered by a cumulative net capital inflow of £2.38bn. During 1983, the contribution to the balance of official financing was made up as follows: balance-of-trade effects of +£8.1bn, net IPD due overseas of –£3.0bn and capital inflow net of imports of goods and services to exploit North Sea resources of +£0.18bn, to give a total effect on the BOF of +£4.18bn.[1]

To calculate the net contribution to the balance of payments is, of course, more difficult. With the exchange rate floating freely, an oil-wealth-induced appreciation will 'crowd out' exports of non-oil manufactures and services, and stimulate competing imports to an extent which depends on the magnitude of the appreciation. This, in turn, depends upon the capital-movement effects of North Sea oil and gas, and the extent to which the authorities wish to turn North Sea surpluses into foreign-exchange reserves. Tentative calculations would indicate that North Sea oil and gas activity had pushed the effective rate for sterling roughly ten to fifteen percentage points higher than the value it would otherwise have taken.[2] Industrialists certainly consider that exploration of the North Sea has reduced UK export potential, imposing damaging losses of capacity which will be difficult to rebuild.[3]

The dramatic collapse in the free-market prices of oil, from approximately $29 per barrel at end-1985 to approximately $11 per barrel at end-April 1986, radically changes the scenario for North Sea oil and its effects on the balance of payments. While the long-term effects of this cannot be but welcomed, the short-term effects will be to cut the oil export surplus by as much as two-thirds (depending on the movement of the dollar/sterling exchange rate). Unless there is a corresponding increase in other export revenues, possibly associated with a greater rate of growth of world trade, some downward adjustment in the effective sterling exchange rate will be required.

II   FOREIGN TRADE OF THE UK
II.1   Structure and Trends 1955–1985

In this section, we shall examine the major structural features and trends in the foreign trade of the UK between 1955 and 1985.[4] In focusing attention upon certain longer-term trends, we will find evidence of a marked decline in

---

1   For further details of the general effects, see 'NS Oil and Gas – Costs and Benefits', *BEQB*, March 1982.

2   Cf. F.J. Atkinson *et al.*, 'The Economic Effects of North Sea Oil', *NIER*, No. 104, 1983, pp. 38–44.

3   House of Lords, *Report from the Select Committee on Overseas Trade* (HMSO, July 1985).

4   Since, over the period, some 65%–70% of total exports and imports reflected commodity transactions, we here concentrate solely on commodity trade. For a treatment of invisible items in the current account, see P. Phillips, 'A Forecasting Model for the United Kingdom Invisible Account', *NIER*, No. 69, 1974. Interest, profit and dividend flows are discussed in section III.7 below. For further details on invisibles, consult the COI pamphlet, *Britain's Invisible Exports* (HMSO, 1970). Delays in the publication of trade figures mean that data is only available up to 1980. The figures for 1981 are unlikely to deviate significantly from these.

the international competitive performance of UK manufacturing industry; a decline which, it may reasonably be claimed, is the proximate source of the unsatisfactory behaviour of the balance of payments noted in the previous section.

Geographical and commodity trade structure: The traditional picture of UK foreign trade was one in which manufactures were exchanged for imports of foodstuffs and raw materials, with the bulk of the trade being carried out with the Commonwealth and overseas sterling area countries. That this picture is now completely out of date is shown in tables 3.3, 3.4 and 3.5, which illustrate the radical changes in trading structure which have occurred in the quarter century since 1955. To some small extent, these changes reflect the relaxation of wartime import restrictions and the general postwar movement toward trade liberalization associated with the several rounds of GATT tariff reductions. But, in general, they are the outcome of more deep-seated changes in competitive forces.

TABLE 3.3
Area Composition of UK Merchandise Trade, 1955–85 (percentages)

	Imports, c.i.f.				*Exports, f.o.b.*			
	1955	1970	1980	1985	1955	1970	1980	1985
Western Europe	25.7	41.5	55.9	63.1	28.9	46.2	57.6	58.3
EEC[1]	12.6	27.1	41.3	46.0	15.0	29.4	43.4	46.3
North America	19.5	20.5	15.0	13.8	12.0	15.2	11.2	17.0
USA	10.9	12.9	12.1	11.7	7.1	11.6	9.6	14.7
Other developed[2]	14.2	9.4	6.8	7.5	21.1	11.8	5.6	4.8
Japan	0.6	1.5	3.4	4.9	0.6	1.8	1.3	1.3
Total developed countries	59.4	71.4	77.7	84.3	62.0	73.2	74.5	80.0
Centrally planned economies	2.7	4.2	2.1	2.2	1.7	3.8	2.8	2.0
Oil-exporting countries	9.2	9.1	8.6	3.3	5.1	5.8	10.1	7.6
Other developing countries[3]	28.7	15.3	11.3	10.0	31.2	17.2	12.4	10.1
Total	100.0	100.0	100.0	100.0	100.0	100.0	100.0	100.0

Sources: *AAS*, various; *TI*, 16 March 1972.
Notes: 1   Excluding Greece.
           2   Japan, plus Australia, New Zealand and South Africa.
           3   Subject to minor changes in classification over time.

The major changes in the geographic composition of UK trade are shown in table 3.3. Several general trends are immediately apparent. Compared to 1955, the following years show a decreased dependence on trade with developing countries, a trend which has been primarily at the expense of

TABLE 3.4
Commodity Composition of UK Imports, Selected Years 1955–85 (percentages)

SITC Group	Description	1955	1970	1980	1985
0, 1	Food, Beverages, Tobacco	36.2	22.6	12.4	10.9
3	Fuel	10.4	10.4	13.8	12.4
2, 4, 5, 6	Industrial Materials and				
	Semi-Manufactures	47.9	42.7	35.2	31.4
7, 8	Finished Manufactures	5.2	22.9	35.6	43.7
9	Unclassified	0.3	1.4	3.0	1.6
	Total	100.0	100.0	100.0	100.0

Source: *AAS*, various.
Imports are measured on an overseas trade statistics basis and are valued c.i.f.

trade with the less developed members of the OSA,[1] and the four major Commonwealth nations, Canada, Australia, New Zealand and South Africa. An interesting development since 1970 is the increased importance, for obvious reasons, of the oil-exporting countries as a market for UK exports. The decline in their importance as a source of UK imports between 1980 and 1985 is the direct result of the exploitation of the UK's North Sea oil resources. As far as trade with the developed nations is concerned, the most striking trend is the increasing importance of trade with the EEC. In 1972, the year prior to entry, the current nine EEC members accounted for approximately 30% of UK exports and imports; but by 1985 the export share had risen to 46.3% and the import share to 46.0%. The growing importance of Japan as a source of UK imports may also be noted. In broad terms, the EEC now occupies the same position in the UK trade structure that the Commonwealth countries occupied in 1955.

The switch towards a greater trade dependence on the industrialized, urbanized, high *per capita* income countries of Western Europe, Japan and North America has been matched, not unexpectedly, by significant changes in the commodity structure of UK trade, particularly in respect of imports. The changing structure of UK import trade is shown in table 3.4. Most important here is the increase in the proportion of imports of finished manufactures, the share of which increased eightfold between 1955 and 1985, and the decline in the proportion accounted for by foodstuffs, beverages and tobacco. Imports of finished and semi-manufactures now account for some 60% of total UK imports. This same trend has also been experienced by other EEC countries, although it remains the case that the UK is more dependent upon imports of non-manufactures than are, for example, France or West Germany.[2] On the export side, table 3.5 shows that changes in structure are less noticeable.

1 In 1955, these countries provided 22.8% of UK imports and absorbed 21.6% of UK exports; the corresponding figures for 1977 were 6.3% and 9.4%.

2 See M.Panic, 'Why the UK's Propensity to Import is High', *LBR*, No. 115, 1975, for an interesting study.

The most obvious trends are the declining shares of textiles and metals and less obviously of road motor vehicles and other transport equipment. Clearly, though, it is the increased share of fuel exports, predominantly North Sea oil-related, which commands most attention and this has largely been at the expense of the sectors noted above. It should also be pointed out that the share of machinery in total exports reached a peak of 30.4% in 1975, from which it had fallen substantially by 1985. The general weakness of the UK engineering sector is a matter of some concern given its dominant position in the UK export structure.

TABLE 3.5
Commodity Composition of UK Exports, Selected Years 1955–85 (percentages)

SITC	Description	1955	1970	1980	1985
7, 87	*Engineering products*	36.5	43.6	37.5	34.3
	Machinery	21.1	27.4	25.3	22.3
	Road Motor Vehicles	8.9	10.7	6.7	4.3
	Other Transport Equipment	5.7	3.7	3.5	5.0
	Scientific Instruments	1.2	1.8	2.0	2.7
5, 65, 67–9	*Semi-Manufactures*	29.7	26.4	22.7	20.4
	Chemicals	7.8	9.5	11.2	12.0
	Textiles	10.1	5.1	2.9	2.2
	Metals	11.8	11.8	8.6	6.2
Remainder 6 and 8	*Other Semi-Manufactures and Manufactures*	12.6	14.7	13.4	12.6
0, 1, 2, 3, 4 and 9	*Non-Manufactures*	21.2	15.3	26.4	32.7
	Food, Beverages and Tobacco	6.5	6.3	6.9	6.3
	Basic Materials	5.6	3.0	3.1	2.6
	Fuels	4.6	2.6	13.6	21.3
	Others	4.5	3.4	2.8	2.5
Total		100.0	100.0	100.0	100.0

Source: *AAS*, various.

It will be apparent from this that UK trade is increasingly dominated by an exchange of manufactures for manufactures with the advanced industrialized nations. These structural changes would imply that UK manufacturing industry has experienced and will continue to experience greater foreign competition in home and export markets. They also help to explain the distintegration in the sterling area system which occurred after 1964.

II.2   The Decline in Competitive Performance

The trend toward increasing visible-trade deficits, which became evident in the early 1960s, has rightly been taken as an indication of a widespread lack of competitive edge in UK industry relative to foreign industry. Evidence to support this view is provided by the progressive decline of the UK's share of world exports of manufactures[1] and by evidence of the increased import penetration of the UK market by foreign competitors. The net effect of these trends is to substantially limit the scope for the UK to grow without coming up against a balance-of-trade constraint. Indeed, this has prompted widespread fears of the imminent de-industrialization of the UK, with the manufacturing base so eroded by foreign competition, that full employment and payments equilibrium cannot be achieved without a substantial reduction in real income.[2]

The statistics of the decline in the UK share of world exports of manufactures are dramatic and indicate that the share fell from 20.4% in 1954, to 17.7% in 1959, 11.9% in 1967 and a low of 8.8% in 1974. Rough calculations for this period would suggest that a 10% increase in world exports of manufactures was associated with a 5% to 6% increase in UK manufactures.[3] Since 1974, however, the position has stabilized. Despite a 36% increase in world exports of manufactures between 1975 and 1983, the UK volume of world trade share appears to have settled at an average figure of 9.0%.

Of itself, the decline in export share need not give rise to concern, since it may simply reflect a decline in the UK share of world manufacturing production, the natural result of her early industrial start. (In 1899, the UK accounted for 32.5% of world exports of manufactures and 20% of world manufacturing production.) However, this is far too complacent a view. Once it is recognized that between 1959 and 1975 the volume of world trade in manufactures grew at historically unprecedented annual rates of between 7 and 13% per annum, and that the UK was alone among the major industrial countries in experiencing a substantial drop in export share, there are grounds for disquiet. Furthermore, the decline in the UK's share in world manufacturing production may itself reflect the same factors which hinder UK trade performance.

On the import side, the evidence for a loss of competitive edge is equally disturbing. Even though all the major industrialized nations, with the exception of Japan, have experienced a rising import share since 1955, the UK seems to be relatively more import-prone than her competitors and to have a relatively high income elasticity of demand for imports.[4] Recent calculations show that over the period 1968–84, the ratio of imports of manufactures to the value of domestic consumption of manufactures increased from 17% to

1 'World', in this context, means W. Germany, France, Italy, Netherlands, Belgium, Luxemburg, Canada, Japan, Sweden, Switzerland, USA and UK. In 1977, they accounted for 75% of manufactured exports from all industrial nations. See *TI*, 7 June 1978, p. 22.

2 Cf. the various contributions to F. Blackaby (ed.), *Deindustrialization* (Heinemann, 1979).

3 *NIER*, No. 73, 1975, p. 12.

4 A.D.Morgan, 'Imports of Manufactures into the UK and other Industrial Countries 1955–69', *NIER*, No. 56, 1971; M. Panic, *op. cit.*; L.F.Campell-Boross and A.D.Morgan, 'Net Trade: A Note on Measuring Changes in the Competitiveness of British Industry in Foreign Trade', *NIER*, No. 68, 1974, suggest that from 1963, UK manufacturing industry had never been sufficiently competitive to restore the country's trade situation to the position held in that year.

33.4%. This trend appears widespread across manufacturing industry and is particularly significant in certain sectors, e.g. motor vehicles, office equipment, construction equipment and miscellaneous metal goods.[1] Some care, however, is required in interpreting these figures since, in part, they reflect the increasing division of labour in the international economy which has occurred since 1958. Similar calculations on the export side indeed show a corresponding, albeit less marked, trend increase in the proportion of UK output which is exported, with the average ratio of UK manufacturing exports to manufacturing production rising from 17.6% in 1968 to 28.4% at end-1984.[2]

To explain these developments in any precise sense is not easy; several interrelated factors are involved and the relative weight to be attached to each is difficult to establish and may vary over time. At the most general level, and since it is trade in manufactures which is crucial, there would seem to be two potential sources of the poor UK trade performance: an increasing lack of price competitiveness; and a failure to produce and market commodities of the right quality, in the face of rapidly changing technologies and world demand structures.

Unfortunately, the precise role of these factors has proved impossible, as yet, to determine, although it is interesting to note that similar explanations of poor British competitive performance were employed at the end of the nineteenth-century.[3]

Explaining trade performance: Some guidance on these matters may be provided by a brief consideration of theories of comparative advantage. Traditional trade theory explains patterns of international trade by reference to national differences in endowments of production factors, a country exporting those commodities which use relatively intensively its abundant factors. While this may have some relevance to the explanation of exchanges of manufactures for raw materials between industrialized and developing countries, it is of less obvious relevance to the explanation of the dominant

---

1   J.J.Hughes and A.P.Thirlwall, 'Trends in Cycles in Import Penetration in the UK', *Oxford Bulletin of Economics and Statistics*, Vol. 39, 1977, pp. 301–17. See also *BB*, 19 June 1981, p. 348.

2   It may be noted that the sectors experiencing the greatest improvement in export performance, e.g. chemicals, electrical engineering, mechanical engineering and scientific instruments, are also the sectors which perform two-thirds of the non-aerospace research and development carried out in UK manufacturing industry. See 'Manufacturing Industry in the Seventies: An Assessment of Import Penetration and Export Performance', *ET*, 1980. Import-penetration ratios and export-sales ratios are now published on a monthly basis in *MDS*. A useful account of some of the pitfalls of interpreting movements in these ratios, pitfalls which arise out of the foreign trade multiplier links between exports, imports and home output, is contained in C.Kennedy and A.P.Thirlwall, 'Import Penetration, Export Performance and Harrod's Trade Multiplier', *OEP*, July 1979, pp. 303–23.

3   R.Hoffman, *Great Britain and the German Trade Rivalry 1875–1914* (Pennsylvania University Press, 1933), pp. 21–80.

component of world trade, exchange of manufactures between industrialized nations. Indeed, the assumptions of traditional theory immediately invite a cautious interpretation of its content, for they specify homogeneous outputs of each industry, equal access to technical knowledge in all countries, and all factors of production of equal quality. *Prima facie*, they do not reflect the reality of modern industrial competition, i.e. conditions of imperfect competition with non-price factors being dominant in competition performance. A powerful indication of the weakness of traditional theory is provided by the phenomenon of intra-industry trade, the simultaneous importing and exporting of products of the same industry, which is estimated to comprise some 60% of trade between developed countries.[1] In part, of course, this phenomenon is a statistical aberration, reflecting the lack of detail within even the finest classification of industrial statistics. For example, within the steel industry, there are many qualities of steel each of which is a poor substitute for the other in many applications but which are treated statistically as if they were perfect substitutes. More fundamentally, it reflects the role of intra-industry product-differentiation as a key element in the competitive process.[2] It is no puzzle that the UK should simultaneously import and export whisky of different brands or equally automobiles, given the many grades of product which exist within this commodity group, each model type defined by a unique set of characteristics. Design, technical sophistication, after-sales service, durability and reliability are easily recognized as elements which successfully differentiate products in the mind of the consumer, whether a household or a firm.

The major determinants of inter-industry trade thus relate to product differences rather than cost differences, and may be outlined as follows. First, the existence of diversity of preferences for commodities of many different kinds within industrial countries, with the degree of overlap of preference distributions being determined by the similarity of *per capita* income levels.[3] Secondly, the importance of a domestic market to the initial development of a new commodity, which implies that the types of commodities produced in an economy reflect the pattern of domestic preferences. The same industry within different countries will then produce different product designs. Thirdly, the importance of economies of scale, including in this category the spreading of overhead marketing and R & D expenses, in leading firms to specialize within particular product niches. In general, specialization will be directed to those products in which home demand is greatest. Economies of scale and diversity of preferences then create the basis for intra-industry trade between industries organized in an

---

1   D. Greenaway and C. Milner, 'On the Measurement of Intra-Industry Trade', *EJ*, 1983, Vol. 93, pp. 900–8.

2   Cf. H. Grubel and P. Lloyd, *Inter-Industry Trade* (Macmillan, 1975), for an exhaustive discussion of this phenomenon. Also P. Krugman, 'New Theories of Trade Among Industrial Countries', *AER*, 1983 (May), Vol. 73, pp. 343–7.

3   Cf. S. B. Linder, *An Essay on Trade and Transformation* (Almqvist and Wicksell, 1961).

imperfectly competitive fashion. The conditions which generate intra-industry trade also make technological innovation an important element in trade performance. Economists have long recognized the connection between technical innovation, technology transfer and changes in the structural pattern of foreign trade. Three factors are recognized as being of proven importance here: time-lags in the inter-country transfer of technology; differences in the national rate of diffusion of innovations; and differences in the rates of growth of national production capacity to exploit innovations.[1] From this perspective, a country's trade performance is determined by the rate at which it acquires and exploits new technologies relative to its major competitors. Moreover, as technologies mature, the inputs which are required for effective exploitation change significantly. A new technology, in a fluid state, requires major scientific and technical manpower inputs to compete effectively. But as it matures, production processes become standardized and the emphasis shifts to exploitation of economies of scale and access to cheap labour.[2]

Although one can recognize the historical force of these arguments in the study of individual industries,[3] it has proved difficult to identify the role of innovation-related factors in UK trade performance as a whole. Some pieces of evidence may, however, be relevant. First, if one divides UK trade according to the R & D intensity of the underlying industries, one finds that throughout the 1970s, R & D intensive industries consistently experience a trade surplus, while other industries are in deficit.[4] Secondly, a variable which reflects the employment of professional and technically qualified manpower is statistically important in explaining UK trade performance.[5] These findings fit naturally with any explanation of trade in terms of human capital inputs. More generally, there is also evidence to show that export success in the advanced industrialized nations is positively related to the resources devoted to R & D and to measures of inventive activity, e.g. patenting.[6] Here, it is important to remember that 44% of UK exports in

---

1   The classic reference is M.V.Posner, 'International Trade and Technological Change', *OEP*, 1961, Vol. 13, pp. 323–41.

2   R.Vernon, 'International Trade and Investment in the Product Cycle', *QJE*, Vol. 80, 1966, pp. 190–207.

3   Cotton textiles and the computer industry are excellent examples. On micro-electronic innovations and trade, see E.Braun and S.McDonald, *Revolution in Miniature* (Cambridge, 1978); E.Tilton, 'International Diffusion of Technology: The Case of Semi Conductors', *Brookings Institution* (1971), and B.A.Majumdar, *Innovations, Product Developments and Technology Transfers* (University Press of America, 1982).

4   *Business Monitor*, QAID. High-technology industries are those with a ratio of R & D expenditures to value added greater than 3%.

5   S.R.Smith *et al.*, 'UK Trade in Manufacturing: The Pattern of Specialization During the 1970s', *GES Working Paper, No. 56*, June 1982.

6   For a review, see the valuable paper by C.Freeman, 'Technical Innovation and British Trade Performance', in F.Blackaby (ed.), *op. cit*. See also the study by K.Pavitt and L.Soete, Ch. 3 of K.Pavitt (ed.), *Technological Innovation and British Export Performance*, Macmillan, 1980.

1985 were in the R & D intensive and high patenting areas of engineering and chemicals.

It will be clear that these dynamic considerations do not fit well with the factor endowments theory of trade. The important endowments of skills available to innovate and exploit new technology quite naturally differ in quality between countries and, moreover, change over time as new knowledge is discovered and transmitted into the workforce via formal education and practical experience. At root, it may be the vague cultural attitudes towards change and innovation, summarized as industrial dynamism, which are impossible for the economist to measure but yet underpin the long historical trends of trade performance.

Much of what we have said stresses the role of non-price factors in trade performance. It must not be read as implying that price factors are unimportant. The econometric evidence suggests that price elasticities are important in determining traded quantities, even if they are not the overwhelming determining factor in trade performance. However, an important aspect of pricing is missing from this conventional view. Namely that the relation of prices to costs determines the financial base from which firms may engage in R & D, investment and competitive marketing. Profit margins are a key determinant of the resources available for innovation and thus of the relative dynamic performance of different national industries. Price elasticity evidence is important, but it is only part of the picture. Nonetheless, indices of relative unit labour costs, adjusted for exchange-rate change, do provide evidence of trends in competitive strength, depending as they do on the relationships between money wages and labour productivity in different countries.

It is not difficult to link together the relative contributions of price and non-price factors, at least in theory if not in practice. The central point is that we have a sequence of interacting and mutually reinforcing, proximate sources of the trend deterioration in UK trade performance. A convenient place to begin is with the well-documented fact that, since 1950, the rate of growth of labour productivity in the UK has been inferior in comparison with the other major industrial nations.[1] A relatively slow growth rate of productivity implies a trend reduction in the relative level of UK industrial efficiency, which contributes to an increasing lack of price competitiveness for UK manufactures and to a relative shortage of resources for investment directed toward capacity expansion, marketing and innovative activities. A low rate of export growth, combined with rising import penetration and a low rate of industrial investment, feeds back to reinforce the relatively slow growth of output. In turn, a low rate of output growth reduces the scope for the UK to exploit static and dynamic economies of scale and scarcely provides a

---

1 See, e.g., E.H.Phelps-Brown, 'Labour Policies', in A.Cairncross (ed.), *Britain's Economic Prospects Reconsidered* (Allen and Unwin, 1971) and A.D.Smith *et al.*, 'International Industrial Productivity: A Comparison of Britain, America and Germany', *NIER*, No. 101, 1982.

climate conducive to risk-taking and successful innovative activity. Consequently, the growth of productivity and quality change is held back, and we come full circle again to the initial source of the poor UK trade performance. A country such as the UK has no option but to maintain its technological level close to 'world best practice', if it is to maintain its historically high standards of living. As technologies mature, the centre of comparative advantage inevitably moves to low real wage countries, so an advanced country can only maintain its living standards by shifting its resources into new areas opened up by technological advance. Like the Red Queen, the UK has to run to stand still, and if it fails, it will enter the ranks of the underdeveloped nations from the wrong direction.

III   ECONOMIC POLICY, THE BALANCE OF PAYMENTS, AND THE EXCHANGE RATE

III.1   Introduction

The coverage of this section is limited in two ways. First, pressure of space precludes more than a passing reference to events and policies prior to the floating of sterling in June 1972. Second, the concept of economic policy is limited mainly to government intervention where the prime concern is to produce alterations in flows immediately affecting the balance of payments.

It may be argued that *all* economic policy affects the balance of payments, since any non-trivial intervention in the economy is likely to produce at least minor alterations in the balance of forces affecting trade and payments flows and the exchange rate. Some policies may well have major implications for trade but, for present purposes, are not regarded as balance-of-payments policies. Thus, policies to control inflation or to stimulate innovation and growth are likely to have substantial impacts on trade flows, but these problems are discussed elsewhere in this book and, in any case, are of interest for reasons other than those concerned with the balance of payments. Equally, policies which are directed explicitly at trade flows may involve related adjustments in 'domestic' policy, as we shall see below in the discussion of exchange-rate management. Manipulation of tariff and other barriers to trade is a legitimate branch of balance-of-payments policy, but, in practice, government action of this nature is circumscribed by international agreements and membership of the EEC. Entry to the EEC was obviously a policy decision with profound implications affecting all aspects of economic behaviour, but this section will confine itself to some balance-of-payments implications of that decision. The external debt problems facing less developed countries and the influence of the international monetary system upon UK policy are so important that we conclude the section by looking at recent developments in these fields.

III.2   The Exchange Market Framework

Modern industrial economies have evolved by means of a progressive specialization of labour and capital, and one important pre-condition for this is the adoption of a single internal currency, to act as an intermediary in all economic transactions. At the international level, specialization has so far proceeded without this advantage. Since nations continue to maintain separate currencies for internal use, it follows that, in general, international transactions must proceed with the simultaneous exchange of national currencies. This exchange of currencies takes place in the foreign-exchange market and it is there that the relative prices of different national currencies – exchange rates – are established.

An important policy issue which faces the government of any country is, therefore, that of the degree of restraint which it wishes to place on the exchange of its own currency with the currencies of other nations. Not only may the chosen restraints limit the type and geographical direction of transactions which domestic residents may make with foreigners, but they will also have an important bearing upon the conduct of policy to achieve internal objectives such as full employment and price stability. Successive UK governments have exercised their options in two ways: by adopting particular forms of exchange-rate policy, and by placing restrictions upon the currencies against which sterling may be exchanged for the pursuit of specified transactions, i.e. by exchange control.

Between 1945 and June 1972, exchange-rate policy in the UK was operated in accordance with the rules of the par-value system.[1] This required the adoption of a fixed spot-market exchange rate for sterling ('the par value'),[2] which was maintained by the authorities buying or selling sterling whenever the exchange rate threatened to move outside a permitted band of fluctuation about the par value.[3] A country with a 'fundamental disequilibrium' in its balance of payments, and after consultation with the IMF, was expected to change its par value, as did the UK government in 1949 and in 1967. In the market for forward exchange, the par-value system imposed no formal restrictions. There are, in fact, good reasons to believe that spot and forward exchange rates will necessarily be fairly closely related. The Covered Interest Parity Theorem states that, provided arbitrage

---

1   This is the name given to the exchange-rate system adopted by the majority of Western nations after the Second World War. The central body of the system is the International Monetary Fund (IMF). The treaty establishing the IMF was signed at Bretton Woods in the USA, and the par-value system is often called the Bretton Woods system. The par-value system was suspended in December 1971 and its rules relaxed; the system was never restored. A fuller discussion of the rules of the par-value system may be found in the tenth and earlier editions of this volume.

2   A distinction must be made between the spot-market and the forward-market exchange rates for a currency. The spot exchange rate is the price of foreign currency for immediate delivery, that is, at the time the rate for the transaction is agreed (or, strictly, within two working days). A forward exchange rate is the price of foreign currency for delivery at a specified date in the future. The most widely traded forward contract in practice is that for delivery in three months.

3   The permitted band of fluctuation was 1% either side of par. Under the Smithsonian Agreement of December 1971, this band was widened to 2.25% either side of par.

funds are in perfectly elastic supply, the percentage difference between the spot and a forward exchange rate in any pair of currencies will equal the interest differential on assets of the corresponding maturity denominated in those currencies.[1] With arbitrage funds not in infinitely elastic supply, the forward rate will deviate from its covered interest parity value. Evidence for the 1960s and 1970s is consistent with the view that forward exchange rates up to three months mostly approximated their interest parity values quite closely.[2] The implication of covered interest parity is that, if spot exchange rates are fixed, similar restrictions on forward exchange rates will either be unnecessary or, in circumstances in which different countries' interest rates diverge very sharply, will probably be unenforceable.

A major change in policy took place in June 1972 when the UK abandoned its commitment to maintain a fixed (though adjustable) exchange rate, and instead allowed sterling to take whatever values the balance of demand and supply for foreign exchange might dictate. This policy of allowing sterling to float does not mean that the exchange market ceases to be an object of concern. The government still has to decide to what extent sterling will float freely without official intervention in the exchange market by the authorities' buying or selling foreign currency. Moreover, even in the absence of official intervention, the authorities have considerable scope for influencing the exchange rate by less direct means. Because of the covered and uncovered interest parity relationships, any policy measure which affects domestic interest rates will, given foreign interest rates, influence the relationship between spot and forward exchange rates and expected future spot rates. When the exchange rate is floating, spot and forward rates as well as exchange-rate expectations may all be influenced in differing degrees by an interest-rate change. It follows that the whole range of monetary policy actions which affect interest rates will also, to some extent, influence the exchange rate, and could therefore be used more explicitly for this purpose.

Exchange control constitutes the other main aspect of exchange-rate policy.[3] Through 1979, various direct controls were placed on the freedom of UK residents to carry out transactions in the foreign-exchange market. However, floating exchange rates remove one of the principal justifications for exchange controls; that is, the restriction of exchange market transactions so as to help maintain the exchange rate of a currency at a particular level. In practice, this usually meant restricting private sales of sterling to

---

1   For a more detailed discussion see for example V. Argy, *The Post-War Money Crisis: An Analysis* (Allen & Unwin, 1981), ch. 19. Reference should also be made to uncovered interest parity, which refers to a similar relationship between the current spot exchange rate, the spot rate which is *expected* to rule at some time in the future, and the interest differential between assets of corresponding maturity denominated in different currencies. Uncovered interest parity holds when speculative funds are in infinitely elastic supply.

2   See the evidence in J. A. Frenkel and R. Levitch, 'Covered Interest Arbitrage: Unexploited Profits?', *JPE*, Vol. 83, No. 2, 1975, pp. 325–38.

3   An account of UK exchange-control regulations can be found in the tenth and earlier editions of this volume. See also B. Tew, *International Monetary Co-operation 1945–1970* (Hutchinson, 1971); and the IMF *Annual Reports on Exchange Restrictions*.

defend an over-valuation of the currency. Following the floating of sterling in 1972, exchange controls were administered in an increasingly liberal way, and the anomaly of combining exchange controls and a floating exchange rate was finally recognized when, in October 1979, they were abolished altogether. The main direct implications of the abolition of exchange controls relate to capital-account transactions, which are discussed in section III.6.

III.3   External Economic Policy with a Floating Exchange Rate

The floating of sterling in June 1972 marked a watershed in postwar British external economic policy and, as it transpired, for the world as a whole. By the middle of 1973, sterling had been joined in floating by all other major currencies. For the advanced industrial nations as a whole, the par-value system was effectively abandoned. With sterling only one of many currencies engaged in a simultaneous float, there is no simple index of movements in the international value of sterling. Sterling may appreciate in terms of some currencies while, at the same time, it depreciates in terms of others. Current practice is to rely upon the 'effective exchange rate', which is a weighted average of the movements of sterling compared to the currencies of those countries which are most important in UK trade.[1] The evolution of the effective exchange rate since 1972 is shown in figure 3.1.

The broad trends in the movement of the effective exchange rate since 1972 can be divided conveniently into four phases. The first, to November 1976, was one of generally steady depreciation culminating in a sharp fall in value after February 1976. In the last quarter of that year, the effective rate (with 1975 = 100) averaged 76.6, compared to an average of 92.5 in the first quarter and an average of 125.1 in 1972. In the second phase, between the end of 1976 and the end of 1978, the effective rate was remarkably stable, rarely deviating more than 2% points either side of an average quarterly value of 81.3. This was followed by a burst of relatively rapid appreciation from January 1979 to January 1981, when it reached a value of 105.2. The final stage, after January 1981, has been one in which the effective rate has once again moved mostly downwards. It reached a low of 70.8 in March 1985;[2] it recovered somewhat during the remainder of 1985; but, following the sharp fall in world oil prices in early 1986, the trend has again been generally downwards.

The movement of sterling relative to individual currencies, particularly

---

1   The terminology should be kept clear. When the price of sterling in terms of foreign currency rises, the pound is said to *appreciate*; when the price of sterling falls, the pound *depreciates*. Thus a move from £1 = US$1.30 to £1 = US$1.40 represents an appreciation of the pound *vis-à-vis* the US dollar and a move in the other direction represents a depreciation. For details of the method of calculating the effective exchange rate, see 'Revision of the Calculation of Effective Rates', *BEQB*, March 1981, pp. 69–70.

2   This does not correspond exactly to the data in figure 3.1, which refers to the last working day of the month.

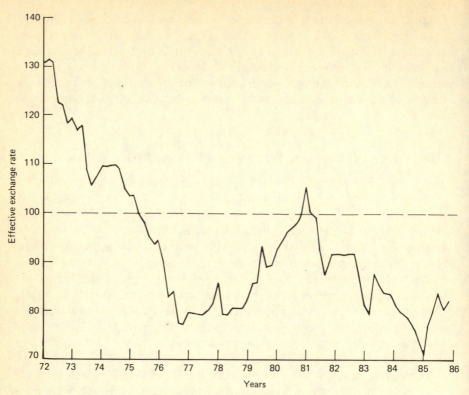

Figure 3.1   Sterling's effective exchange rate 1972–85 (monthly)

the dollar, has been more volatile although, until 1981, the broad trends have been very similar to that of the effective rate. From 1981, however, the movement in the effective rate has concealed important changes in the pattern of sterling's behaviour *vis-à-vis* the US dollar on the one hand, and the Japanese and European currencies on the other. The predominant feature of international currency markets over this period was the appreciation of the US dollar from an effective rate of 95.0 (1975 = 100) in January 1981 to a high of 155.4 in March 1985, a remarkable 64% rise. This was followed by a yet more precipitate depreciation to an effective rate of 119.0 by end-March 1986. The fall and subsequent partial recovery in the pound over the same period has, to a large extent, mirrored the movement in the dollar; sterling's movement against other European currencies and the yen was much less marked and, with the exception of a few months in mid-1985, has generally been one of steady depreciation.

Before we consider the likely causes of these movements, it will prove useful to outline some of the more important economic implications of floating exchange rates.

Floating rates and economic policy: In its simplest form, the case for floating exchange rates rests upon the efficiency and automaticity of the free-market mechanism in reallocating resources in response to changing circumstances. In a dynamic world in which comparative advantages change over time and national inflation rates differ, changes in exchange rates are necessary if widespread misallocation of productive resources is to be avoided. The advantage of floating rates, it is argued, is that the amount and timing of the necessary changes can occur progressively at a pace dictated by the costs and profitability of resource allocation, and not, as with the par-value system, by periodic, discrete jumps dictated by speculative pressures and political expediency.

Floating exchange rates also have important implications for macro-economic policy and these implications are the more immediate concern of this chapter. Under a floating-rate regime, the government is under less pressure to decide precisely what constitutes an equilibrium exchange rate, as this will be decided automatically within the foreign-exchange market. This does not, however, imply that the conduct of domestic economic policy, particularly demand management, can proceed independently of developments in the foreign-exchange market. Balance-of-payments problems do not disappear with the adoption of a floating exchange rate, they simply appear in different forms. Developments that would lead to a loss of reserves with a fixed exchange rate, lead to a depreciation in the foreign-exchange value of the currency if the exchange rate is allowed to float. In the first case, a continuing loss of reserves will result in a policy-induced contraction in domestic income; while with a floating rate, the loss in real domestic purchasing power occurs as the prices of tradeable commodities rise with the currency depreciation.

The main advantage of a floating exchange rate was traditionally thought to be that it allowed greater independence in domestic macroeconomic policy-making. As there is some value of the exchange rate which will give exactly a zero BOF at any level of employment, the objective of full employment may be more consistently pursued. Likewise, a floating rate tends to isolate the level of demand for domestic goods from changes in foreign incomes and preferences. An increase in foreign demand which, under a fixed rate, would generate a multiple expansion in UK output and employment, now generates an appreciation of the sterling exchange rate until the final increase in the value of UK exports is exactly matched by an appreciation-induced increase in the value of UK imports. The total demand for UK goods, and therefore UK output, will remain unchanged.[1]

The experience of the 1970s, however, suggests that this case for floating exchange rates may have been misstated. Although the substantial external disturbances which occurred in that era would have generated insoluble policy problems if the UK had adhered to the par-value system, floating rates did not fully insulate the UK economy from these disturbances, and

---

1   A more detailed discussion would have to modify this argument in respect of any change in the aggregate savings ratio which followed the exchange appreciation and the possible effects on demand of any changes in international interest-rate levels.

floating itself posed new policy problems for the authorities. The traditional arguments for floating rates overlook the fact that, in a relatively free international capital market, the exchange rate affects not just the prices of internationally traded products but also the prices of internationally traded assets. The exchange rate which is determined in a free market depends on the demand and supply of foreign currency emanating from both trade in products and trade in assets. There is no reason to expect any immediate relationship between day-to-day transactions in foreign currency generated by product markets and those generated by asset markets, and the equilibrium exchange rate implied by product-market considerations may be very different from that implied by asset-market considerations. The volume of international transactions in financial assets has mushroomed in the last fifteen years[1] and it is now generally recognized that, in the short run, exchange rates in the industrial world are determined mainly by asset-market considerations, particularly by relative international interest rates and expectations of future economic trends. Product-market factors may reassert themselves in the longer term, but it is unclear just what 'longer term' means in calendar time. Certainly, the four-year appreciation of the US dollar to March 1985 must have been caused to a large extent by a worldwide portfolio shift in favour of US dollars. The current account of the US balance of payments worsened continuously from a surplus of $6.347bn in 1981 to a deficit of $102bn in 1984 but this appeared to have little effect in checking the simultaneous rise of the dollar.

Floating exchange rates, asset markets and 'overshooting':   It was recognized for many years that floating rates might be volatile because of speculation in financial markets. If the markets for foreign exchange are to be cleared continuously without the intervention of the monetary authorities and without undue fluctuations in the exchange rate, it is essential that speculators take over the role of the authorities and operate in a stabilizing manner, selling sterling when the rate is temporarily 'too high' and buying sterling when the rate is temporarily 'too low'. Proponents of floating rates argued that speculative activity will be stabilizing because destabilizing speculation (buying when the rate is 'high' and selling when it is 'low') is unprofitable.[2] However, this presumes that speculators can predict the 'true' equilibrium value of the exchange rate. Opponents fear that the exchange market will be dominated by too much uncertainty for speculators to recognize the equilibrium rate. Waves of optimism and pessimism will follow the

---

1   A precise estimate of the volume of international transactions in financial assets is impossible to obtain. A rough measure is provided by the size of commercial banks' foreign-currency liabilities. According to *IFS*, worldwide commercial bank foreign-currency liabilities increased from $176bn in 1970 to $1,838bn in 1980 and $2,572bn by mid-1985. This represents an increase of nearly 20% per annum sustained over 15 years.

2   See M. Friedman, 'The Case for Flexible Exchange Rates', in *Essays in Positive Economics* (University of Chicago Press, 1953).

frequent revision of expectations and will generate substantial movements in exchange rates, out of all proportion to the volume of trading. The difficulty with the above arguments is that we have little factual evidence to decide either way. Certainly the period with floating rates has witnessed some sudden, sharp movements in exchange rates. There is evidence, too, that exchange rates respond to the publication of new economic statistics, no matter how provisional the data. However, it is unclear whether movements of this kind can be regarded as excessive.

It must not be overlooked that destabilizing speculation can disrupt any exchange-rate framework and clearly did so with the par-value system. One of the major drawbacks of the par-value system was that it gave a one-way option to currency speculators. A currency under pressure would be pushed to one edge of the permitted band of fluctuation. This immediately signalled the possibility of a change in par value which could be in one direction only. This encouraged a large and cumulative movement of funds across the exchanges which tended to precipitate the very par-value adjustment which speculators had predicted. An important advantage of floating exchange rates is that the problem of a perpetual one-way speculative option at the expense of the authorities is eliminated.

It has also been argued that floating rates increase the uncertainty faced by international traders and investors to the detriment of the international division of labour. It is the volatility of exchange rates which may deter trade, and volatility depends to some extent on the role of speculation in stabilizing floating exchange rates.[1] Moreover, many exchange risks involving trade in goods and services can be covered with simultaneous deals in spot and forward markets. For sterling transactions involving the major currencies, the forward exchange market currently provides active dealings for contracts up to one year in duration. Since some 92% of UK exports are financed on credit terms of less than six months' duration,[2] with, no doubt, a similar proportion for imports, there should be no difficulty in traders covering their exchange risks. Longer-term trade contracts and international investment projects will face problems, but then in an uncertain world they always will. Moreover, new markets in futures and options considerably widen the range of possibilities for traders to hedge their exchange risks.[3]

A more subtle argument which has gained credibility in the light of experience is that exchange rates 'overshoot': thus if a disturbance requires an appreciation of the pound, it will tend to over-appreciate in the short run and subsequently depreciate to its equilibrium value. This is explained by the flexibility of the exchange rate relative to other prices in the economy,

---

1 For a review of the impact of exchange-rate volatility on international trade flows, see 'The Variability of Exchange Rates: Measurement and Effects', *BEQB*, September 1984, pp. 346–9.

2 See Business Statistics Office, *Business Monitor MA4: Overseas Transactions 1977* (HMSO, 1979).

3 G.T.Gemmill, 'Financial Futures in London: Rational Market or New Casino?', *NWBQR*, February 1981.

particularly money wage rates. If a general adjustment in wages and prices is required, this will take time; in the meanwhile, asset prices, particularly the exchange rate, must 'over-adjust' to compensate for the sluggishness of wages and product prices. As before, evidence is hard to find because of the difficulty of identifying the equilibrium exchange rate. However, as described below in section III.4, some of the broader movements in sterling during the seventies and eighties do appear consistent with the overshooting hypothesis.

If undue volatility and overshooting of exchange rates is a problem, it is possible for the authorities to engage in 'official' speculation, or exchange-market intervention. This implies that, even with a floating exchange rate, the authorities must maintain a stock of exchange reserves. Widespread adoption of exchange-management practices also requires the institution of international co-ordination and surveillance of exchange-rate practices, and these are precisely the functions of the IMF under its revised Articles (see section III.8 below).

In assessing the arguments and evidence on floating exchange rates it is important to distinguish between the concept of *volatility* and that of *misalignment*. The exchange rate may be highly volatile on a day-to-day basis but nevertheless stay relatively close to its equilibrium value. When the exchange rate overshoots its equilibrium value for long periods, however, it can be said to be misaligned, and such misalignment may cause a systematic misallocation of resources in the economy. In this situation, a freely floating exchange rate may be detrimental rather than advantageous. Nevertheless, the balance of argument and evidence is that flexibility in exchange rates is desirable as a means of promoting efficient resource allocation and reducing the vulnerability of the economy to external disturbances. However, there is still considerable room for debate about the optimum balance between flexibility and management by the authorities.

III.4   The Exchange Rate and the Balance of Payments 1972–85

In section I.4 we outlined the considerable changes in the UK's external position in the period since 1972, showing that from an initial surplus the current account moved into deficit during 1972–8 and then recovered, with substantial surpluses from 1979 onward. The purpose of this section is to outline some of the major factors leading to the changes in the current account and the exchange rate during the period, and their relation to domestic and international events. To conduct the analysis it is helpful to distinguish between those factors which are related to changes in national price levels, and those which are related to the forces of production, consumer preferences, productivity and thrift. It is to the former that we turn first. In interpreting the events of the period, it must also be emphasized that the exchange rate for sterling has not been allowed to float freely; rather it has been managed quite actively, and this policy has produced economic effects which are a mixture of those occurring under the extremes of fixed and freely floating rates. We return to this point subsequently.

Purchasing-power parity: A convenient place to begin is the theory which relates the values taken by a currency's exchange rate to its purchasing-power parity (PPP). Broadly speaking, this suggests that the equilibrium exchange rate between the currencies of two countries is proportional to the ratio of the price levels in the respective countries. Providing this factor of proportionality remains constant, the proportionate rate of change of the exchange rate will be approximately equal to the difference between the inflation rates in the two countries.[1] With the exchange rate in equilibrium, the current account would be in balance. In this framework, the proximate source of the rapid depreciation of sterling between 1972 and 1976 can be found in the excess of the UK rate of inflation over a suitably weighted average of the inflation rates in our major trading partners; it being a matter of indifference what the source of this inflation differential may be, whether it be related to excessive monetary expansion in the UK or to excessive wage-push by UK trade unions. Similarly, the rise in sterling after 1978 would be related to a lower UK inflation rate in comparison to that of our major trading partners.

Figure 3.2 shows the monthly movements from 1974 to 1985 in an index of PPP, measured as the ratio of the sterling effective exchange rate (EER) (in the computation of which the OECD countries have a weight of 100%), to the consumer price index (CPI) in the combined OECD countries relative to that in the UK. In symbols:

$$PPP = \frac{EER}{OECD\ CPI/UK\ CPI}$$

The larger the value of this index, the more appreciated is the sterling exchange rate relative to its PPP value. It should be emphasized that the index only measures relative movements. It is normalized to 1975 = 100, but we cannot infer that sterling was at its purchasing-power value in that year. In fact, the purchasing-power value of sterling corresponds to the equilibrium exchange rate and would therefore be exceedingly difficult to compute. Finally, it should be noted that the consumer price index is not the only possible index which can be used for PPP calculations but it is adequate for the present purpose.

From 1972 to 1976, sterling depreciated more quickly than PPP would suggest. This was followed by a period of relative quiescence and then,

---

1 Probably the clearest statement of the purchasing-power parity theory is still contained in J.M. Keynes, *A Tract on Monetary Reform* (Macmillan, 1923), pp. 70–93. For a recent survey, see L.H. Officer, 'The Purchasing Power Parity Theory of Exchange Rates: A Review Article', *IMF Staff Papers*, Vol. 23, 1976. The exact formula for the percentage change in PPP between two dates is $(P' - P)/(1 + P)$, where P and P' are the proportionate changes in the domestic and foreign price levels.

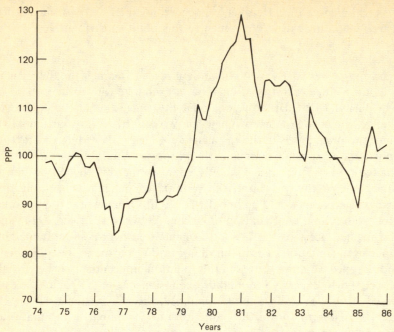

Figure 3.2   Purchasing-power parity 1974–85 (monthly)

during 1979 and 1980, a rapid appreciation, despite a simultaneous 7.4% decline in its purchasing-power value. As a consequence, sterling stood well above PPP during 1980, a very sharp reversal from the position in 1976. Between 1980 and 1985, UK prices rose by about 40% compared to the OECD average of about 31%. Meanwhile, the effective exchange rate for sterling depreciated by some 19%, so that by end-1985 its value had approximately returned to the same purchasing-power level as in 1975. These are very approximate calculations but they indicate clearly that, even though PPP may capture the longer-term trend in the effective exchange rate, it is not a very useful guide to its short-term movements.[1]

How are we to explain the substantial deviations from PPP? A vital point to remember here is that PPP is only relevant if three stringent conditions are met during the relevant period: the national inflation rates must be correctly anticipated by economic agents; there must be no net capital movements across the exchanges, including government intervention; and there must be no relevant changes in economic structure affecting the current account of the balance of payments. Not one of these conditions can be said to have applied over the period since 1972, and it is convenient to seek the proximate sources of deviations from purchasing-power parity in terms of capital movements, structural change, particularly in relation to the exploitation of North Sea oil, and official intervention policy. As far as

1   There is fairly considerable evidence that the major currencies (including sterling) have deviated substantially from PPP. Cf. G. Hacche and J. Townsend, 'A Broad Look at Exchange Rate Movements for Eight Currencies, 1972–80', *BEQB*, December 1981.

capital movements are concerned, a full analysis is contained in section III.6; for the present the reader is reminded of the earlier discussion of the possible discrepancies between exchange-rate movements resulting from current-account transactions and those resulting from capital flows.

Structural determinants of the exchange rate: On the question of economic structure, several factors are relevant. The first is the effect of UK membership of the EEC and the associated longer-term trends in UK trade patterns, referred to in sections II and III.7 *A priori*, it is impossible to say how these factors have affected the purchasing-power parity value of sterling. Certainly they are slow-moving, persistent forces which could reasonably be relegated to a minor role in this account. Of much greater importance have been sharp changes in the terms of trade and the progression of the UK toward self-sufficiency in oil production. Without question, the most significant price change was the quadrupling of the posted price of oil by the OPEC nations at the end of 1973, from $3.45 to $11.58 per barrel.[1] The implications of this development were considerable and worldwide, affecting not only individual economies but also the international monetary system as a whole. (Some of the wider issues are treated in sections III.8 and III.9 below.) Between 1975 and 1978, the market price of oil remained within the range $12 to $14 per barrel but rose sharply again from June 1979, with a price at the beginning of 1981 of $36 per barrel. However, the deepening world recession and the declining demand for energy gradually created a world oil glut so that, beginning in the first quarter of 1982, there has been a downward trend in the market price of oil culminating in an unprecedented collapse during the early months of 1986. This may well prove as significant for the world economy as the 1973 and 1979 price increases.

The problem for OPEC in the 1982–86 period has been that member countries have invariably failed to adhere to agreed limits on their individual production levels in the face of slack world oil demand. This, combined with the expansion in output by non-OPEC countries, notably Mexico, Norway and the UK, has created persistent downward pressure on prices. The decline would have been more severe were it not for a substantial cut in output from Saudi Arabia, the world's largest oil-exporting country. Saudi output was reduced from an average of 9.8m barrels a day in 1981 to an average of about 3.1m barrels a day in 1985,[2] in a deliberate effort to prevent an undue decline in prices. Finally, at a meeting of OPEC ministers in December 1985, OPEC countries agreed to take steps to restore their share of the world oil market. The logic of this position calls for a substantial increase in

---

1 The posted price should not be confused with the market price of oil. The posted price is the administrative price from which the OPEC countries assess the royalty payments and tax payments from the oil-extracting companies.

2 An estimate based on the first eight months' production.

Saudi output and a fall of unknown magnitude in oil prices. Spot market prices for Brent crude (the main price for North Sea oil) responded with a precipitate fall from $29 a barrel in early December 1985 to $18 in early February 1986. With the onset of spring in the industrial northern hemisphere, spot prices declined further to reach just $10 a barrel early in April 1986.

As the short-run elasticity of demand for oil and associated products is extremely low, the impact effect of the first oil-price increase in 1973 was simultaneously to worsen the trade balance and to generate deflationary pressures on the UK economy while also raising prices. It is as if the UK government had raised indirect taxes and had then transferred the proceeds to the oil-producing nations. In addition, the similar effects on other industrial economies produced cuts in the demand for UK exports and so provided a further deflationary stimulus; while very little help could be expected in the short run from the spending of OPEC funds on UK-produced goods. A further complication was that the pervasive use of oil as an energy source for industry provided an upward impetus to costs and prices. This combination of circumstances produced the terminology of 'stagflation' to describe the coexistence of falling demand and rising inflation.

The problem faced by the UK government in 1973 was that it was already known that the North Sea contained oil reserves, though of an unknown quantity. If the UK had carried out the substantial adjustments needed to eliminate the current-account deficit, it would have imposed possibly severe costs on the economy. With oil in the North Sea there was then every prospect that the UK would subsequently have to undertake further costly adjustments to accommodate a possibly substantial balance-of-payments contribution from domestic oil production. Although the potential size of the North Sea contribution was not known at the time, its existence suggested the need for caution before initiating major adjustments on the assumption that the UK would remain indefinitely a major oil importer. At the time, too, there was some uncertainty about the durability of the price rise initiated by the OPEC countries. In the context of these considerations, the government in fact adopted a policy of substantial foreign borrowing, combined with a broadly neutral stance toward domestic aggregate demand.[1] Foreign borrowing took place under three headings: sterling deposits of surplus oil revenues by OPEC producers; medium-term (3–7 year) nationalized industry and local authority borrowing under the Treasury Exchange cover scheme; and official borrowing by the UK government. During the period 1974–7, total public-sector foreign-currency borrowing under these heads amounted to more than $14bn. Although this policy allowed the UK to accommodate its payments deficit in anticipation of the benefits of North Sea oil, it also prevented the exchange rate from

1   Over the period 1975–7, the net effect of fiscal policy has been estimated as being mildly expansionary. See 'Why is Britain in Recession?', *BEQB*, March 1978.

dropping even further below PPP than it did. As pointed out in section I.4, this increased external debt also implied the need for a substantial UK current-account surplus in the 1980s to service the interest and amortization payments.

Turning now to the period after 1978, the most important fact to be explained is the rapid appreciation of sterling during 1979 and 1980. The major structural factor of relevance here is the growth in production from the North Sea oil fields, which has made by far the largest contribution to the improvement in the current account since 1977. The direct effect on the current account has been reinforced by the indirect effects on confidence and capital flows. From 1979 there was, in effect, a reassessment of the long-term prospects for sterling and the associated exchange-risks of holding sterling-denominated assets. The renewed confidence in sterling as a 'petrocurrency' is reflected in the annual rate of recorded ('inward') overseas investment in the UK, which rose from £1.7bn per annum during 1972–6 to £4.3bn per annum in 1979–81 and £4.1bn per annum in 1982–4. However, there was, over the same period, an even sharper rise in the annual rate of private ('outward') investment by the UK in foreign countries, from an average of £1.4bn in 1972–6 to £8.4bn in 1979–81 and £12.1bn in 1982–4. A further structural influence on the exchange rate was the depth of the UK recession. Between 1978 and 1981, UK industrial output fell by 6.8%. GDP did not fall so sharply because of the buoyancy of North Sea oil production. However, industrial output is probably a better indicator, as the change in the composition of output corresponds to a switch from relatively labour-intensive industries (manufacturing) to the relatively capital-intensive oil production and related activities. As discussed in Chapter 1, unemployment rose sharply. The depth of the recession was associated with a decline in domestic demand and therefore an improvement in the current account. This in turn would have contributed to the buoyancy of sterling. A final factor was the rise in UK nominal interest rates, particularly short-term interest rates, relative to those in other OECD countries. Throughout 1979 and much of 1980, UK short-term rates were between 2% and 4% higher than comparable rates in the United States. This would tend to induce a capital inflow into the UK and hence raise the value of sterling. However, the 1979 abolition of exchange controls should, by facilitating a capital outflow, have moderated the rise in sterling to some extent. Overall, there remains some disagreement both about the relative contribution of each factor to the appreciation of sterling and about whether, when put together, they provide a complete explanation of this appreciation.[1] It seems likely that increased confidence in sterling as a petrocurrency must have contributed to a substantial part of the appreciation, but this is to assert little more than that we cannot fully explain why the pound rose so strongly in 1979–80.

---

1 For an appraisal of the causes of the rise in sterling see W.H.Buiter and M.H.Miller, 'Changing The Rules: Economic Consequences of the Thatcher Regime', *Brookings Papers*, 1983:2, pp. 305–65.

Since 1981, movements in the pound have, in large part, reflected changes in the value of the US dollar. However, the pound continues to be affected by changes in the world price of crude oil. For example, in early 1986 sterling depreciated in response to the fall in oil prices until the depreciation was checked by a rise in UK short-term interest rates. Nevertheless, the UK's dependence on North Sea oil and gas should not be exaggerated. Oil and gas production and processing contributed some 22% of the output of UK production industries (manufacturing and energy) in 1984 but they contributed only 8% of total GDP in the same year, and this percentage is likely to fall in future years as oil and gas production levels out and then declines.

Intervention and the exchange rate: So far we have looked at deviations from PPP in terms of shifts in various real factors impinging upon the exchange rate. Equal weight must also be given to government intervention in the foreign-exchange market. The next section deals with the theoretical pros and cons of intervention, so here we simply record that the float of sterling has been heavily managed since 1972. In addition to foreign-currency borrowing, the management of sterling has been effected in two main ways: by the use of reserves and by variations in interest rates. Between 1974 and 1976, annual reserve losses of $1.3bn were incurred to prevent an even more rapid slide of the exchange rate, while during 1977 the reserves were allowed to increase by the historically unprecedented sum of $16.4bn when the effective rate was stabilized. Further reserve gains of approximately $9bn during 1979 and 1980 also prevented even greater appreciation above PPP. Since 1979, interest-rate policy has played an increasing role in exchange-rate management, with short-term interest rates being raised to generate an inflow of funds to prevent a depreciation of the pound and vice-versa. This switch in emphasis is reflected in less volatile movements in the reserves, particularly during 1983–5. In October 1985, the authorities announced that they would use short-term interest rates more actively than previously and this would include adjustments required to help maintain the external value of the pound within a desired range. This point is discussed further in section III.5.

To sum up, it is clear that sterling has deviated very substantially from PPP for long periods. The reasons for these deviations can be catalogued in general terms, but on some occasions it is not easy to see precisely why the pound moved as strongly as it did. This puzzle is to some extent accentuated by the knowledge that the pound would on occasion have moved more strongly still were it not for various forms of intervention by the authorities.

III.5   Management of the Exchange Rate

In the previous section we have indicated how the sterling exchange rate has been influenced by the activities of the authorities since 1972, their primary instruments being foreign-currency borrowing, domestic interest-rate policy, and changes in the stock of UK foreign-exchange reserves. There are several reasons why a government may wish to manage the exchange rate. These may loosely be classified into those based on longer-term and those based on shorter-term objectives.

Industrial competitiveness and anti-inflation policy: We turn first to two competing longer-term objectives of exchange-rate policy. First, it can be argued that the UK should engineer a systematic *depreciation* of sterling to maintain or improve the international competitiveness of UK industrial products. The mechanism of a managed depreciation can be argued as follows. The impact effect will be a deterioration in the terms of trade as sterling import prices rise relative to sterling export prices.[1] These changes induce substitutions in patterns of production and consumption, which grow in magnitude as contracts are renegotiated and as new plant and equipment is installed to take advantage of changed profit opportunities. In the long run, the trade balance will improve provided domestic and foreign elasticities of demand for import goods and elasticities of supply of export goods are 'sufficiently' large.[2] Available evidence suggests that these conditions are satisfied for the UK,[3] but there may be an initial deterioration as the immediate effects on relative prices precede the longer-term quantitative responses of trade flows. The deterioration and subsequent improvement in the trade balance is known as the 'J' curve effect. However, to the extent that the trade balance improves in terms of home currency, the aggregate demand for UK goods will be increased and, if the economy is near to full employment, this will be inflationary unless domestic expenditure is reduced to 'make room' for the improvement of the trade balance. Account must also be taken of the import content of domestic production, and the effects of the devaluation in raising domestic costs and in creating pressure for higher money wages.[4] Unless the depreciation is associated with a reduction in real wages, its only effect will be to lower the long-run profitability of UK manufacturing industry. Moreover, if in addition, domestic firms follow pricing policies to maintain rates of return, then a *real* depreciation will be prevented, and the ultimate effect of the *nominal* depreciation will simply be

---

1 However, this depends in part on the pricing policies of domestic and foreign firms. For evidence on the pricing policies of UK firms following the 1967 devaluation, see P.B.Rosendale, 'The Short-Run Pricing Policies of Some British Engineering Exporters', *NIER*, No. 65, 1973, and the valuable study by D.C.Hague, E.Oakeshott and A.Strain, *Devaluation and Pricing Decisions* (Allen and Unwin, 1974).

2 In the special case in which trade is initially balanced and supply elasticities of traded goods are infinite, then a depreciation improves the trade balance provided that the sum of the foreign and domestic elasticities of demand for imported goods exceeds unity. For a more general statement, see Lindert and Kindleberger, *International Economics* (7th edition, Irwin, 1982), chapter 15 and Appendix H.

3 For a discussion of recent evidence on import and export elasticities, see J.Williamson, 'Is There an External Constraint?', *NIER*, August 1984, pp. 73–7.

4 The average import content of UK manufacturing output is currently 21%.

to increase all prices and the level of official foreign-exchange reserves without any long-run effect on flows of exports and imports.

The conclusion to be drawn from this is that powerful forces are at work to offset the initial effects of a managed depreciation on the balance of trade. Indeed, recent calculations show that the effects of a hypothetical depreciation in sterling are largely transitory with respect to the level of output and the current balance of payments and that, after six years, a devaluation of 5% would produce a 4% increase in the UK's retail price index. These calculations also make clear that the effects of a devaluation depend on policies to control money income which should accompany the depreciation.[1]

In contrast, a second possible longer-term goal of exchange-rate management might be to engineer an *appreciation* of sterling to help combat domestic inflation. The main proposition here is that the rate of inflation is influenced by the pressure of demand in the labour market and by expectations of inflation, so that a currency appreciation reduces inflation in three ways: it directly lowers domestic production costs via the cost of imported inputs; it reduces the demand for labour by its adverse effects on total demand for UK output, and, since many of these effects take time to work, it also has the indirect effect of lowering the anticipated rate of inflation, thus moderating money wage demands. The effectiveness of such a policy must be questioned for similar reasons to those which cast doubt on the value of a managed depreciation. Moreover, even if an appreciation were to work in the way described, it is hard to see how a *continuing* reduction in inflation could be brought about by a *once-over* appreciation; a continuing appreciation would seem to be required. In addition, exchange-rate changes appear to have substantial real effects in the short term and an appreciation could prove a rather costly way (in terms of output forgone) of achieving a purely temporary fall in the inflation rate.

Exchange-rate targets: The argument so far suggests that it is rather unlikely that the exchange rate can be managed to achieve permanent effects: on the balance of payments, inflation, or employment. Other considerations support this view. First, in a world where all the major currencies are floating, governments may follow mutually inconsistent exchange-rate targets and find themselves in a situation of competitive exchange-rate management in which one country's policies are nullified by the action of others. Second, the experience of the 1970s and 1980s suggests that there are limits to the ability of national authorities to set an exchange rate which is very

---

1   Cf. *TER*, March 1978, No. 96. It is particularly important that the money supply is not allowed to expand and negate the effects of depreciation in reducing real money balances and absorption. A more recent study suggests that, holding money wages constant, a 10% effective depreciation of sterling would be followed after three years by a 4% increase in wholesale prices and a 2.5% increase in consumer prices. See the article, 'Sterling and Inflation', *BEQB*, September 1981.

different from that which would be set by the private market. When the authorities step outside these limits, the resulting flows of speculative short-term capital tend to force a change in policy. Third, any disequilibrium exchange rate will, in general, be associated with a non-zero BOF and thus with changes in the stock of foreign-exchange reserves and the domestic money supply.[1] Changes in the domestic money supply will change domestic prices until the exchange rate returns to equilibrium. This must be so since, as long as the exchange rate is out of equilibrium, the money supply and therefore domestic prices will be changing; when the exchange rate is in equilibrium there are no forces impelling any further price or exchange-rate changes. It must be stressed that this is true only in the very long run and that the links between reserve changes and the domestic money supply can, to some extent, be offset by domestic monetary policy. Nevertheless these arguments underline the point that the scope for exchange-rate management is confined mainly to the short run.

In the short run though there are several arguments to suggest that some degree of exchange-rate management might be desirable. First, the authorities may view changes in the demand and supply of foreign exchange as temporary and so act as a speculator to prevent such changes influencing the exchange rate and causing costly changes in trade flows. The difficulty with this argument is that it presumes that the authorities are substantially better informed than private investors as to what constitute 'permanent' and 'transitory' changes. On some occasions this presumption may be correct but it is certainly not true *in general*.[2]

A more complex argument for exchange-rate management in the short run is related to the interaction between interest rates, the exchange rate and monetary policy when international capital is highly mobile. In this environment it may be sensible for the authorities to pursue a target value or range of values for the exchange rate. This can be achieved by varying domestic interest rates to influence the flow of international capital. If the authorities were to attach overriding importance to the achievement of an exchange-rate target, they could not in general simultaneously expect to attain a target for the quantity of money, for it is by varying the quantity of money that the authorities can influence interest rates and thus accommodate shocks to the economy in such a way that they do not unduly affect the value of the exchange rate. The relative merits of monetary and exchange-rate targets are too complex to be debated in full here.[3] The choice of one or other should be determined by its ability to 'insulate' the economy from unwanted

---

1 For useful accounts of the links between external transactions and the domestic money supply, see 'Of DCE, M_3 and Similar Mysteries', *MBR*, February 1977; 'External and Foreign Currency Flows and the Money Supply', *BEQB*, December 1978; and 'External Flows and Broad Money', *BEQB*, December 1983.

2 The assessment of the effectiveness of official stabilization operations is fraught with difficulty. See 'Intervention, Stabilization and Profits', *BEQB*, September 1983, pp. 384–91.

3 For a clear exposition of the issues involved, see M.J.Artis, 'From Monetary to Exchange Rate Targets', *Banca Nazionale del Lavoro Quarterly Review*, September 1981, pp. 339–58.

exogenous disturbances. Roughly, exchange-rate targets are likely to be preferable if the main disturbances to the economy originate in financial markets. An exchange-rate target helps prevent such disturbances from being transmitted to domestic production and prices.

Since 1976 the UK authorities have attached considerable importance to monetary targets. In the last few years, however, there have been signs of a switch in emphasis towards using short-term interest rates to regulate the exchange rate.[1] Notably, there were sharp increases in short-term interest rates in July 1984 and again in January 1985 and January 1986 which appeared to owe little to domestic monetary conditions but were implemented largely to arrest or attentuate a fall in sterling. The problem with this strategy is that if the target value of the exchange rate is chosen wrongly or too inflexibly then maintaining the target will have adverse effects on either output or inflation which may persist for some time. This suggests the need for making the targets *conditional* on other aspects of the economic situation, including domestic monetary conditions and the level of demand. In practice it is far from easy to judge the 'right' level of a target. The difficulties are likely to be particularly acute in the immediate future: current innovations in financial markets make monetary targets difficult to judge, while continued turbulence in exchange markets makes it equally difficult to judge an exchange-rate target. One possible method of increasing exchange-rate stability would be for the UK to join the European monetary system; this is discussed in section III.7 below.

In summary, exchange-rate management is fraught with problems although it seems clear that some degree of management is desirable. As far back as 1973, the UK authorities set out their broad objectives of exchange-rate policy as being '. . . not to oppose any well-defined trend but merely to smooth excessive fluctuations'.[2] These relatively modest goals may be about the best that can reasonably be expected.

North Sea oil and exchange-rate policy: We have already described the direct effects on the balance of payments of the growing production of North Sea oil and gas since 1973, and argued that this was one of the key factors behind the appreciation of sterling between 1979 and 1980. The UK's benefit from North Sea oil amounts to a windfall gain resulting from the discovery and exploitation of oil reserves. The effects of oil-price changes are more complex. On the one hand, the UK benefits from a rise in oil prices because of the improvement in its terms of trade. On the other hand, insofar as the rest of the world goes into recession as a result of higher oil prices, the total demand for UK goods and services falls and unemployment increases. On balance the UK is probably a net beneficiary from higher oil prices, and

---

1   See in particular the Chancellor of the Exchequer's 1985 Mansion House speech, reported in *The Financial Times*, 18 October 1985.

2   Bank of England, *Annual Report and Accounts*, 1973, p. 21.

therefore a net loser as a result of the lower oil prices of 1985 and 1986. The principal benefit, however, arises from the production rather than the price effects.

The policy implications of North Sea oil have been hotly contested.[1] Crude oil has certain specific uses, and therefore the benefits of oil resources can be spread across the whole community only if the oil is sold on the market and the government follows 'appropriate' monetary and fiscal policies to assure distribution of the benefits. Since all UK oil production represents an equivalent gross gain to the balance of visible trade,[2] an increase in production will improve the current account and put upward pressure on the exchange rate. This depresses the production of non-oil tradeables in the UK and, since these are labour-intensive relative to oil, has the effect of reducing the aggregate demand for labour at current levels of real wages. The non-oil tradeable sector consists largely of manufacturing industry and the adverse effects on manufacturing of a high exchange rate consequent on a resource discovery are known collectively as the 'Dutch disease', following the evolution of the Dutch economy after the discovery of natural gas in the sixties. The question is how far a sustained real appreciation of the currency, with its Dutch disease implications, is a necessary consequence of a resource discovery.

The Forsyth and Kay position is that a high real exchange rate is the principal, if not the only mechanism by which the benefits of North Sea oil can be realized. Since oil has to be traded for consumer goods, the terms-of-trade improvement allows UK consumers to purchase foreign manufactured goods more cheaply than would otherwise be the case. On this view, the real appreciation did not imply a general deterioration in UK competitiveness but rather reflected a change in the UK's comparative international advantage: from a manufacturing exporter to a resource exporter. It does not follow that the authorities should have allowed an unchecked appreciation of sterling. It does, however, follow that the correct way to limit the appreciation was for the UK government to invest the oil proceeds largely overseas, or to encourage the private sector to perform this task by, for example, abolishing exchange controls as occurred in 1979.

The contrary argument is that the decline in UK manufacturing industry was caused by the real appreciation of sterling, was largely unnecessary and might be difficult to reverse as it is more costly to open new factories than it is to close old ones. On this view, North Sea oil revenues should be invested by the UK government in the UK in a programme of industrial regeneration. In addition, the authorities should expand demand in a deliberate effort to depress sterling and reduce the unemployment rate.

---

1 The path-breaking contribution was P.J.Forsyth and J.A.Kay, 'The Economic Implications of North Sea Oil Revenues', *Fiscal Studies*, 1980, pp. 1–28. For a rebuttal see T.Barker, *Energy, Industrialization and Economic Policy* (Academic Press, London, 1981). An official viewpoint is given in 'North Sea Oil and Gas: A Challenge for the Future', *BEQB*, vol. 22, 1982.

2 Forsyth and Kay, *op. cit.*

In assessing these views it is difficult to resist the conclusion that some real appreciation must follow from North Sea oil. We have seen that the scope for a managed depreciation is inherently limited. Moreover a demand-led expansion of the economy is constrained by the need of the UK to run balance-of-payments surpluses to repay foreign debt incurred in the mid-seventies. Indeed sterling's appreciation has not prevented such surpluses from appearing, which would suggest that the currency has not been over-valued. Turning now to the utilization of oil resources, it is difficult not to be sceptical of a programme of industrial regeneration since this would involve investing in sectors rendered relatively unprofitable by the change in the UK's terms of trade. Investing in these sectors will not of itself make them more profitable nor will it reverse the terms-of-trade shift. More plausible is the argument that there should be investment in non-traded goods industries whose profitability would increase as a result of the appreciation of sterling. In the public sector this would include investment in roads and in health, education, and training. Through such investments, the North Sea oil benefit could be translated into physical and human capital assets, with positive effects on UK industrial competitiveness in the medium and long term when North Sea production declines.[1] These arguments should not be taken to imply that the 'Dutch disease' is of no concern. However, there is now a respectable body of evidence to suggest that the decline in UK manufacturing industry in the last decade cannot be attributed solely to North Sea oil or a high real exchange rate. Indeed, in a recent survey, many industrialists were as concerned as much about the *stability* of the exchange rate as they were about its level.[2]

In summary, it seems clear that North Sea oil involves a higher sterling exchange rate than would otherwise prevail. Some structural change is certain to follow from this, with adverse consequences for employment in the production of tradeable goods. The pattern of comparative advantage has changed in a way which allows a higher *average* level of UK income than would otherwise prevail. The proper response is surely not how change can be prevented but how the consequences of North Sea resources can be accommodated with a minimum of transitional cost and a maximum of longer-term benefit.

Unemployment and import controls: Aside from North Sea oil, the main and to some extent associated structural problem facing the UK is that of high and seemingly persistent unemployment. This problem is associated with North Sea oil because the terms-of-trade shift is responsible in part for a decline in demand for UK manufactured goods. In the frictionless world of

---

1   Cf. *The Challenge of North Sea Oil*, Cmnd. 7143 (HMSO, 1978).

2   House of Lords, *Report From The Select Committee on Overseas Trade* (HMSO, 30 July 1985).

textbooks the resulting unemployed labour would be reabsorbed in non-traded goods industries at a new structure of relative wages. Such adjustments are not in practice immediate and an unknown fraction of the high unemployment of recent years is certainly due to the adjustment problems associated with North Sea oil. A full analysis of the causes of unemployment is contained in other chapters. Here we will confine our attention to a proposed remedy which impinges particularly on the balance of payments, namely the argument that to reduce unemployment and revive UK industry some substantial protection in the form of import restrictions (quotas and tariffs) is required.[1] The case for import restrictions rests partly on the probable non-viability of a managed depreciation. Import restrictions, it is argued, provide an alternative and more selective route to protect and provide incentives to UK industry.

Objections to such a policy are numerous. A *general* tariff or quota works in much the same way as a depreciation of the currency, relying for its effectiveness on price elasticities and changes in the structure of real wages.[2] If these are ineffectual in the context of a depreciation, a tariff or quota is unlikely to be more successful. The argument that import controls can be administered selectively is also unconvincing, as it is generally recognized that a direct subsidy to a particular industry is more efficient than the indirect support provided by a tariff or quota on the foreign trade of the products of that industry.[3] A practical objection to import controls is that they are likely to provoke foreign retaliation. It is true that any measure intended to improve the UK balance of payments must lead to a worsening of the balance of payments of some other country and is therefore open to the possibility of retaliation. However, the UK is particularly unlikely to get a sympathetic hearing at international bodies which are concerned with trade restrictions such as the IMF, GATT and the EEC for as long as the UK current-account balance is in overall surplus, as is presently the case. The existence of such a surplus underlines the weakness in the argument for import restrictions; the structural problems of UK industry are related only tangentially at best to the state of the external accounts. Thus, there is no guarantee that import restrictions will persuade industry to undertake more productive investment, or introduce more

1   The most persistent advocates of this view have been the Cambridge Economic Policy Group. See, e.g., their *Economic Policy Review*, No. 4, March 1978, and the contribution by R. Nield to the book by R.L. Major cited at the end of this chapter.

2   It is well known that import tariffs and quotas are in most essential respects equivalent. A quota will induce higher import prices which have identical effects to some rate of tariff. See Lindert and Kindleberger, *op. cit.*, Chapter 8. The main difference is that the benefits of higher import prices accrue chiefly to the taxing authority in the case of a tariff (in this instance the UK government) and mainly to foreign suppliers and domestic holders of import licences in the case of a quota. The recent experience of the United States with quotas on Japanese car imports strongly confirms this logic.

3   This is argued in detail by J.N. Bhagwati and V.K. Ramaswami, 'Domestic Distortions, Tariffs, and the Theory of Optimum Subsidy', *JPE*, Vol. LXXI, No. 1, February 1963, pp. 44–50.

flexible working practices.[1] If such changes did not occur, import restrictions could prove a recipe for stagnation rather than industrial regeneration. In short, whatever the problems of UK industry, it is exceedingly improbable that import restrictions would form part of any viable programme of industrial regeneration.

III.6   Capital Flows and Balance-of-Payments Policy

In this section we shall investigate the relationship between capital movements, the balance of payments and the exchange rate. As noted in section I.2, the distinction between short-term and long-term capital flows is to a large extent a matter of convenience. By short-term capital movements, we shall mean transactions between UK and overseas residents, in currency, bank deposits and securities: transactions which are typically related to the finance of foreign trade or the optimal allocation of stocks of wealth between assets denominated in different currencies. In the case of long-term capital flows, we shall primarily be concerned with the international direct investment operations of companies and public-sector bodies.

Short-term capital movements have traditionally played an important role in the overall UK balance-of-payments situation. Some short-term capital movements reflect changes in the sterling balances which foreign governments and individuals have acquired as matters of commercial and financial convenience. The remainder reflect the role of London as the major centre for the Eurocurrency, Eurobond and other international financial markets, with banks in the UK lending and borrowing extensively in dollars and other currencies. The development of the Eurocurrency markets since 1958 has meant the increasing integration of European and American capital and money markets.[2] The net assets of the Eurocurrency market increased from $85bn in 1971 to $1,265bn in 1984. The volume of deposits and the ease with which they may be switched between currencies have important implications for the stability of exchange rates and the conduct of national monetary policies.

The significance of short-term capital flows for the conduct of UK policy arises from their magnitude relative to the official reserves and from their volatility. It is convenient, though artificial, to divide these flows into two broad classes: speculative and non-speculative. The motive behind speculative capital flows is one of making a capital gain from anticipated movements in spot exchange rates or interest rates. A risk-neutral currency

---

1   The 7th edition of this volume contains a brief account of the temporary import restrictions employed by the UK in the 1960s.

2   Eurocurrency deposits are bank deposits in currencies other than that of the country in which the banks in question are located. For the working and development of the Eurocurrency markets, consult R.B.Johnston, *The Economics of The Euro-Market* (Macmillan, 1983). See also 'Eurobanks and the Inter-Bank Market', *BEQB*, September 1981.

speculator would be indifferent between holding sterling- or dollar-denominated assets, for example, if the interest rate on sterling assets equalled the interest rate on dollar assets plus the anticipated depreciation of sterling relative to the dollar. If the anticipated sterling devaluation exceeds the sterling interest advantage, holders of sterling assets will switch their assets into dollars while UK importers will accelerate (lead) dollar payments for imports and UK exporters will try to delay (lag) dollar payments due from foreigners. Non-speculative activities are undertaken to avoid the risk of capital gains or losses associated with exchange-rate movements, and typically involve simultaneous transactions in both spot and forward currency markets so that the risks associated with currency transactions may be shifted onto speculators.[1] In sum, short-term capital movements depend on a complex set of interactions between national interest rates, spot and forward exchange rates and expectations of future changes in spot rates.

With a floating exchange rate, the impact effect of a net capital flow falls directly upon the spot exchange rate[2]: a capital outflow will tend to depreciate sterling, and an inflow to appreciate sterling. Moreover, any such change in the exchange rate acts upon the current account in the same way as a policy-induced parity change. Hence, a capital inflow which generates an appreciation also has the effect of discouraging exports, encouraging imports, and depressing the inflation rate. It should be clear therefore that large and sudden capital flows can provide difficult policy problems for economies operating with floating exchange rates and, in the light of this, it is relevant to enquire if the UK authorities can exert any substantial influence over short-term capital flows. In the first instance, some restraint on UK residents would be obtained via exchange-control provisions which, until 1979, were a major element in UK policy. Following the abolition of exchange controls in October 1979, the capital and money markets of the UK became fully integrated with those of the rest of the world. The effects of this should not be exaggerated, since the exchange regulations applied only to UK residents and left untouched the activities of non-resident holders of sterling, who since 1958 have been free to switch between sterling and other currencies. To be sure, the relaxation of exchange controls allows an adjustment of the asset portfolios of UK individuals and financial institutions. But this is likely to be of a once-for-all nature. Recent calculations do, indeed, indicate an effect of this kind, portfolio capital outflow in real terms during 1980 to 1984 being roughly nine times greater than in the years 1975 to 1979.[3]

---

1   See the 6th edition of this volume for a discussion of forward market transactions. More detailed treatments will be found in Grubel, *International Economics* (Irwin, 1977), chapter 12, and Lindert and Kindleberger, *op. cit.*, chapter 13 and Appendix G.

2   Under certain circumstances, capital flows may also affect the money supply, even under floating exchange rates. See 'External Flows and Broad Money', *BEQB*, December 1983.

3   See also the article, 'The Effects of Exchange Control Abolition on Capital Flows', *BEQB*, September 1981.

To the extent that these figures accurately reflect the abolition of exchange controls, then it is clear that this policy could be justified as one means of limiting the oil-wealth effect on the sterling exchange rate. Exchange controls apart, the main weapon for influencing capital flows is the manipulation of domestic interest rates. This has already been discussed in some detail in sections III.3 and III.5 and the arguments there do not need repetition.

By far the most significant structural element influencing short-term capital movements since 1973 has been the changes in the price of oil. The price increases of 1973 and 1979 created a massive capacity to lend by the OPEC nations and the second price increase enhanced the desirability of depositing surplus funds in sterling as a 'petrocurrency'. The falling oil prices of 1985 and 1986 must, to some extent, have the opposite effect. Between 1978 and 1985 the outstanding sterling obligations of the UK monetary sector and other financial institutions to the overseas sector increased more than fivefold, from £7.9bn to £40.8bn.[1] Since the balance-of-payments surpluses of OPEC countries have evaporated, the share of oil-exporting countries in the sterling balances has fallen sharply, from 26% in 1981 to 15% in 1985. Meanwhile, the shares of other countries have risen, particularly that of other EEC countries which amounted to 23% in 1985.

We turn now to consider long-term capital flows, and direct investment overseas in particular. Foreign direct investment is one mechanism by which modern corporations seek to gain competitive advantages relative to their rivals, and the rate and direction of investment is determined by anticipated profit opportunities. Avoiding tariff barriers and taking advantage of cheap foreign labour are two underlying motives, although, increasingly, foreign direct investment must be considered in relation to exporting and foreign licencing of technology, as ways in which the firm may extract maximum advantage from its knowledge and human capital base.[2] Throughout the postwar period to 1979, investment overseas by UK firms was strictly controlled with the object not of preventing such investment but of ensuring that it was financed either from the retained profits of foreign operations or from foreign currency borrowing.[3] Indeed, over the period from 1965 to 1978, roughly half of UK direct investment overseas was financed out of retained profits and the remainder largely from foreign borrowing. Quite how the relaxation of exchange controls will affect this financing pattern, it is too early to say. But the initial indications are that finance from UK retained profits is being substituted for foreign borrowing.

---

1   These obligations are usually known as 'sterling balances'. The 9th edition of this volume contains an extended discussion of the evolution of sterling balances in the 1960s and 1970s and of the official measures taken to support the maintenance of overseas sterling holdings.

2   Cf. R.Caves, 'International Corporations: The Industrial Economics of Foreign Investment', *Economica*, Vol. 38, 1971, pp. 1–27.

3   The 9th edition of this volume contains details of the capital controls on overseas direct investment.

It might be expected that entry into the EEC would have had a marked effect on the pattern of the UK's overseas investment. Of the total stock of UK direct investment assets in the mid-1970s, it has been estimated that 28% was located in Western Europe and 23% in North America compared to figures of 13% and 23% in 1962.[1] This would appear to suggest a trend of increasing investment in Western Europe. However, recent balance-of-payments data suggest a reversal of this trend. During the period 1974–83, 51% of total outward direct investment went to North America, with only 8% being directed to the EEC. Apart from noting that data on direct investment are among the least reliable parts of the balance-of-payments accounts, it is difficult to think of a plausible explanation for these figures. One possibility is that a major motive for outward investment is for large firms to avoid tariffs and other import restrictions imposed by the host country. On this interpretation, the dismantling of such barriers within the EEC largely obviates the need for UK firms to invest in other EEC countries, and provides incentives for them to concentrate their foreign investment activities instead in non-EEC markets where barriers to imports may be more important. However, this explanation is necessarily very tentative in nature.

The movements of capital funds across the exchanges cumulate over time to determine the net asset position of the UK *vis-à-vis* other countries. The balance of payments on current account is the chief element in this process, but valuation effects due to exchange-rate and national interest-rate changes are also an important factor. At end-1984, identified *net* assets amounted to £73.5bn or 26% of GNP at factor cost. Largely as a consequence of North Sea oil exploitation, the ratio of *gross* external assets to GNP has risen from 0.9 in 1970 to 2.2 in 1984.[2]

Associated with the stocks of foreign assets and liabilities are return flows of interest, profits and dividends (IPD) which appear in the current account. For the UK, roughly 53% of the IPD credits are related to past direct investments by UK manufacturing firms, and 7% are derived from portfolio investments. It is worth noting that, throughout the period since 1960, the outflow of foreign investment from the UK has been smaller than the return flow of IPD credits on the existing stock of assets. Surprisingly perhaps, the discrepancy has widened recently. In 1984, private and official long-term outward investment totalled £14.9bn while gross IPD credits were £50.7bn. The net flow of IPD into the current account is also positive, from year to year, although the net receipts of foreign income are now only about 1.2% of GDP at factor cost.

---

1   For further details, see J. H. Dunning, 'The UK's International Direct Investment Position in the Mid-1970s', *LBR*, April 1978.

2   Cf. 'The External Balance Sheet of the United Kingdom: Developments to End-1984', *BEQB*, September 1985, pp. 427–35.

III.7   The UK and the European Economic Community

The UK became a full member of the EEC along with Denmark and Ireland in January 1973. Since then, the EEC has been enlarged to twelve countries with the entry of Greece (in January 1981) and Portugal and Spain (in January 1986). Within the UK the question of EEC membership has always involved a certain degree of controversy. The Labour government of 1974 declared its intention to renegotiate the original terms of entry,[1] completed the renegotiations in March 1975[2] and then settled the question in favour of membership with a referendum in July 1975. Although there remains a strand of opinion in the UK which still favours withdrawal, this option looks increasingly less likely than a continued debate within the EEC itself about the appropriate size of income transfers between member countries. Moreover, with the enlargement of the EEC, it is only to be expected that agreement on detailed matters of economic policy will continue to prove elusive.

In this section we shall concentrate chiefly on balance-of-payments and exchange-rate implications of UK membership of the EEC; other implications are treated in Chapters 2 and 4 of this volume.

Calculation of the economic costs and benefits of EEC membership can be made under two heads. First are the 'static' gains and losses, which themselves arise from two sources: the formation of a customs union between the UK and other EEC members with a common external tariff; and the inter-country transfers which result from aspects of the Common Agricultural Policy (CAP) and the Community budget. The second head includes 'dynamic' gains and losses which may result from selling in a larger market; allowing, for example, the exploitation of economies of scale in production and consequent improvement in competitiveness. If the combined static and dynamic effects led to a deterioration in the balance of payments, the UK would have to restore external balance, typically by a combination of a depreciation in the exchange rate and cuts in public spending or tax increases. These policies would impose a measurable real resource cost on the UK. Clearly the reverse would be true if entry were to produce an improvement in the balance of payments. Calculations made at the time of pre-entry negotiations were virtually unanimous in finding that entry would impose a static balance-of-payments cost, probably of around one per cent of GDP in the long run.[3] Acceptable estimates of dynamic gains or losses have not so

---

1   *Renegotiation of the Terms of Entry into the European Economic Community*, Cmnd. 5593 (April 1974).

2   *Membership of the European Community: Report on Renegotiation*, Cmnd. 6003 (March 1975).

3   The 1970 White Paper (*Britain and The European Communities: An Economic Assessment*, Cmnd. 4289, February 1970) suggested a balance-of-payments cost ranging between £100m and £1.1bn per annum. For a comparison with other estimates, see J. Pinder (ed.), *The Economics of Europe* (Charles Knight, 1971), chapter 6 by M. Miller.

far been made. In fact, the UK's relative economic position in the EEC has not changed markedly since entry. Between 1972 and 1983, per capita GDP in the UK declined slightly, from 96 to 94% of the EEC average.[1] This does not, however, answer the question: Would this performance have been better or worse if the UK had not been an EEC member?

In more detail, the effects of EEC membership on the UK balance of payments can be considered under three headings: changes in the pattern of trade in manufactures, adoption of the CAP, and contributions to the Community budget.

The main implications for trade in manufactures follow from the customs union aspects of the Community. All tariffs on trade between the UK and other members were reduced to zero in 1977 when the UK adopted the final stages of the common external tariff (CET) on trade with non-Community countries.[2] The discrimination which is now imposed against former Commonwealth countries (excluding signatories of the Lomé Convention[3]) and the associated loss of UK export preferences in the same countries must also be taken into account. We have already shown, in section II.1, that the direction of UK trade in the 1950s and 1960s swung progressively toward Western Europe and away from traditional markets in North America and the OSA. It is clear that entry into the EEC has accelerated this trend. Over the years 1963 to 1973, UK exports of manufactures to the EEC increased at an average annual rate of 10.7%, while imports from the EEC increased by 16.6%. Between 1973 and 1983, these average annual growth rates of trade in manufactures increased dramatically, with exports to the EEC increasing by 21.1% and imports from the EEC increasing by 19.1%.[4] However, it remains the case that the UK trades with the EEC somewhat less intensively than do her fellow members of the Community. Thus, in 1984, roughly 45% of UK exports and imports were exchanged with EEC countries, compared to an average intra-trade of the whole Community of about 53%. This divergence of trading patterns, which applies to agriculture as well as manufacturing, is an important factor behind the adverse net budgetary position of the UK which emerged after 1979.

Assessments of the balance-of-payments cost of entry for the UK have

---

1   The average is taken over the same ten countries in 1972 and 1983, i.e. before the accession of Spain and Portugal. Such calculations are, however, fraught with difficulty.

2   The necessary tariff changes were to be achieved in stages. For details, see *The United Kingdom and the European Communities*, Cmnd. 4715, July 1971. Following the completion of the Tokyo Round of multilateral tariff reductions in 1979, the average CET on industrial products will fall from 9.8% to 7.5% over an eight-year period.

3   For additional details of the Lomé Convention, which grants tariff preferences on exports to the EEC of industrial products and some agricultural products from signatory developing countries, see P.L.Coffey, 'The Lomé Agreement and the EEC: Implications and Problems', *TBR*, No. 108, December 1975.

4   For a more detailed analysis of the increasing intensity of UK–EEC trade, see A.E.Daly, 'UK Visible Trade and the Common Market', *NIER*, No. 86, November 1978. In the period 1973–83 the value of total intra-EEC trade increased by approximately 14% per annum.

tended to concentrate on the effects of adopting the CAP system of agricultural support. The original purpose of the CAP was to increase farm incomes with the twin aims of preserving family farms and promoting rural industrialization. These are laudable goals, but they can be achieved in different ways. Three are worth mentioning: direct income payments to farmers; producer price support through deficiency payments (the pre-entry UK system); and general price support by variable import and export taxes (the CAP). A detailed discussion of the relative merits of these schemes can be found elsewhere.[1] However, it is generally recognized that, on strict efficiency grounds, direct income payments are typically superior as they involve the smallest 'deadweight' loss. In practice, governments throughout the world have intervened in agriculture with a variety of price support schemes. Possibly, these are thought to be more 'arms length' in nature than direct income transfers.

Under its pre-entry deficiency payments system, the UK imported and consumed foodstuffs at world prices and subsidized (less efficient) UK farmers out of general taxation. Under the CAP, a set of common EEC farm prices are agreed annually. The prices of imports from non-EEC countries are then brought up to EEC prices by a system of variable import taxes. Likewise, EEC food exports receive a variable subsidy. The main economic differences between deficiency payments and the CAP are two in number. First, CAP taxes and subsidies impose a cost on more efficient non-EEC producers. Such producers affected by UK entry consisted mainly of Commonwealth countries. This was recognized in the 1974–5 renegotiations, which produced a guarantee of continued access to the Community for Commonwealth sugar and New Zealand dairy produce.[2] Second, EEC consumers suffer a loss under the CAP through having to pay higher than world prices for their foodstuffs. Thus, as compared with deficiency payments, the CAP shifts the cost of price support from general taxation onto foreign producers and domestic consumers of foodstuffs. Given that the UK has a much smaller and mostly more efficient farm sector than other EEC countries, it is easy to see why the UK should prefer a system of deficiency payments.

The exact cost of the CAP to the UK balance of payments and to EEC consumers in general depends largely on the gap between EEC prices and world market prices for foodstuffs, which varies over time. Since EEC farm prices are set by an annual round of bargaining, they are far more stable over time than world prices. Agricultural price stability has often been regarded as a desirable goal in its own right, but recent theoretical work casts some doubt on this view.[3] Moreover, the EEC bargaining process is subject to intensive

1   See T. Josling, 'The Common Agricultural Policy of The European Economic Community', *Journal of Agricultural Economics*, May 1969, pp. 175–91.

2   Cmnd. 6003.

3   For a comprehensive but difficult analysis of price stabilization schemes, see D.M.G.Newbery and J.E.Stiglitz, *The Theory of Commodity Price Stabilization* (Oxford University Press, 1981).

lobbying and it has proven much easier to raise intervention prices than to lower them. The fundamental fact is that, over the last one and a half decades, EEC intervention prices have almost always been above world market prices and often far above these prices. The result has been substantial over-production of many commodities, much of which has had to be stockpiled, forming the notorious 'food mountains'. In addition to costs already cited, the management of such stockpiles imposes a substantial additional burden on the Community. It should be apparent that food stocks on such a large scale are wasteful and absurd.

Substantial problems in the administration of the CAP have also arisen because EEC food prices are set in terms of units of account and then translated into the respective member currencies at representative exchange rates, the so-called 'green currencies', fixed by administrative decision. As long as the ratio between any two green-currency rates is equal to the spot-market exchange rate between the corresponding national currencies, the system works as intended, in that any agricultural commodity will sell at a common price throughout the EEC. However, since 1971, spot-market rates for several EEC currencies have diverged substantially from the green-currency rates.[1] Such divergences are extremely disruptive to agricultural trade and production in the EEC, since they undermine the principle of common prices for foodstuffs and create profitable opportunities for arbitrage between commodities and EEC currencies. To prevent this, border taxes and subsidies are levied on agricultural trade between EEC countries, the total amounts of subsidy involved being known as monetary compensation amounts (MCAs). The MCA system began as a temporary measure following the collapse of the par-value system in 1972. But it continued in effect until March 1984, when the EEC agreed to phase out MCAs over a period of four years. This agreement leaves unsolved the problem of managing the CAP when exchange rates are flexible. Elimination of MCAs implies that green exchange rates must be tied to actual exchange rates and this would pose formidable administrative problems. A stable currency area provided by a widened European Monetary System would resolve these problems. The objection to this argument is that it is the structure of the CAP which is deficient; it would be ironic if the EMS were broadened and strengthened for the sole object of shoring up the CAP.

Reform of the CAP has become particularly pressing in the last few years. Between 1980 and 1985 world food prices increased by only 10%, well below the EEC average inflation rate of 51% (or 8.6% per annum) over the same period. Since intervention prices have also increased, EEC food stocks have built up to record levels (see table 3.6). The accession of Spain and Portugal

---

1 For further discussion, consult R. W. Irving and H. A. Fern, *Green Money and the Common Agricultural Policy* (Wye College, Occasional Paper No. 2, 1975), and C. Mackel, 'Green Money and the Common Agricultural Policy', *NWBQR*, February 1978. The values for the green currencies are published monthly in *Bulletin of the European Communities* (Secretariat General, Brussels). An excellent account of the CAP and the green-currency system is given in A. E. Buckwell *et al.*, *The Costs of the Common Agricultural Policy* (Croom Helm, 1982).

to the Community will accentuate the pressures on the CAP as both are major producers of Mediterranean foodstuffs. Finally, and perhaps most pertinently, CAP expenditures absorbed some two-thirds of the Community budget in 1984 and 1985 and, in the absence of reforms, would have considerably exceeded total EEC resources in 1986, thus creating a situation of technical bankruptcy.

TABLE 3.6
EEC: Estimated Surplus Farm Stocks, November 1985

	in million tonnes (except wine)
Butter	1.2
Skimmed Milk Powder	0.5
Beef	0.8
Wheat	12.2
Barley	4.6
Rye	1.1
Sugar	4.8
Wine (in billion litres)	3.3

Source: EEC Commission and Trade Estimates.

As long as the basic principles of the CAP are adhered to, the two major avenues for economy are to link EEC prices more closely with world prices, and to place limits on the amount of farm production which will receive support. Very little progress has been made in either direction. The 1984 farm price review produced an average 0.5% cut in prices paid to farmers, and in 1985 no change on average was agreed. The 1986 review again produced a price freeze but, following the April 1986 EMS currency realignment, all green currencies except the Mark and the Guilder were devalued. This had the effect of permitting an increase in local currency prices of farm produce in all EEC countries apart from Germany and The Netherlands. In addition, the 1984 review introduced production quotas for all sectors in surplus. Such quotas are only effective if backed up by sanctions against over-production, and the portents are not encouraging. Cereal production exceeded the quota by 8% in 1984. Accordingly the Commission proposed a 3.6% cut in prices for 1985; this was scaled back to a 1.8% cut by national farm ministers. In 1986, farm ministers agreed to a 3% tax on cereal production, dubbed 'the co-responsibility levy'. However, until more vigorous action is taken to cut prices, the CAP will continue to absorb a high volume of resources in an extremely wasteful manner.

The third and final aspect of UK membership of the EEC concerns contributions to and receipts from the Community budget, each of which involves transfers of funds across the foreign exchanges and may in turn require compensating exchange-rate adjustments. The EEC budget is financed from the 'own resources' of the Community, which consist of all import duties and agricultural levies from non-EEC sources (less 10% to cover costs of collection and administration) plus a VAT contribution which in January 1986 was raised from 1% to 1.4% of proceeds of a VAT levied on a uniform basis in the Community. The contribution to own resources is known as the 'gross contribution', the 'net contribution' being the gross contribution less receipts from the budget in the form of regional aid, agricultural support and the like.[1] For the UK, the fundamental problem is that structural features of the economy mean that its net budget contribution is certain to be always large and positive. The fact that the UK is relatively heavily dependent on food imports from (more efficient) non-EEC producers enhances her gross contribution, while the small size and greater efficiency of her agricultural sector mean that receipts from the agricultural funds are relatively small.[2]

Budgetary reform has become an increasingly pressing concern for the UK since 1980 when it shouldered for the first time the full budgetary cost of entry. For 1985 for example, the UK would have contributed some 20% of the Community's own resources and received only 10% of the Community's expenditure which would have amounted to a net budgetary contribution, prior to any rebate, of about £1.2bn. In 1980, a special system of rebates for the UK was negotiated which reduced the net contribution to an average of £400m in 1981 and 1982 and to £440m in 1983. Longer-term reform of the budget was discussed in a lengthy series of ministerial meetings, culminating in an agreement at the June 1984 Fontainebleau summit. This agreement confirmed the 1983 budget rebate which had previously been frozen by the EEC parliament, and settled on rebates of £590m (1bn ECUs) for 1984 and £630m (1.07bn ECUs) for 1985. The 1985 rebate is equivalent to 66% of the gap between UK VAT payments to the Community and EEC expenditures in the UK, and it was agreed that rebates would continue according to this formula from 1986 onwards. The UK's rebates will be financed by other member states according to their relative shares of the EEC's VAT income although, exceptionally, West Germany will pay two-thirds of its share. In addition the summit agreed on the rise from 1% to 1.4% of VAT revenues to be paid to the EEC's own resources, effective January 1986. The UK rebates will continue until a further increase in EEC revenues, to 1.6% of member states' VAT income, is agreed.

Although the Fontainebleau summit produced a more durable-looking agreement than previous efforts, neither the tortuous negotiating process nor the agreement itself give much encouragement for future reform. The principal measure in the agreement is an increase in the EEC's own resources through the higher VAT contributions and these will go chiefly to fund the inefficiencies of the CAP, which will absorb more than two-thirds of the Community budget for the foreseeable future. Moreover, the increase

---

1 Cf. Cmnd. 4715, paras. 91–6 and Annex A.

2 During 1986/7 the UK is expected to receive £1.3bn from the agricultural fund; total receipts from the EEC excluding the special rebates will amount to £2.0bn. On the other hand, the UK's gross contribution is expected to be £4.0bn.

in own resources is expected to prove barely adequate to prevent an overall budget deficit even in 1986. It is clear that, until the reform of the CAP is squarely faced, the EEC will continue to remain bogged down in an unending sequence of budgetary problems.

The European Monetary System (EMS):　　The origins of the EMS can be traced in particular to the 1970 Werner Report, which proposed the achievement of a full monetary union within the European Community by 1980. The timetable was abandoned almost immediately, but monetary union ostensibly remains a long-term goal of the Community. Monetary union would involve the establishment of a single Community-wide currency issued by a Community central bank with powers to determine monetary policy throughout the EEC. Moreover, since any national government can issue currency as a means of financing its own budget deficit, acceptance of a single EEC currency would necessarily require a considerable measure of Community-wide agreement on national *fiscal* policies as well as on national *monetary* policies.

The case for monetary union in the EEC is often presented as analogous to the case for having a common market in commodities. Creation of a single currency reduces transactions costs and promotes exchange and the division of labour which, it could be argued, is necessary if the benefits of the EEC are to be fully realized by member countries. Furthermore, it can be argued that as EEC members develop intensive trade and investment links with one another, then adoption of a single currency is the only foreign-exchange-market policy consistent with price stability. Stable (though not irrevocably fixed) exchange rates are, of course, an essential part of the operation of the CAP and other Community-wide policies. However, the costs of complete monetary unification may also be considerable. With a single currency throughout the EEC, each country becomes a region within a larger currency area. A country in balance-of-payments deficit to the rest of the EEC would have to adjust in much the same way as a region of the UK in deficit to the rest of the UK currently has to adjust. Since an exchange-rate change is ruled out, adjustment must be by a combination of domestic deflation and changes in regional taxes and subsidies. Within the EEC, of course, the latter are largely ruled out for balance-of-payments purposes by the CET. In practice, the process of balance-of-payments adjustment by a region within a single currency area depends to a large extent on the monetary effects of a balance-of-payments imbalance. A deficit for example will generate flows of money out of the region, depressing demand and, ultimately, prices and wages within the region. The effectiveness of this process in restoring regional balance-of-payments equilibrium without a sustained regional recession depends to a large extent on the flexibility of wages and prices, and on the mobility of labour and capital between occupations and regions in response to changed profit opportunities. There is no reason why the optimal areas for separate currencies should coincide with the jurisdictions of existing nation states. However, there is no general agreement as to what does constitute an optimal currency area.[1] Clearly a high degree of wage and price flexibility and of labour and capital mobility within the currency area are likely to be necessary conditions, but they may not be sufficient conditions for optimality. Certainly, it would be wishful to assume that the entire EEC with its evolving membership has ever constituted an optimal currency area, although it seems clear that stable exchange rates among certain subgroups of EEC members (notably Germany and the Netherlands) do appear desirable.

Following the collapse of the par-value system in 1971, the first steps towards greater monetary co-operation in the EEC were taken in April 1972 with the establishment of 'The Snake in the Tunnel', the name commonly given to the agreement to limit the margins of fluctuation between EEC currencies to one-half the permitted 'Smithsonian' limits.[2] In practice the snake proved to be mainly an enlarged Deutschmark zone. Sterling and the Lira were never full participants and the French Franc spent more time out of the snake than inside. Renewed impetus for greater co-operation began in 1978 when, at the Bremen conference of the European Council of Ministers, a timetable for monetary integration was discussed. These proposals subsequently formed the basis for the EMS, which came into existence on 13 March 1979.

The EMS has as its objective the creation of greater monetary stability in the EEC, and is generally seen as a key element in plans to improve the harmonization of national economic policies. It consists of three principal components: an exchange-rate structure, an intervention mechanism based on the European Currency Unit (ECU), and a system of credits for financing payments imbalances between members called the European Monetary Co-operation Fund (EMCF).[3] The exchange-rate structure consists of a 'currency grid' within which each member's currency is assigned a central rate against other EEC currencies, together with a permitted band of fluctuation of 2.25% either side of this central rate.[4] Central banks are obliged to keep their currencies within the margins of fluctuation but, as became clear during the operation of the snake, this creates an asymmetric burden of

---

1 The interested reader may consult Y. Ishiyama, 'The Theory of Optimum Currency Areas: A Survey', *IMF Staff Papers*, Vol. 22, 1975, pp. 344–83. For a discussion of the monetary union between the UK and Eire, see Whitaker, 'Monetary Integration: Reflections on Irish Experience', *Moorgate and Wall Street*, Autumn 1973.

2 The snake represented the set of closely linked EEC currencies which, under the pressure of market forces, was free to move up and down relative to the dollar in the 'tunnel' defined by the exchange-rate limits (see section III.8). The 'tunnel' disappeared in March 1973 when the EEC currencies engaged in a joint float against the dollar.

3 Full details of the EMS mechanisms are given in Commission of the European Communities, *European Economy*, July 1979. A useful exposition is given in: 'Intervention Arrangements in the European Monetary System', *BEQB*, June 1979. The arguments for monetary integration are set out by the then President of the European Commission, R. Jenkins, in 'European Monetary Union', *LBR*, No. 127, January 1978.

4 Exceptionally, the Italian Lira is permitted margins of 6% around its central rate.

obligation. The weak-currency country loses reserves and is always under pressure to adjust its internal policies to a greater extent than is the strong-currency country. In the EMS, an ingenious intervention mechanism has been introduced to try and eliminate the asymmetries of adjustment and therefore to enhance the convergence of exchange-rate and economic policies. The key to this is the ECU, a basket of EEC currencies which acts as numeraire for the exchange-rate mechanism. Using the currency-grid exchange rates, each currency is assigned its central value. From this basis, a divergence threshold is defined whereby a currency may not diverge from its central ECU rate by more than three-quarters of its divergence rate.[1] The point of these restrictions is that, in general, a currency will reach its divergence threshold before it reaches any of the bilateral intervention limits defined by the currency grid, and, once this occurs, there is a presumption that consultation will be initiated with *all* Community members to decide upon intervention policy, possible changes in central parities and any necessary internal policy measures. While the onus is on the country whose currency is divergent to alter its policies, the divergent currency could be either depreciating or appreciating. Thus, it is hoped that burdens of adjustment will be more equally shared within the Community and the asymmetries of bilateral intervention avoided.

Table 3.7 shows EMS exchange rates as of 7 April 1986, the date of the latest realignment of member currencies at the time of writing. From the establishment of the EMS to 7 April 1986 there have been nine realignments of member currencies, involving a total of 33 changes in the exchange rates of individual EEC currencies *vis-à-vis* the ECU. Of these changes, 14 were devaluations and 19 revaluations. This is in sharp contrast to the experience of the world as a whole during the Bretton Woods era, when virtually all exchange-rate changes were devaluations, generally precipitated by the weight of external pressures. Thus, on the basis of this admittedly crude statistic, the EMS must be judged at least a partial success in initiating a more equitable sharing of the burden of adjustment between deficit and surplus countries.

Besides acting as numeraire in the EMS, the ECU has an important role as an instrument of settlement between Community central banks and ultimately as the planned reserve asset of the Community. Member countries deposit 20% of their gold and gross dollar reserves with the EMCF on a

1   The maximum range of divergence for each currency is determined by $\pm 2.25 (1 - w_i)\%$, where w_i is the weight of that currency in the value of the ECU basket. When a currency diverges from its central rate it also pulls pulls the value of the ECU with it to some extent. The adjustment $(1 - w_i)$ reflects this fact and ensures that the divergence range reflects deviations of a currency from other individual currencies in the ECU basket. An adjustment is also made for the wider margins specially applicable to Italy and for the fact that sterling and the drachma, while components of the ECU, are not participants in the EMS adjustment mechanism. Any divergence of these currencies in excess of 2.25% is excluded when the value of the ECU is calculated for the purposes of the divergence indicator. The notional weight of sterling in the ECU at 7 April 1986 was 14.9%, giving a notional divergence range of $\pm 1.91\%$ for sterling against the ECU. The divergence threshold for sterling would be 75% of this, or $\pm 1.44\%$.

TABLE 3.7
EMS Exchange Rates, 7 April 1986

	ECU central rates (currency units per ECU)	Composition of the ECU:	
		Currency amounts	Percentage currency weights
Belgian franc	43.68	3.71	8.2
Danish krone	7.919	0.219	2.7
Deutschmark	2.138	0.719	32.1
French franc	6.963	1.31	19.1
Irish punt	0.7130	0.00871	1.2
Italian lira	1,496.00	140.00	10.1
Luxemburg franc	43.68	0.14	0.3
Netherlands guilder	2.409	0.256	10.2
Greek drachma	135.7	1.15	1.3
UK pound	0.6303	0.0878	14.9

Source: EEC Commission.

three-month renegotiable basis, and in return have access to a variety of credit facilities, to the total value of 25bn ECU, to finance payments imbalances within the Community and to support the currency grid.[1] Of this total, 14bn ECU has been allocated to short-term monetary support and the remainder to medium-term credit facilities.

Although the UK participated fully in the setting up of the EMS, and contributes to the ECU credit arrangements, it has thus far declined to join the exchange-rate mechanism of the EMS. At the time of the establishment of the EMS, academic and government opinion in the UK was almost universally hostile to the idea.[2] Drawing on the apparent lessons from the collapse of the par-value system, it was widely agreed that the substantial disparities of economic performance within the EEC made it unwise to fix exchange parities within the narrow limits set by the currency grid and the divergence indicators. Other factors which appeared to weigh specifically against UK membership included the possibility that oil-price changes would pose unacceptable strains on the EMS because of the divergence of interest between the UK as an oil exporter and other EEC countries as oil importers. In addition, there was thought to be a potential conflict between the Medium Term Financial Strategy (MTFS), which emphasized the money supply as an intermediate policy target, and the EMS, which emphasized the exchange rate as an

1   The gold contribution is valued at the average London fixing price during the six months prior to valuation, and the dollar portion is valued at the market rate of the two working days prior to valuation.

2   For a considered evaluation of the EMS, see 'The European Monetary System', *NIER*, February, 1979, pp. 5–12. Official viewpoints are contained in HC (1978–9) 60: *First Report of The Expenditure Committee*, 1978–9, para. 15; and in *The European Monetary System*, Cmnd. 7405, November 1978. See also previous editions of this book.

intermediate target. To date, these and other arguments have mitigated against UK membership.

It now seems clear, however, that the actual experience of the EMS as well as other factors have forced a reappraisal of the position of many commentators *vis-à-vis* UK membership. First, there is some very tentative evidence that EMS membership may have contributed to greater stability of member countries' exchange rates and may therefore have promoted some convergence of economic policies and performance within the system. The obverse of this is the general dissatisfaction which is felt by UK manufacturing industry in particular at the relative volatility of the sterling exchange rate.[1] The two specific concerns of North Sea oil and the MTFS also seem less important. With oil production now at its peak, there is the prospect of a steady depreciation of sterling in the coming years. Likewise, and as noted in section III.5, the MTFS has increasingly become an exchange-rate strategy as much as a money-supply strategy. The authorities are, in practice, already committed to a more active mangement of the exchange rate than was the case in the early 1980s.

Perhaps the most important factor is that it is now clear that there is a major difference between currency unification, the ostensible long-term aim of the EMS, and relative exchange-rate stability, which appears to be a practical short-term implication of the system. Any move towards currency unification clearly requires far-reaching changes in the sovereignty of each nation's monetary and fiscal policies, which may be neither practicable nor desirable and which are certainly not even in distant prospect. As argued in section III.5, however, there are some strong arguments for greater stability of exchange rates and there are equally powerful arguments suggesting small but useful gains from the co-ordination of international economic policy-making.[2] These considerations may suggest the desirability of UK membership of the EMS in the not-too-distant future, if not necessarily in the very near term.

III.8   The Reform of the International Monetary System

If the quarter century from 1945 had one dominant characteristic in the international economic arena, it was the integration of national commodity and capital markets into a unified and rapidly growing system of world trade and investment. A key role in this process was played by the international

---

1   On all these issues see HC (1984–5), 57-IV, *Thirteenth Report from The Treasury and Civil Service Committee*, 1984–5. While the Select Committee came down against UK membership of the EMS, it clearly felt that the balance of argument had moved towards membership since the previous Select Committee report on the subject. For an analysis of exchange-rate variability see 'The Variability of Exchange Rates: Measurement and Effects', *BEQB*, September 1984.

2   For a non-technical exposition of the issues involved, see M.J.Artis and S.Ostry, 'International Economic Policy Co-ordination', *Chatham House Papers No. 30*, Royal Institute of International Affairs, 1986.

financial rules established at the Bretton Woods conference of 1944, the supervisory institution of which is the International Monetary Fund (IMF).[1] The principal features of the Bretton Woods system were, in brief, its emphasis on mutual international co-operation and its creation of a system of fixed, but, in principle, adjustable exchange rates, the par-value system, together with the provision of temporary and conditional balance-of-payments finance by the IMF to supplement reserve media in the form of gold and foreign exchange.

Throughout the 1960s, it became clear that the Bretton Woods system suffered from potentially lethal inconsistencies and that, in particular, it placed the United States in an economic position which the European industrial nations became increasingly unable to accept. The first weakness was the general unwillingness of the main industrial countries to adjust par values in the face of obvious fundamental disequilibria until the tide of events, aided by currency speculation, forced governments into belated action. The case of sterling in the mid-1960s and of Germany and Japan in the late 1960s are obvious examples of this failure to use the par-value adjustment mechanism in the way originally intended by the architects of Bretton Woods. Related to this was the asymmetry between deficit and surplus countries, in that the pressure of reserve losses bore far more heavily on the deficit countries than did the converse phenomena of reserve gains in the surplus countries. In practice, the 'scarce currency' provisions of Article 7 of the IMF Agreement, which were meant to act as a sanction against persistent surplus countries, were never invoked.

The second weakness involved the supply of global reserve media, which under the IMF system consisted mainly of gold and foreign-exchange holdings, and in particular, of US dollars. The problem was that the supply of monetary gold depended on the vagaries of mining and speculative activity, and the supply of foreign exchange depended upon the balance-of-payments deficits of the US, which could prove to be temporary and, more important, unrelated to global reserve needs. In the light of this, there was considerable discussion in the 1960s of the alleged inadequacy of world reserves which took as its basis the observed decline in the ratio of world reserves to world imports, from a value of 68% in 1951 to one of 30% in 1969; the latter being less than the equivalent ratio for the depressed years of the 1930s. A difficulty with this type of discussion was that it failed to make clear that the demand for foreign-exchange reserves is a demand to finance balance-of-payments *disequilibria*, not a demand to finance the volume of trade. It failed, therefore, to recognize that the demand for reserve media will be smaller the more frequently exchange rates are adjusted in line with economic pressure, the more co-ordinated are national policies of demand management, and the greater the willingness of national governments and private capital markets to engage in mutual international borrowing and lending to finance payments imbalances. In the limit, for example, with a

---

1 Cf. R.N.Cooper, *The Economics of Interdependence* (McGraw Hill, 1968).

perfectly freely floating system of exchange rates, the demand for official reserves would be zero.

Finally, there was the so-called 'confidence' problem, which followed from the increasing degree of dependence of world reserve growth on foreign exchange in the form of the dollar and to a lesser extent sterling. The problem was simply that by 1964, the total of outstanding dollar liabilities exceeded the gold reserves of the United States and, from then on, this disparity between dollar liabilities and gold 'cover' increased. By December 1971, the US gold stock amounted to only 16% of the total of US short-term dollar liabilities held by overseas monetary authorities. *De facto* this meant that the dollar was no longer convertible into primary reserve assets and so with willingness to hold dollars in official reserves decreased and the danger of a dollar crisis increased. As R. Triffin pointed out in 1960, the gold-exchange standard contained an automatic self-destruct mechanism,[1] with the potential risk of a severe liquidity crisis in which dollar and sterling reserves were liquidated and destroyed, while a given total of gold reserves was redistributed between countries.

Throughout the 1960s, the strains inherent to the system were manifested in a variety of ways. Most significant, perhaps, were the *ad hoc* measures taken by the industrial countries to supplement the existing sources of balance-of-payments finance. At one level were the General Arrangements to Borrow (GAB), organized in October 1962, in which the Group of Ten countries (UK, France, Germany, Belgium, Netherlands, Italy, US, Canada, Sweden and Japan) agreed to lend their currencies to the IMF should the latter run short of one of their respective currencies. These arrangements have been renegotiated on several occasions, most recently in February 1983, and the amount of support now totals about SDR 17bn, with the Swiss National Bank added to the list of participants. Recent years have seen increasing use of the GAB, indeed 76% of the finance for the standby arrangements negotiated by the UK in 1976 come from eight of the GAB countries. A second important manifestation of strain related to the official price of gold and the clear possibility that its price might have to be increased to boost world reserves and improve the asset : liability ratio of the US. Attempts to stabilize the free-market price of gold by the major central banks which had begun in 1961 had to be abandoned in March 1968 following the loss of $3bn in monetary gold stocks, sold in an attempt to hold down the free-market price during the previous five months. The Washington Agreement of that time created a two-tier market for gold and effectively prevented national monetary authorities from using monetary gold stocks to finance payments disequilibria in the face of an ever-widening differential between the free market and the official price of gold. This two-tier system was abandoned in November 1973.

---

1   R. Triffin, *Gold and the Dollar Crisis* (Yale, 1960) and R. Triffin, 'Gold and the Dollar Crisis: Yesterday and Tomorrow', *Essays in International Finance*, No. 132, Princeton, December 1978.

The final, and some would say most significant, manifestation of strain was the increasing volume of speculative capital flows which from 1967 onwards repeatedly disrupted the working of foreign-exchange markets and threatened the parities of sterling, the deutschmark, the yen and the dollar. It became increasingly clear that the par-value system could not survive unless more effective methods for adjusting exchange rates in line with changing economic circumstances could be devised, and unless some means could be found for absorbing the increasing volume of short-term capital flows made possible by the growth of the Euro-dollar market. Not surprisingly, in the face of such obvious strains, many proposals for reforming the system were put forward during the 1960s. On the fundamental question of the adjustment mechanism, proposals ranged from the adoption of freely floating exchange rates to mechanisms for ensuring the gradual and automatic adjustment of par values to payments disturbances – the crawling-peg proposal. However, the response of the IMF to such proposals was lukewarm; a study by the executive directors concluded by reaffirming faith in the viability of the par-value system, with the only concessions to flexibility being the suggestion of wider margins of fluctuation around par values and the temporary abrogation of par-value obligations.[1]

By far the most important development of the 1960s was international agreement on the creation of a new reserve asset, the Special Drawing Right. The outcome of several years of discussion, this scheme came into operation in 1970.

Special Drawing Rights: SDRs are book entries in the Special Drawing Account of the IMF, by means of which countries can give and receive credit on a multilateral basis to finance balance-of-payments deficits. At the outset, SDRs were to be held only by those national monetary authorities which participated in the IMF arrangements and which agreed to accept the provisions of the SDR scheme. The total of SDRs is agreed collectively by the members of the IMF, so that the supply of this new reserve asset is agreed by international decision; the basis for their creation being the provision of an adequate, but not inflationary, long-term rate of growth of world reserves. SDRs are thus superior to gold and foreign exchange in that their supply is not arbitrary but is, in principle, the outcome of rational discussion. The total of SDRs is revised on a five-year basis, the last revision in January 1981 taking the cumulative allocation to SDR 21.4bn.[2] Each country is assigned a net cumulative allocation of SDRs, in proportion to its quota in the general account of the IMF, and can treat this allocation as 'owned reserves' to finance payments imbalances. A country in deficit, for example,

---

1 *The Role of Exchange Rates in the Adjustment of International Payment: A Report by the Executive Directors* (IMF, 1970).

2 The revised Articles of Agreement to incorporate SDRs may be found in the *IMF Annual Report* for 1968, or in the book by F. Machlup listed at the end of this chapter.

may use its SDR quota to purchase needed foreign exchange from other countries. One of the most ingenious features of the scheme is that utilization of a country's SDR quota is subject to the supervision of the IMF, the object being to ensure a balanced and widespread activation of the SDR facility. Use of SDRs was initially subject to several provisions, of which the most important was the reconstitution requirement, that a country's average holding over a period of five years must not fall below 30% of its net cumulative allocation, a measure designed to prevent the persistent, as distinct from temporary, financing of a deficit with SDRs.

The fundamental question surrounding the SDR has always been that of whether SDRs simply co-exist with other reserve assets or whether they are destined to replace gold and foreign exchange, or both, as the reserve base of the system. In the initial arrangements, SDRs were effectively a gold substitute, they had a gold guarantee and carried a low rate of interest on net holdings of 1.5%. On the understanding that the dollar is not devalued relative to gold, then SDRs were inferior to the dollar as a reserve asset because of their lower interest yield and lesser convenience of use. However, the dollar devaluations of 1971 and 1973 upset this situation, as did the resort to a general floating of the important currencies relative to gold during 1973. In response to these changing circumstances, a series of steps have been taken since 1974 to enhance the use of the SDR as a store of wealth and as a standard of value. The first step in July 1974 was to value SDRs in terms of a basket of sixteen currencies, rather than in terms of the US dollar alone, and to set the interest rate on net SDR holdings at 60% of an average of short-term interest rates in the financial centres of the five countries with the largest SDR holdings. These rules have been progressively revised since 1974, and the latest revision in 1981 set the SDR interest rate at 100% of the market rate and based the valuation basket on the currencies of the same five countries.[1] Steady progress has also been made to promote the SDR as the logical, principal reserve asset of the international monetary system. The most important changes came into effect with the adoption of the second amendment to the IMF Articles of Agreement in April 1978 (see below). These developments greatly extended the range of transactions for which SDRs may be employed by mutual agreement between countries without Fund authority, and reduced from 30% to 15% a country's minimum permitted holding of its SDR allocation over a five-year period. From 1 May 1981, this reconstitution requirement was eliminated.[2]

With effect from the Seventh General Increase in Quotas in 1980, members now contributed 25% of their additional quota in SDRs. Finally, a

---

1   For details, see the article, 'The New Method of Valuing Special Drawing Rights', *BEQB*, September 1974, and *IMF Annual Report*, 1981. For further analysis of the issues discussed below, see F. Hirsch, 'An SDR Standard: Impetus, Elements and Impediments', *Essays in International Finance*, No. 99, Princeton, 1975, and K. A. Chrystal, 'International Money and the Future of the SDR', *ibid*, No. 128, December 1978.

2   *IMF Annual Reports*, 1978 and 1981, Ch. 3, give relevant details.

multitude of developments have taken place, extending the right to hold SDRs to non-member organizations and legalizing the use of SDRs for currency swaps and forward transactions.[1]

Despite these developments aimed at enhancing the status of SDRs, the simple fact remains that SDRs only accounted for 4.6% of total world reserves (excluding gold) at end-1985 and only 2.7% when gold reserves are valued at their market price. At best, all the IMF can press for is a continued enhancement of SDRs relative to currencies. In this respect, the proposed Substitution Account at the IMF, in which members would deposit currency reserves in return for SDRs, could be an important means of increasing the weight of SDRs in world reserves. Whether the proposals will come to anything during 1986 is doubtful, unless there is a sustained collapse in the dollar relative to other currencies.[2]

The future of the SDR is thus, for the moment, uncertain, not least because the tremendous growth in world reserves and rapid inflation over the 1970s has created fears of an excess of world liquidity rather than a shortage. Even valuing gold at the old official price of $35 per ounce, world reserves increased by 42% between end-1979 and end-1985. Of course, after allowing for inflation, these nominal reserve gains look less impressive, as can be seen by comparing the value of world reserves relative to the value of world imports. In particular, if gold is valued at its market price rather than old official price, this ratio fluctuates narrowly around an average of 36% between 1973 and 1985. Indeed, on reflection, it is plausible to argue that the downfall of the Bretton Woods system proved to be its propensity to generate world liquidity, and from this stemmed the inflation tendencies of the 1970s and the collapse of the par-value system in 1973.

To the Second Amendment and beyond: Any illusions that the creation of the SDR had inaugurated a new period of stability for the par-value system was rudely shattered in August 1971, when the US government announced that the US dollar was no longer convertible into gold. The negotiations which followed this announcement set in train a review of the international monetary system under the direction of the so-called Committee of Twenty, but by the time of its final report in June 1974, its central concern with the maintenance of stable, but adjustable, par values had been overtaken by events.[3] Indeed, by April 1973, a succession of speculative crises meant that the exchange rates of all the major industrial countries were floating

---

1 *IMF Annual Report*, 1985. The total number of prescribed 'other holders' is currently fourteen.

2 Cf. 'The Proposed Substitution Account in the IMF', *MBR*, Winter 1979, and P.B.Kenen, 'The Analytics of a Substitution Account', *Banca Nazionale del Lavoro*, Quarterly Review, December 1981.

3 Cf. *IMF Survey*, June 1974, and J.Williamson, *The Failures of World Monetary Reform 1971–74* (Nelson, 1977).

independently of their par values, while in December 1973 the increase in the price of oil dealt the final blow to the Bretton Woods consensus on exchange rates. The fact that the oil producers could not rapidly convert export revenue into imports left them with little alternative but to invest in the industrialized countries, so returning on capital account the revenues extracted on current account. The oil surplus raised three problems for the stability of the international monetary system. First, the potential havoc that can be wrought in foreign-exchange markets if surplus oil funds are invested in liquid assets and switched between currencies in search of interest return and the expected capital gain from exchange-rate alterations. Secondly, and more important, is the fact that the attractiveness of different oil-importing nations as havens for OPEC investment need bear no relation to the way in which their respective current-account balances have been affected by oil-price increases. The possibility is, therefore, reinforced that individual countries will try to eliminate their deficits by deflation, trade restrictions or currency depreciation, the only outcome of which would be to depress world trade and output. Finally, there are the problems faced by the developing nations which have seen the real values of aid inflows virtually eliminated by the increase in oil prices, of which more will be said in section III.9 below.[1]

One response to these pressures has been to augment the resources at the disposal of the IMF, in fulfilment of its traditional function as provider of temporary balance-of-payments assistance. A number of temporary Financial Facilities were created from 1974 onwards, the latest example of which was the Supplementary Financing Facility which came into effect in February 1979 with resources of SDR 7.8bn which members could borrow for longer than the normally allowed periods. Of greater important have been the greatly increased levels of general quotas in the Fund which stood at SDR 39bn in 1976 and have been raised to SDR 90bn in the Eighth General Review which came into effect in 1984.

The second major response has been a thorough reappraisal of the exchange-rate mechanism of the international monetary system, culminating in the Second Amendment to the Articles of Agreement of the IMF in April 1978.

Without doubt, the most fundamental element is the amendment to Article 4 of the IMF Agreement. The main points of the new Article are as follows:[2] (i) a general return to stable but adjustable par values can take place with the support of an 85% majority in the IMF; (ii) such par values may not be expressed in terms of gold or other currencies but can be expressed in terms of SDRs, the margins of fluctuation around par values

---

1   For discussion of the adverse effects on developing countries and possible means of easing their problems, consult C.Michalopoulus, 'Financing Needs of Developing Countries: Proposals for International Action', *Essays in International Finance*, No. 110, Princeton, 1975.

2   The text of the proposed new Article 4 is contained in *IMF Survey*, 19 January 1976, pp. 20–1. Full details of the revised articles of agreement may be found in *The Second Amendment to the Articles of Agreement of the International Monetary Fund*, Cmnd. 6705 (HMSO, 1977).

remaining at ±2.25%; (iii) with the concurrence of the IMF, any country may abandon its par value and adopt a floating exchange rate; (iv) the exchange-rate management of a floating currency must be subject to IMF surveillance and must not be conducted so as to disadvantage other countries; (v) the agreed practices with respect to floating rates will operate until such time as a general return to par values is attained. In effect, these changes legitimize floating exchange rates within the framework of the IMF system and without any diminution of the powers of the IMF.

A second aspect of the Second Amendment dealt with the relative positions of SDRs and gold. We have commented above on the attempts to enhance the reserve status of the SDR; the associated measures to demonetize gold were equally significant. In particular, the official price of gold was abolished and members were no longer allowed to use gold to make their general quota contributions. Furthermore, members were again allowed to trade in gold at gold-market prices.[1]

The reforms embodied in the Second Amendment are undoubtedly important and reflect well on the IMF as an effective forum for international co-operation. However, they fall short of the ideals outlined by the C-20 and their long-run effects may be in doubt.[2] Of particular concern have been the large swings in nominal exchange rates that have occurred since 1978, swings well in excess of those which might be predicted by reference to purchasing-power parity, imperfect indicator though that may be. The volatility of capital flows at a time when capital restrictions in the UK and Japan were relaxed, the differing success of governments in controlling inflation, the structural problems induced by the OPEC cartel, and nominal interest-rate structures which have not reflected inflationary expectations, no doubt have each played a role in the appreciation of the dollar and the decline of the yen since 1980. These swings have been viewed with sufficient concern to result in a statement of objectives following the 1982 Versailles summit of world leaders which emphasized, *inter alia*, the need to avoid competitive exchange-rate policies and the legitimacy of exchange-market intervention to avoid disorderly market conditions.[3] The IMF response to exchange-rate volatility has been to emphasize the role of surveillance with the purpose of identifying unwelcome economic developments including exchange-rate practices, which arise from inappropriate economic policies such as fiscal

1 At a meeting in Jamaica in 1974, it was agreed that the Fund divest itself of one-third of its stock of gold, with the profits on the free-market sale of one half of this amount allocated to a special Trust Fund to provide balance-of-payments assistance on concessionary terms to very poor countries.

2 For somewhat jaundiced views of the Jamaica Agreement, see Bernstein *et al.*, 'Reflections on Jamaica', *Essays in International Finance*, No. 115, Princeton, 1976, and A.Kafka, 'The IMF: Reform Without Reconstruction?', *Essays in International Finance*, No. 118, Princeton, 1976.

3 Cf. P.B.Kenen (ed.) 'From Rambouillet to Versailles: A Symposium', *Essays in International Finance*, No. 149, Princeton, 1982, and R.M.Dunn Jr., 'The Many Disappointments of Flexible Exchange Rates', *Essays in International Finance*, No. 154, 1983.

expansion or exchange-market intervention. However, it is doubtful whether this procedure can ensure greater harmonization of domestic economic policies – divergences between which are a powerful source of exchange-rate movements. It is for this reason that a most significant development in 1985 was the September accord of the Group of Five finance ministers to engage in a co-ordinated policy to reduce the value of the US dollar. This was an explicit recognition that exchange-rate levels cannot be determined by the independent action of single national governments but require joint action if orderly conditions are to prevail. Clearly, there is little prospect at present of a return to stable par values, whatever mechanisms may be invoked to ensure this adjustment to underlying circumstances. For the foreseeable future, the world will have to cope with managed flexibility. Relative to the problems associated with the world debt situation, however, those of exchange-rate management seem relatively innocuous.

III.9   World Debt and Bank Lending

A considerable degree of concern has been expressed in recent years over a further consequence of the oil price shocks, namely the implications for the international debt structure of non-oil-exporting, less developed countries (non-oil LDCs) and the associated risks of an international banking crisis. This is an important issue but one which should be kept in its proper perspective.

It should be remembered, at the outset, that the efficient allocation of resources on a world scale will generally require international lending and borrowing. Countries with a surplus of savings will find it advantageous to lend to countries with a savings deficiency through the medium of international capital flows. In the postwar world, the major savings-deficient nations have, of course, been the LDCs. The conditions for the international flow of capital to be sustainable are essentially twofold: the borrowing must be used to build up productive capacity in the debtor nation, with a gross rate of return on investment at least equal to the gross cost of borrowing; and, the debtor country must be in a position to earn the foreign exchange required to service and repay the debt. This transfer requirement does not imply that the growth of debt-financed capacity be restricted to the direct production of traded goods, but simply that the traded-goods sector expand at a rate consistent with the rate of foreign borrowing. In fact, it is possible to identify for any country a set of circumstances which determines its capacity to accumulate external debt in a sustainable fashion. The simplest index of this capacity is measured by a ratio of foreign debt to gross domestic product. It may be shown that this sustainable ratio will be higher the greater the ratio of the trade surplus to national product, the greater the rate of growth of national product, and the lower the gross interest and amortization cost of borrowing. A country which is developing rapidly will enjoy a higher equilibrium debt : income ratio, and its total debt can increase over time at the rate of growth of income without any fear of insolvency.[1] The picture is complicated slightly by capital-market imperfections, which mean that the interest rate at which any country can borrow is likely to rise with the debt : income ratio, so that a country enjoying a higher elasticity of supply of finance will, *ceteris paribus*, enjoy a higher equilibrium debt : income ratio. It is important to remember that sustainable debt : income ratios will be as varied as the circumstances which determine the respective country's international credit rating, capacity to generate a net export surplus and rate of economic growth.

One final point concerning the foreign debt mechanism is worth noting before we turn to the events of the 1970s and this concerns the potential volatility of actual debt : income ratios. The problem is that when the actual debt : income ratio of a country diverges from the equilibrium value, a process of cumulative divergence is set in train, so driving the debt : income ratio further from the equilibrium level unless corrective action is taken. For example, a reduction in net exports below the level required to service the current debt : income ratio requires recourse to further foreign borrowing to meet the foreign-exchange shortfall.[2] The increase in borrowing adds to the servicing burden and creates the need for even greater borrowing, and so the process of cumulative divergence is reinforced. Conversely, the effects of an improvement in the net export position will permit a cumulative contraction of debt. Of course, in practice, such movements are likely to be halted by remedial structural changes but, nevertheless, debt : income ratios are likely to show significant short-term instability.

We turn now to the practical implications of this analysis. Throughout the postwar period to 1970, the LDCs had been net importers of foreign capital obtained primarily through direct foreign investment, official aid and official credits transferred through institutions such as the World Bank. The total foreign debt of LDCs increased against the backcloth of steadily expanding world trade and production, without servicing problems apart from those associated with export earnings instability in selected countries. The oil-price shocks of 1974 and 1979 changed this situation rather drastically, creating a rapid growth in LDC debt and simultaneously reducing their capacity to borrow in a sustainable fashion. For non-oil LDCs as a whole, the ratio of outstanding debt to exports rose from 1.15 in 1973 to 1.40 in 1982, with a particularly sharp rise occurring after 1979. However, the

---

1 Thus, for example, a country exporting (net) 20% of its output, growing at 3% per annum and paying 10% gross on its foreign debt, would have a sustainable debt : income ratio of 2.85. Throughout the 1970s, the actual debt : income ratio of non-oil LDCs fluctuated between the values of one and five. The original statement of this condition is contained in E. Domar, *Essays on the Theory of Economic Growth* (Oxford, 1957), Chapter 6.

2 We exclude here any temporary respite gained by drawing upon foreign-exchange reserves. For most LDCs, this option is of negligible importance. Instability depends upon the gross interest rate exceeding the growth rate of income in the LDCs. The average interest rate on total LDC debt averaged 6% in 1976/9 but rose to 10.25% in 1981. The median growth rates in non-oil LDCs are 5% and 3% for the same two periods. Cf. IMF, *World Economic Outlook* (1983), Appendix B, Table 2.

aggregate figures conceal the extent to which external debt is concentrated in a small number of large and relatively developed countries of Europe, the Far East and Latin America, each enjoying good links with the international capital market. Taking the twenty largest borrowers (accounting for 85% of total debt to private creditors in 1982 but only 50% of non-oil LDC exports), we find the ratio of debt to exports rising from 1.50 in 1973 to 2.00 in 1982.[1] The connection with the oil-price increase has both demand and supply aspects. On the demand side, the oil-price shock had two adverse effects on the LDCs: it directly increased oil import bills, and indirectly reduced export revenues as the effect of the oil-price-induced recession in the industrialized countries worked its way through to lower export volumes and worsening terms of trade.[2] In these circumstances, rapid structural adjustment was not to be expected, and between 1979 and 1982 the non-oil LDCs accumulated trade deficits of $257bn and current-account deficits of $344bn. By contrast, the corresponding figures for the industrial countries were $136bn and $50bn respectively. The associated increase in demand to borrow was readily satisfied due to supply-side changes in international credit markets which involved an increasing role for commercial banks in the industrial countries. BIS figures show that the gross foreign liabilities of commercial banks within the reporting area increased sixty-fold between 1973 and 1979, and that an increasing proportion of the lending was in the form of short-term 'roll-over' credits often with a floating interest rate. In 1982, some 30% of non-oil LDC borrowing was of this nature. The pressures for commercial bank lending to LDCs are not difficult to identify. The recession reduced the demand for credit within the industrial countries at the same time as their banking systems were receiving large flows of funds from the OPEC producers. Profit-seeking commercial banks were more than willing to lend to credit-worthy LDCs on competitive terms which appeared to minimize risks, for each bank taken by itself.

The denouement came in 1982, as the full effects of the decline in sustainable debt:income ratios became clear. The combination of world recession (world trade volume fell by 2.3% in 1982) and high interest rates on commercial loans put an increasing number of LDCs in a position in which they could not meet the repayment schedules on a debt burden which was increasingly sensitive to short-term changes in interest rates. In quick succession, a small number of major borrowers, such as Mexico and Brazil, and for different reasons, Poland, announced their inability to meet immediate obligations. This naturally raised questions that bankers, in general, would prefer not to be asked. Was default a possibility? If so, would any commercial bank find that bad debts exhausted its capital resources? Indeed so, for some banks found themselves with such debts amounting to 1.5 to 2 times their capital reserves. Would the appropriate national central bank act as lenders

---

1   IMF, *Annual Report* (1983), p. 32.

2   For example, the real export value of primary commodities fell by 24% between January 1980 and January 1982.

of the last resort in order to prevent a cumulative collapse in the credit structure, and what role might the IMF play in supporting this delicate situation?

At this stage, it seems reasonable to report that the serious danger of a collapse of the international capital market has passed. In the short term, LDCs have drawn on reserves where possible but otherwise turned to the IMF for direct finance of their current-account deficits. However, IMF resources are limited, even after the Eighth General Review on quotas and the additional GAB arrangements which have been discussed in the previous section. Moreover, financing the problem does not deal with the structural changes necessary to raise sustainable debt:income ratios. In general terms, a resolution requires that the net export-earning capacity of debtor nations be increased while, at the same time, their debt is rescheduled onto a longer time-scale, cutting the amortization burden and reducing sensitivity to short-term interest-rate change. The IMF has made significant efforts to impose import-reducing policies on countries in difficulty, while at the same time making its financial support conditional on continued lending by commercial banks in the industrialized countries. Fund-assisted stabilization programmes of this kind resulted in the rescheduling of 21% of LDC banking debt in 1984.[1] It is vitally important that the flow of credit should continue, for fear of precipitating a default at a time when IMF resources are severely stretched. In the longer term, relief will come from more rapid world growth and a decline in nominal interest rates, although it may take several years for this to work to the benefit of the debtor nations. There can be no question that the present decline in the oil price, and the momentum this will give to world trade and production, is the most important event raising the ability of LDCs to repay external debt – even though major oil-exporting debtors such as Mexico will be adversely affected.

Further indication of the continuing concern about LDC debt to Western banks is provided by the so-called Baker initiative, which focused upon the ten major debtor countries of Latin America (and five others) and combined an emphasis on more rapid economic reforms with an increased flow of private and official capital to support this development. Hopefully it will continue the trend towards enhanced balance-of-payments performance of these countries, which is the only long-term solution to their debt problems.

REFERENCES AND FURTHER READING

Sir Alec Cairncross (ed.), *Britain's Economic Prospects Reconsidered* (Allen and Unwin, 1971).

Sir Alec Cairncross, *Control of Long-Term Capital Movements* (Brookings Institution, 1973).

---

1 Cf. T.Killick (ed.), *Adjustment Financing in the Developing World* (IMF/ODA, 1982). IMF, *Annual Report* (1985), p. 60.

R.E.Caves and Associates, *Britain's Economic Prospects* (Brookings Institution and Allen and Unwin, 1968).

R.E.Caves and L.B.Krause (eds.), *Britain's Economic Performance* (Brookings Institution, 1980).

H.G.Grubel, *International Economics* (Irwin, 1977).

H.G.Johnson and J.E.Nash, *UK and Floating Exchanges*, Hobart Paper, 46, Institute of Economic Affairs, 1969.

R.B.Johnston, *The Economics of the Euro-Market* (Macmillan, 1983).

C.P.Kindleberger and P.H.Lindert, *International Economics* (7th edition, Irwin, 1982).

F.Machlup, *Remaking the International Monetary System* (Committee for Economic Development and Johns Hopkins, 1968).

R.L.Major, *Britain's Trade and Exchange Rate Policy* (Heinemann, 1979).

C.McMahon, *Sterling in the Sixties* (Oxford University Press, 1964).

J.E.Meade, *UK, Commonwealth and Common Market: A Reappraisal*, Hobart Paper, 17, Institute of Economic Affairs, 1970.

R.L.Miller and J.B.Wood, *Exchange Control for Ever* (Institute of Economic Affairs, London, 1979).

W.B.Reddaway, *Effects of UK Direct Investment Overseas: An Interim Report* (Cambridge University Press, 1967); *Final Report* (Cambridge University Press, 1968).

B.Tew, *International Monetary Cooperation, 1945–70* (Hutchinson, 1970).

B.Tew, *The Evolution of the International Monetary System, 1945–77* (Hutchinson, 1977).

S.J.Wells, *British Export Performance* (Cambridge University Press, 1964).

J.Williamson, *The Failure of World Monetary Reform, 1971–74* (Nelson, 1977).

Official Publications

Bank of England Quarterly Bulletin.

Commission of the European Communities, *European Economy*, Brussels (quarterly).

Economic Trends (regular analyses of balance of payments in March, June, September and December issues).

IMF *Annual Report* and IMF *Survey* (twice monthly).

Report of Committee on the Working of the Monetary System, Radcliffe Report, Cmnd. 827 (1959).

British Business (weekly) (previously *Trade and Industry*). Department of Trade and Industry, *UK Balance of Payments* (Pink Book annual), CSO.

4

Industry
J.R.Cable

I   INDUSTRIAL PERFORMANCE AND POLICY
I.1   The Industrial Decline of Britain

The beginnings of Britain's decline relative to other industrial countries can be seen as far back as the latter part of the nineteenth century, when competition began to be felt in key, staple industries, like textiles, chemicals and iron and steel, from the newly industrialized countries of that era, in particular Germany and America. However the full consequences for Britain's international standing in world trade and living standards have not been felt until the period after the Second World War. From the end of the war until the early 1970s all the industrialized countries expanded more or less continuously, as did most sectors within them, albeit at different and fluctuating rates. The problem for Britain in this period was that, while our industry continued to grow in line with an historic trend rate of 2–3% per year, it failed to match the much faster growth achieved by our main competitors. The first column of table 4.1 gives some comparative figures for the latter part of this period, from 1960 to 1973.

TABLE 4.1
Growth of Industrial Production, Selected Countries, 1960–85

	Annual average increase (%)		
	1960–73	1973–85	1960–85
UK	3.0	0.6	1.9
USA	4.9	2.3	3.6
Japan	12.6	3.4	8.2
France	5.9	1.0	3.5
West Germany	5.5	1.1	3.4
OECD average	5.7	1.9	3.8

Source: Derived from *NIER*.

After 1973 all countries grew much more slowly (table 4.1, column 2), with sharp recessions after the oil 'shocks' of 1974 (when crude oil prices rose by 254%) and 1978–80 (when the oil price rose a further 140%), during one or both of which industrial output actually fell in absolute terms in all countries. Over this period British industrial performance was affected not only by the worldwide change in relative fuel prices, but also by our entry into the EEC, and by the fortuitous and extraordinarily rapid growth of North Sea oil and gas production (table 4.2), at a time of unprecedentedly high oil prices (up to 1986). Despite the oil bonus, however, Britain still managed only to bump along the bottom, relative to our major trading competitors, and our performance relative to OECD countries as a whole continued to decline (figure 4.1). In 1983 Britain became a net importer of manufactures for the first time since the Industrial Revolution, and by 1984 ranked only thirteenth in terms of national income per head among 18 industrial economies, just in front of Italy

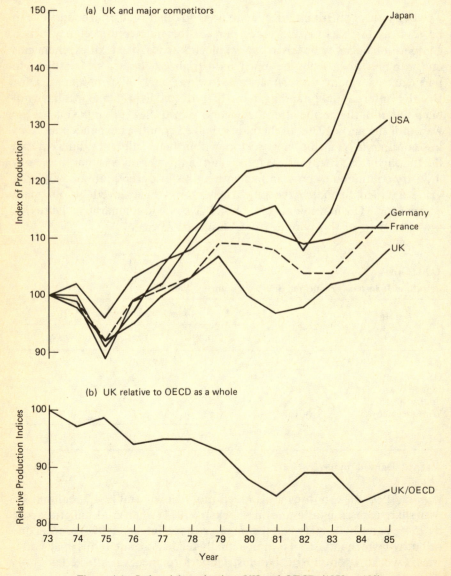

Figure 4.1 Industrial production, UK and OECD (1973 = 100)

and Spain, with Ireland, Greece and Portugal bringing up the rear (table 4.3).

Output series for different sectors and industries after 1973 are given in the Statistical Appendix table A–8, while table A–9 shows how the industrial composition of the economy has changed over the longer period from 1960 to 1985 as a result of differing sectoral growth rates. Two main points stand out. The first is the more than doubling of energy output since 1975. This again reflects the impact of North Sea oil, production of which rose from only 1.6m tonnes in that year to the levels shown in table 4.2; coal production, the other main activity in the energy sector, fluctuated at around 125m tonnes up to 1982, before falling drastically to only 51.2m tonnes in 1984 (due to pit closures and the effects of the miners' strike), and recovering to 94.1m tonnes in 1985. By 1984 oil and gas production contributed no less than £16.2bn to GDP, or 5.8% of the total, which is nearly a quarter of that accounted for by the whole of manufacturing industry in the same year. It also generated approximately ten per cent of total exports.

TABLE 4.2
North Sea Oil Production and Revenues 1978–90

(a) *Production (m. tonnes)*

	Outturn		Forecast [1]
1978	54.0	1986	127.5
1979	77.9	1987	120.0
1980	80.5	1988	112.5
1981	89.4	1989	105.0
1982	103.2	1990	100.0
1983	114.7		
1984	125.9		
1985	127.4		

(b) *Revenues[2] (£bn, current prices)[3]*

1983/4	84/5	85/6	86/7	87/8	88/9	89/90
9	12	11.5	6	4	4	4

Source: Treasury Statement on North Sea Revenue, 1986 Budget.

Notes: 1 Figure shown is mid point of range of estimated output.
2 Total government revenue from the North Sea consists of royalties, petroleum revenue tax, and corporation tax. In 1985/6 these contributed 18%, 56% and 26% respectively to total revenues as shown.
3 The price of oil is assumed to be $15 per barrel from the second quarter of 1986 to end-1987, and thereafter to rise broadly in line with inflation.

Secondly, the statistics reveal an overall absolute decline in both the manufacturing and the construction sectors, where output has fallen substantially over the period. The most dramatic falls in both sectors occurred between 1979 and 1981, over the first two years of the first Thatcher government, with output reductions of 14.1% and 14.9% for manufacturing and construction respectively. Despite subsequent recovery at around 2.5% per annum (which the government optimistically refers to as years of 'continuous boom'), manufacturing output in 1985 remained a full 5% below its 1979 level, and 8.9% below the level of 1973; for construction the comparable figures are 5.4% and 18.4% respectively. As a result of this decline, manufacturing industry now contributes less than a quarter of GDP, compared with nearly 32% previously, and construction less than 6% compared with 7.6% in 1973 (see Statistical Appendix, table A–9).

TABLE 4.3

International Living Standards in 1980 and 1984 (USA = 100)[1]

	Real, 1980	*GDP per head, 1984*
USA	100	100
Canada	100	95
Japan	71	75
Belgium	76	74
Denmark	79	81
France	79	75
Germany	82	79
Greece	41	38
Ireland	44	45
Italy	63	57
Netherlands	75	69
Spain	51	52
UK	66	66

Source: P. Hill, *Real Gross Product in OECD Countries and Associated Purchasing Power Parities*, OECD Working Paper 17, December 1984.

Note: 1 Figures based on purchasing-power parities. Comparisons based on official exchange rates only should not be used. See also I.B. Kravis *et al.*, 'Real GDP for more than one hundred countries', *EJ*, June 1978.

At the time of writing, the government is playing down the decline of manufacturing, pointing to the growing importance of the service sector as a source of new jobs, and stressing that a shift in the balance of production from primary and secondary activities (i.e. agriculture, mining, manufacturing, etc) to tertiary activities (like services) is perfectly normal as economies become more advanced. The government also asserts that there will be an automatic resurgence of manufacturing when, in the foreseeable future, oil production ceases. Severe doubts have been expressed, however, by independent observers, representatives of industry and, amongst others, a House of Lords select committee.[1] There are at least five major problems with the government's position.

Firstly, while the share of services in GDP has in fact increased in most of the leading industrial nations over the last twenty years (with the notable exception of Japan), it is questionable whether services will be dominant in the long run, not least because of a tendency for luxury 'service functions' increasingly to be embodied in tangible goods (e.g. as car purchase and

---

1 House of Lords, Report from the Select Committee on Overseas Trade, HMSO, 238–I, July 1985.

private motoring replace commercial transport services).[1] In any case, the *relatively* faster growth of services is generally supposed to accompany a still-expanding or at least static manufacturing sector, not an absolute decline in manufacturing output such as Britain has seen.

Secondly, while the service sector as a whole is very large (accounting for 56.5% of GDP in 1984), it is also very heterogeneous, with a mixed growth record. Over the last ten years, productivity in services as a whole rose more slowly than in manufacturing or the economy at large, and rapid growth of output has been confined to relatively small sectors, in particular banking and finance etc. with an annual rate of growth of 5.7% compared with distribution, hotels and catering (0.4%), transport and communications (1.3%), and public administration, health, education, R & D, and cultural, recreational and other services (1.7%).

Thirdly, as the government's critics have pointed out, the service sector could not be counted on to make up for further serious losses in manufacturing (and petroleum) exports, and avert balance-of-payments problems as the oil runs out. Only about 20% of services are directly tradeable, and while manufacturing generates only a quarter of GDP, it accounts for around 40% of exports (oil and gas, as we have seen, contributing a further 10%). Overall a 3% rise in service exports is needed to offset a 1% fall in those of manufacturing. Moreover, in the ten years to 1983 the UK actually lost more ground in the world service market than in the world manufacturing market, our share falling by 3.4 percentage points (to 7.3%) in services, compared with 1.3 percentage points (to 6.2%) in manufacturing.

Fourthly, while it is true that the service sector has been the major source of new jobs in the recent past, these have so far been both insufficient in number and of the wrong type to make up for job losses in manufacturing and construction. Thus, employment in services increased by 1.3m between 1974 and 1984, but most of the addition consisted of female part-time workers (+36%) rather than full-time workers (+3–4%), whereas the 3m or so jobs lost elsewhere have been primarily those of full-time male workers.

Finally, the government has yet to explain the mechanism through which an 'automatic', self-correcting resurgence of manufacturing will occur, especially if there is meanwhile further erosion of its assets and capacity (which fell by 24% between 1980 and 1983), and of its technological base.

Despite the current government's optimism, it is difficult to avoid the conclusion that Britain faces extremely serious industrial problems, the full severity of which remains masked by the presence of oil.

I.2   Causes and Remedies

The search for explanations of Britain's economic decline has produced a

---

1 J.Gershuny and J.Miles, *The New Service Economy* (Francis Pinter, 1985). See also G.F.Ray, 'Productivity in Services', *NIER*, February 1986, and *BEQB*, 'Services in the UK Economy', September 1985.

formidable catalogue of ills: underinvestment (gross fixed capital formation in Britain was only 18.6% of GDP from 1973 to 1982, compared with 34.4% in Japan, 22.4% in France, 22.6% in Germany, but only 18.8% in the USA); inefficient use of new capital (Britain's incremental capital/output ratio in the period 1973–79 was around 5, compared with 3.1 in Germany, 1.7 in the USA and 2.6 in Canada);[1] low productivity growth and high growth of wage costs (table 4.4); inadequate education and training; poor management; intransigent trade unions; bad industrial relations; strikes; poor product design and service arrangements; failure to meet delivery dates; inadequacies in the system of financing industry; technological backwardness, with underinvestment in R and D, too much concentration of scientific effort on military defence projects, and failure vigorously to pursue the commercial exploitation of new inventions; 'excessive' public-sector development at the expense of marketed goods; and so on. However, major and largely unanswered questions remain over which of all these, and others, represent fundamental underlying causes, and which may be merely symptoms of other more deep-rooted problems.

TABLE 4.4
Productivity and Wage Costs, 1965–84

| | *Annual average growth of:* | | | |
| | *Output per person-hour in manufacturing* | | *Wage costs per unit of output in manufacturing* | |
	1965–80	*1980–84*	*1965–80*	*1980–84*
UK	2.9	5.1	8.7	4.7
USA	3.1	4.2	3.5	1.7
Japan	8.5	2.9	5.1	1.5
France	5.4	3.8	5.5	8.0
W. Germany	4.6	3.3	3.5	0.7

Source: Derived from *NIER*.

Further questions arise over what role the government could and should play in promoting industrial development or, as in Britain's case, reversing the decline. Unlike some of our competitors, notably Japan and France, Britain has never had an industrial policy in the sense of sectoral output targets, or even a list of priority industries towards which the government would assist the mobilization of resources. In fact it can be argued that there has never been a coherent overall approach to industrial policy – only a series of individual strands, introduced at different times, and addressing specific issues or problems. In the remaining sections of this chapter we consider in turn a number of these policy strands. Most can be rationalized as intervention to correct for various kinds of 'market failure' – market instability, monopoly divergences between public and private returns, information failure, etc – though it should not be supposed that this is so

---

1   OECD, *Economic Surveys 1984/85: United Kingdom*, January 1985.

because of any systematic and sustained attempt to develop an overall policy on this principle. Finally, in section VII we shall consider briefly whether, in the light of past policy and present circumstances, there may be a case for an alternative kind of industrial strategy.

II   AGRICULTURAL DEVELOPMENT AND POLICY[1]

As in other developed countries, agricultural production in the UK has been maintained and developed since the Second World War at a higher level than would otherwise be the case, given the costs of domestic production and world price levels for agricultural products. Different methods of agricultural support were in force before and after Britain's entry into the EEC in 1973. It is primarily for this reason that table 4.5 shows agricultural developments separately for the two periods. Because agricultural harvests are subject to considerable annual fluctuation, the levels of output and inputs are shown as three-year averages centred on the years 1961, 1973 and 1983. The statistics show that production has risen substantially faster in agriculture than in other production industries over the period as a whole. They also reveal a big increase in the mechanization of production and capital intensity over the period, with a halving of total employment and an 80% expansion of the capital stock. The resulting increase in labour productivity is very much greater than in most other industries. However, the reduction in employment, and the growth in output, capital employed and productivity all slowed after 1973. In part this reflects the very much smaller emphasis on increasing efficiency and productivity in agriculture (as

TABLE 4.5
Agricultural Development 1961–83

| | 1960/62 | 1972/4 | 1982/84 | Annual average growth (%) | | |
				1961–73	1973–83	1961–83
Index of real output (1980 = 100)	62.6	87.2	112.1	2.8	2.5	2.7
Employment (000s)	666	403	328	−4.1	−2.0	−3.2
Capital stock (£bn at 1980 replacement cost)	13.8[1]	20.6	24.8	3.4[2]	1.9	2.7
Index of labour productivity (1980 = 100)	32.0	73.5	116.2	7.2	4.7	6.0

Source: *AAS* and *NIE*.

Notes: 1 Estimate.   2 1964–1973.

1   See also 'The Common Agricultural Policy', *MBR*, Winter, 1984; 'Agriculture and its Finances', *MBR*, Autumn/Winter 1982; A.M.El-Agraa, 'The CAP: Theory and Practice', *Economic Review*, September and November 1984; M.J.Roarty, 'The EEC Common Agricultural Policy and its Effects on Less-Developed Countries', *NWBQR*, February 1985; and J.K.Bowers and Paul Cheshire, *Agriculture, the Countryside and Land Use* (Methuen, 1983).

opposed to price-support) under the EEC's agricultural policy, as compared with the previous UK scheme.

Under the pre-1973 system, farmers received assistance in two main ways: deficiency payments, and direct grants for capital investment and farm improvement. Under the *deficiency payments scheme*, agricultural products sold in the UK at world price levels, with more or less free access to the UK market for foreign producers, and some preferential treatment for Commonwealth producers. Where these prices were below the level of a guaranteed price, set by the government to encourage a certain level of home production taking production costs and farm incomes into account, the deficiency payment received by farmers was equal to the difference. Thus the UK maintained open markets to foreign producers, and consumers enjoyed the relatively low world food price-levels. At the same time, home production was encouraged and farm incomes were stabilized and controlled. The cost to the Exchequer varied inversely with the level of world prices. Early experience of an open-ended support scheme, with no upper limit on quantities produced at home and hence on the liability of the Exchequer, led to the introduction of 'standard quantities' for most products in the early 1960s; thereafter the guaranteed price fell on a sliding scale as these were exceeded. The farm *capital grants scheme* provided assistance for investment in buildings and machinery and also projects such as land drainage, hill-land improvements and remodelling works for farm amalgamations. The rates of grant-aid tended to differ among projects, although steps were taken in 1970 towards a comprehensive scheme with a basic rate of 30%. Some subsidies were also offered for current expenditures, e.g. those associated with the use of fertilizers and lime. The guaranteed prices, grants and subsidies were reviewed annually. In the years up to 1973 about 60% of total support took the form of capital grants and subsidies, and 40% went on deficiency payments.

Through this policy the government was able not only to maintain domestic production at a higher level than would have been achieved without official support (assuming other countries continued to support their own farmers), but also to influence the composition of agriculture and the efficiency of the industry. Especially in the later years of the policy, guaranteed prices were manipulated to produce a selective rather than a general expansion. Similarly, grants and subsidies were used to bring about desired changes in the structure of the industry and to mechanize and modernize it. The developments up to 1973 shown in table 4.5 were thus very much influenced by government policy.

Since 1973 agricultural support has come under the Common Agricultural Policy (CAP) of the EEC. The objectives are in principle very similar to those which governed previous UK policy. Thus Article 39 of the Treaty of Rome speaks of securing increases in agricultural efficiency, stabilizing agricultural markets, guaranteeing regular supplies, and ensuring reasonable prices to consumers and fair living standards for the agricultural population. The two policies are also similar in that support to farmers comes partly in the form of price guarantees and partly in capital and current grants or subsidies.

There are two major differences, however. Under the CAP the food prices paid by consumers reflect not world prices but EEC production costs. In general these are very much higher: 50–60% higher in the production of pork, wheat and barley, for example; roughly twice as high in the case of beef, maize, olive-oil and rape-seed; and around four times as high for butter and powdered milk production.[1] Secondly, very little of the total support under CAP is devoted to improving efficiency rather than to maintaining prices: a mere 3.5% of total expenditure over the past three years,[2] compared with the 60% or so previously mentioned as going on grants and subsidies under the old UK system. This represents a failure of the EEC to implement policy initiatives which as long ago as 1968 were intended to shift the emphasis of CAP away from price support, and towards structural reform.

The CAP is administered by the European Agricultural Guidance and Guarantee Fund (EAGGF). Grant aid is supervised by the Guidance section, though grants are actually paid out on its behalf by each national government. Price support is managed by the Guarantee section of the EAGGF. The aim is to bring about free intra-Community trade in agricultural products, with uniform prices among the members and a common external tariff. 'Target prices' are negotiated for most products which make domestic production profitable. To maintain market prices at or close to this level there is a system of variable levies on imports from the outside world, broadly designed to equalize the supply price of foreign products (including transport costs) and the target price. In addition, there is provision for support buying of unsold produce when prices fall below an 'intervention-price' level. In some cases, such as grain, the intervention price is set close to the target price. In certain other cases, however, such as fruit and vegetables, prices can fall significantly before support buying occurs.

Because of the difference in the pre-1973 and CAP systems, Britain experienced severe adjustment problems of joining the EEC. One arose from the need to raise consumer price levels from world to EEC levels. Food prices rose very rapidly after entry, at a rate of 19.5% per annum in the five years up to 1977, and nearly twenty per cent more than other retail prices over the whole period. Subsequently the index of food prices has risen less than prices in general, suggesting that the once-for-all adjustment was by then complete. A second, continuing problem arises from the structure of UK agriculture. As we have seen, the pre-1973 system did not seek to bring about a high degree of self-sufficiency in agricultural products in the UK. Indeed it to some extent encouraged Britain's relatively large import trade

1 Eurostat, *Yearbook of Agricultural Statistics*, 1981. The relevant table has not been published in more recent issues.

2 See European Commission, *General Reports on the Activities of the European Communities* (annual editions).

with non-EEC countries, and left the UK with a small agricultural sector, by European standards. Under the CAP, the imports became subject to levies, while there was only a comparatively small agricultural sector to benefit from the largesse of its other provisions. Since 1973 the degree of UK self-sufficiency in food products has increased sharply in some areas (at the expense of some Commonwealth and Third World countries), but it remains well below the EEC average for fresh fruit, sugar and butter and, to a lesser extent, cheese, rye and meat (table 4.6), and there remains a very large deficit, from Britain's point of view, on the agricultural account. This is the overwhelming reason for our being, with Germany, the principal net contributors to the overall EEC budget. Since 1980 the British government has been pressing both for greater control over the rapidly escalating costs of the CAP, and for budgetary reforms to ensure a 'broad balance' between national inpayments and outpayments.

TABLE 4.6

Degree of Self-Sufficiency in Agricultural Products in the UK and EEC (value of domestic consumption as % of domestic production)

	UK		EEC	
	1975/6	1981/2	1975/6	1981/2
Wheat (soft)	54	100	101	122
Rye	27	73	92	96
Barley	105	153	103	115
Oats	93	99	95	99
Potatoes	83	89	98	102
Sugar	29	47	105	154
Vegetables	75	62	95	101
Fresh Fruit	30	23	79	82
Skimmed Milk	169	315	109	153
Cheese	61	70	101	107
Butter	20	67	107	128
Eggs	100	99	100	103
Meat	74	78	96	100

Source: *Yearbook of Agricultural Statistics 1984*, Eurostat.

Both the CAP and its pre-1973 predecessor have involved major, long-term distortions in the prices of agricultural products paid to farmers, in land values and in farm incomes. They have consequently resulted in a much greater allocation of resources to agricultural production than would otherwise occur through an undistorted price mechanism, with further, indirect allocative effects on industries supplying agricultural inputs or using agricultural products. Permanent support of agricultural production at an artificially high level in this manner could in principle be in the public interest, but requires some welfare explanation. However, vested interests and the farm vote apart, it is quite hard to find *any* explanation for the CAP's objective of European self-sufficiency in most foods. One that is sometimes advanced is in terms of defence strategy: an ability to feed the population in time of war. However the nature of modern warfare casts doubt on such an argument. Moreover in global terms, European self-sufficiency represents a highly questionable international division of labour, and protective measures against non-Community produce impede Third World development.

There have also been substantial distributional consequences of agricultural support policies. In the UK, farmers' incomes have on average risen from about 80% of male manual workers' earnings in 1938 to more than 200% by the mid-1970s, and the inflation of land values has simultaneously made the owners of quite modest farm holdings extremely wealthy. Agricultural workers, it should be pointed out, have not done so well, their earnings rising only from 53% of male manual workers earnings in 1939 to 75% in the mid-1970s; and according to a recent report of the Low Pay Unit, 40% of agricultural workers earn so little as to qualify for supplementary benefit. A second distributional effect occurs under the CAP because of its high consumer price aspect (in contrast to the 'cheap food' policy up to 1973). This is because food expenditure accounts for a higher proportion of total expenditure among poorer families, so that the cost of agricultural support falls disproportionately on them.

The existence of large agricultural subsidies has also created an incentive for farmers to apply intensive cultivation methods, and these have raised doubts over possible environmental damage and loss of amenity to the public. Intensive farming encourages the heavy use of fertilizers and pesticides, which may be resulting in gradual but cumulative damage to the soil, river pollution and loss of wildlife. Similarly, high crop-prices make it attractive to farmers to plough up marginal land, remove hedgerows and drain wetlands, which can further endanger wildlife and also reduce the recreational, visual and leisure value of the countryside. Under the provisions of the 1981 *Wildlife and Countryside Act*, farmers may now be paid compensation not to do some of these things. While this may alleviate the countryside and wildlife problem, it can also result in paying farmers not to produce crops which would be unprofitable but for CAP price-support, and in any case would only add to existing, embarrassing and costly surpluses of unsold produce.

The CAP has a built-in weakness in this respect. The regime of high consumer prices and support-buying arrangements stimulates production and removes the normal market sanction on oversupply (downward price adjustment), while simultaneously discouraging demand. In the absence of widespread, non-market production quotas, surpluses cannot be prevented. Table 4.6 shows some of the areas in which there is serious oversupply, in particular dairy produce, sugar and some cereals. In fact, as well as the infamous European butter and beef 'mountains' and the 'wine lake', there have also at various times been major surpluses of grain, sugar, and fruit. Thus the CAP today suffers from the problem of open-ended financial support like that which was largely dealt with by the introduction of 'standard quantities' twenty years ago under the pre-1973 UK system.

The cost of the CAP is huge and rising rapidly. In 1985 the budgetary cost to the EEC was no less than 20.7bn ECU, accounting for 72.8% of all official Community spending. When the cost of high consumer food prices is also taken into account, EEC agricultural support has been estimated to cost no less than £650 per annum for a family of four throughout the Community. In 1984 and 1985 the financial demands of the CAP exceeded available resources, the limit on which was then set by the 1% VAT in member states which was payable to the Community. In both years the shortfalls were covered by 'advances' from the member states, which in 1984 were repayable but in 1985 were not. This budgetary expedient involved procedures other than those laid down in the Treaty of Rome. Then, in May 1985, the budget constraint was eased by a Council decision raising the VAT rate to 1.4% with effect from January 1986 (on which date the Community was also enlarged by the accession of Spain and Portugal – both with large agricultural sectors).

There is widespread recognition of the need to reform the CAP, but a long history of inability to reach an agreement due to differences in national interests. In financial terms Britain, Germany and to a much smaller extent Italy have in the past been net contributors to the budget, while other countries have either benefitted or received roughly what they gave, and therefore do not have the same direct incentive to seek reform. Moreover, all countries have specific and often conflicting national interests to protect in particular branches of agriculture. However, the looming insolvency of the CAP did produce a first tentative step towards reform in April 1984, when production quotas were introduced to cut milk production, and most other agricultural products received a 1% price cut. As a result, butter and skimmed milk production fell by 6% and 9% respectively in 1985 (though surplus butter 'stocks' remained 11% above the corresponding 1984 level at 1.2m tonnes in November 1985), while changes in agricultural prices for 1985/6 ranged between −2% and +2%, with an average increase in ECU terms of only 0.1%. Subsequently, new long-term guidelines for the CAP were drawn up, and submitted to the Council of the EEC in the form of a policy document in December 1985, and the latest report on agriculture in the Community includes a key sentence that 'agriculture must obey the laws of supply and demand'.[1]

Thus there are some signs of movement which might eventually result in reform of what must rank as one of the most outstanding economic absurdities of the twentieth century, the CAP. On the other hand, the relaxation of the budget constraint which also occurred in 1985 leaves grounds for suspicion that the farming lobby may yet still have the last word.

---

1   Bull E.C. 12-1985, and European Commission, *The Agricultural Situation in the Community: 1985 Report*.

III THE NATIONALIZED INDUSTRIES
III.1 Introduction

The nationalized industries are run by publicly-owned undertakings, set up by government to supply marketed goods and services (as opposed to 'public goods' like defence and broadcasting, or social services like health and education which are provided at prices unrelated to use). In recent decades the bulk of the nationalized industries in Britain have been concentrated in two broad sectors of the economy: energy, and transport and communications. The principal undertakings in the energy sector have included the Central Electricity Generating Board and Area Electricity Boards, British Gas (at the time of writing), BNOC and the National Coal Board. In transport and communications they included British Rail, British Airways, the British Airports and Civil Aviation Authorities, the National Bus Company, the National Freight Corporation (until 1982), the Scottish Transport Group, the Post Office, and British Telecom (until 1984). Tables 4.7, 4.8 and 4.9 provide a statistical outline of production trends in these public-enterprise-dominated sectors since the late 1960s. Outside these sectors the main public-enterprise undertakings have included British Steel, British Shipbuilders, and two famous companies rescued from bankruptcy by state intervention in the early 1970s: British Leyland (BL) and Rolls-Royce (RR). In the early 1980s, just prior to a massive programme of 'privatization' embarked on by the Conservative government, the nationalized industries employed nearly 8% of the total working population, and accounted for approximately 11% of UK capital stock (excluding dwellings).

The UK has not been alone in having a substantial sector of industry under public ownership. In the EEC, this is the norm for postal services and telecommunications, electricity and gas distribution, the railways, parts of road transport, and coalmining. All major countries have national airlines, and the steel, aerospace and shipbuilding industries are usually subject to at least a degree of state participation. Vehicles production is likewise carried

TABLE 4.7

GB Inland Passenger Transport 1968–84[1] (000m passenger kilometres)

	Air	Rail	Road Public-service vehicles	Private Transport[2]	Total
1968	2 (0.5%)	33 (8.9%)	59 (15.7%)	280 (74.8%)	374 (100%)
1973	2 (0.5%)	35 (7.7%)	53 (11.6%)	364 (79.4%)	459 (100%)
1978	2 (0.5%)	35 (8.0%)	50 (11.4%)	351 (80.1%)	438 (100%)
1984	3 (0.6%)	35 (7.0%)	42 (8.4%)	422 (84.1%)	502 (100%)
Total change 1968–84	+50.0%	+6.1%	−28.8%	+50.7%	+34.,2%

Source: *AAS*.
Notes: 1 % figures in brackets show respective contributions to the total in any one year.
      2 Includes cars and taxis, motorcycles and pedal cycles.

TABLE 4.8

GB Inland Freight Transport 1968–84[1] (000m tonne-kilometres)

	Road	Rail	Inland Waterways	Pipelines[2]	Total
1968	79.0 (74.8%)	24.0 (22.7%)	0.2 (0.2%)	2.3 (2.2%)	105.6 (100%)
1973	90.4 (74.6%)	25.5 (21.1%)	0.4 (0.3%)	4.8 (4.0%)	121.1 (100%)
1978	99.1 (76.6%)	20.0 (15.5%)	0.4 (0.3%)	9.8 (7.6%)	129.3 (100%)
1984	106.9 (82.0%)	12.7 (9.7%)	0.4 (0.3%)	10.4 (8.0%)	130.4 (100%)
Total change 1968–84	+35.3%	−47.1%	+100.0%	+352,2%	+23.5%

Source: *AAS.*
Notes: 1 % figures in brackets show respective contributions to the total in any one year.
2 Excludes movements of gases by pipeline.

TABLE 4.9

Total UK Inland Energy Consumption by Final Users 1968–84: Heat Supplied Basis (bn therms)

Type of fuel	1968	%	1973	%	1978	%	1984	%	Total change 1968–84
Coal (direct use)	13.6	(24.6)	8.1	(13.3)	5.7	(9.6)	3.9	(7.2)	−71.3%
Gas	4.9	(8.9)	11.0	(18.0)	15.4	(26.0)	17.5	(32.3)	+257.1%
Electricity	5.8	(10.5)	7.5	(12.3)	7.7	(13.0)	7.7	(14.2)	+32.8%
Petroleum	24.1	(43.7)	29.6	(48.5)	27.1	(45.8)	22.7	(42.0)	5.8%
Other Fuels [1]	6.8	(12.3)	4.8	(7.9)	3.3	(5.6)	2.3	(4.3)	−66.2%
Total	55.2	(100)	61.0	(100)	59.2	(100)	54.1	(100)	−2.0%

Source: *AAS.*
Note: 1 Includes coke, breeze, solid and liquid fuels derived from coal.

on elsewhere than the UK in public or mixed enterprises (i.e. under joint public and private ownership); while Britain has (at the time of writing) BL, France has Renault, Italy has Fiat and Germany has VW. The public sector is particularly large in France, and Italy has two giant state companies: IRI, a wide-ranging holding company; and ENI, an oil and chemicals firm. There are also certain state monopolies for taxation purposes; that is, the state retains a monopoly profit as part of its fiscal revenue. The match industry (in France, West Germany and Italy) and the tobacco industry (in France and Italy) are examples.

In the USA, on the other hand, public ownership is unusual, though for many years a significant number of industries were subject to regulation of their tariffs, profits and services, even though their assets remained in private hands. The list of industries included railroads; motor and water carriers; airlines; electric, gas, water and sanitary services; telephones, telegraph and broadcasting; and financial institutions. Recently, however, there has been a substantial programme of 'deregulation'.

Most of the major nationalized industries in Britain were set up in the immediate postwar period. In the three decades thereafter, there was a broad political acceptance of the mixed economy, although the boundaries of the publicly-owned segment were prone to change somewhat according to which party was in power.[1] (The steel industry, in particular, was first nationalized in 1951, denationalized in 1953, and returned to public ownership in 1967.) This political consensus has now collapsed, and the Conservative government in power at the time of writing is in the midst of a programme to raise an expected £21.8bn over ten years up to 1989 from the sale of public assets. Table 4.10 shows the build-up of this programme since 1979. Section III.3 considers the issues raised by privatization and the details of the government's programme. But first let us consider the evolution of policies towards the nationalized industries in the period prior to the present, denationalization, era.

TABLE 4.10

Privatization Receipts, 1979/80–1988/9 (£bn)

79/80	80/81	81/2	82/3	83/4	84/5	85/6	86/7	87/8	88/9
0.37	0.21[1]	0.49	0.38[2]	1.10	2.5[3]	2.5[3]	4.75[4]	4.75[4]	4.75[4]

Notes: 1 Plus £0.20bn North Sea oil licences.
2 Plus £0.11bn oil licences, oil stockpiles and miscellaneous.
3 Estimated.
4 Target sales announced in the Chancellor's autumn statement, 1985.

III.2 Past and Present Policies towards the Nationalized Industries

The first phase of policy towards public enterprise was set down in the postwar nationalization Acts, which required the industries to break even, taking one year with another. This requirement did little to ensure efficiency in production or that a socially desirable level of output would be chosen, since it can be met by setting prices equal to average cost, at any level. In 1961 the financial responsibilities of the industries were tightened in a number of ways, and financial targets were introduced.[2] However, policy remained open to the earlier criticism until explicit pricing and investment procedures were adopted in 1967. An important White Paper of that year

---

1 For contrasting views on the virtues of the mixed economy see, e.g., S. Holland (ed.), *The State as Entrepreneur* (Weidenfeld and Nicolson, 1972), and S. Littlechild, 'The Fallacy of the Mixed Economy', Hobart Paper 80, second edition, *IEA*, 1986.

2 *The Financial and Economic Obligations of the Nationalised Industries*, Cmnd. 1337 (HMSO, April 1961).

introduced marginal-cost pricing and net-present-value procedures for investment decisions.[1]

The rationale for marginal-cost pricing is as follows. On the one hand the demand curve for a product tells us how much consumers will pay per unit for different quantities supplied; it represents consumers' marginal evaluation of the good or service as output is varied. On the other hand, the marginal-cost curve tells us the incremental cost of producing each unit. Provided the money costs incurred in production reflect the true opportunity cost of diverting extra resources from alternative uses, the marginal-cost curve records consumers' evaluation of the forgone alternative product. Hence, if consumers value the good in question more than the alternative (demand price exceeds marginal cost) then welfare can be increased by diverting more resources to its production and increasing output, and vice versa. Thus, the optimal level of output is determined where price equals marginal cost.

There are difficulties and limitations, however, over and above those of simply identifying and measuring the marginal cost of individual goods and services provided by complex industries like electricity, railways, coal, etc. For example, departures from marginal-cost prices may be called for where prices elsewhere in the system are not equal to marginal cost, as they generally will not be since oligopoly rather than perfect competition is the rule in the private sector, and only under perfect competition does profit-maximizing behaviour ensure that price equals marginal cost. Secondly, where there are 'externalities' such as pollution or other environmental damage or traffic congestion, account should be taken of these, and price set equal to marginal *social* cost, rather than the purely private costs entering the accounts of the undertaking in question. Thirdly, except under conditions of constant returns, marginal-cost pricing will not necessarily ensure that total costs are recovered (since marginal and average costs are equal only where the latter are at a minimum and price equals average revenue), so that a problem arises of financing deficits or disposing of surpluses. Finally, it has to be remembered when considering the marginal-cost pricing rule that it takes no account of the interpersonal distribution of income in the economy. Strictly speaking, the rule is valid only for whatever distribution happens to exist, and if this is not regarded as fair and reasonable, nor are the marginal-cost prices which the rule produces.

The idea behind the net-present-value (NPV) rule in investment decisions is to relate the future streams of benefits and costs during the lifetime of a project to the period when the decision must be made. Thus we define

$$\text{NPV} = \sum_{t=1}^{n} \frac{B_t - C_t}{(1+r)^t} - I$$

1   *Nationalised Industries: A Review of Economic and Financial Objectives*, Cmnd. 3437 (HMSO, November 1967).

where B_t, C_t are benefits and costs respectively in year t, r is the discount rate and I is the initial cost. The formula allows for the fact that net benefits in the more distant future are worth less in today's values (since £1 invested now would be worth more, with interest, as time elapses). Any project is worth investing in if its NPV is positive, and the relative returns from different projects may validly be compared by reference to their NPVs.

To preserve a correct balance in resource allocation, the discount rate r used in evaluating public-sector projects should be comparable with that used elsewhere (and any allowance made for uncertainty should also be the same). The 1967 White Paper laid down a public-sector rate of 8%, which was later raised to 10%. These rates were expressly chosen to match the rate looked for by private industry on marginal, low-risk investment at the time in question. Because of differences in financing methods and tax liability, the equivalent private-sector rate will be higher than any given nationalized industry rate; the original 8% was held to be equivalent to 15–16% in the private sector.

The 1967 White Paper retained the existing system of financial targets for nationalized industries, in order to provide measures of expected performance against which to compare actual achievements. This may be viewed as an attempt by the government to apply a similar sanction on the efficiency of the nationalized industries as the capital market imposes on private firms. Finally, the White Paper recognized that nationalized industries may provide so-called 'non-economic services', by which is meant services which yield greater social benefits than their social costs, but which can only be provided at a financial loss. Examples include rural postal, telephone and transport services, the free emergency telephone service and, arguably, commuter rail transport. From 1967 the policy intention was for the government to provide specific subsidies or grants for such non-commercial operations.

The 1967 policy had sought to achieve optimal resource allocation within nationalized industries by focusing on the pricing of individual goods and services and on individual investment projects. However, difficulties were encountered in practice, and in 1978 a subsequent White Paper,[1] while retaining the objective of optimal resource allocation, marginal-cost pricing and NPV methods, shifted the focus of policy towards the opportunity cost of capital in a nationalized industry as a whole. A 'real rate of return on assets' (RRR) was defined, to be achieved by the industries on new investment. The RRR is related to the real rate of return in the private sector, taking into account questions of the cost of finance and of social time preference. It was set initially at 5%, and was to be reviewed every three to five years. The RRR is not the same as the financial target rate of return for each industry, which varies, and takes into account the earning power of existing assets, sectoral and social objectives and so forth. Thus the main matters over which the government has sought to exercise control since 1978

1 *The Nationalised Industries*, Cmnd. 7131 (HMSO, March 1978).

are the RRR and the financial target, together with the 'general level of prices'. Individual prices and investment priorities have been left largely up to the industries themselves, subject to the vague instruction to 'pay attention to the structure of prices and its relation to the structure of costs' and to the need to consult sponsoring departments on certain major investment proposals.

Establishing an appropriate working relationship between the nationalized industries, Ministers and their departments, and Parliament has, however, proved difficult. The central problem is to ensure an adequate degree of public accountability without restricting unduly the day-to-day operations of the industries. The original intention was that Ministers should lay down broad principles but not intervene in management. However, in 1968 the Select Committee on the Nationalized Industries concluded that Ministers had tended to do the opposite of what Parliament intended, giving very little policy guidance but becoming closely involved in many aspects of management. A 1976 NEDO report proposed various structural reforms to counteract these difficulties, but these were rejected by the 1978 White Paper. However, the White Paper did propose that explicit ministerial directions should replace the existing system of informal persuasion, in order to clarify the extent of Ministers' responsibility for the industries' performance. It was also proposed that a civil servant be appointed to corporation boards, to improve the understanding of industry problems on the part of sponsoring departments.

Particular difficulties have arisen over government 'interference' with nationalized industry policies in pursuit of macroeconomic objectives, e.g. imposing public-sector price and/or earnings restraint as an anti-inflationary measure. For example, severe price restraint was applied in the years up to 1974 and investment programmes were cut, with damaging effects on the implementation of the 1967 White Paper's policy. In a more recent example the government forced a 2% increase in electricity prices on an unwilling electricity supply industry in early 1984, in what the House of Commons Select Committee on Energy saw as a 'largely fiscal policy', i.e. a tax. Government interventions of this kind do not breach the letter of official policy towards the nationalized industries, as the relevant White Papers reserve the government's right to bring national economic considerations to bear. However, they have at times frustrated attempts to achieve socially efficient resource-allocation decisions in the nationalized industries, and have also affected their reported financial performance one way or the other.

Assessing the comparative performance of public and private enterprise is a complex matter, complicated by a number of factors.[1] Firstly, public-enterprise surpluses and deficits to not correspond exactly with private profits and

1   See R. Pryke, *The Nationalised Industries: Policies and Performance since 1968* (Martin Robertson, 1981) and 'The Comparative Performance of Public and Private Enterprise', *Fiscal Studies*, July 1982; R. Millward and D. Parker, 'Public and Private Enterprise: Comparative Behaviour and Relative Efficiency', in R. Millward *et al.*, *Public Sector Economics* (Longmans, 1983); and J. D. Tomlinson, 'Ownership, Organisation and Efficiency', *Royal Bank of Scotland Review*, March 1986.

losses; allowance must be made for differences in funding, tax liability and accounting practice (e.g. certain items, including capital costs, being deducted as costs which would be paid out of profits in private industry). Then, in interpreting performance on any measure, account must be taken of governmental responsibility, as above, and also of the declining markets and general unprofitability of certain nationalized-industry activities throughout Western Europe (e.g. rail, coal, shipbuilding and steel).

The efficiency of the nationalized industries has been subject to a limited amount of official scrutiny since 1965, when their prices became subject to review by the National Board for Prices and Incomes. This continued during the life of the Price Commission. On its disbandment in 1980, responsibility for a vestige of price control was transferred to the office of the Director General of Fair Trading and at the same time the nationalized industries became liable to investigation by the Monopolies Commission. However, the reviews made under the auspices of all three bodies have related to particular price increases or specific monopoly situations, and do not amount to a regular system of internal efficiency audits, for which a case could be argued, though MMC enquiries come much closer to such audits than did earlier investigations.

EEC policy towards public enterprise has so far been concerned mainly with the use of subsidies. These could be contrary to the rules and spirit of the Community, if subsidization of loss-making industries in particular countries prevented the free play of competition within the Community-wide industry. However, a distinction should be drawn between subsidies granted to undertakings supplying strictly non-commercial services, and general revenue support for operating deficits. It is the latter which would be most likely to meet with disapproval, though it could be hard for the Community to apply meaningful sanctions. The emphasis of policy to date has been towards securing 'transparency' of financial arrangements for public enterprise; that is, as a first step the aim is to elicit information which would reveal what subsidies are in fact being given and their size.

III.3 Privatization

Principles: 'Privatization' is a vague term. It could include charging for services previously supplied at prices unrelated to use by government agencies; injecting private (non-voting) capital into the financial structure of nationalized undertakings; opening up their markets to competition from private-sector firms; or full-scale denationalization – setting up public limited companies in place of nationalized undertakings, with the sale of 51% or more of the shares in these companies by the government to private investors. It is privatization in the last sense on which we focus here, because it is on privatization in this sense that the government is intent at the time of writing.

The theoretical arguments concerning privatization have mostly to do with competition, and its effects on the technical and social efficiency of enterprises; for the effect of privatization is to expose the enterprise to direct market forces in the product and/or the capital markets. Supporters of privatization argue that increased product-market competition will make suppliers more responsive to consumers' preferences, provide goods and services of the quality and variety demanded at lower prices than would otherwise be charged, and adapt more quickly to changes in demand and in technical opportunities through greater innovation.[1] The profit motive is seen to provide the incentive to compete in this way, reinforced by the need to satisfy capital-market requirements for future borrowing, and by the ultimate threat of bankruptcy or takeover. Moreover, it is argued, privatized firms are better able to adapt and grow than their state-owned predecessors, because of their greater freedom to change and diversify their activities.

Thus there are three main parts to the pro-privatization argument: increased product-market competition; exposure to capital-market sanctions; and enhanced flexibility. Let us consider them in reverse order. The third is not a strong argument for privatization *per se*, because the inability of public enterprises to diversify arises merely from the fact that they are not permitted to do so by statute; it would be quite possible for the government to vary the relevant statutes and thereby give public enterprises the flexibility privatization would bring, without their leaving the public sector.

The effectiveness of capital-market sanctions is likely to vary from case to case. Recent history suggests that for both privatized public undertakings *and* existing private-sector firms, the ultimate bankruptcy threat applies strongly only where the closure of the enterprise would have no serious unemployment or strategic implications at national or regional level, or other politically unacceptable consequences. In other cases it is doubtful whether any government, however committed to the verdicts of market forces in principle, could resist pressure to mount a rescue operation; and it only has to be believed that the government, not necessarily the present one, might intervene for the effectiveness of the capital market's most drastic sanction to be severely moderated. Similarly, the capital-market sanction of takeover threat would be attenuated if, for example, it were believed that the government would not allow control of a strategically important enterprise to pass into foreign ownership.[2] While some of the companies and

---

1   See M. Beesley and S. Littlechild, 'Privatisation: Principles, Problems and Priorities', *LBR*, 149, July 1983, pp. 1–20. However, for alternative assessments of the privatization exercise see, e.g., J.S. Vickers and G.K. Yarrow, *Privatisation and the Natural Monopolies* (Public Policy Centre, London, 1985); G.K. Yarrow, 'Privatisation in Theory and Practice', *Economic Policy*, April 1986; the special issues of *Fiscal Studies*, Vol. 6, No. 4, November 1985 (with articles by Hammond, Helm and Thompson; Starkie and Thompson; and Mayer and Meadowcroft); and J. Kay and D. Thompson, 'Privatisation: A Policy in Search of a Rationale', *EJ*, March 1986.

2   In a number of privatizations the government has retained a 'golden share' which carries an exlusive right of veto over certain major issues, of which takeover is one.

undertakings already sold off or scheduled for disposal no doubt would not raise sensitive employment, strategic or political issues, the very nature of the nationalized industries is such that others would. Thus it is not credible that a government would allow British Telecom or privatized gas, electricity and water utilities to fail; and there is little reason to suppose that closure of a re-privatized RR, or of BL's volume car production, would be any more acceptable in the future than it was once before in the 1970s (when a Conservative government previously committed to putting down 'lame duck' firms found itself impelled to intervene).

Likewise, the extent to which product-market competition is likely to increase after privatization is highly variable. In automobiles, shipbuilding and international airline operations, for example, there is already intense market rivalry due to chronic world overcapacity. Changing the ownership of UK producers in these cases cannot be expected to have any significant effect on the level of product-market competition; the privatization case must rely solely on increased capital-market pressure, as previously discussed. In other areas, problems of natural monopoly are likely to be encountered, for example where production depends on a network like the national electricity grid, gas distribution pipelines, and local telephone and rail systems. Here single-seller industries are to be expected, unconstrained by any credible threat of entry by potential competition. Thus in these cases also privatization will not serve to unleash natural forces of competition. Elsewhere, technical economies of scale and scope in production are likely to result in markets with very few firms of minimum efficient size, e.g. in electricity generation, gas exploration and extraction, steelmaking, shipbuilding, volume car production, airlines and airports, and so on. Thus post-privatization competition will frequently be of the 'small numbers' or oligopolistic kind in which, as we shall see later in section IV.1, market rivalry does not necessarily lead in socially desirable directions, and market behaviour depends strongly on the ease of entry of new competitors, or market 'contestability'. Hence it is to be expected that in many, perhaps most cases, competition alone will not be a sufficient safeguard of the public interest, and some form of continuing government controls or *regulation* will be needed.

Continued government responsibility for, and involvement with, privatised public enterprises is also called for where non-commercial services are provided, for example British Telecom's maintenance of public callboxes, and certain rural services, as part of the national emergency system. The principles in such cases are straightforward and no different from those under nationalization. The government should decide the type and level of service to be provided on behalf of the community, and pay the privatized firms supplying it an explicit subsidy, thus ensuring 'transparency'. The subsidy would require periodic review and adjustment to take account of the cost of materials, technological advances and so on, and some monitoring of output and perhaps costs would be necessary. The relationship between the government and firms would in many ways resemble that which already exists under defence contracts. Where there is multiple, as opposed to single firm supply, competitive tendering might even be a possibility. But whatever form the arrangements take, the general point is that, once again, competition alone is not enough, and must be supplemented by a continuing government-industry relationship.

Finally, there is a third reason why government responsibility for public enterprises should not cease at the point of privatization. The production activities involved frequently generate significant external effects, such as the environmental impact of nuclear power stations, and the traffic congestion effects of decisions made by transport undertakings (e.g. the closure of a rail link or other public service). Where the enterprises concerned are publicly owned, the government automatically has access to powers to moderate and influence decisions, and so take externalities of this kind into account. Unregulated private companies, on the other hand, as is well known, tend to ignore such externalities, because the costs (or benefits) are borne not by themselves but by some other individual or group, or by the community at large. Yet it is important that these external effects, which loom large in the nationalized industry areas, should be taken into account if the welfare of the community is to be maximized. Hence they may constitute a further ground for post-privatization regulation.

In general we may conclude that denationalizing any industry is a major decision, involving social benefits and costs that are likely to vary greatly from case to case, and potentially require appropriate regulatory arrangements. Each decision should therefore be preceded by an analysis of the benefits and costs and the regulatory arrangements. The analysis should take account of consumers' gains (or losses) due to changes in prices, outputs, the quality and variety of services provided, and the rate of innovation. The effects on total employment, imports and exports, raw-material and component suppliers, regional development, and taxpayers should all be considered. In a democratic society one would expect that the case for privatization would then be publicly debated, in the light of this evidence, before privatization takes place.

The privatization programme: The privatization programme began in a comparatively modest way after the election of the first Thatcher government in 1979, with receipts averaging roughly £0.5 billion a year up to 1983/4 (see table 4.10). In this period the sales included between 5 and 100% government holdings in a wide range of companies – British Petroleum, ICL, Ferranti, Fairey Aviation, British Aerospace, British Sugar, Amersham International, the National Freight Corporation, Britoil, Associated British Ports, and Cable and Wireless; but with the exception of the National Freight Corporation, none of the major nationalized industries, in particular the public energy and transport utilities, was touched.

The second phase was heralded by the introduction of a programme of planned sales of £2bn a year for five years from 1984/5. In the first year this included the BL luxury car division Jaguar, Enterprise Oil, and Wytch Farm Oilfield in Dorset (previously owned by British Gas), Sealink cross-channel ferries and, most importantly, 51% of British Telecom (BT). This last spectacular disposal alone raised £1.6bn in November 1984 (which compares with only £1.4bn of new ordinary shares raised by the whole of the private sector in the same year), and an eventual £3.9bn including two subsequent tranches.

In only the second year of this ambitious programme the target rate of disposals was escalated to £4.75bn a year in the Chancellor's autumn statement of November 1985. By far the most important individual sales in prospect at the time of writing are British Gas (scheduled to raise some £3bn in November 1986, and a further £2.5bn in each of the next two years) and the regional water authorities (up to £6bn from 1987/8 onwards). Also on the schedule for 1986/7 are management 'buyouts' of the Vickers and Cammell-Laird shipyards (previously part of British Shipbuilders); sale of the Royal Ordnance Factories and the British Airports Authority; and the break-up and disposal of the National Bus Corporation. Rolls-Royce and further parts of British Shipbuilders, and British Steel are candidates for sale in later years. However, both the proposed sale of BL's truck and Land-Rover divisions to General Motors of America, and the flotation of British Airways have at the time of writing been indefinitely postponed.

In all this, no cost-benefit analyses have been published, or are expected. Thus the privatization programme is going forward on a general belief in the superiority of competition and private ownership *per se*, rather than as a result of research into the likely consequences in particular circumstances. In fact, it has become clear as the programme advances that the government's objective has less to do with enhanced competition and efficiency than with simply augmenting government revenue. Thus, on the one hand, there has been little emphasis on competitive aspects in the selection and treatment of individual cases: no attempt was made to separate the national and local operations of BT, as had been advocated,[1] and the government has made it clear that only one competitor (Mercury, a subsidiary of Cable and Wireless) will be allowed to enter the industry for seven years; British Gas is to be sold as a single entity rather than a number of parts, and to retain monopoly North Sea gas publishing rights; and regional water authorities come as close to the textbook definition of a natural monopoly as one is likely to find. On the other hand, contrary to most informed opinion,[2] the government has persisted in treating asset sales receipts as normal revenue, which can then be set off against equivalent amounts of public expenditure and so allow the true fiscal deficit to be much higher than otherwise, while still

1   See e.g. Beesley and Littlechild, *op. cit.*

2   Including the Select Committee on the Treasury, which recommended treating assets sales as exceptional items or as an alternative method of financing PSBR. See *Treasury and Civil Service Committee Report on the Government's Economy Policy: Autumn Statement* (HMSO, 1984).

apparently meeting targets for the public-sector borrowing requirements (PSBR); the sale of British Gas was brought forward and pursued to an extraordinarily tight time-schedule primarily, it is believed, to maintain the flow of receipts when the sale of BA had to be postponed (due first to litigation arising from the Laker Airways affair, and then to the need to renegotiate the Bermuda Agreement on transatlantic air routes); and the privatization programme now clearly forms an indispensable part of the Chancellor's general macroeconomic strategy (see Chapter 1). In short, the overriding aim now seems to be to carry out the denationalization programme as rapidly as the capacity of the stock market will allow.

In order to guarantee 'successful' flotations, most public asset sales have been underpriced, apparently deliberately. In principle, the sale price is important not so much for the decision to privatize (which should turn solely on the existence of a net social benefit, larger than the transactions cost of effecting the change), but from the point of view of fairness and the distribution of wealth. This is because the sale price simply represents the payment for which ownership is transferred from taxpayers at large to a smaller group of private investors. The aim should therefore be to ensure that the price reflects a true value of the assets, with no undue capital gains or losses to purchasers and underwriters. Judging an equilibrium price is by no means easy, especially as the sums involved are orders of magnitude greater than those normally traded on the stock market; but the government appears to have erred consistently on the low side. As a result, most of the share issues have been heavily oversubscribed. In the case of BT the oversubscription was by a factor of almost ten, and the new shares registered an instant 90% capital gain when first traded on the stock market. In total this meant the government had received about £1.3bn less than the initial market value of the shares, and the total 'loss' on some £5.5bn of assets sold up to and including BT has been estimated to be about £2.1bn at the end of 1984.[1] In addition, the sales have involved substantial transactions costs; in the case of BT, fees and commissions to the City alone amounted to £128m, and the total cost of the sale (including the issue of free shares to employees and telephone vouchers as inducements to share-purchasers) has been estimated at up to £320m.

Regulatory provisions have been made for BT, and are proposed for British Gas and the future WSPLCs (Water Service Public Limited Companies) after privatization. In the case of BT, a Director General and Office of Telecommunications (OFTEL) have been set up, to receive complaints, monitor developments, and administer price and service-charge regulations. Call charges are governed by an '(RPI$-x$) formula', under which consumers are assured that they will not rise by more than the rate of retail price inflation less an amount x, determined by bargaining between BT and

---

1   Note, however, that such calculations should be adjusted for changes in underlying market value which may have occurred in the period after privatization, and would not be reflected in the initial market valuation.

the government, and currently set at 3 percentage points. The idea is that, while consumers are protected, the industry has an incentive to secure increased efficiency, since it keeps the benefits (over and above those needed to comply with the formula).[1] Rental charges are not included, however, and are allowed at present to rise by the amount of retail price inflation plus 2 percentage points. Moreover the call-charge formula applies to the average increase for a basket of individual charges, and in 1985 B T increased charges by more than the inflation rate for domestic consumers, where there is no competitive pressure, in order to increase its price competitiveness in the business sector, where competition from Mercury is faced. The price formula is, in any case, a temporary measure only, due to expire in 1990 beyond which, on current plans, 'competition' is looked to as the principal regulator. Details of the regulatory arrangements for the gas and water industries have not been finalized at the time of writing, but are expected to conform to the BT model.[2]

It is too early yet to assess the performance of privatized undertakings. Some political commentators have been quick to point out increases in profitability achieved, for example, by Jaguar and BT in the first years after privatization (though Jaguar's profits had in any case been rising strongly before privatization). But the relevant comparison is not with past performance, but with what the enterprises would be achieving if still under public ownership – a much more difficult comparison to make. Moreover profitability is not necessarily the appropriate yardstick, since it may as easily reflect the effects of monopoly pricing as of increased efficiency. From the social efficiency standpoint, the verdict on privatization must await an analysis of at least five years' evidence on the behaviour of prices, costs and the quality and range of services in denationalized undertakings.

IV COMPETITION POLICY AND CONSUMER PROTECTION
IV.1 Competition, Market Power and Welfare

Efficient market co-ordination of economic activity depends on competition and on consumers' exercising free and well-informed choices. If, on the other hand, there is market power or consumers have poor information, the 'invisible hand', which is supposed to reconcile individually self-interested behaviour with the communal good, falters or is overruled. Public policies in this area therefore seek to monitor market competitiveness and consumer interests, and apply remedies where these are infringed. However, the general assumptions about the relationship between competition and the

---

1 For a discussion see S. Littlechild, *Regulation of British Telecommunications' Profitability*, DI, London (HMSO, 1983).

2 But see S. Littlechild, *Economic Regulation of Privatised Water Authorities*, HMSO, January 1986.

public interest which are governing policy at the time of writing seem to be rather different from those which have applied in the past. Moreover the context in which competition policy operates is undergoing rapid change, in part as a consequence of the government's privatization programme which, as we have seen, raises important regulatory and potential market power issues in certain cases. In the following discussion of competition policy we therefore consider first the 'orthodox' or traditional view on competition and welfare, on which the framework of existing policy measures has been largely based, and then the current view, which helps explain how policy is presently being applied.

The traditional view of competition: The traditional view focuses primarily on the relationship between various *structural characteristics of markets*, and the welfare implications arising from their effects on the behaviour of firms within them. Consider first the sole-supplier case of pure monopoly (figure 4.2). DD' is the monopolist's downward-sloping demand curve, the slope and position of which reflects the degree of competition from close substitute products. Costs are for simplicity assumed constant, so that CC' represents both marginal and average costs. For reasons given in section III.2 above, maximum welfare requires that the 'competitive' output Q^* is produced, at which price equals marginal cost. The profit-maximizing monopolist, however, equates marginal cost with marginal revenue (not shown) and restricts output to Q, which is sold at price P. In consequence of this distortion in resource allocation there is first of all an *allocative welfare loss*; the triangle of consumers' surplus AEB, which is present under competition, is lost, and represents the 'deadweight welfare loss' due to monopoly. Secondly, the rectangle $PABC$, which was consumers' surplus under competition, becomes supernormal profit, π, under monopoly due to the elevation of price above average cost; thus there is also a *distributional effect*, in which welfare is transferred from consumers to producers. The first estimate of the magnitude of deadweight welfare loss – for the USA in the period between the two world wars – was minuscule: equivalent to less than one tenth of one per cent of GNP. More recent estimates, taking into account certain technical issues and adopting a broader view of the social costs of monopoly (including the costs of acquiring monopoly positions), suggest much larger losses: 7 to 13% of gross corporate product in the USA, and 3 to 7% in Britain.[1] However, as we shall see shortly, proponents of the new thinking on competition do not accept these estimates.

While pure monopoly is clearly a special case, in which sales are concentrated in the hands of a single firm, the degree of allocative distortion and of supernormal profit is expected under the traditional view to increase with market power as we move from the polar case of competition to that of pure monopoly; and market power may be measured in the degree of *seller con-*

---

1   K.G.Cowling and D.C.Mueller, 'The Social Costs of Monopoly Power', *EJ*, 1978.

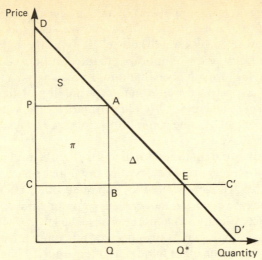

Figure 4.2   Monopoly and welfare

centration – the extent to which production is concentrated in the hands of a few large firms. This is primarily because as concentration increases, so does the probability of collusion amongst sellers in a market. This may be explicit in the form of cartel arrangements and restrictive trade practices involving price-rings, quota systems, geographical market sharing, etc; or it may be tacit, in the form of mutually accommodating behaviour on the part of sellers in accordance with an unspoken understanding between them. By such means, colluding firms may be able to assume some or all of the market power of a monopolist. In the limit, theory shows that a group of joint-profit maximizing firms behave exactly as would a single, multi-plant monopolist.

Alternatively, where there is 'small numbers' competition in oligopolistic markets, competition may take place primarily not in terms of price, but in what are often considered less socially desirable ways, such as product differentiation and advertising. Thus competitive energy may be channelled into producing finely differentiated brands of products offering little real variety of choice to consumers, and into the manipulation of consumers' preferences; and while enlarged consumer choice and knowledgeability can increase welfare up to a point, there seems to be no natural constraint in the system to prevent this being exceeded in oliogopolistic markets, and suspicions of 'wasteful' product competition and 'excessive' advertising enter.

Of course, the behaviour of both monopolists and oligopolists may be constrained by *potential competition* in the form of the threat of new entry to the market, and since at least the mid-1950s the traditional view of the competition-welfare relationship has recognized the importance of *barriers to entry* for new competitors.[1] But it is also recognized that this, too, can

---

1   The pioneering work on entry barriers is J. S. Bain, *Barriers to New Competition* (Harvard University Press, 1956). For an up-to-date account see M. Waterson, *Economic Theory of the Industry* (CUP, 1984), Ch. 4.

become an aspect of the monopoly problem, inasmuch as entry barriers may be not inherent (e.g. due to patents or exclusive access to specialized resources), but contrived by established sellers (e.g. through 'predation' – undercutting entrants' prices temporarily to force withdrawal – or the threat of predatory moves through investment in overcapacity). In some circumstances we may expect to observe market instability, with a sequence of initially high prices inducing entry, leading to market rivalry and price cutting and the collapse or exit of some competitors, followed by restoration of high prices, and so on.

Because the structural conditions of markets play a central role in the traditional analysis, so mergers between existing firms are a potentially important aspect of competition policy, where they impinge on market structure. This is most likely in the case of *horizontal mergers*, between firms competing in the same marketplace. Clearly, such mergers raise the level of seller concentration, other things being equal, with expected anti-competitive consequences as outlined above. On the other hand, it is often argued in merger cases that they are necessary to reap economies of scale and rationalize production as circumstances change, yielding benefits to consumers. Thus horizontal mergers pose a trade-off problem for competition policy, offering potential benefits on the one hand, but also potential losses.[1] Strictly, the balance of advantages cannot be assessed *a priori* and must be determined through empirical study.

Vertical mergers between firms at different stages in the same production chain pose a similar policy dilemma. Again, they may permit efficiency gains either in production or via improved information exchange and co-ordination. But they can also raise competition policy issues, where, for instance, a manufacturer takes over the firm supplying raw material both to himself and to his competitors, and would be able to charge disadvantageous prices to them, or where a manufacturer secures control over the sales outlets for both his own and his competitors' products.

Conglomerate mergers are mergers between firms where there had previously been neither a horizontal nor a vertical link. These are generally thought to raise less serious anti-competitive risks but also fewer potential efficiency gains. Thus neither scale economies in production nor gains from improved production scheduling are available and seller concentration does not increase. However, firm-level scale economies may occur, e.g. in raising finance and planning investment. On the other side, competition-policy concerns have arisen over conglomerate merger cases in two areas. One is associated with the ability of conglomerate concerns to cross-subsidize activities, which could be used to exclude a competitor in one industry by incurring temporary losses there. The other concerns the practice of 'reciprocal buying' between divisions of a conglomerate organization, which again can be used to weaken competition. Furthermore, conglomerate mergers may represent

---

1   The merger-welfare trade-off framework is discussed in ch. 2 of K. G. Cowling *et al.*, *Mergers and Economic Performance* (CUP, 1980).

pursuit of purely managerial objectives, including growth of the firm *per se*, with few benefits to the community, while large economic power blocs develop with potentially far-reaching socio-political as well as economic consequences.

Empirical work on mergers has not been able to identify a single, dominant motive for merger, which is perhaps not surprising since there are so many possible reasons why firms might wish to merge. Extensive studies of merger effects indicate a general absence of observable, post-merger efficiency gains.[1] Thus it appears that mergers are not a major force making for improved industrial performance. On the other hand there is fairly widespread, though not universal, agreement that they contribute significantly to increased market power, as measured by the extent to which economic activity is concentrated in the hands of relatively few producers. Thus the general conclusion from a substantial number of studies is that at least 50% and, on some estimates, a much greater percentage of the change in concentration in recent decades can be attributed to mergers. Moreover, this applies both to *market concentration* (the concentration of sales in the hands of relatively few sellers in individual industries or markets) and to *aggregate concentration* (the concentration of economic activity in the hands of giant firms in the economy as a whole). The level and recent trends in both types of concentration are discussed further in section IV.3 below.

The Austrian view: Proponents of the so-called Austrian school reject the essentially static, structural view of competition they detect in the traditional analysis, and emphasize what they regard as the creative role of entrepreneurship, and the dynamic aspect of competition as a process. Though newly fashionable, the basic ideas go back half a century, in particular to the work of Schumpeter, who stressed the role of the entrepreneur as innovator and first argued the case that monopoly may have 'compensating dynamic gains'; that the cushion of profit and relative market security are necessary enabling conditions for firms to undertake risky and high-cost R & D expenditures. Other important influences on the new school include Hayek, von Mises and Kirzner.

An influential supporter of the Austrian viewpoint reinterprets the traditional monopoly welfare-loss analysis of figure 4.2 to analyse the behaviour of an entrepreneur who discovers a new product ahead of the field, as follows:

> Assume he charges a monopoly price P, since for the moment he is the sole seller. It is true he is restricting output compared to what he could produce, or compared to what would be produced if all his rivals

---

1 See e.g. G. Meekes, *Disappointing Marriage: A Study of the Gains from Mergers* (CUP, 1977); D.C.Mueller (ed.), *Determinants and Effects of Mergers: An International Comparison* (Oelgeschlager, Gunn and Hain, 1980); and K.G.Cowling *et al.*, *op. cit.*

shared his own insight. But they do *not* share his insight; this is not the relevant alternative. For the time being *the relevant alternative to his action is no product at all*. It would therefore be inappropriate to characterize his action as generating a social loss given by the welfare triangle △. On the contrary, *his action generates a social gain given by his own entrepreneurial profit π plus the consumer surplus S*.[1]

Notice the Austrian ingredients: the case selected is one of innovation; profit is regarded in a positive light, as a just reward for entrepreneurial activity and as an incentive to other firms to imitate and enter the market; and the monopoly element is temporary ('. . . for the moment . . . For the time being . . .'). However, the Austrians have yet to show what proportion of monopoly situations are of this kind, how far new product innovations add usefully to consumer choice, and how long is the interval 'before competition arrives'. In general, empirical work has so far been unable to establish a clear superiority of monopoly over competition in securing technical progress, or vice versa, though some evidence at variance with the Austrian analysis has been produced, showing the persistence of excess profits in individual firms over long periods of time.[2]

In merely stressing market entry and exit as a dynamic aspect of competition, the Austrians do not distinguish themselves from the traditional position which, as we have seen, also recognizes the importance of entry conditions as a structural characteristic of markets. Where the Austrians do appear to differ is in holding much more optimistic beliefs about the magnitude of entry barriers and the force of potential competition. Equally optimistic on this front are the adherents of the recently introduced theory of 'contestability'. A contestable market is one which is prone to 'hit-and-run entry'; that is, a market where if supernormal profits were earned an entrant could come in, make a profit and costlessly depart. The policy significance of the 'new' theory, it is claimed, is that the existing structure of the market – the number and size distribution of sellers – is irrelevant; as long as the market is contestable, firms will be forced to behave competitively. In fact this is not a new proposition, but simply the case of perfect free entry, of which traditional economists have long been aware, but considered of little practical importance because it is unlikely to occur at all widely. In terms of the 'new' theory, the problem is that there must be no 'sunk costs', i.e. costs which would not be recoverable by an entrant or exit.[3] Some instances have been suggested, notably in the field of transport where, for example, an airline operator may be able to switch between, say, intercity routes at

1 S.C.Littlechild, 'Misleading Calculations of the Social Costs of Monopoly Power', *EJ*, 1981.

2 D.C.Mueller, 'The Persistence of Profit above the Norm', *EC* 1977.

3 'Sunk' and 'fixed' costs are not the same. For example the cost of a factory or piece of equipment is not itself a sunk cost, since the asset can be resold. However, transactions costs of the asset purchase are sunk costs, since these are non-recoverable.

virtually no cost (provided of course licensing is not required), and so exert a competitive threat to even a single, existing operator. But non-trivial sunk costs are to be expected in most manufacturing and service industries. Moreover the entry barriers and entry-deterring strategies open to incumbent firms that are recognized in the traditional analysis, and observed practice, would operate in just the same way for a 'hit and run' entrant as for one hoping to stay in the market, in the traditional analysis.

Consumer protection: The question of consumer protection has not so far proved as contentious in the UK as has competition, though 'deregulating the product' has been more of an issue in the USA. The economic theory of consumer protection remains relatively undeveloped. In the textbooks, consumers are assumed to have a complete ordering of their preferences for different goods and services, based on full information about the characteristics of the commodities and the utility to be gained from consuming them. Consumers then attempt to maximize their utility, faced with their income and market-determined prices. Provided these prices (including the price of labour and hence income) are competitively determined, the theory implies that all is well with the consumer. In practice the consumer is not fully and costlessly informed, and may not be able to judge the utility he will derive from a certain good. He may not, for example, realize that a drug may be unsafe under certain conditions, or that food may be too old for use, and he may be faced by confusing packaging or subject to misleading claims by advertisers or retailers. Furthermore, he may not be able to choose how much or how little service he obtains with a good, and his right of redress against suppliers of unsatisfactory goods or services may be either unclear or impractical to exercise via the courts. There is nothing to guarantee that it is in the interests of all manufacturers and suppliers for consumers to exercise a totally free and informed choice. It is this potential divergence of interests which creates the need for policy measures.

IV.2 Policy Measures

Competition: A 'wide-ranging' review of competition policies is under way at the time of writing, the final results of which are expected in late 1986 or possibly 1987. The following account describes the situation prior to any changes to which this review may lead.

The first major policy measure was the 1948 *Monopolies and Restrictive Practices Act*. Several further measures followed until the 1973 *Fair Trading Act* consolidated the existing law and codified and extended legislative safeguards for consumers. It also provided for the appointment of a Director General of Fair Trading (DGFT), to centralize the application of competition and consumer law; previously this responsibility had been rather widely shared. The 1973 Act is now the basis of current policy, along with the subsequent *Restrictive Practices* and *Resale Price Maintenance Acts* of 1976 and the 1980 *Competition Act*. In competition policy there are two main strands, embodying different approaches to the control of monopolies and mergers and of restrictive agreements between firms. Let us consider them in turn.

Monopolies and mergers which meet certain criteria may be referred for investigation by an independent administrative tribunal, the Monopolies and Mergers Commission (MMC). The Commission's task is to determine whether the case in question is or is likely to be detrimental to the public interest, and make recommendations for corrective measures as appropriate. Responsibility for implementing recommendations lies with the appropriate Minister, and statutory orders may be made binding on the companies concerned, or a settlement reached in the form of voluntary undertakings.

Section 14 of the 1948 Act defined the public interest as 'production . . . by the most efficient and economical means . . . in such volume and at such prices as will best meet the requirements of home and overseas markets'; progressive increases in efficiency and the encouragement of new enterprise; the 'fullest use and best distribution of men, materials and industrial capacity' . . .; and '. . . the development of technical improvements and the expansion of existing markets and the opening up of new markets.' Section 84 of the 1973 Fair Trading Act reformulated this comprehensive definition, but still left it rather vague. However, this has at least allowed the MMC wide discretion in evolving practical criteria.

Monopoly references may be made either by Ministers or the DGFT. The latter is expected to provide a broader-based view of the state of competition in the economy, and has a responsibility to collect data on market structure and the behaviour of the firms on which the MMC may draw. An economic information system now operates in the Office of Fair Trading for this purpose. Merger references are the prerogative of the Secretary of State, acting on advice from a Merger Panel. The panel screens merger proposals falling within the scope of the law, to determine the economic significance of each case and priorities for investigation.

From 1948 a monopoly could be referred where one firm supplied one third or more of a total market. In 1973 this was reduced to 25%, which from then on could apply to sales in a particular locality, rather than the national market. Cases of 'complex monopoly' – in effect tight oligopolies – were also brought within the scope of the legislation. Mergers which would result in a monopoly were not covered until 1965. Thereafter they became liable either via the monopoly market-share test or if the gross assets involved exceeded a certain value: £5m initially, £15m from 1980 and £30m from 1984. The 1980 *Competition Act* extended monopoly control to certain public-sector bodies. The Act defined these as corporate bodies supplying goods and services whose members are appointed by a Minister under legislation, plus public bus services and water undertakings, certain agricultural boards and others. A principal object was to provide a mechanism for enquiring into the efficiency of nationalized industries. Previously this had been possible via the

Price Commission and before that the National Board for Prices and Incomes, in the context of price and incomes policies. The 1980 Act abolished the Price Commission, but retained a last vestige of price control, authorising the Secretary of State to refer 'any price' to the DGFT for investigation.

Restrictive-practice agreements were originally treated in the same way as monopolies, and occupied the MMC almost entirely in its first years after 1948. In 1956 a separate procedure was introduced. Agreements under which there were restrictions relating to the price of goods, conditions of supply, quantities or descriptions, processes or areas and persons supplied were *presumed* illegal (though not prohibited) unless the parties could establish a case for exemption before a specially constituted Restrictive Practices Court. A register of agreements was set up, and a Registrar was appointed to bring cases to the Court. This has the status of a High Court and consists of five judges and ten lay members.

The basic procedure still applies, though the definitive law is now the 1976 *Restrictive Practices Act*, which consolidated previous legislation, and the role of the Registrar has been taken over by the DGFT. To be exempted, the agreement must pass through one or more of eight escape clauses or 'gateways'. Thus, paraphrasing the legislation slightly, it must be shown that the agreement is necessary: (a) to protect the public against injury; or (b) because its removal would deny to the public 'specific and substantial benefits'; or (c) to counteract measures taken by others to restrict competition; or (d) to enable the parties to negotiate 'fair terms' with others; or (e) because its removal would have 'serious and persistent' adverse effects on employment; or (f) because its removal would cause a 'substantial' reduction in exports; or (g) to maintain another agreement, accepted by the Court as not contrary to the public interest on other grounds; or, finally, it may be shown that, while not necessary, the agreement (h) does not restrict or discourage competition to any material degree.

This last gateway was framed with 'information agreements' particularly in mind. Here no restrictions are accepted, but information concerning prices and so forth is exchanged. Information agreements were not covered by the legislation from the outset but were brought within its scope from 1968 onwards. Otherwise, it is gateway (b) which has been most frequently argued in cases which came to court, either alone or in conjunction with other clauses. If an agreement passes through one or more of the gateways, there remains a further obstacle: the so-called 'tailpiece' requires the Court to be satisfied that, on balance, benefits to the public outweigh detriments.

Originally the restrictive-practice legislation applied only to the supply of goods, but was extended to services in 1976. There is a time-limit for the registration of agreements, with (rather mild) penalties for non-registration, and interim orders may be made while a final decision is being made. The Minister may exempt certain agreements which he deems to be in the national interest or intended to hold down prices.

Resale price maintenance (RPM) is a particular type of restrictive practice which is now dealt with by the separate *Resale Prices Act* of 1976. Prior to

1964, when individual RPM was first controlled, it was a common manufacturers' practice to specify actual prices at which their product should be retailed, with sanctions for non-compliance. The procedure for controlling RPM is very similar to that for restrictive practices in general, involving a general prohibition and 'escape clauses'. Although RPM remains in a few trades, for instance in the supply of books, it has in many cases been superceded by the device of 'recommended' retail prices, which are in effect maximum prices. This device has been investigated by the MMC which concluded that it operated with different effects in different industries, not always contrary to the public interest.

The 1973 *Fair Trading Act* also empowers the MMC to investigate uncompetitive practices in monopoly situations. The 1980 *Competition Act* added a further provision for control of anti-competitive practices.[1] These may now be subject to a preliminary investigation by the DGFT, and subsequently referred to the MMC if satisfactory undertakings are not forthcoming after the preliminary report.

Finally, as a member of the EEC Britain is covered by the regulation dealing with monopolies, mergers and restrictive practices in Articles 85 and 86 of the Treaty of Rome. The European Commission is the body responsible for applying the policies and investigating breaches in them.

The most fully developed parts of the regulations are those relating to restrictive practices. These prohibit all agreements, such as price-fixing and market-sharing, which prevent, restrict or distort competition in the EEC and extend over more than one member country. As in the UK, however, exemption may be gained via a 'gateway' if the agreement improves production or distribution or promotes progress. There is also provision for block exemptions.

EEC monopoly regulations are less clear-cut since, although any abuse of dominant position within the EEC is prohibited if it affects trade between member countries, it is not clear what sort of market-share criterion constitutes dominance, or what abuses will be covered by the regulations. EEC case-law on monopoly is virtually non-existent as yet. Even less clear up to 1971 was the position of mergers. Until the case of Continental Can (an American firm) in that year, it was unsettled whether Articles 85 and 86 could be applied to merger cases. Although this particular merger was allowed on appeal to the European Court of Justice, the implicit extension of the legislation to mergers has been approved by the European Parliament. Since then a proposed regulation concerning mergers has been put forward. As originally proposed, it would have prohibited mergers involving firms above a specified size or market share, with provision for exemption in special circumstances, and with compulsory advance clarification for very large mergers. However there was very slow progress towards its implementation, and late in 1981 the European Commission submitted an amendment

---

1 See J. A. Kay and A. E. Sharpe, 'The Anticompetitive Practice', *Fiscal Studies*, November 1982.

to its original, 1973 proposal with a view to reopening discussions. The amended proposal restricts control more closely to mergers with a Community dimension and involves member states more closely in the decision-making process. Little progress has, however, since been made.

Consumer protection: The concept of overall government responsibility for consumer protection (as opposed to piecemeal responsibility) is relatively recent. Under the 1973 Act, the DGFT was again assigned a key position. He has a duty to collect and assess information about commercial activities, in order to seek out trading practices which may affect consumers' economic interests. If he finds areas in which there is cause for concern, he then has two options. The DGFT may either make recommendations to the relevant Minister as to action which might be useful in altering the malpractice, whether it concerns consumers' economic interest or their health, safety and so on. Or, presumably where more severe action is demanded, he may set in motion a procedure which could lead to the banning of a particular trade practice. To do this he makes a 'reference' along with proposals for action to the Consumer Protection Advisory Committee (CPAC), which considers whether his proposals are justified, and that the practice is covered by the legislation. After taking evidence from interested parties, this body reports to the relevant Minister, who may then make an Order, subject to the agreement of Parliament.

Another of the DGFT's main functions in the area of consumer protection is to make sure that those who are persistently careless of their existing legal obligations to consumers mend their ways, either by his seeking a written assurance, or failing this in the courts. Lastly, he has obligations to pursue an informal dialogue with industry; to publish information and advice for consumers; and to encourage trade associations to use voluntary codes of practice to protect consumers.

IV.3 Policy Appraisal

The degree of policy intervention: By the end of 1984 the MMC had investigated less than 50 monopoly supply situations – not a large number in relation to the total number of monopolies and oligopolies in existence, though covering a diverse range of goods, including beer, breakfast cereals, fertilizers, cigarettes, colour film, soap and detergents, contraceptives, wallpaper, building bricks and tampons, and a range of services including those supplied by architects, barristers and solicitors, veterinary surgeons, stockbrokers, surveyors, the cross-channel ferriers, and credit-card companies. Moreover there have been criticisms of both the quality of the MMC's analysis of individual cases, and successive governments' unaggressive approaches in applying remedial measures, which have relied heavily on informal undertakings from the firms concerned. More generally, the policy has not succeeded in establishing clear guidelines on the kinds of abuse of dominant market positions which should be controlled, with a predictable prospect of strong countermeasures being taken where such abuses can be proven.

Since the introduction of merger controls in 1965 many proposals falling within the legislation have been screened, though only a small proportion have been referred to the MMC. For example, between November 1973 (when the Fair Trading Act came into force) and the end of 1984 nearly two thousand cases were reviewed, but only 64 referred. Of those referred, only a relative handful were stopped, though several more were allowed to proceed only after certain assurances had been given. Once again, however, merger verdicts and reports have failed to evolve clear guidelines on permissible levels of market concentration in merger cases, or to establish uniform criteria for assessing barriers to entry of new competition, or substitutability by consumers of one product for another. As with monopoly policy, this has led to an unpredictability of outcome in merger cases, and probably mitigated against the policy's impact.

In purely numerical terms, restrictive-practice control appears to have been more successful than monopoly and merger policy. By the end of 1984 the cumulative total of goods agreements registered since 1956 had reached 4,215 and that for services agreements (since 1976) a further 984. Of these, about half had been abandoned, and about two-fifths of the remainder had had all restrictions removed. Not all these cases were heard by the Court; most abandoned agreements were either terminated voluntarily after the results of key cases became known, or were simply left to expire. By the mid-1970s the DGFT was able to say that no more significant, known cases remained to be dealt with (though this was before the extension of the legislation to cover services agreements). However, both the escape clauses in the 1956 Act and the quality of the Court's reasoning and decisions have been adversely criticized. Indeed, doubts have been expressed over the suitability of judicial practices for resolving complex economic issues. Thus it is not clear whether the right decisions have been taken.

On the consumer protection side, a number of references have been made to the CPAC, and more than twenty voluntary codes of practice have been introduced covering, amongst others, package holidays, new and used car sales, shoe sales and repairs, funeral services, mail-order trading, laundering and dry-cleaning. Various other practices have been investigated, including advertising, bargain-offer claims, party-plan and door-to-door selling, as has the conduct of a large number of individual firms. The 1968 Trades Description Act has been reviewed, and the 1974 Consumer Credit Act implemented (under which the OFT is responsible for licensing traders). A working party on advertising reported in 1980, and a wide range of leaflets has been published containing various kinds of consumer information. In general, the variety and detail of the consumer protection activities undertaken since 1973 is impressive. As expected, however, in the light of competition policy developments, the overwhelming emphasis has been on voluntary solutions: negotiated codes, assurances and the like; and the problem then is that in this sphere voluntary co-operation is perhaps most likely to be forthcoming where it is least needed.

The level of merger activity and concentration trends: Whatever impact monopoly and merger policy may have had in individual cases, it has not prevented a strong trend towards increased seller concentration both in individual markets and at the aggregate level (though this trend has de-celerated since about 1968).[1] Moreover there has been little sign of a secular decrease in merger activity that might be attributed to policy; and it is even possible that the introduction of restrictive-practice control may have con-tributed to very high rates of merger activity in the 1960s, as merging firms 'internalized' the agreements they were no longer able to make between themselves as legally independent companies.

TABLE 4.11
Merger Activity 1970–84

	Proposals covered by Fair Trading Act			*Business Monitor MQ7 Series. Industrial and commercial: number*
	Numbers	*Assets acquired[1] (£m)*	*Industrial & commercial: number* [1]	
1970–74 (p.a.)	116	4,074	92	919
1975–9 (p.a.)	215	7,945	165	450
1980	182 (115)	22,289 (21,042)	141 (89)	469
1981	164 (105)	43,597 (42,537)	126 (79)	452
1982	190 (122)	25,939 (24,494)	144 (93)	463
1983	192 (129)	45,495 (44,275)	143 (104)	447
1984	259 (223)	80,688 (79,957)	200 (165)	507

Source: Director General of Fair Trading, *Annual Report* (HMSO, 1984).
Note: 1 Figures in brackets show the outcome if a £30m assets criterion had been in operation throughout 1980–84. The assets criterion was also revised from £5m to £15m in 1980.

Table 4.11 shows both the general level of merger activity (*The Business Monitor*, MQ7 series) and the incidence of mergers within the scope of the Act. On average the latter accounted for approximately a quarter of the total (considering industrial and commercial mergers only), though this proportion had risen to nearly 40% in 1984. In the main this increase in the effective coverage of the Act was due to a rising number of larger mergers within the total. Table 4.12 shows that horizontal mergers remain the largest category, though they now tend to account for around two-thirds of the total, compared with over 80% in the late 1960s. Vertical mergers account

---

1   See L.Hannah and J.Kay, *Concentration in Modern Industry* (London, 1977) and P.E.Hart and R.Clarke, *Concentration in British Industry 1935–75* (CUP for NIESR, 1977).

TABLE 4.12

Percentage of Proposed Mergers by Number and Value of Assets Acquired, Classified by Type of Acquisition, 1965–84

	Horizontal		*Vertical*		*Diversified*	
	number	*assets*	*number*	*assets*	*number*	*assets*
1965–69[1]	82	89	6	5	12	7
1970–74[1]	73	65	5	4	23	27
1975–79[1]	62	67	9	7	29	26
1980	65	68	4	1	31	31
1981	62	71	6	2	32	27
1982	65	64	5	4	30	32
1983	71	73	4	1	25	26
1984	63	79	4	1	33	20

Source: Director General of Fair Trading, *Annual Report* (HMSO, 1984).
Note: 1 Annual average.

for a very minor amount of merger activity, while the incidence of conglomerate (or 'diversified') mergers has risen substantially from the late 1960s to around 30% (by number) in the 1980s. However, this last development is perhaps as likely to reflect reduced opportunities for horizontal mergers (so many firms having been taken over already), as any differential impact of policy on horizontal mergers themselves as the category of most potential significance for market power.

The latest available statistics on the level of concentration in UK markets are for 1977. Table 4.13 gives a frequency distribution of the degree of concentration in broad (MLH) industries and more disaggregated product markets, in terms of the commonly used five-firm concentration ratio – the combined market share of the top five firms (CR_5).[1] Amongst other things this underlines how the broader MLH data understate the true level of seller concentration at market level; thus in over half the product groups, CR_5 exceeded 70%, compared with just under 30% of MLH industries. Note that in nearly one in six product-groups, five firms controlled 90% of the market or more. Overall, the statistics strongly suggest that oligopoly is the prevailing market structure. Earlier data for 1963 suggested the UK level of market concentration was much higher than in France and Italy, and much the same as in Belgium and the Netherlands. Strictly comparable data for West Germany is not available, but the data which does exist suggests a pattern similar to that in the UK.

Alongside the trend towards a higher degree of seller concentration in individual markets there has been a similar, accelerating increase in overall concentration, as measured by the share in net output of the 100 largest firms in the economy. Before World War I this was less than 20%, rising to 33% in 1958. Over the next twelve years, the rate of increase roughly trebled, and in

---

1   For a discussion of alternative concentration indices, see Hannah and Kay, *op. cit.*

TABLE 4.13

Seller Concentration in Selected UK Markets, 1977

Concentration class (range of five-firm concentration ratio, %)	Number of markets in class			
	Product group basis[2]		MLH basis	
	No. [1]	%	No.	%
0–9	0	0.0	0	0.0
10–19	6	0.1	6	3.7
20–29	25	3.1	15	9.3
30–39	37	4.5	21	13.0
40–49	102	12.5	34	21.0
50–59	101	12.4	22	13.6
60–69	124	15.2	16	9.9
70–79	145	17.7	15	9.3
80–89	140	17.1	18	11.1
90–100	137	16.8	15	9.3
Total	817	100.0	162	100.0

Source: Business Monitor (PO 1006): *Statistics of Product Concentration of UK Manufacturing.*

Notes: 1 The meaning of this column is that there is no product group in which the largest five firms account for less than 10% of total sales, six in which they account for 10–19%, and so on.

2 The markets included are sub-Minimum List Heading product groups in mining and manufacturing, for which five-firm concentration ratios are available.

1970 the largest 100 firms accounted for nearly 50% of net output.[1] The precise connection between overall concentration and seller concentration in individual markets is not well documented. But of the largest 100 manufacturing companies between 1968 and 1974, approximately half were known to have two or more 'monopolies' (25% shares in particular markets) and, of these, twenty companies had five or more monopolies.

Other evidence: Evidence on the degree of competition other than structural indicators of the sort considered above tends to be of an unsystematic and often impressionistic nature, but may nevertheless be informative. One apparent improvement due to policy is that the great mass of overt price-fixing and resale price maintenance which existed prior to the 1956 and 1964 Acts has now gone. However, there is a question over how far the abandonment of restrictive practices has actually affected behaviour in the markets concerned. As we have seen, cartel arrangements are most likely in fairly concentrated, oligopolistic markets, where they may merely formalise the mutually accommodating behaviour which would in any case occur.

---

1   S.J.Prais, *The Evolution of Giant Firms in Great Britain: A Study of Concentration in Manufacturing Industry in Britain 1909–70* (CUP, 1976).

Removal of an agreement in these circumstances would not touch the
underlying, structural cause of this behaviour. Moreover where restrictive
agreements have been abandoned, firms may have been able to substitute
alternative arrangements; the extension of the law to embrace information
agreements in 1968 was in response to such a development. It is also
possible, as we have seen, that the introduction of restrictive-practice control in 1956 may have intensified merger activity while, as we have also
seen, many firms have substituted 'recommended prices' for RPM.

However, in his more recent Annual Reports, the DGFT writes rather
optimistically about some recent competition-increasing trends, saying, for
example, that 1984 saw 'the walls of some institutional Jerichos begin to
crumble under the eyes of various Joshuas'. Amongst other things, the
DGFT mentions in particular increased competition in the professions and
The City; the breaking of the opticians' dispensing monopoly and ending
of restrictions of advertising; the introduction of display advertising for
solicitors and accountants; the ending of the solicitors' monopoly on house
conveyancing; proposals which would allow Building Societies to broaden
their actitivies; removal of Stock Exchange restrictions – e.g. on minimum
commissions, single capacity dealing (separating the function of brokers
and jobbers), and restrictions on outside shareholdings and participation in
member companies – which, though now proceeding 'voluntarily', were
prompted by five years' work in the OFT in preparation of a case that
would have come to court in 1984, had not the government introduced a
Bill exempting the Stock Exchange from Restrictive Practice legislation,
conditional on the introduction of self-regulatory measures; and proposals
for increased competition among airlines by the Civil Aviation Authority,
including the ending of exemption from competition laws.

Other developments which might be mentioned include the extension of
competition policy to public-sector bodies under the 1980 Act, and government deregulation in various markets (often in the context of privatization
policy, for example in ending the Post Office monopoly on mail-carrying,
and in liberalizing licensing arrangements for express coach services). On
the consumer protection side, the DGFT also argues that, while vigilance
against individual rogue suppliers is an unending task, the present-day
consumer is historically speaking much more protected than formerly, in
part as the result of legislation (e.g. in relation to dealings with credit
companies following the 1974 Act), but also as a result of voluntary guarantee and accreditation schemes, and other developments on the part of
suppliers, that are taking place with changes in the climate of opinion on
consumers' rights, and increasing public awareness of both those rights and
the problems they seek to address. The very existence of an official consumer protection policy since 1973, with the OFT as overseer, may
reasonably be assumed to have contributed to this development of public
opinion and awareness. Thus, while catalogues of this sort only give part
of the overall picture, they do at least show that the picture is not all
bad.

Prospects for future policy: Quite how 'wide-ranging' the review of competition policy now under way will turn out to be is an open question. It can safely be assumed that the basic, 'neutral' stance and principle of case-by-case review in UK competition policy will not be changed in any fundamental way, since the flexibility which this affords has been favourably commented upon both by the DGFT and recent Secretaries of State. So there is no real prospect of a radical shift, for example, to an American style, *per se* approach, with widespread prohibitions on monopoly situations and practices, and no reference to their effects in individual cases. However, in the specific case of certain kinds of restrictive practice the DGFT has recently mooted the possibility of introducing a prohibition (rather than merely a presumption of illegality), backed up by stronger sanctions than the very mild penalties which now attach to non-registration, and this may or may not be taken up in the review.

Many observers would argue that a second specific issue should be reconsidered, namely a change in the 'onus of proof' in merger cases. Specifically, they would propose requiring firms to demonstrate positive benefits from the merger, in place of the present requirement for the DGFT to show actual detriments to the public interest. In the previous major review of policy in 1978/79, such a change was widely anticipated, but in the event did not happen.[1] Had it occurred, there is little doubt that shifting the 'benefit of the doubt' in this way would have affected the rate of merger activity. In the present political climate, however, the question is perhaps unlikely to come up again, since the government's stated policy on mergers since 1984 has been that, provided competition is not materially weakened, it is for the market to adjudicate on the merits of individual cases.

One area which it is clear at the time of writing is likely to be covered, is that of the criteria applied in referring merger cases for investigation. As we have seen, the sole criterion since 1984 has in principle been how competition is affected. However, there have been criticisms of inconsistency and unpredictability in referral policy since 1979, coming from the CBI and other groups. Moreover the question of referral has lately taken on a new dimension following a wave of merger proposals involving £1bn-plus assets deals from late 1985 onwards (including Allied-Lyons/ Elders IXL, £1.8bn; Habitat-Mothercare/BHS £1.5bn; Imperial Group/United Biscuits £1.2bn; Guiness/Argyll Group/Distillers £2.5bn; and GEC/Plessey £1.2bn). So large are these mergers that fears have been expressed that the 'market test' – central to the government's present policy – will become distorted. Already one of these mergers (Allied/ Elders) has been referred on grounds which appear to be concerned not primarily with effects on competition, but with unusual financing arrangements (to make the bid, Elders had borrowed most of the money from a

---

1 See *A Review of Monopolies and Mergers Policy*, Cmnd. 7198 (HMSO, May 1978) and *A Review of Restrictive Trade Practices Policy*, Cmnd. 7512 (HMSO, March 1979).

consortium of banks). Whatever else it may or may not do, the forthcoming review seems bound to consider the special problems raised by mega-mergers.

V   REGIONAL POLICY
V.1   Introduction

Regional policies seek to reduce or eliminate disparities in incomes, industrial growth, migration and, above all, unemployment between different geographical areas of the country. If markets operated in a smooth friction-less fashion there would be no need for such policies, since the disparities would be self-eliminating. In particular, regional unemployment would signal labour-market disequilibrium with excess supply of labour at the ruling wage levels, to which the market would respond with lower real wages and product prices. In practice, however, there are market frictions due to downwards rigidities in nationally determined wages and prices, and due to the immobility of capital and labour (the latter on account of such factors as rehousing problems, imperfect knowledge of job opportunities elsewhere, and social ties).

Moreover, government intervention would be justified even with friction-less markets if private and social costs and benefits diverge. Thus a firm might choose a location in the south-east of England on the basis of the costs actually entering its accounts. But the socially optimum location could be elsewhere, e.g. in Wales, Scotland or the North, when account is taken of social costs such as traffic congestion, the availability of social overheads like schools, hospitals, etc., as well as less tangible benefits such as the preservation of existing community life in areas which might otherwise become depopulated.

If the firm's private production costs are higher at the socially optimum location, there is a real resource cost in diverting it there, and also a subsidy may be required. However, welfare is raised and policy intervention remains justified as long as the benefits exceed the costs. In practice, UK policy has been based on a premise that location does not significantly affect costs, at least for much of manufacturing, for which there is some evidence.

For the purposes of regional policy, the UK is divided into eleven standard regions: Northern, Yorkshire and Humberside, East Midlands, East Anglia, South East, South West, Wales, West Midlands, North West, Scotland and Northern Ireland. The imbalances between the regions which policy seeks to redress originate from complex geographical, technological and historical causes. Falling employment in agriculture, and the decline of the former staple industries, especially coal, cotton-textiles, steel and shipbuilding, have been a major influence since the mid-1950s. In the earlier phases of industrialization in Britain these had located close to sources of power and raw materials in the North, Scotland and Wales. More modern industries, particularly those using electrical power, have developed elsewhere. Thus structural developments in the economy create tendencies for centres of economic activity to shift, while demographic developments remain largely shaped by the past, and it is against these tendencies that regional policies must pull. However, the UK regions are nearly all mixed urban-rural areas with a fair spread of activities, and the imbalance between them is not as severe as in some other countries, e.g. Italy, where there are extreme differences between the industrialized north and the largely agricultural south of the country.

Problems of declining employment and population and structural decay in inner cities are considered by the present Conservative government as separate from the regional problem. However, as we shall see, urban and regional policies may interact, not always favourably, and logically the two must be seen as dealing with part of the same, overall problem of the spatial distribution of economic activity. Similarly, the British problem must be seen in a wider European context, especially as the Treaty of Rome was intended, above all, to ensure the free mobility of resources and production within the European Community.

Like Britain, the EEC has a number of regional problems in older industrial areas developed around iron ore and coal. These include the Ruhr, Saar and Lorraine. A further, serious EEC regional problem stems from the existence of low-income agricultural areas to which industrialization has never come. Originally these were mainly in parts of France and, especially, the south of Italy (where GDP per inhabitant is little more than half the level in the industrial north of the country, and only a quarter of that in Hamburg, the richest part of the EEC). With the expansion of the Community, this aspect of the EEC regional problem has been intensified by the addition of the Irish Republic, Greece, Spain and Portugal. The flourishing industrial centres of the EEC, on the other hand, lie mainly along the Rhine-Rhône valleys, from the Netherlands to Northern Italy. These are estimated to have accounted for some 60% of the Gross Product of the EEC before its enlargement in 1973. Some commentators now speak of a 'golden triangle' in Europe, lying roughly between Hamburg, London and Milan.

V.2   Policy Measures

UK policy: The strategy of regional policy has been to identify specific areas requiring assistance, primarily on the basis of above-average unemployment rates. Firms located in or moving to these areas have then been offered various financial incentives, while administrative controls have been placed on industrial expansion elsewhere. Both the qualifying areas and the type and value of financial incentives have been changed frequently in the last forty years, and the degree of control on industrial development outside the assisted areas has also fluctuated. Policy measures were first introduced in the prewar Special Areas Act of 1934. Postwar policy has been implemented through the Distribution of Industry Acts since 1945, the Local

Employment Acts from 1960, various Finance Acts, the 1972 Industry Act
and the 1982 Industrial Development Act.

Current regional policy provisions have been in force only since November 1984, following the publication of a White Paper a year earlier.[1] Details
of earlier main policy phases – from 1945–60, 1960–66, 1966–75, 1975–79,
1979–82 and 1982–84 – may be found elsewhere;[2] here we focus on the latest
revisions leading to current policy. The 1984 revision abolished an existing
category of special development areas, which had been designated as areas
of most acute need, to leave a two-tier structure: *development areas*, and
intermediate areas (the so-called 'grey areas', lying mainly outside the more
seriously affected development areas, but suffering similar problems). Firms
in intermediate areas are eligible for *regional selective assistance* (RSA) in
the form of negotiable project grants based on capital costs and job creation.
Those in development areas are eligible for both RSA and *regional development grants* (RDGs). With the abolition of special development areas and
the 22% RDG rate previously available there, a 15% flat-rate grant towards
eligible fixed capital costs now applies in all development areas. Under
current policy, RDGs are made on a (job-creating) project basis (previously
they were based on qualifying premises), and are subject to a new, lower
ceiling of £10,000 per job (not applicable in the case of small firms) or a fixed
sum of £3,000 for each job created, whichever is the greater. This compares
with £30–£40,000 per job under previous policies. To reduce a perceived
bias in favour of manufacturing in previous policy, certain service activities
are now eligible for RDGs.

Together with government provision of land and factory units, these are
the main financial incentives in operation at present in Great Britain.
(Special provisions apply to Northern Ireland.) In addition, assisted area
status also brings eligibility for assistance towards infrastructural and other
projects from the European Regional Development Fund.

Altogether, the assisted areas now cover 35% of the working population.
This is less than the 47% at one time benefitting from regional policy, but
more than the 28% covered prior to 1984. However, the latest increase in
coverage is due primarily to the award of intermediate area status, for the
first time, to the recently prosperous and densely populated Birmingham/
West Midlands area, together with parts of Manchester and its northern
satellite towns; and in fact only 15% of the working population is now
covered by development areas, compared with 22% by the previous
development and special development areas. The development areas which
remain are mainly located around the old industrial centres of Glasgow,
Liverpool, Newcastle and South Wales, together with geographically
remote areas of Cornwall, and small areas such as those seriously affected by
steel works closures in Corby, Rotherham and Scunthorpe. Intermediate

---

1   *Regional Industrial Development*, Cmnd. 9111 (HMSO, December 1983).

2   For a succinct outline see B. Moore, J. Rhodes and R. Tyler, *The Effects of Government
Regional Economic Policy*, HMSO, 1986.

areas mostly adjoin development areas or take in remote parts of the country such as the Scottish highlands and Hebridean Islands and parts of North Wales and Anglesey. Except for certain parts of the extreme West Country, there are no assisted areas at all in the Conservative Party heartland south of a line from the Bristol Channel to The Wash.

In redrawing the map of the assisted areas, the government's aim appears to have been for a wider outer tier of intermediate areas, receiving only modest UK incentives, but maximizing access to the European regional development fund, coupled with a more tightly drawn, inner tier qualifying for higher levels of UK support. The government's stated intention is thereby to achieve a more cost-effective policy involving, in particular, a shift of emphasis from the essentially *automatic* RDGs towards the *discretionary* RSA. RGDs (historically by far the largest expenditure category) are set to fall for several reasons: abolition of the higher 22% rate in the former special development areas; the reduced coverage of development areas; ending of grants for replacement of plant and machinery; and the new, lower grant ceiling of £10,000 per job. The government's hope is that, in conjunction with the switch from a qualifying premises to a qualifying project grant basis, this will permit greater concentration of resources on net new job creation rather than on subsidizing developments which would have occurred in any case. However, it should be noted that total assistance given under regional industrial policy, which has already been drastically cut back from the levels of the early 1980s in the previous revision of policy in August 1982, will be subject to a massive further reduction – the latest step in a progressive descaling of regional economic policy since 1979. Table 4.14 reveals how the trend in regional policy expenditure has been reversed under Conservative governments since 1979. Because of transitional arrangements which involve an overlap in the operation of the old and the new RDG schemes and the old and new maps, the full effects of the latest

TABLE 4.14

Regional Industrial Assistance 1977/8 to 1984/5, GB (at current and constant prices, £m)

	77/8	78/9	79/80	80/81	81/2	82/3	83/4	84/5
Regional Development Grants	393	417	441[1]	491	617	540[1]	439	417
Regional Selective Assistance	44	104	78	74	76	90	149	176
Total (at outturn prices)	437	521	519	565	693	630	588	593
Total (at constant, 1980 prices)[2]	646	697	595	545	608	517	462	446

Source: *Annual Reports* under the Industry Act 1972[3] and Industrial Development Act 1982 (HMSO, various years).
Notes: 1 1979/80 figure includes £110m deferred expenditure on approved grant applications; 1982/3 excludes £150m for the same reason.
2 Outturn prices deflated by implicit GDP deflator, adjusted to fiscal-year basis.

cuts will not be felt until 1987/8. Then spending is expected to approach £400m, nearly £300m less than it would be under pre-1984 arrangements. Thus cost-effectiveness will have to increase by over 40% for the new policy merely to equal the impact of the old, which many observers would consider in itself inadequate.

As was mentioned earlier, the second main strand of regional policy alongside financial incentives (the 'carrot') has historically been administrative control over industrial expansion outside the assisted areas. When in operation this has been exercised mainly via *Industrial Development Certificates* (IDCs) relating to new factory buildings or extensions (the 'stick'). Up to 1972, they were required in all areas for projects above a certain minimum size, and after 1966 their issue was strictly controlled in the Midlands and South East. From 1972, IDCs have not been required in development areas, and after 1974 a three-tier system was applied to the rest of the country although, in the continuing recession which followed, IDC control was not strictly applied. Finally, IDCs were suspended in 1982. Office development has at times been subject to similar controls, though this has never been regarded as a major policy instrument for dispersing jobs to the regions.

Policies to alleviate inner city problems have been comparatively small and *ad hoc* in nature. Initially in the postwar period, central and local government policies to relieve congestion and assist urban renewal in large conurbations encouraged an exodus to the suburbs and new towns; under the 1946 New Towns Act and the 1952 Town Development Act more than twenty new towns have been established, and rather more enlarged. This policy may actually have conflicted with regional policies, since the new towns have by no means all been in development areas, and may have been a counter-attraction to firms which otherwise might have responded to regional incentives. More recently there has been recognition of the existence of serious problems that remain in inner cities, leading to among other things the creation of 'enterprise zones' from 1981; the designation of free ports from 1984; and, following riots in Liverpool, Birmingham and London, specific local urban aid programmes operated through the Department of the Environment.

Enterprise zones are very small districts, averaging around only 500 acres, primarily in older urban areas. The provisions relating to the 25 designated zones reflect an underlying belief on the part of the Conservative government that private initiatives can be stifled by excessive public-authority involvement and government rules and regulations. Therefore, in addition to financial benefits (100% capital allowances, and exemption from both general rates on industrial and commercial property and development land tax), firms are intended to benefit from simplified government procedures and speedier administration of controls over development. For example, firms in enterprise zones are excluded from the scope of Industrial Training Boards, were exempted from any remaining requirement for industrial development certificates (IDCs), and are promised speedier processing of requests for customs warehousing, etc. and minimal request to supply statistics to government. *Free ports* are areas to which goods can be imported free of customs duties and other levies provided they are sent abroad again after processing. The six free ports designated in 1984 were in Belfast, Cardiff, Prestwick, Liverpool, Birmingham and Southampton.

EEC policy: EEC regional policy came into operation with the establishment of a European Regional Development Fund (ERDF) in 1975. The ERDF now accounts for around 9% of the Community budget. This is of course very much less than the 73% spent on agriculture, and also represents only about 5% of total spending on regional support policies by member states. Nevertheless the UK has been a substantial beneficiary, receiving 3.3bn ECU up to 1985 (24% of the total); only Italy has to date received more, with 5.1bn ECU (37%). In principle the EEC funds are intended to be additional to government spending in the regions, but in 1980 there was some dispute between Britain and the European Commission (EC) as to whether this had actually been the case. The ERDF originally worked solely on a national quota basis, within which the fund could contribute up to 20% towards job-creation schemes and 50% towards infrastructural development under the national policies of member states. After 1979, however, a small proportion of the fund was earmarked for 'non-quota' purposes. This was intended to provide finance for projects negotiated between member governments and the EC, which would direct funds towards the most pressing problems and at the same time permit a more integrated, Community-wide policy to emerge. In 1984, the last year in which the non-quota section was in operation (see below), just over 5% of the total Regional Fund was earmarked for non-quota purposes (though not all of this was spent).

In 1981 the EC put forward radical proposals for revision of the ERDF. These reflected concern that regional disparities within the Community had widened over the preceding ten years, sought to focus policy more sharply on the most serious problems, and emphasized the need to knit regional policy and other Community programmes more closely together. The main proposals were to abolish national quotas and focus attention on specific regions (including Northern Ireland, parts of Scotland and Wales, and the North and North West of England) and to raise the non-quota section of the fund to 20%, thereby increasing the influence of the EC over the national policies of member states. Studies of the regional side-effects of all major Community programmes were also proposed, in particular of agricultural support under the CAP, and assistance for the restructuring of coal and steel production under the ECSC Treaty.

However, these proposals met with considerable resistance from member states unwilling to relinquish their quotas and control over national policies. As a result, revised proposals emerged in 1983, and new policy provisions took effect from January 1985. The quota and non-quota sections of the fund were amalgamated into a single fund, and higher, more simplified rates of assistance introduced (including grants of 50%, compared with 20–30% previously). National quotas were retained, but in the form of upper and lower bounds on a given country's share, giving more flexibility in the allocation of funds, and providing the EC with some scope for a *de facto* increase in what was previously non-quota type assistance. Finally, a gradual switch was initiated from the previous emphasis on assisting national projects – a bridge, a stretch of road, clearing the environment – to supporting longer-term, Community-based 'programmes', e.g. for small firms, employment-creating activities, advanced technology, environmental improvement and priority areas. The intention is that these will become the core of a central Community-wide policy, over which the EC will take the initiative. Thus a compromise was reached, in which national shares in the benefits were guaranteed within certain ranges, but policy became more explicitly Community-oriented and 'Communautaire', rather than a matter of the EEC simply financing nationally determined projects.

Under the new provisions, Britain will remain a major beneficiary, with guaranteed minimum allocations of 21.42% and 28.56% of the ERDF, respectively, as set in 1985. These shares will fall by approximately one third after the entry of Spain and Portugal in 1986, in line with those of other existing members, but absolute benefits are not expected to decrease, as the total fund will be increased to take account of the new members. Quite apart from this once-for-all enlargement, the ERDF has been growing by about 5% per annum – in sharp contrast, as we have seen, with UK levels of national support for the regions.

V.3   Regional Policy Impact

Latest estimates suggest that government regional economic policy in the UK created some 630,000 permanent jobs in the assisted areas from 1960 to 1981, after allowance for local multiplier effects,[1] at an exchequer cost of about £40,000 per job in constant (1982) prices. The rate of job creation was much lower in the late 1970s than the late 1960s, when it reached a peak. All three major types of policy instrument – IDCs, capital subsidies of various kinds, and contributions towards operating costs – have exerted a separate, significant influence. About two-thirds of the extra jobs may be accounted for by RDGs (or corresponding financial incentives operating via tax allowances), 16% by IDCs, 9% by RSA, and 6% by the one-time regional employment premium (REP) – a labour subsidy paid to manufacturing firms in development areas, in addition to capital subsidies, from 1967 to 1976. (In

---

1   B.Moore *et al.*, *op. cit.* See also *Cambridge Economic Policy Review*, Vol. 6, No. 2, July 1980, and Vol. 8, No. 2, December 1983; and B. Moore and J. Rhodes, 'Evaluating the Effects of British Regional Policy', *EJ*, Vol. 83, 1973, pp. 87–110; 'Regional Economic Policy and the Movement of Manufacturing Firms to Development Areas', *Eca*, 43, pp. 17–31, February 1976; and *Methods in Evaluating the Effects of Regional Policy*, Paris, OCED, 1977.

interpreting these figures it must be remembered that different policy in-truments have been in force for varying lengths of time.)

Since the objective of regional policy is to mitigate regional disparities, its impact should ultimately be seen in regional indicators of industrial output, incomes and, especially, unemployment. Statistical Appendix table A–10 gives regional unemployment rates for 1966 and for each year since 1975. As can be seen, there has been a significant narrowing of regional differentials in purely proportionate terms; for example, unemployment in Northern Ireland, the worst affected area, was only 56% above the national average in 1985, compared with nearly four times the national average in 1966, and so on. But at the same time, overall unemployment has risen more than nine-fold. Moreover the four main problem areas in 1966 – Northern Ireland, Wales, Scotland and the North – still provide three of the worst affected areas in 1985, only Scotland having improved its relative position from ninth to fifth. Thus, though the context is now one of high national unemploy-ment, a regional problem still exists and, with some exceptions, including the dramatic decline of the West Midlands from lowest to sixth highest place in the regional unemployment league, the main problems are where they always have been.

Meanwhile structural factors continue to favour the South East (for example, much of the investment in new 'sunrise' industries involving micro-electronic technology is taking place within 50 miles of London) and East Anglia (within the European 'golden triangle'); and the problem in assess-ing regional policy effects is to disentangle them from these other, structural forces at work. This requires careful research. Results so far suggest that up to 1966 structural factors were operating very strongly against the most depressed regions (Northern Ireland, Scotland, the North and the North-West); however, policy exerted a beneficial effect in each case.[1] In the period 1966–1975, the adverse structural effects were less adverse (and in fact became favourable in the case of the Northern region), while policy, as we have seen, was at its height. In general, we may conclude that policy contributed substantially to the narrowing of differentials up to 1975, especi-ally after 1966. Since 1975, as we have seen, the strength of regional policy was very much reduced, and the continued narrowing of differentials and a much higher average figure may be seen as largely due to the spread of very deep recession to previously more prosperous industries and regions.

While the effectiveness of regional policy must ultimately register in re-gional statistics of the kind just considered, questions may also be asked about the nature of the policy instruments used and their cost-effectiveness. Here a number of criticisms of previous policy have been made. Firstly, most of the financial incentives have related to capital expenditures, imparting a capital bias to the policy as a while. Thus the firms most likely to be attracted to assisted areas have been those with highly capital-intensive technologies

---

1 See B. Moore and J. Rhodes, *op. cit.*

(e.g. oil refining), offering relatively few new jobs for a given total expenditure (the 'catalytic cracker syndrome'). Moreover, the distortion of relative prices for labour and capital in the assisted regions will have encouraged all firms in them, including those not attracted by regional policies, to substitute capital for labour so far as technological constraints will permit. Significantly, the highest job-creation rates of regional policies occurred in the late 1960s and early 1970s, when the capital bias of the policy was offset by REP.

Secondly, it has been argued that the use of automatic financial incentives (like RDGs, tax allowances and REP), as opposed to discretionary regional grants tied to specific programmes of job-creation (like RSA), has reduced the cost-effectiveness of regional support, since aid is given to firms already in development areas, as well as to those moving in or setting up. Thirdly, the use of cash grants as opposed to incentives in the form of reduced tax liability has been criticised on the grounds that it does not differentiate between efficient and inefficient firms (i.e. those making profits and others). On the other hand, industrialists argue that cash grants have more influence over firms' decisions, because their size is known and the monies are recoverable at or soon after capital expenditures, whereas the magnitudes and timing of future tax remissions is much more uncertain.

As we have seen, securing greater cost-effectiveness has become the major objective in regional policy since the latest policy change in 1984; and the switch of emphasis from RDGs to RSA, and lower grant-per-job ceilings, may be seen as correcting features of past policies which have been criticised on the foregoing grounds. The main question which remains over current policy, however, is one of level: whether it will prove adequate in the face of structural forces at work in the future, especially after the full effect of the latest, 43% cut in expenditure is felt in 1987/8. A cause for concern here is that the traditionally depressed areas of the UK, in Northern Ireland, Scotland, the North, North-West, Wales and the South-West, are geographically even more remote from the economic centre of gravity of the EEC than they ever were in the UK alone.

On the inner cities front, the freeport development has so far been disappointing, while the principal effect of enterprise zones seems to have been to redistribute jobs over a rather narrow area. Thus an independent report found that some 10,700 jobs had been generated up to end-1983 in the first eleven zones designated in 1981, at a cost of around £16,500 per job.[1] However, 75% of companies opening in a zone came from the same county, and at least 85% originated within the region; only 14 companies had moved between regions. So far, it seems, 'enterprise' has been mostly on the part of firms responding to the lure of, in particular, a 10-year rates 'holiday' by moving down the road, rather than on the part of new firms setting up and creating jobs which did not exist before.

---

1   Roger Tim and Partners, *Monitoring Enterprise Zones: Year Three Report*, 25 Craven Street, WC2.

VI   TECHNOLOGY, INDUSTRIAL STRUCTURE AND PLANNING

VI.1   R & D, Hi-tech and Information Technology

In Britain, as in other industrialized countries, there is a long-standing history of government intervention to promote the technological development of industry, via support of R & D and industrial innovation. The basic economic rationale is that the social rate of return from innovation exceeds the private benefits, because the innovator will not be able to appropriate all the returns from his innovation. Thus if R & D and other innovative effort is left entirely to market forces, too little will be undertaken. Early US case studies suggested a social rate of return of 56% compared with a private return of only 25%.[1] The analysis also highlighted the inherent riskiness of R & D effort, and large variations in private returns, and showed that in nearly one third of cases it would not have been rational for firms to invest in the projects if the returns had been known in advance with certainty; yet in nearly all these cases the social return was positive. Similarly large gaps between social and private returns have been found in subsequent studies, and have influenced thinking on innovation policy. This has had a number of strands, including financial subsidies, institutional measures and, more recently, special programmes of support for research and innovation.

Tables 4.15 and 4.16 give figures of R & D spending in Britain and elsewhere.[2] As can be seen, total spending in Britain is roughly on a par with that in other major industrialized countries, in relation to GDP. As in France, more than half is financed by the government, compared with somewhat less than half in the US, and much smaller fractions in West Germany and, especially, Japan, where industry is by far the predominant source. However, it must be remembered when interpreting these figures that UK GDP is itself relatively low, and in absolute terms the US spends 6–7 times as much as the UK, Japan nearly 3 times as much, and West Germany 1½ times as much. Moreover, UK spending has been growing very much less rapidly than in other countries, and actually falling as a proportion of GDP. Nor is this all, from the point of view of developing the technological base of industry as a whole. For around half of UK government R & D is on defence, the industrial spin-off from which is necessarily limited by secrecy, and the international comparison of spending on civil projects only is very much less favourable to the UK (table 4.15). Moreover, UK civil R & D spending by government in the past has itself tended to be concentrated heavily in certain narrow fields, notably aerospace and the nuclear programme. Although this has become less pronounced in more recent years, when there has been rapid growth in areas like electronic components and

---

1 See E. Mansfield, 'Measuring the Social and Private Rates of Return on Innovation' in *Economic Effects of Space and Other Advanced Technologies* (Strasbourg, Council of Europe, 1980).

2 See also P. L. Stoneman, 'Research and Development Policy in the UK', *Economic Review*, March 1986.

computers, British R & D still remains much less evenly spread than in most other countries, notably Japan.

TABLE 4.15

R&D Expenditure, UK and Selected Countries

	France	*W.Germany*	*Japan*	*UK*	*US*
Total R&D as % of 1983 GDP of which:	2.2	2.6	2.5	2.3	2.8
Private Sector	0.8	1.5	2.0	1.0	1.6
Government	1.4	1.1	0.5	1.3	1.2
of which: defence	(0.5)	(0.1)	(0.0)	(0.7)	(0.8)
civil	(0.9)	(1.0)	(0.5)	(0.6)	(0.4)
Total civil R&D[1]	1.7	2.5	2.5	1.6	2.0
Annual growth of R&D 1967–82 (% p.a.)	5.9	5.9	9.8	0.9	4.1

Source: Derived from *Annual Review of Government Funded R&D* (HMSO, 1985) and *FT*.
Note: 1 Total domestic expenditure on R&D, less government expenditure on defence R&D, expressed as % of GDP.

TABLE 4.16

UK Government Expenditure on R&D, 1981/2–1987/8 (£bn)

	81/2	*82/3*	*83/4*	*84/5[2]*	*85/6[3]*	*86/7[3]*	*87/8[3]*
Civil	1.76	1.86	1.94	2.06	2.14	2.17	2.10
Defence	1.74	1.76	1.98	2.18	2.39	2.48	2.56
Net Total[1]	3.50	3.62	3.92	4.24	4.53	4.65	4.66
% defence	49.8	48.7	50.6	51.3	52.7	53.4	55.0

Source: *Annual Review of Government Funded R&D* (HMSO, 1985).
Notes: 1 Excluding receipts from industry, overseas, etc.
2 Estimated.　3 Planned.

Thus the present level, disposition and trend in total UK R & D effort give cause for some concern, and future government plans at the time of writing offer no relief. Total nominal expenditure is planned to rise by about 10% in the three years up to 1987/8, but virtually all of the increase is in defence spending, whose share of the total will rise to 55% (table 4.16) and, after allowing for inflation, the real value of government R & D is likely to fall in absolute terms, as well as in relation to GDP. Moreover, there are apparently no major plans to stimulate private-sector spending, for example by special tax provisions.

Institutional measures to encourage technical progress in Britain began with the establishment of the National Research and Development Corporation (NRDC) in 1948, to finance the development of inventions made in universities, government laboratories and by private individuals, where this was in the public interest. The total resources at its disposal were, however, not large, some £15m a year towards the end of its existence. In 1982 the NRDC was merged with what remained of the National Enterprise Board (NEB), to form the British Technology Group (BTG). The government also sponsors work on behalf of industry in its own research establishments, funds research in universities and through Research Councils, and supports co-operative research associations in a number of industries.

Specific technological support programmes have become a major feature of government policy only in the last 5–10 years, and have focused in particular on micro-electronics and information technology (IT). Initially the programmes were nationally focused, and have included a Microprocessor Application Project (MAP), initiated in 1978 to increase computer awareness and training at senior levels in industry, the trade unions and public-sector bodies, and develop specific microprocessor applications; a schools microcomputer programme; specifically funded programmes for postgraduate training and staff appointments in IT in the universities; and the £350m, 5-year Alvey programme for joint research by firms and universities, focusing on the development of 'fifth generation' computers for the 1990s. In 1982 a variety of separate aid programmes were brought together into an overall 'Support for Innovation' scheme, under the auspices of the then recently created Minister for Information Technology. Expenditure rose rapidly up to November 1984, when a five-month freeze on further spending was imposed. Since then, spending has been cut back, to a planned £280m in 1986/7, compared with £298m in the previous year, and £378m in the year before. In addition, the government has at the time of writing indicated that no large-scale funding will be forthcoming for any successor to the Alvey programme after 1988. Present policy, insofar as there is one apart from cutting all expenditure possible, appears to favour confining national policy to promoting technological 'awareness' and exploiting the international pool of technology, and looking increasingly to international programmes as the way of increasing that pool. This, it should be said, is not the way that the USA and Japan have built up the technology gap which is widely perceived to exist between them and the rest of the world. It also represents a further abandonment of one earlier policy concern, to preserve a British capability in key areas. Among other things, this had involved state support both for Britain's only mainstream producer of microchips, INMOS (now a subsidiary of Thorn-EMI), and for Britain's only remaining mainframe computer manufacturer ICL (now taken over by STC, a British-registered company, but thirty per cent owned by the American company, ITT).

So far, programmes for international collaboration on civil technology projects have been mainly at the European level. In 1983 the EEC adopted its first general framework for research policy, envisaging the preparation of action programmes and an expenditure of 3.8 bn ECU over four years, directed mainly towards energy (47%) and industrial competitiveness (28%).[1] Guidelines for the period 1987–91 are under discussion at the time of writing. These propose 9 bn ECU expenditure, and a shift of emphasis away from energy (65% of expenditure in 1982, recommended to fall to 21%) towards industrial competitiveness, and with 60% of expenditure going on programmes (compared with 17% in 1982). A draft new chapter of the Treaty of Rome on research and technology has been submitted which, if adopted, would define the extent of Community action and introduce new decision-making machinery. Among the specific programmes so far adopted are ESPRIT, an Alvey-type IT drive involving 1.4 bn ECU expenditure from 1984 to 1988, with 50% EEC funding of participating firms' costs; RACE, a telecommunications programme of research into integrated broadband communications; and a much smaller programme, BRITE, or 'basic research in industrial technologies for Europe', involving 125 m ECU over four years from 1985.

Other international research initiatives include a French-inspired EUREKA agreement, adopted by 18 EEC and EFTA nations and the Commission of the EEC in November 1985. This, however, seems likely to result more in a diversion of existing national support than a major new source of funds. There is also President Reagan's 'Star Wars' (SDI) research programme, though this is expected by many observers not to outlast his term of office. Finally, Japan has mooted an at present rather loosely defined and tentative proposal for a 10–20 year, £3.8 bn basic research project on human and organic processes (the 'Human Frontier Project' or 'Human Earth Sciences Programme') which, however, is not intended or expected to yield immediate industrial benefits.

VI.2   Structural Reorganisation

Under this heading we are concerned both with government assistance to declining industries and failing firms, and with intervention to promote growth, exploit scale economies and encourage the birth and development of small new enterprises. In textbook models these adjustments come about naturally via the long-run competitive process of entry and exit, merger and internal growth. However, capital market sanctions can be slow to operate in practice, financial institutions may not be responsive to the needs of companies at all stages of their growth and development, and the private and social costs of redeploying inputs (e.g. due to the duration of unemployment) may be greater through widespread bankruptcy and subsequent market responses than under a more gradual, government-assisted process. Where the government acts merely as a catalyst, aiding adjustment that would ultimately occur through the operation of market forces, its actions

---

1 For details of EEC developments see European Commission, *General Report on the Activities of the European Communities*, annual editions.

may be considered uncontroversial. If, however, the end result is to maintain industries permanently at an artificial level of production, as in the case of agriculture, other considerations of resource allocation arise.

The government has been directly involved with the major contraction or expansion of several public-sector industries, especially coal, rail, steel, tele-communications and gas. Action in the private sector was initially undertaken by means of schemes for specific industries facing changed trading conditions, intensive foreign competition and decline. Thus the 1959 *Cotton Industry Act* provided for government contributions to encourage contraction and rationalization of the industry, hit by competition from the Far East. In the case of the *aircraft industry*, the government used its position as the industry's dominant consumer to force a reorganization of nineteen companies into five groups in the 1960s. Assistance to the *shipbuilding industry* also began in the early 1960s, with credit subsidies, and continued with a £68 million re-organization of 27 major yards into large regional units in a three-year period after 1967. In both the aircraft and shipbuilding cases, government Committees of Inquiry had concluded there was no case for maintaining production at artificially high levels, for reasons concerning the balance of payments, unemployment or defence, etc.

Government intervention across private industry as a whole was facilitated by the establishment of the Industrial Reorganization Corporation (IRC) in 1966 and by the 1968 Industrial Expansion Act. The IRC was intended to seek out opportunities for rationalization in private industry, and in these cases to initiate and finance mergers which might not otherwise occur. During its existence the IRC was associated with some spectacular mergers (including Leyland–BMC and GEC–AEI–English Electric) but it was quickly abolished by the Conservative government in 1971. The Industrial Expansion Act permitted government support for schemes to improve efficiency which would benefit the economy but required financial backing. There was some scope for helping rationalization, but the aim was to extend and amplify the work of the IRC, rather than overlap with it.

Under the 1970–74 Conservative government the emphasis swung away from 'structural' solutions and towards greater reliance on the pressure of competition as a stimulus to reorganization and greater efficiency. The first expression of this was a declared intention to allow market forces to put down 'lame duck' firms, but this was soon modified when concern about the social and national implications of the failure of Rolls-Royce and Upper Clyde Shipbuilders led the government to intervene in early 1971.

Measures to help small firms were also presented as a means of fostering new competition. The small firms policy began with the establishment of a small firms division within the then Department of Trade and Industry, to safeguard their interests, and local advisory centres were subsequently set up and various financial reliefs given. However, powers to grant selective financial assistance to industry contained in the 1972 Industry Act were less pro-competitive, and more in the spirit of the earlier Industrial Expansion Act. The 1972 Act also provided for grants in exchange for state shareholding in the companies concerned. This was not used by the Conservative government, but was subsequently implemented by its Labour successor, in particular during its rescue of BL in 1975.

The emphasis on extending state ownership in the provision of assistance to industry appeared to have been greatly extended by the Labour government when it set up the National Enterprise Board (NEB), also in 1975. In some ways a successor to the IRC, the NEB had an initial finance of £1bn to assist firms and promote industrial reorganization. At the time there were some expectations that the NEB would lead to a major extension of public ownership, to include at first 100 and then 25 of the largest UK companies. But this did not materialize and in practice the NEB was mostly occupied in dealing with the securities and other property in public ownership which had been transferred to it, including Alfred Herbert, Ferranti, Rolls-Royce and BL. The return of a Conservative government in 1979 heralded the end of the NEB in its original form. The 1980 Industry Act ended its function to extend public ownership, promote industrial reorganization and encourage industrial democracy, and the Secretary of State for Industry subsequently took over its responsibility for Rolls-Royce (after the resignation of the entire NEB) and later BL. What remained of the NEB was ultimately merged with the NRDC to form the British Technology Group, its focus thus shifting to new ventures, including the previously mentioned INMOS project.

Since 1979 the Conservative government has predictably returned to the policy of encouraging enterprise and small firms. A wide range of measures has been introduced, many of which involve some form of tax relief, e.g. the preferential 'small companies' rate of corporation tax; tax relief for pre-trading expenditure by new companies; and income-tax relief on up to £40,000 of shares subscribed to unquoted companies by individuals under the Business Expansion Scheme (originally set up in 1981 as the Business Start-Up Scheme, and confined to new companies). Other kinds of measure include arrangements to encourage profit-sharing and employee share-option schemes, relaxation of planning controls and a Loan Guarantee Scheme involving government underwriting of small-company borrowing from banks.

The current emphasis on small business in government policy is not confined to Britain, and various schemes for its encouragement and assistance are in force throughout Europe. According to an independent study,[1] Britain has the most favourable climate for small business in only one respect, namely taxation. When other factors are taken into account, including labour conditions, the cost of premises and (lack of) discriminatory legislation, Britain ranked in ninth place overall in a league of ten European countries, surpassing only Italy, and with West Germany, France and Greece in the top three places.

---

1   Economist Intelligence Unit, *The European Climate for Small Business: A Ten Country Study* (EIU, 1983).

When attempting to assess any of the foregoing policies for structural reorganization, it is important to see them in the context of the existing distributions of firm and plant size. These are highly skewed; the great majority of plants and firms are small, but output is heavily concentrated in a comparatively tiny number of very large units. Thus in 1982 over 90% of manufacturing plants employed less than one hundred employees (and over half in fact had no more than ten workers), but contributed less than a quarter of total net output (table 4.17a). At the other end of the scale, less than 400 plants with more than 1,500 employers were responsible for over 30% of net output. A similar pattern can be seen in the case of firms (table 4.17b). The average number of plants per firm is only 1.2, and the vast majority of firms are small, single-plant enterprises, while a few very large firms have many plants.

TABLE 4.17

Distribution of Plants by Employment Size, 1982

Employment size category	No. of units	%	Total employment (000s)	(%)	Total net output (£m)	(%)
(a) *Establishments*[1]						
1–99	93,937	(91.7)	1,351	(25.2)	16,579	(22.2)
100–499	6,697	(6.5)	1,416	(26.4)	18,994	(25.4)
500–1499	1,367	(1.3)	1,100	(20.5)	15,819	(21.1)
1500 and over	,386	(0.4)	1,494	(27.9)	23,426	(31.3)
Total	102,387	(100)	5,361	(100)	74,818	(100)
(b) *Enterprises*[2]						
1–99	80,782	(94.6)	1,078	(21.1)	12,772	(17.7)
100–499	3,441	(4.0)	705	(13.8)	8,922	(12.4)
500–1499	733	(0.9)	597	(11.7)	8,445	(11.7)
1500 and over	406	(0.5)	2,738	(53.5)	41,910	(58.2)
Total	85,362	(100)	5,119	(100)	72,049	(100)

Source: Business monitor PA 1002, *Report on the Census of Production*, 1982.
Notes: 1 An establishment is the smallest unit capable of supplying census information, usually a factory or plant at a single site or address. Data relate to manufacturing and construction.
2 An enterprise means one or more establishments under common ownership or control. Data relate to manufacturing.

Over time, there has been a long-term trend towards large-scale production; for example, plants with more than 1,500 workers accounted for some 15% of total employment in private-sector manufacturing industry in 1935, but for 28% in 1982. On the other hand, there has also been a very large increase in the total number of firms and plants over the last two decades; after remaining static in the 1960s, the number of manufacturing establishments rose from around seventy thousand in 1968 to seventy-five thousand in 1972 and then to the figure shown in table 4.17. All of this increase occurred in the smaller size-categories, with the number of plants with more than a hundred workers actually falling over the period. Despite this, the shares in total output of the different size-categories have not changed dramatically. Thus while it may be that there are ICIs and Unilevers of the future among the small firms of today, it should be borne in mind that the present policies encouraging small enterprise affect only a small proportion of existing production activity.

VI.3   Planning

British industrial policy has never adopted an industrial plan in the sense of binding sectoral output targets, or even a coherent list of priority industries towards which the government would assist the mobilization of resources. The nearest approach to such a strategy was the National Plan of 1965. The plan was the culmination of a strand of development influenced by the contemporary French system of 'indicative planning'. This had seen earlier expression in the establishment of the National Economic Development Council (NEDC) in 1962. This is a tripartite body representing employers, trade unions and government at a very senior level, supported by a permanent staff. Some twenty-one EDCs for individual industries were also set up on a similar basis. The general hope was for a consensus approach in analysing and helping overcome impediments to faster growth, at both the national and the industry level.

The National Plan itself was not a plan in any *dirigiste* sense but a set of industry-by-industry projections of the implications of an assumed growth of the economy at 4% a year from 1964 to 1970. Though it followed a NEDC report on the obstacles to faster growth, the plan was the work of the newly created Department of Economic Affairs, set up in an aura of enthusiasm for the age of the 'white-hot technological revolution' following the election of a Labour government in 1964.

In the event the planning exercise was short-lived, brought to an end by the national economic crisis measures of 1966. The plan's 1969 successor, entitled *The Task Ahead*, was originally to have been the Second Plan, but turned out to be a much less detailed and ambitious document, merely discussing the possible use of resources under alternative growth rates. However, the institutional structure of the NEDC and EDCs survived. During the Conservative government of 1970–74 the focus of their activities shifted towards more low-key activity concerning problems of growth and efficiency at industry level. A wide range of analyses was carried out and the results were disseminated within industries via newsletters and reports, with some inter-industry exchanges.

The industrial strategy concept was revived in 1974, with Labour once again in power. This time the strategy was launched by NEDC. Once again the first stage was to analyse the short-term difficulties facing individual sectors and recommend ways of overcoming them. The emphasis was then to turn to analysing performance and agreeing medium-term programmes of action to improve competitive performance. A further set of tripartite bodies was set up for this purpose, the Sector Working Parties (SWPs). In selecting the sectors, the governing idea was 'picking winners', i.e. industries which were 'intrinsically likely to be successful' or potential growth centres. Forty SWPs had been created by 1979, covering about 40% of manufacturing output, and including eleven remaining EDCs which had taken over the role of SWPs.

The work of the SWPs has, like that of the EDCs, been very varied, involving studies and recommendations on things like investment and productivity, manpower and training, product design, development and standardization, the identification of markets, marketing techniques and export finance. Management and union representatives are intended to see that the programmes are practically viable, and government representatives to see that the programmes are harmonized nationally. Under the 1975 industrial strategy, the government was also committed to take steps in support of the sectoral programmes, such as providing extra financial assistance for investment (as in the case of microelectronics), for entry into export markets, and for industry training schemes. The government also undertook to 'identify the industrial implications of the whole range of government policies' and give more weight to the needs of industry in shaping them.

The value of the work undertaken by the SWPs and EDCs and co-ordinated under NEDC is hard to judge. Jointly they provide a forum for dialogue between government and industry, and this could result in the government discovering more about the micro implications of its macro policies, so avoiding some of the adverse effects of unduly sharp and frequent changes in economic regulations, pre-emption of resources for the public sector and personal consumption, and intervention in the nationalized industries. At industry level, many topics have been discussed and many reports issued dealing with specific problems affecting performance. There is, however, a doubt about the effectiveness of the tripartite, consensus line of attack in the UK, which may be quite good at diagnosing the causes of poor performance, but much less able to agree on remedies and go on to implement them.

The current (Conservative) government's approach to industrial policy is one of deep scepticism towards the value of planning and government interference, and of great confidence in the ability of market forces to reveal growth potential and solve co-ordination problems. As a result, institutions like the NEDC and SWPs tend to occupy a less prominent position in government policy, which instead focuses on liberating the 'supply side' of the economy by breaking up restrictive practices, liberalizing the labour market, making training and education more responsive to industrial needs, curbing inflation, restoring incentives and profitability, and reducing the public sector.

VII   CONCLUSIONS AND POLICY ALTERNATIVES

Britain's poor industrial performance in recent decades has led to a serious decline in living standards relative to those in other advanced industrialized countries. With self-sufficiency in oil expected to come to an end around 1990, and with a finite stock of saleable public assets, adverse fiscal and balance-of-payments constraints may be expected to affect developments and policy options in the foreseeable future. Though productivity has been rising more rapidly in Britain than elsewhere over the last few years, it is not yet clear whether this represents anything more than a short-term effect of the recovery from the disastrous collapse of output in 1979–81, which may not be sustained over the longer term.

As we have seen, the current government has drastically scaled down the level of support for regional development, is disengaging from the promotion of R & D, and is transferring major sections of the nationalized industries to private ownership. It is also withdrawing incentives to invest in industry as a whole.[1] By these actions the government is implying that the divergences between social and private costs and returns, and other forms of market failure in these areas, do not warrant past levels and kinds of public intervention – a view which many observers do not share. Competition policy continues, but is being applied under a view of the competition process that gives less weight to the possible adverse effects of monopolistic structures and practices than does the mainstream, 'traditional' view, and the direction of future policy is under review at the time of writing. Agricultural support policies cry out for reform but, while the UK government has some room for independent action, the main lines of policy are EEC-determined.

The positive side of the current government's industrial policy consists of its policies and exhortations to foster 'enterprise' and share ownership, and its measures to encourage small firms with, as we have seen, an emphasis on the service industries, and a strong underlying preference to 'let the market decide'. Taken together with its macroeconomic and labour-market-liberalizing policies, all this may be regarded as a gigantic, free market, supply-side experiment. Whether this will succeed in solving Britain's current and future industrial problems only events will show, but as we have seen there are several grounds for reservation, and it should be added that it was not by measures such as these that Japan, Germany and France, for example, have each achieved industrial records far surpassing our own in the postwar period.

The main alternative industrial policy would involve the formulation of an overall economic strategy – a priority system of industrial areas where a potential advantage is seen to lie – coupled with a willingness to channel resources in their direction; to set up whatever institutional machinery might be called for; and to co-ordinate basic policies for education and

1   See Chapter 2.

training, infrastructural development, the provision of industrial finance, and so on, in relation to a projection or 'plan' of the direction in which the industrial economy is expected to go. Such thinking is very much out of fashion at the time of writing, when the fashionable thing is rather to dismiss out of hand the idea of 'picking winners', and to stress the futility of attempting to 'second-guess the market'.[1] But in Japan, for example, exactly this was done in the 1950s, when some farsighted decisions over the industries on which to base the country's postwar industrial recovery were taken.[2] Thus, resisting short-run market pressures to concentrate on traditional and labour-intensive industries in a situation of commodity shortage and excess labour, Japanese strategy focused on capital-intensive, high technology industries (such as steel, oil refining, petrochemicals, automobiles, aircraft, industrial machinery and electronics) which were rightly judged to have long-run export and growth potential (since they produce goods with high income elasticities).

Moreover, the very process of formulating sectoral targets or projections can have considerable consultative value, as was found in France, especially in the earlier phases of 'indicative planning' in the 1950s and 1960s,[3] and at least help lead to consistent expectations about future developments among industrialists and policy-makers. In any case, supporters of the alternative policy would argue, what is being asked of the government is in principle no different from what actually happens in large firms, who also have to plan their future production, and make provision for their expected resource needs. But involving the government in a parallel, overall strategic exercise means that factors beyond the influence of individual firms or short-run market considerations can be taken into account.

FURTHER READING

General Texts

D.A. Hay and D.J. Morris, *Industrial Economics, Theory and Evidence*, (OUP, 1979).

F.M. Scherer, *Industrial Market Structure and Economic Performance* (second edition, Rand McNally, 1980).

M. Waterson, *Economic Theory of the Industry* (CUP, 1984).

---

1 See, however, P. Hare, 'Planning a Market Economic: Problems and Lessons', *Royal Bank of Scotland Review*, September 1985.

2 See, e.g., C.J.F. Brown, 'Industrial Policy and Economic Planning in Japan and France', *NIER*, August 1980, and J. Hillis, 'The Industrial Policy of Japan', *Journal of Public Policy*, February 1983.

3 See S. Estrin and P. Holmes, *French Planning in Theory and Practice* (Allen and Unwin, 1983).

Industrial Performance

S.J. Prais, *Productivity and Industrial Structure* (CUP, 1983).

M. Panic (ed.), *The UK and German Manufacturing Industries* (NEDC, 1976).

G.D.N. Worswick (ed.), *Education and Economic Performance* (Gower Press, 1985).

R. Bacon and W. Eltis, *Britain's Economic Problem: Too Few Producers* (Macmillan, 1976).

J.C. Carrington and G.T. Edwards, *Financing Industrial Investment*, (Macmillan, 1979) and *Reversing Economic Decline* (Macmillan, 1981).

Agriculture

J.K. Bowers and Paul Cheshire, *Agriculture, the Countryside and Land Use: An Economic Critique* (Methuen, 1983).

European Commission, *The Common Agricultural Policy* (revised edition, 1981.

Nationalized Industries

R. Rees, *Public Enterprise Economics* (Weidenfeld and Nicolson, 1976).

R. Pryke, *The Nationalised Industries: Policies and Performance since 1968* (Martin Robertson, 1981).

NEDO, *A Study of the UK Nationalised Industries: Their Role in the Economy and Control in Future* (1976).

Symposium on 'Privatisation and After', *Fiscal Studies*, Vol. 5, No. 1, February 1984.

Competition Policy

A Symposium on Competition Policy, *Fiscal Studies*, February 1985 (articles by George, Waterson, Hay, Fairburn, and Shaw and Simpson).

K.G. Cowling *et al.*, *Mergers and Economic Performance* (CUP, 1980).

G. Meekes, *Disappointing Marriage: A Study of the Gains from Mergers* (CUP, 1977).

D.C. Mueller (ed.), *Determinants and Effects of Mergers: An International Comparison* (Oelgeschlager, Gunn and Hain, 1980).

L. Hannah and J. Kay, *Concentration in Modern Industry* (London, 1977).

P.E. Hart and R. Clarke, *Concentration in British Industry 1935–75* (CUP, 1980).

S.J. Prais, *The Evolution of Giant Firms in Great Britain* (CUP, 1976).

European Commission, *Competition Law in the EEC and ECSC* (1981).

Regional Policy

H. Armstrong and J. Taylor, *Regional Economics and Policy* (Philip Allan, 1985).
B. Moore, J. Rhodes and P. Tyler, *The Effects of Government Regional Economic Policy* (HMSO, 1986).
K. Allen, H. Begg, S. McDowall and G. Walker, *Regional Incentives and the Investment Decision of the Firm* (HMSO, 1986).

Industrial Policy

C.F. Carter (ed.) *Industrial Policy and Innovation* (Heinemann, 1981).
F.M. Scherer, *The Economics of Multi-Plant Operation* (Harvard University Press, 1975).
C.F. Pratten, *Economics of Scale in Manufacturing Industry* (CUP, 1971).
NEDC, *Industrial Policies in Europe* (1981).
NEDC, *Industrial Policy in the UK* (1982).
P. Hare, *Planning the British Economy* (Macmillan, 1985).

5

Labour

David Metcalf and Ray Richardson

I EMPLOYMENT
I.1 The Working Population

Out of a total population of roughly 56.5 million, the working population in the UK in September 1985 was officially estimated to be 27.6 million. This represents an aggregate labour-force participation rate, or activity rate, of nearly 49 per cent. It should be noted that the working population is defined to include the unemployed, officially estimated at 3.3m in September 1985. In addition, there were 21.3m employees in employment, 2.7m employers and self-employed and just over 300,000 members of H.M. Forces.[1]

The working population tends to grow over time. The precise trend is not clear because the detailed definitions of, and methods of estimating, the different components of the working population both change from time to time. A recent official estimate, however, was that the civilian working population in Great Britain grew by 1.6 million, an average of nearly 125,000 a year, between 1971 and 1984. There are considerable fluctuations around this trend. The working population is estimated to have fallen in 1981 and 1982, whereas it rose by 400,000 between 1975 and 1976 and by 500,000 between 1983 and 1984. These changes, both the underlying growth and the fluctuations, reflect the operation of two factors. First, there are changes in the size of the population of working age, i.e. demographic factors. Secondly, there are variations in activity (or labour-force participation) rates, i.e. the proportion, for any age or sex group, of working to total population.

In the last 10 years, the population of working age has been expanding quite fast. This has been a consequence of relatively small numbers of people reaching retirement age, a reflection of low birth rates in the First World War, and of a sharp rise in the number of teenagers, a reflection of the very high birth rates of the 1960s. These factors have become less powerful by the mid-1980s and the population of working age is now officially projected to peak by 1990, at 34 million, and then to be slightly smaller for the rest of the century.[2]

Activity-rate analysis is a good deal more complex and speculative. Activity rates differ sharply between demographic groups, and, for some groups, vary substantially over time. Thus, females generally have relatively

---

1 *DEG*, February 1986, p. S8.

2 *DEG*, 'Labour Force Outlook for Great Britain', July 1985, pp. 255–64.

low but rising activity rates, while younger and older males have relatively low and falling activity rates.

The standard economic analysis of male activity rates sees them as being principally affected by earnings in real terms, non-wage income and educational opportunities. For example, long-run economic growth tends to reduce male activity rates. In particular, younger males stay in the educational system longer and older males retire earlier, especially when growth is accompanied by improved retirement pensions. For older men, for example, the reported activity rates have fallen in each successive Census of Population; thus, the activity rate of 65–69-year-olds fell from 48% to 31% between 1951 and 1971, and fell again to only 16% by 1981. It is officially projected to fall to 8% by 1991. In part, these long-run changes reflect the fruits of economic growth, both directly through increased incomes and indirectly through greater government support to education and retirement pensions.

Superimposed on the inverse relation between long-run growth and male activity rates is a complex, and not necessarily stable, reaction to fluctuations in growth. The dominant postwar reaction of the male working population to fluctuations in growth has been a tendency to contract (or grow less rapidly) during economic recessions and grow (or contract less rapidly) during periods of economic expansion. Between September 1979 and September 1983, for example, male unemployment rose by about 1.3m, male employment fell by about 1.5m and the male working population diminished.

The typical response to long-run growth is that the male working population contracts; the typical response to short-run growth is that it expands. These two responses, the negative and the positive, are not contradictory, as they might seem at first sight. The first reflects people's responses to a permanent increase in wealth levels; the second reflects their responses to a more temporary change. This may be interpreted as an application of the fundamental notions in economics of income and substitution effects. If a worker is not planning to supply the maximum amount of labour at all times, he can choose the most advantageous periods when the supply is to be offered. On many calculations the most advantageous periods occur when wages are high and jobs are easy to find; that is, in expansionary conditions. Consequently, a recession is a period during which there is less point in offering one's services. This view therefore predicts that over the business cycle the size of the working population will be positively related to the state of the economy. It is usually termed the 'discouraged worker effect', meaning that as the economy contracts, the number of people in employment falls by more than the increase in the number counted as unemployed.

There is an alternative and opposite view to the one just described, labelled the 'added worker effect'. It suggests that as 'primary' (i.e. permanent) members of the working population are made unemployed in recessions, 'secondary' (i.e. temporary) workers are drawn into the workforce so as to provide an additional source of income for the family; the result is that the number of unemployed rises more than the number disemployed. This view obviously has some validity but it is basically a qualification to the 'discouraged worker' hypothesis. It stresses that many households plan imprecisely, that unpredicted events are important and force changes even in carefully laid plans, and that savings, credit and social welfare payments may be inadequate to maintain family living standards for more than a relatively short period. These and other factors are all of obvious practical importance, but they should not be taken to imply that the 'discouraged worker' hypothesis, with its emphasis on rational calculation, is thereby unrealistic and likely to be misleading.

Whereas male activity rates have declined over the long run, female activity rates have increased very sharply. Females accounted for nearly 42% of the civilian labour force in 1985, as compared with just over 30% in 1950. In discussing long-run changes, however, a distinction should be made between married and non-married females. The activity rates for young non-married females have fallen, while those for older non-married females have risen; for example, between 1951 and 1981 they are estimated to have fallen for 20–24-year-olds from 91% to 78%, and to have risen for 45–49-year-olds from 61% to 77%.[1]

The reasons for the distinctive pattern for young non-marrieds are not clear, but they are probably connected with (a) the rise in the extent of girls and young women staying on at school and attending universities, and (b) the rise in the number of one-parent families financially supported either by the state or by alimony or by other family resources.

For married women the picture is unambiguously one of increased activity rates, albeit at different rates for the different age-groups. Table 5.1 shows the striking changes that are officially estimated to have taken place.

TABLE 5.1
Wives' Activity Rates (%) by Age, Great Britain, 1951, 1971 and 1981

Age-Group	1951	1971	1981
16–19	38	42	49
20–24	37	46	57
25–44	25	46	59
45–59	22	57	67
60+	5	14	12
All ages	22	42	50

Source: ST, 1979, p. 84 and *ST*, 1984, p. 58.

The importance of these changes can hardly be overstated, and their implications extend far beyond the labour market. Even after a great deal of research, however, it is still not clear precisely why they have occurred. One possibility is that there has been a widespread reduction in the extent of sex

---

1   *ST*, 1979, p. 84 and *ST*, 1984, p. 58.

discrimination in the labour market. For this to have happened, however, there would have to have been either a consistent rise in the wages of females relative to those of males or a significant shift in the employment structure, with large numbers of females joining the better-paid and more attractive occupations. Neither of these developments has taken place, certainly not on a major scale. Whether or not sex discrimination, however defined, has been extensive, there have been no conclusive studies demonstrating changes in its extent.[1]

Turning to influences primarily affecting married women, we can point first to the fact that the average number of children per family has fallen over time. Whether this is a cause or effect of higher participation is not known. What is known is that activity rates have risen for younger wives as well as for older wives, and that activity rates have also risen for married women with young children. This suggests that declining family size is, at most, a partial explanation of rising activity rates.

Another possibility is that, due to the introduction of new products, there has been a rise in the productivity of the housewife, effectively allowing her to produce the same amount of services as before but in less time. By itself, this improved productivity does not necessarily make for greater participation by the wife in the labour force because, at the same time, everyone's income has risen. With the rise in income one might expect both the family's demand for housewifely services and the housewife's demand for personal leisure to increase, thereby decreasing the incentive to join the labour market. Only if the domestic productivity effect is strong will the net effect be to release housewives for market work.

Yet another explanation of the rise in activity rates for married women is that social attitudes have become increasingly tolerant of wives, and even of mothers, working. This explanation is probably the most popular of all and there is certainly no doubt that attitudes have changed. Again, however, there is the difficulty of deciding the extent to which changes in attitudes were an independent cause or were themselves a response to changes in practice. It does seem plausible that the two world wars were very influential in this matter. They were, as far as the labour market was concerned, exogenous events inducing many women to join the market for the first time. This process surely changed social attitudes in favour of wives working.

The above explanations all run in terms of supply influences, implying that progressively more married women are willing to work in the market. Demand influences may also have been important. One possibility is that the growing similarity of regional employment structures, in part perhaps a result of the attempts by successive governments to induce greater regional evenness of employment, have been successful in bringing work to women

---

1 For an analysis that suggests that there have only been small changes in the extent of occupational segregation by sex, see C. Hakim, 'Sexual Divisions Within the Labour Force', *DEG*, November 1978, pp. 1,264–8, and C. Hakim, 'Job Segregation Trends in the 1970s', *DEG*, November 1981, pp. 521–9.

who previously had very limited job opportunities. It is certainly the case that female activity rates have tended to rise more rapidly in those regions where they were historically low.

But there has not been merely a geographical redistribution of jobs. Between the end of the 1930s and the end of the 1970s the UK economy was generally run at unprecedented and persistent tightness. This must explain a major part of the rise in the female working population.

A second, structural argument relating to demand influences can be made. Female activity rates might have risen because expansion has been particularly marked in industries employing a high ratio of female to male workers. On the other hand, these sectors are not inherently female-intensive and, in the absence of full employment, they might well have used significantly more male labour over the years. Again, it seems reasonable to put the major emphasis on the general expansion of the economy when considering demand influences which account for the long-established rise of female participation in the labour market. Essentially, what has been happening here has been the tapping of a labour reserve.

It has not been easy for economists to do convincing empirical work explaining the patterns of wives' activity rates over time, because suitable data have not been readily available. One recent study found that the growth in real wages had played a part in attracting more women into the labour market, but they found the evidence to be suggestive rather than conclusive.[1]

In addition to this time-series work, there have been studies looking at cross-sectional patterns, i.e. patterns at a point in time, which can be translated into explanations of the time-series developments. One study investigated the variation in married females' activity rates between towns and cities in Great Britain. It was shown that wives' activity rates were greater, the higher were female wage rates and the lower were male wage rates; wives' activity rates were also higher for the foreign-born, for those who lived in the larger cities and for those who lived in towns with low male unemployment rates.[2]

Some of these results were confirmed in a study using survey data on nearly 4,000 wives. It was shown that wives were more likely to be in the labour force if their own potential wage was high, if their husband's wage was low, if they did not have young children, if they were West Indian or Irish born and if their husband was in employment.[3]

As with males, there have been considerable fluctuations in the female labour force superimposed on the longer-run trends. Again, the usual

1   H. Joshi, R. Layard and S. Owen, 'Why Are More Women Working in Britain', *Journal of Labour Economics*, January 1985.

2   C. Greenhalgh, 'Labour Supply Functions for Married Women in GB', *EG*, August 1977. Somewhat similar, but not identical results can be found in R. McNabb, 'The Labour Force Participation of Married Women', *MS*, September 1977.

3   R. Layard *et al.*, 'Married Women's Participation and Hours', *EC*, February 1980.

pattern has been for the female working population to expand most rapidly when the economy is growing fast, and to expand slowly or even to contract when the economy moves into recession.

I.2   Aggregate Employment Patterns

Between 1950 and 1965 the number of male employees in employment in the UK followed an upward trend, from 13.6m to 14.9m. Since 1965 there has been a trend in the reverse direction, so that by September 1985 the number was down to below 11.8m. Within the latter period, the rate of decline has varied substantially. It was fairly rapid up to 1972, much slower between 1973 and 1978, and exceedingly fast until the end of 1983. In the period from December 1978 to September 1983, the number of male employees in employment fell by about 1.5m, or nearly 80,000 per quarter. Such a sustained and substantial fall is without precedent in the postwar period.

In contrast to the pattern for males, female employment continued to rise until 1979. Between 1959 and 1979 there was a 25% increase in the number of females in work and only three years during which female employment fell. From September 1979, however, the latter fell in each quarter until mid-1983, from a total of 9.7m to one of about 9.0m. Thereafter, it recovered strongly and was back to nearly 9.6m by the end of 1985.

One of the important differences between the male and female labour forces is the degree to which they work on a part-time basis. In 1981, more than 40% of the female labour force worked part-time (i.e. normally worked for less than 30 hours per week), as against only 5% of men. Part-time work has also been strongly on the increase.

A final aspect of aggregate employment patterns that is worth stressing is the recent growth in the number of self-employed workers. At the beginning of 1979, it was officially estimated that there were 1.9m self-employed; by September 1985, it was thought that there were 2.7m, though this latter estimate is subject to perhaps substantial revision. Relatively little is as yet known about the characteristics of the newer self-employed or why they have apparently increased so rapidly and so suddenly.

I.3   Employment by Industry and Occupation

In September 1985 the manufacturing sector of the British economy employed fewer than 26% of all employees at work. Adding the number of employees in agriculture, mining, construction, gas, electricity and water, we still get less than 35% of all employees, implying that the service sector now accounts for well over half of the employment in the country. The tendency for the service-sector labour force to grow relative to the whole labour force began in the mid-1950s, when the manufacturing and service sectors each employed about 42.5% of the total number of employees. The marked absolute decline in manufacturing employment began in 1966. In that year, manufacturing employment stood at 8.4m; subsequently it has fallen in nearly every year (1969, 1973, 1974 and 1977 are the exceptions) an in nearly every individual manufacturing grouping, so that in December 1985 there were fewer than 5.4m workers employed in manufacturing.

Within the service sector, the main growth areas have been professional and scientific services, particularly in education and medical and dental services. In the fifteen years to June 1985, the numbers employed in professional and scientific services rose by roughly three-quarters of a million. Some service sectors have become smaller over this period, for example transport and communications (due mainly to the rapid decline in railway employment), but the general long-run tendency has been one of growth.

The principal reasons for these employment shifts are the differences between the sectors in their rates of growth (a) of final, including foreign, demands and (b) of labour productivity. There are changes in the final demand for an industry's products as a result of movements in the income and wealth of the economy as a whole, the structure of prices and the appearance of substitute products, particularly of rival products produced abroad. Thus, between December 1979 and December 1981, in conditions of generalized recession and an unusually high exchange rate, employment in manufacturing fell with unprecedented rapidity, by 17% or nearly 1,200,000 workers.

In addition to changes in final demand, changes in labour productivity can also affect the structure of employment. Over the long run it is clear that labour productivity has grown faster in manufacturing than in most of the service trades and that this has resulted in a contraction in the relative demand for labour in manufacturing. It is also the case that labour productivity has been tending to increase at an unusually rapid rate in British manufacturing since 1979. What is said to be happening is that, in order to survive extreme recessionary pressures, many employers are able to or are being forced to reorganize work practices and introduce new standards of efficiency. An alternative explanation is that the changes in measured labour productivity largely reflect the scrapping of marginal, low-productivity capacity. The implication would be that the remaining facilities are no more productive than they were before and that the measured rise in productivity is a statistical illusion. No doubt the truth lies somewhere in between these two extremes.

Another way of examining the composition of the labour force is to examine the division between the private and the public sectors. Over the period 1961 to 1980, there was an increase in the proportion of the employed labour force working in the public sector, from 24% to nearly 30%. The rate of increase was most rapid in the years 1966–7, 1969–70 and 1974–5, when the level of private employment fell sharply and public employment was fairly stable. After 1980, however, new patterns began to emerge. First, in spite of the very rapid fall of employment in the private sector, the share of the public sector in total civilian employment was roughly constant, at 28%, between 1980 and 1983. The share then fell to 25½% by 1985. In part, these developments reflect privatization, i.e. the transfer of existing activity from the public to the private sector. They also reflect the Conservative government's attempt to reduce public employment. Between 1979 and 1985, the number of public-sector workers fell by 13%, to 6.5 million.[1]

Within the public sector, local authority employment rose very sharply, by more than 60%, in the 1960s and 1970s. Between 1980 and 1983 it fell by about 80,000, or about 3%. Central government employment also grew fast in the 1960s and 1970s, by 30%, mainly because of growth in the National Health Service. Subsequently it has changed hardly at all. Finally, employment in the public corporations (i.e. roughly the nationalized industries) was fairly constant for many years, despite an increase in the number of corporations. Since 1980, however, there has been a nearly 20% fall in public corporation employment, in part because of privatization and in part because there have been substantial run-downs in certain industries.

These structural changes are also reflected in the relative growth of female employment, referred to above, because much of the service sector has made intensive use of female labour. Thus, approximately 68% of the employees in professional and scientific services are female, as against 28% in manufacturing, only 4% in mining and 7% in shipbuilding. It is true that the textile and clothing industries are also female-intensive, but their decline has not been great in comparison to the expansion of the service sector. It is also worth emphasizing again that a significant number of females, particularly in the rapidly expanding service sectors, work only part-time. Thus 55% of the females working in education and 40% of those in medical and dental services are part-time workers. This compares with less than 25% for manufacturing, and it may suggest that some of the sectoral shifts that have occurred are not a purposeful move away from manufacturing but the use of a previously unused labour reserve that would not be available for full-time work, or perhaps even for part-time work in other sectors.

I.4 Hours Worked

To clarify discussion of work, one should distinguish between normal basic hours, normal hours and actual hours of work. The first term relates to the number of hours a person is expected to work at basic rates of pay; the second includes any guaranteed overtime paid at premium rates; the third, and for most purposes much the most interesting notion, includes all over-

---

1 The most detailed discussion of public-sector employment trends is to be found in M. Semple, 'Employment in the Public and Private Sectors, 1961–78', *ET*, November 1979, pp. 99–108. More recent figures are to be found in S. Briscoe, 'Employment in the Public and Private Sectors, 1975–1981', *ET*, December 1981, pp. 94–102, and I.G. Richardson, 'Employment in the Public and Private Sectors, 1979–1985', *ET*, December 1985, pp. 90–98.

time, guaranteed or not. Actual hours are typically in excess of normal hours, but by including absenteeism and sick days in the picture the situation may be reversed.

As with activity rates, two lines of enquiry can be distinguished for hours worked by the labour force as a whole. First, one wants to explain the trend; second, one wants to explain temporary variations around it. Further, it is revealing to examine the structure of hours worked, e.g. by occupation or wage level.

Over a long period, average actual hours of work have fallen, from around sixty hours per week in the early part of the century to around forty hours now. Initially, the fall was in hours per day; subsequent reductions have been first in days worked per week and second in weeks per year. There is therefore a clear tendency for extra leisure to be bunched, there being 'economies of scale' in leisure activities.

For many years, normal hours fell more rapidly than actual hours, implying an increase in the number of overtime hours. Thus, between 1948 and 1968 normal weekly hours of male manual workers fell from 44.5 to 40.1. Actual hours in the same period tended to rise until the mid-1950s and fall thereafter. Since the late 1960s, however, normal hours have been relatively constant but actual hours have tended to fall.

Hours of work fluctuate a good deal from year to year. The changing tempo of the economy is the principal explanation of these variations, with the length of work-weeks falling in recessions and rising in expansions. Thus, the proportion of operatives in manufacturing industry who worked any overtime fell from just under 35% in 1978 to under 27% in 1981; subsequently, as the economy began to expand somewhat, it rose above 32%.

There are wide variations between industries in actual hours worked. In 1978 the average annual hours worked per manual employee in Great Britain was 2,144 in construction, as against 1,655 in mining and quarrying. Within manufacturing, the range was from 1,992 in the timber and furniture sector, to 1,694 in clothing and footwear.

Some of the variation observed in such a cross-section is due to different industries being at different stages in their own business cycle. Additionally, some industries have relatively old labour forces whose work-weeks are naturally shorter. Nevertheless, there are persistent real variations across industries and occupations in hours worked, and these certainly affect the attractiveness of the different jobs. Some research work has shown that for a sample of ninety-six industries in Britain the number of hours offered by the average manual male worker was positively affected by the hourly wage rate and low skill levels, and negatively affected by the number of fellow workers employed in the factory, residence in the South East and Midlands, and residence in conurbations. Further, the number of work-hours demanded from the male worker was greater when the worker was more skilled, aged between 25 and 54, and working in industries that were fast-growing or highly concentrated; fewer hours were demanded from young males and from those who tended to work alongside females.[1]

I.5   The Quality of the Working Population

As time goes on, the average skill level of members of the labour force rises. This is one component of the increased quality of the working population, implying that, from a given number of workers and a given quantity of supporting factors of production, potential output grows over time. Other important sources of higher quality are better health levels, an improved spatial distribution of employment and, up to a point, shorter working weeks. In quantitative terms the increase in skill levels has had much the largest impact on productivity of any of these sources.

There is no precise, independent measure of the increase in average skill level in the UK over any period and no comprehensive indication of the allocative efficiency of labour between various skill levels. A number of relevant studies have been made, however, mainly of the educational system. The formal education sector is not the only source of skill augmentation but the model testing its efficiency has general applicability. The problem at issue may be described as follows. If the sector is organized efficiently, the net social value of a pound of expenditure will be the same at the margin for all types and levels of education. What we must do, therefore, is to equalize the social profit on all educational activities.

The terminology employed here may be disagreeable to some people. However, as long as account is taken of all sources of cost and benefit, whether they be material or psychic, there can be no real objection. It is true that some sources may not be measurable in practice and that others may be measured only imperfectly. These defects do not suggest that no measurement should take place, merely that decisions and judgements should not be based solely on what is measurable.

In fact the measurement of the profitability of education and training programmes is decidedly imperfect. The usual measure of benefits is some estimate of the expected increase in monetary earnings enjoyed by the trainee, i.e. his expected full earnings minus the earnings he would otherwise expect were he not to undertake the training under consideration. To take a concrete example, in estimating the profitability of a university degree a comparison is made between the observed earnings of people already graduated and those of people who stopped just short of going to university. This provides an earnings differential for each age-group, which stands for the earnings increase expected by the current trainee at each stage of his working life.

This estimate is extremely crude, and a number of adjustments can be

---

1   D. Metcalf, S. Nickell and R. Richardson, 'The Structure of Hours and Earnings in British Manufacturing Industry', *OEP*, July 1976.

made to improve on it. For example, not all of the crude differential can be attributed to education, because ability and motivation levels differ between the two groups from which data are drawn. Consequently, an effort should be made to estimate the independent effect of ability differences.

Once the estimate of benefits has been obtained, it is necessary to estimate the costs of the training. The principal cost is the output that could have been produced by the trainee had he been in full-time work. Its value is usually measured by the monetary earnings he forgoes while being trained or educated. Added to the forgone earnings are the direct costs of instruction, represented by salaries of teachers, cost of buildings, etc.

Two early research efforts for the UK were by Blaug and by Morris and Ziderman, and both contain a clear account of the procedures and difficulties involved. The latter was more comprehensive and among its conclusions were (1) that post-graduate qualifications were not very profitable for society, and (2) that higher national certificates were very profitable indeed. If these calculations were correct, they suggest that the UK educational system was inefficiently structured and was turning out the wrong mix of graduates.[1]

Many workers receive considerable amounts of training after they leave school, and successive governments, particularly during the last twenty years, have attempted to influence the provision of such training. Prior to 1964, the great bulk of industrial training was provided on the initiative of individual employers, often within a context of industry-wide understandings between trade unions and employers' organizations. This voluntary system was widely believed to be defective. In particular, it was said to lead to inadequate provision of training, especially for certain highly skilled manual trades. The principal argument here was that many firms who would otherwise be willing to provide training did not do so on a sufficient scale because they could not be sure of retaining the skilled labour after training had finished. This argument carries with it some implicit assumptions concerning who pays for the training (as opposed to who provides it or makes it available) but it was nevertheless influential in leading to the 1964 Industrial Training Act.

The 1964 Act created a system of Industrial Training Boards (ITBs). By 1969 there were 27 ITBs, of widely differing size, which together covered about 65% of the working population. The principal function of the Boards was to improve the quantity and quality of training provided in industry, and their principal mechanism was a system of levies and grants. Each Board imposed a levy, essentially a payroll tax, on all but the smallest firms in their industry. The revenue raised was then returned to those firms in the industry

1 M. Blaug, 'The Rate of Return on Investment in Education in Great Britain', *MS*, September 1965; V. Morris and A. Ziderman, 'The Economic Return on Investment in Higher Education in England and Wales', *ET*, May 1971. For a useful, though complex, survey of the relevant work on Britain, see G. Psacharopoulos and R. Layard, 'Human Capital and Earnings', *RES*, July 1979. See also the interesting article by A. Dolphin, 'The Demand for Higher Education', *DEG*, July 1981.

which ran approved training schemes. The intention was to make all potential users of the skilled labour contribute to the costs of training.[1]

Certain adjustments were made to this system under the 1973 Employment and Training Act, but more radical changes were introduced with the 1981 Employment and Training Act. Using the powers given to him under this Act, the Secretary of State for Employment announced in November 1981 that he had decided to abolish all but seven of the ITBs. Elsewhere, he indicated that he was satisfied that 'the training requirements of the sector concerned can be effectively met on a voluntary basis with less cost and bureaucracy'. It is too early to judge whether this assessment was well founded. At the same time, the government introduced what was advertised as 'the most far-reaching and ambitious set of proposals for industrial training ever put before Parliament'. The scheme was complex, and its centrepiece was the youth training scheme, discussed below in section II.3.

II   UNEMPLOYMENT

If unemployment is to be cut to 2m by 1991, we need to create over the five years 1986–91 at least 1,200 net new jobs every day. Every month for those five years, extra jobs equivalent to the 37,000 people employed by British Petroleum or Whitbread's must be created. Unemployment is truly the problem of our time. In this section we first describe the composition of the unemployed. Then we analyse why unemployment is so high. Finally we consider the prospects for lowering unemployment.

II.1   Composition of the Unemployed

Stocks, flows and durations[2]:   In 1985 unemployment in the UK averaged 3.3m, equivalent to 14% of the labour force. Males accounted for over two-thirds of the total. The unemployment count refers to those claiming benefit. Two corrections might be made to this count. First, some people claiming benefit are not actually seeking work (740,000 in 1984). Second, some people who would like work, and consider themselves unemployed (e.g. some married women and men aged over 60) are not claiming benefit (870,000 in 1984). Thus these two corrections roughly offset each other. In addition, a further 0.5m individuals were kept out of unemployment by the special employment measures in December 1985.

In 1985 the inflow of individuals into unemployment in the UK was 4.7m and an identical number left unemployment. These flows do not all refer to

---

1   For a good discussion of the issues involved in training, see A. Ziderman, *Manpower Training: Theory and Policy* (Macmillan, 1978); see also B. Showler, *The Public Employment Service* (Longman, 1976), especially chapter 5.

2   The sources of information for this section include OPCS, *General Household Survey* (GHS) (annual); *Labour Force Survey*, 1984; DE *Gazette*, especially July 1985.

separate people because some individuals have more than one spell of un-employment. The average duration of each completed spell of unemploy-ment was over two-thirds of a year (3.3m stock/4.7m inflow), or 37 weeks.

This average-spell duration is an important statistic, because the main reason the stock of unemployed people rises is that the average duration of unemployment rises and not that more people become unemployed. For example in 1955 when unemployment was at an all-time (peacetime) low of 1.1%, the average duration of each spell of unemployment was only 3½ weeks. Since 1966 flows into unemployment have been remarkably stable at around 4m per year, so the higher unemployment rates primarily reflect longer-spell durations.

The incidence of unemployment among people is very unequal. With 4m registrations a year and a labour force of 27m, in nearly 7 years the number of registrations equals the size of the labour force. Therefore if a person is in the labour force for 49 years he would, if unemployment were distributed equally, expect to have 7 spells of unemployment during his lifetime. Yet we know many people never suffer a single spell of unemployment. Indeed, in any year some 3% of the labour force account for 70% of the total weeks of unemployment. Clearly a fraction of our labour force must be constantly at risk of long-term unemployment and/or recurrent spells of unemployment. Unfortunately the group who bear the burden of unemployment are also concurrently towards the bottom of the pay distribution, work in the most risky occupations, and are those who also suffer a high incidence of ill-health – i.e. labour-market disadvantage is cumulative.

Demographic and occupational characteristics[1] : In October 1985 unem-ployment rates by age had the following pattern (DE *Gazette*, December 1985, table 2.15):

	under 25	25–54	55–59	All ages
Males %	24	13	19	16
Females %	19	8	9	10

Prime-age men and women have lower unemployment rates than younger and older groups (changes in coverage of unemployment statistics for men aged 60–64 have rendered their unemployment statistics meaningless). Young workers have high unemployment rates because they have a high propensity to become unemployed and many have recurrent spells of unem-ployment: the inflow to unemployment of the under-25s is treble that of the prime-age group. Older workers are less likely than prime-age groups to become unemployed, but once unemployed they have very long spell dura-tions – they remained unemployed for a long time.

---

1   See in particular W. Wells, *The relative pay and employment of young people*, DE Research Paper 42, 1983, and L. Lynch and R. Richardson, 'Unemployment of young workers in Britain', *BJIR*, November 1982.

There is no doubt that youth employment prospects have worsened in the last decade or so. In 1973 males under 20 had an identical unemployment rate to the all-male rate (3.5%), but now their rate is half as large again as the all-male rate. There are two main reasons. First, young workers are harder hit in recession than adult workers and, conversely, their employment prospects pick up faster when the economy improves. Firms economize on labour in a recession and they reduce recruitment. This hits young workers because of their higher turnover rates and lack of labour-market experience. Second, the cost of employing young workers has risen relative to the cost of employing adults. These cyclical and cost effects have a stronger impact on the employment of males aged under 18 than on other teenagers. It can be calculated from Wells' thorough study of the youth labour market that a rise of 3% in the relative cost of employing males aged under 18 is associated with a fall of around 60,000 in their employment. Of this 60,000 figure, 15,000 represents a loss in aggregate employment but the remaining 45,000 is made good in the form of an increase in adult male employment and female employment as employers substitute adult for teenage employment because the adults have become cheaper relative to the teenagers.

The higher unemployment experienced by older workers partly reflects the fact that the structure of jobs and wages within the firm makes it difficult to allow for the waning productivity of older workers, who are therefore specially prone to redundancy. And once older workers become unemployed, they suffer long spells because firms tend to prefer younger workers. A quarter of all vacancies and a third of labouring vacancies have an explicit upper age-limit of 50. The higher unemployment of older workers also reflect their higher incidence of illness and disability.

Single men experience unemployment rates double those of married men of the same age and socio-economiic group. It is not clear whether this reflects the institution of marriage – single men have less pressure to take up another job – or whether married men are simply higher quality than single men and so are desired both by women and by employers. The fact that unmarried men are more likely to suffer from mental instability and alcoholism than their married counterparts hints that the labour-quality point is important.

Once men are married their incidence of unemployment increases with the number of their dependent children. There are many reasons. First, the level of family support for those in work is substantially below that for those out of work. Second, families with a large number of dependent children are less mobile. Third, lower-skilled groups – those most at risk of unemployment – have slightly larger families, but the positive relation between family size and unemployment also holds for particular skill groups. Fourth, sociological literature suggests that groups who are alienated from society and who suffer a feeling of powerlessness are prone to both higher fertility and higher unemployment.

There are also marked disparities in the incidence of unemployment by occupation. The likelihood of a spell of unemployment for manual workers is well over twice that for non-manual workers. Further, people classified by the Employment Service as general labourers account for around a third of the unemployed. Their lack of training causes unskilled workers to bear the brunt of macroeconomic fluctuations and firms' expansions and contractions. The persistently low level of the vacancy to unemployment ratio also reflects lack of demand for these workers, which prolongs their unemployment spells.

Geographical structure[1]:   During the half century to 1975 the main geographical focus was 'the regional problem'. Although this had a number of dimensions, it was encapsulated in the variation in unemployment rates by region. For much of the postwar period Scotland, Wales and Northern England had unemployment rates some three times as large as those in the Midlands and South East. More recently, regional differences in unemployment relativities have become much less severe. The coefficient of variation (standard deviation/mean) of unemployment rates across the 10 British regions fell from .42 in 1966 to .21 in 1985. The five regions with the highest unemployment rate in 1985 – North, Wales, West Midlands, North West, Scotland – had an average rate of 17%, only half as high again as the average 12% rate in the remaining regions.

One reason for the narrowing in unemployment rates is the impact of regional policy. In 1981 employment in the Assisted Areas was around 0.5m higher than it would have been without the array of capital and labour subsidies operating over the period 1960–80. Most of these 0.5m jobs were diverted from the rest of Britain. Even so, unemployment remains stubbornly high, relative to the rest of Britain, in Scotland, Wales and the North. The recent DTI report suggested this is because, as compared with the South East, these areas have 'an industrial milieu less favourable to successful entrepreneurship; a somewhat unfavourable rate of product innovation; a relatively low level of employment in the business service sector; an occupational structure characterized by a low proportion of managerial and professional jobs; a high level of dependence for manufacturing employment on branch plants owned by national or international companies whose UK head offices are concentrated in the South East'.

Perhaps because the regional disparity of unemployment is now less, the focus of attention has shifted towards local labour markets, urban-rural movements and the decaying cores of our inner cities. Within each region, the three local labour markets with the highest unemployment rates have roughly treble the amount of unemployment experienced by the three local labour markets with the lowest unemployment rates. Thus in January 1986 the fun palaces of Margate and Clacton had an unemployment rate of 21%,

1   The facts in this section are taken from Department of Trade and Industry, *Regional Industrial Policy: Some Economic Issues* (1983). See also B. Moore, J. Rhodes and P. Tyler, *The Effects of Government Regional Policy* (HMSO, 1986).

while salubrious, boring Guildford, Aylesbury and Alton had rates of under 7%.

An important spatial employment trend in the last two decades is the net shift of manufacturing employment out of the major conurbations into small towns and rural areas. Thus between 1961 and 1986 London lost approaching two-thirds of its manufacturing employment (nearly one million jobs) and the other conurbations lost more than a third of theirs. By contrast, manufacturing employment rose by more than a quarter in small towns and rural areas. This trend happened in every region.

The most pressing spatial unemployment problem now is the high rates of unemployment in the cores of our great towns and cities. The male unemployment rates (%) given by the 1981 Census for the inner areas (containing one third of the relevant population) and outer areas of four major towns were:

	Inner area	Outer area
Birmingham	25	17
Liverpool	31	21
London	14	8
Manchester	28	18

In all major towns the inner-area rate is typically half as large again as the outer-area rate. This reflects the residential concentration of groups in the population least able to compete for available jobs within the wider labour-market area of which they form a part.

II.2   Why has Unemployment Risen?[1]

Recorded UK unemployment is now some ten times as large as it was in the 1950s:

Average of the year	Male unemployment%
1951–55	1.3
1956–60	1.8
1961–65	2.1
1966–70	2.9
1971–75	4.4
1976–80	7.3
1981–85	15.1

Two sets of factors account for the higher unemployment. First, the long-run rate of unemployment has risen. Second, there are fluctuations around this long-run unemployment rate and in the 1980s the actual rate has exceeded the long-run rate. Fear of inflation and balance-of-payments deficits has inhibited policies to reduce the actual rate to nearer the long-run rate.

The long-run rate of unemployment is sometimes called the natural rate, the equilibrium rate or the NAIRU – the non-accelerating inflation rate of

---

1   For a fuller discussion see C. Greenhalgh, R. Layard and A. Oswald (eds.), *The Causes of Unemployment* (Clarendon Press, Oxford, 1983); R. Layard and S. Nickell, 'The causes of British unemployment', *NIER*, February 1985; D. Metcalf and S. Nickell, 'Jobs and pay', *MBR*, Spring 1985; DE, *Employment: The Challenge for the Nation*, Cmnd. 9474 (HMSO, March 1985).

unemployment. It is important to understand that there is nothing 'natural' about it. It is *not*, as is sometimes believed, the rate that would hold in perfect competition. On the contrary, if union monopoly power increases and real wages are bid up, this is likely to increase the long-run rate, so a reduction in union power would, by implication, cut it. Probably the best way of thinking about the long-run rate is in terms of the NAIRU. Have certain things changed – union power or unemployment benefits, for example – such that the government now needs a higher or a lower level of unemployment to control inflation? We shall discuss a number of changes which have taken place in the labour market which might have raised the NAIRU. These include unemployment benefits, employers' labour taxes, union power, and any mismatch between unemployment and vacancies.

The factors associated with the rise in unemployment in the last thirty years have recently been comprehensively investigated by Professors Layard and Nickell. Their main findings are reported in table 5.2. Over the period 1956–83, male unemployment rose by 11.8 percentage points. We now discuss each of the factors responsible for this rise.

Changes in the level of unemployment and supplementary benefits relative to income from working, and changes in the administration of benefits, might both influence unemployment. The effect of the level of benefits works through two channels. First, if the benefit-to-pay ratio rises, this could cause workers to substitute unemployment for work, either by becoming unemployed or, more likely, by prolonging unemployment. It is this channel that is considered here. Second, benefits may set a floor to real wages, with the resulting level of real wages making it uneconomic to hire unproductive workers. This scale effect is considered below under the real wage discussion. The benefit-to-wage ratio (the replacement rate, RR) accounts for a rise of only 0.35 percentage points – a far more modest contribution to the rise in unemployment than saloon bar pundits would have us believe.

The RR rose in the decade 1968–78, and by 1978 over a quarter of the

TABLE 5.2
Breakdown of the Change in the Male Unemployment Rate 1956–83

Variable	% Increase in unemployment 1956–83
Benefit replacement ratio	0.35
Employers' labour taxes	1.87
Unions	2.27
Real import prices	−0.02
Mismatch	0.76
Demand factors	6.43
Incomes policy	0.12
TOTAL	11.78
(Actual change)	(11.83)

Source: R. Layard and S. Nickell, 'The causes of British unemployment', *NIER*, February 1985.

working population had an average potential RR of over 90% for a 13-week spell of unemployment, although only 5% had such a high RR for the marginal week after a year of unemployment. However, since 1978 the RR has fallen substantially. This reflects the combined influence of the axeing of the earnings-related supplement to unemployment benefit, the taxation of benefits and the fall in the real value of unemployment benefit. In addition, more people *in* work receive housing benefits. Those who asserted that the rise in benefits was an important contributory factor in the rise in unemployment in the 1970s will presumably now be arguing that the fall in the RR over 1978–85 should have cut unemployment. Certainly the tendency for benefits to lead to substitution of unemployment for work is unlikely to have contributed to any rise in unemployment in the 1980s. Anyway, when there are few vacancies, if one person is deterred by benefits from taking a job someone else will snap it up, so it is hard to see how benefits increase or decrease aggregate unemployment via this substitution mechanism.

It is possible that changes in the administration of benefits are associated with changes in unemployment. The divorce in the 1970s of the job-finding and benefit-paying functions of employment exchanges may, for example, have reduced pressure on unemployed people to seek work and reduced the resources devoted to helping longer-term unemployed individuals into work.

Since the early 1960s, non-wage labour costs – mainly employers' National Insurance contributions and pension contributions – have risen by over 13 percentage points. This has made labour more expensive to employ and it is estimated that this has added nearly two percentage points to unemployment. We should note, however, that this result is a bit speculative because we know rather little about the *incidence* of these taxes. It is possible that the taxes are not, in fact, borne by the firm – causing its profits to be lower – rather, they may be passed backwards to employees or forwards to consumers.

Union militancy may raise real wages above that warranted by productivity. Such militancy might reflect, for example, a shift in the relative valuation of real wages and employment. Union militancy can be measured by the union mark-up, i.e. the pay of union members relative to otherwise similar non-union members. This union mark-up rose substantially over the period and, consequently, it is calculated that the direct impact of unions on unemployment since 1956 is over two percentage points. This may, in fact, understate the impact of unions on unemployment. For example, if wages do not adjust properly to changes in employment taxes, is this also because of unions?

Another factor which influences the warranted level of real wages is real import prices. Taking the period as a whole this variable had no significant impact, but it was important after the oil shock of the mid-1970s. When the oil price went up in the 1970s, Great Britain should have reduced real wages to have accommodated the oil price rise. As we did not do so, unemployment in the late 1970s was 1 percentage point higher than it otherwise would have been. However, in the 1980s falling real import prices have tended to cut unemployment.

The long-run unemployment rate will rise if the mismatch between unemployment and vacancies worsens. There is little evidence that this has happened by region or by occupation. However, the industrial structure of the economy has changed substantially in the last two decades, and particularly since 1979. In 1966, half the employed labour force was in the index of production industries (mining, manufacturing, construction, utilities), but by 1985 this production sector only accounted for a third of employment. And between 1979 and 1983, 2m jobs were lost in this sector. The larger switch out of production industries worsened the industrial matching of vacancies and employment and so may have raised the rate of unemployment. But the table indicates that any worsening mismatch between jobs and vacancies accounts for – at most – less than 1% of the rise in unemployment.

Over half the increase in unemployment over the period is associated with inadequate demand. This is measured by our fiscal stance, world trade trends and our international competitiveness. In the period since 1979 these demand factors are particularly important in accounting for the rise in unemployment.

There is a complication here which needs to be understood. When a structural factor – say union militancy – moves adversely, it has both a direct and indirect effect. The direct effect is that reported in table 5.2. The indirect effect of the adverse change arises because it serves to reduce the level of demand consistent with unchanging inflation. Thus some of the unemployment associated with the demand factors reflects the government's attempt to keep inflation stable in the face of worsening structural factors. This brings us back to the notion of the natural rate of unemployment or the non-accelerating inflation rate of unemployment (NAIRU). An increase in the natural rate of unemployment consists of two components. First, the direct impact of structural factors like increased union militancy or higher employer taxes. Second, the indirect effect, working through macroeconomic policy to keep inflation constant in the face of the worsened structural factors. Layard and Nickell calculate that the rate of unemployment consistent with unchanging inflation rose over the period from around 2% in the 1950s to around 11% in the 1980s.

This way of thinking about unemployment emphasizes two important policy implications. First, as actual unemployment (male unemployment is 17% in January 1986) is substantially above the natural rate (11%), it can be cut, without fuelling inflation, via measures which increase aggregate demand. Second, the essence of 'supply side economics' is improving the underlying structural factors. So if, for example, union power is lessened (perhaps by an incomes policy?), this has a favourable direct effect on unemployment, but also a favourable indirect effect, because the economy can now be run at higher aggregate demand without compounding inflationary pressures.

Before concluding this section we should briefly discuss some factors which are often advanced as causes of higher unemployment but which – in fact – are unlikely to contribute much to the increase in unemployment.

First, the size and composition of the labour force changed substantially in the decade 1976–86. The civilian labour force grew by 1.1m, from 25.7m in 1976 to 26.8m in 1986. It may simply be difficult for the economy to absorb an extra 2,000 people a week into jobs. However, this argument should not be pushed too hard: in the decade 1950–60, for example, the working population rose by 1.5m but unemployment remained below 0.5m. Nevertheless it is possible that the labour market has become less flexible and adaptable between the 1950s and the 1970s/1980s, and it is now more difficult to absorb a growing labour force into jobs.

Younger workers now account for a higher fraction of the labour force than previously. Youths aged 16–24 comprised 20% of the labour force in 1976, but 23% ten years later. As youths have an unemployment rate approaching double that of prime-age (25–54) workers, this composition effect might also have raised the underlying rate of unemployment. However, this effect is offset by the fact that older workers, who also have relatively high unemployment rates, account for a smaller fraction of the labour force: those aged 55 and over comprised 17% of the workforce in 1976 but only 13% in 1986. Further, women – who have a somewhat lower unemployment rate than men – increased their share of the labour force from 39% to 42% over the decade.

Second, the various strands of employment-protection legislation introduced since the 1960s have raised the cost of employing labour – increased notice periods, unfair dismissal provisions and strengthened maternity rights all make it more difficult to shed labour. Further, where a dismissed worker qualifies for a redundancy payment, the firm's share of that payment rose from 30% in 1969 to 100% in 1987. These legislative changes have reduced cyclical employment fluctuations, and this is reflected in the continuing decline in turnover rates since the 1960s. However, the impact on unemployment is not clear-cut. If it becomes more difficult or expensive for firms to reduce employment, this will reduce flows into unemployment but, by making employers more choosey, it will also increase unemployment duration. The tentative evidence so far suggests that the net effect of these factors was to reduce rather than increase unemployment.

Third, it is often argued that technical change causes unemployment. For this to be so it would be necessary to show that the rate of technical progress was faster in the 1970s and 1980s than in the 1950s and 1960s. This seems unlikely. Anyway, there is a weak *positive* association across industries between labour productivity and employment growth: sectors where technical progress is most rapid appear to have the largest rise or smallest fall in employment, quite the reverse of what would be expected if technical change is a major factor in determining unemployment.

II.3   Moderating Unemployment

Background: If unemployment (on current definitions) is to be cut to 2m over the five-year period to 1991, at least 2.5m extra jobs must be created by 1991:

		(m)
1.	Current unemployment (Jan. 1986)	3.41
2.	Aim: 1991 unemployment	2.00
Jobs needed		
3.	To absorb the increase in the labour force	0.43
4.	To make the simple cut in unemployment (2–1)	1.41
SUB-TOTAL		1.84
5.	Encouraged-worker effect, ratio 1.4:1	0.74
TOTAL		2.58

DE data indicate that the labour force will grow by 0.43m during this period. Add to this the simple cut from 3.4m to 2.0m in unemployment. So far 1.84m jobs are needed. But expansionary policy results in employment rising by more than registered unemployment falls. If we assume, conservatively, that this 'encouraged-worker effect' results in 14 extra jobs needed for every 10 cut in unemployment, this gives us a net job-creation effort of 2.58m. Further, some 0.5m are at present being kept off the unemployment register by special employment measures (see below). The 2.58m figure is equivalent to over 1,400 jobs a day, nearly twice as much again as the previous six-year fastest postwar growth rate, when employment grew between 1959 and 1965 by 750 extra jobs a day. But we must not be too pessimistic: between 1933 and 1937 employment rose by 2m, and in the USA employment rose from 70m in 1960 to 108m in 1984.

Unemployment will be cut if the structural factors discussed in the previous section move favourably, for example if employer taxes are lowered or if union power is reduced. But unemployment can also be reduced via tax cuts or increases in public spending. The cost effectiveness of the various methods of cutting unemployment was recently studied by collating evidence from the various macroeconomic models of the UK economy and from other sources such as DE surveys. There is a clear-cut ranking in the relative effectiveness of different measures. After 2 years, the cut in unemployment per £1 billion of PSBR is as follows:

	Cut in unemployment
Income-tax cut	21,300
Public investment	38,200
Current public spending	65,400
Special employment measures	487,800

Income-tax cuts are an expensive way of creating jobs; they tend to create jobs abroad rather than at home because so much of the extra income is spent on imports. Public infrastructure investment on things like building hospitals, schools and roads is less employment-intensive than current public spending on nurses, teachers and other public-sector employees. But by far the biggest bang for the buck comes from the special employment measures (SEM), so it is not surprising that these measures are used extensively.

Special employment measures[1]:   In December 1985, 669,000 people were covered by the SEM. The DE calculates that, but for these SEM, unemployment would be 495,000 higher. Public spending on these measures is around £2bn in 1986/7. The main schemes can be divided as follows:

	Numbers covered, Dec. 1985
Job creation etc.	
Community Programme	174,000
Enterprise Allowance	52,000
Schemes to cut labour supply	
Job Release Scheme	48,000
Youth measures	
Youth Training Scheme	329,000
Young Workers Scheme	57,000

In deciding whether to establish, expand or contract a particular measure, Whitehall compares it with what would happen if the same money were used for income-tax cuts. The criteria on which such comparisons are based include the impact of the measure on employment, unemployment, the balance of payments, the inflation rate, and the level and distribution of output. The main criterion from this list is unemployment. Here there are two basic steps used by the DE. First, a register effect is calculated. Next, the net cost per person off the register is estimated.

The register effect of a SEM is usually less than the number of participants. This may be due to:

(a) deadweight: windfall payments for actions consistent with a scheme, which would have occurred in its absence (e.g. Job Release payments in respect of employees who would have retired anyway).

(b) substitution: where employees or trainees covered by a scheme take the place of ineligible employees.

(c) displacement: where the output subsidized by the SEMs competes with the output of unsubsidized firms, so that their demand for labour is reduced.

The next step in the evaluation procedure is to estimate the net Exchequer

1   For a fuller discussion see D. Metcalf, 'Special employment measures: an analysis of wage subsidies, youth subsidies, youth schemes and worksharing', *MBR*, Autumn/Winter 1982, pp. 9–21; House of Commons, Fourth Report of Public Accounts Committee 1983–1984, *Special Employment Measures*, HC 104, November 1983; G. Davies and D. Metcalf, 'Generating Jobs', *The Economics Analyst*, April 1985.

cost of the measure : that is, its gross cost less savings on benefit payments and additions to revenue ('flowbacks') which accrue to the government as a result of the measure. The net cost of the SEM may, in turn, be compared with the average net cost per unemployed person, estimated to be some £7,000 in 1985.

The *Community Programme* provides temporary jobs for long-term unemployed adults on projects of benefit to the community. Recruitment to job opportunities is normally restricted to people in receipt of benefit aged 18–24 who have been unemployed at least 6 months in the last 9 months, and those aged 25 and over who have been unemployed for at least 12 months in the past 15 months. Participants are paid the hourly rate for the job, and projects combine full and part-time jobs. The average wage for a project, or group of projects, is £67 a week. Projects involve, for example, clearing and landscaping waste land, adapting buildings, setting up adventure playgrounds or renovating canals. Currently there are 174,000 year-long places. Not all participants stay the full year so more than 200,000 people pass through the 174,000 places. By Spring 1987, it is intended that there will be 255,000 places, but even then the Community Programme will cover less than 1-in-6 of those eligible to be on it. The net annual cost per person removed from the unemployment count by the Community Programme was £2,200 in 1985.

The *Enterprise Allowance Scheme* helps unemployed people who want to start up in business but who may be deterred by the fact that they would lose their entitlement to unemployment or supplementary benefit. Under the scheme they are paid a flat-rate taxable allowance of £40 a week for a maximum of 52 weeks. Applicants have to be in receipt of unemployment or supplementary benefit, unemployed for at least 13 weeks, and aged between 18 and state pension age. They must also have at least £1,000 available to invest in the business. Current coverage is to be doubled to 100,000 by 1987. The net annual cost per person removed from the unemployment count by the Enterprise Allowance Scheme in 1985 was £2,650.

The *Job Release Scheme* (JRS) was introduced in 1976 and is the longest-running adult measure. The JRS makes it easier for older people to give up work early and to release their jobs to unemployed people. It offers a weekly allowance from the date the applicant leaves work until the state pension age, provided the applicant's employer agrees to replace him or her by an unemployed person, though not necessarily in the same job. The scheme is at present open to two categories of people : one for all men aged 64 and women aged 59, and one for disabled men aged 60 or over. The 1986/7 weekly tax-free allowances are £65.50 for a married person with a dependent spouse and £51.95 for a single person. The DE calculate that the net annual cost per person taken off the unemployment count by JRS in 1985 was £1,650.

Although the labour-supply-reducing JRS is very cost-effective, it should not be concluded that worksharing is therefore generally desirable. First, worksharing involves income sharing. Indeed the debate on how to combat unemployment would be improved if worksharing were called income sharing. If annual or weekly pay is cut in line with the cut in weekly or annual hours, then worksharing has considerable potential for lowering unemployment. But if, as unions demand, weekly pay remains constant in the face of a cut in hours, unit labour costs rise, which is either purely inflationary or, to the extent that firms feel unable to pass on higher unit costs fully into prices, is more likely to cause a fall rather than a rise in employment. Second, the present government may well believe that with present trade-union attitudes heavy unemployment is necessary to maintain single-digit inflation. So, in its eyes, reducing the labour force would not help at all because the same amount of unemployment would still be needed. Third, it is not clear how hours 'saved' by worksharing can be parcelled up into full-time equivalent jobs. For example, the production-line process may require fixed manning levels. And the structure of employment is different from the skill and area composition of the unemployed.

The DE has calculated that if normal weekly hours were cut from 40 to 35 without any corresponding loss in nominal weekly pay, and if the potential loss of output was accounted for as follows:

	%
increased employment	35
higher output per man	20
more overtime	35
lower output	10

then registered unemployment would be reduced by 350,000, while labour costs would rise by 8.5%. The PSBR would fall by around £2 bn. This all looks quite attractive, but it is very important to understand that it is solely a first-round estimate. The rise in unit labour costs will, in time, cause employment to fall back and unemployment to rise again. *Work-sharing is also real income sharing*. Unless individuals are prepared to sacrifice some real income, there is little scope for permanently reducing unemployment by this route.

The *Youth Training Scheme* is the biggest measure in terms of both coverage and spending. The DE describe it as providing 'a high quality integrated programme of training and planned work experience lasting up to a year, including a minimum of 13 weeks off-the-job training or further education'. It is designed to give school-leavers a range of practical transferable skills to enable them to compete more effectively in the labour market. The majority of places are work-based with employers. The scheme provides training for three groups of youngsters: 16-year-old school-leavers (whether employed or unemployed), unemployed 17-year-old leavers in the first post-school year, and disabled leavers up to age 21. Under the YTS, the firm gets the youngster at zero cost. The lion's share of the public spending on YTS is the weekly allowance of £27.60 paid to the youngster.

At present there are some 350,000 year-long places on YTS (though a few are not filled). The scheme is being extended in 1986 and 1987 so as eventually to provide 2-year places for 16-year-olds and 1-year places for 17-year-olds not in full-time education; 16-year-olds leaving school in 1985

will be eligible for a second year's training in 1986. Chancellor Lawson
has commented on the expansion as follows:

> The main aim of the scheme is a better qualified workforce. But it
> would also be a major step towards our objective of ensuring that every
> youngster under the age of 18 will either be in full-time education, in a
> job, or receiving training, with unemployment no longer an option.
> But first we have to get the expanded scheme in place. It will require
> the active co-operation of employers, trade unions, and school leavers,
> which I am confident will be forthcoming.

Around 130,000 extra places will be required in the extended scheme. The
government has stated that it intends the employers to bear a major part of
the costs of this expansion once the extended YTS is on stream.

The *Young Workers Scheme* started in January 1982 and closed for applications in March 1986. Its purpose was described by the DE as 'to encourage
employers to take on more young people at realistic rates of pay'. Originally
there were two levels of subsidy, *inversely* related to pay levels. Currently
employers are able to claim £15 a week for up to one year in respect of young
people on their payroll whose earnings do not exceed £50 a week, who are
under 18 and in their first year of employment. At present, around one-third
of the relevant age-group earn under £50 a week. This scheme has the
highest proportion of deadweight payments of all the SEM. Most of the
subsidy is paid to employers who would have taken the youngster on
anyway. The YWS essentially becomes redundant when the YTS is expanded into a 2-year programme for 16-year olds. Therefore it is to be
replaced by a similar subsidy for 18–20-year-olds. The *New Workers
Scheme* will pay employers £15 a week for a year for each 18- and 19-year old
they hire paid up to £55 a week and each 20-year-old paid up to £65. It seems
likely that the new subsidy will have the same problems of deadweight and
displacement that rendered previous youth-recruitment subsidies
ineffective.

Special employment measures started in 1975. A decade of experience
suggests the following characteristics of SEM. First, they are a very cost-
effective way of cutting unemployment, with a net PSBR cost per person
taken out of unemployment of around £2,500 in 1985. Second, it is unlikely
that SEM compares unfavourably with income-tax cuts or other public
spending on either balance-of-payments or inflation criteria. Third, SEM
score well on equity grounds. Finally, the big question mark over SEM concerns the value of the output. One way of thinking about this is as follows. The
short-term choice is between no output and the sometimes 'unreal' output of
the special measures. The measures may delay the eventual shift back to 'real
output' and employment. So in some years' time output may be higher if there
had never been any SEM. The problem then turns on comparing the outputs
in the two cases over time – is the present value of the stream of current and
future output higher with or without the measures? We believe it is higher

with the measures. In any event unemployment, alas, seems unlikely to drop much in the 1980s, so the SEMs will continue, in one form or another, for some years to come.

The long-term unemployed[1]:   In early 1986, 1.3m people had been unemployed over one year, and half a million over three years. The longer a person has been unemployed the less likely he or she is to get a job: two-fifths of those unemployed 0–3 months leave unemployment in the next three months, but under 1 in 50 of those unemployed 27–30 months leave unemployment in the next three months.

Current government policy to the long-term unemployed has two main strands. First, a quarter of a million year-long places are available under the Community Programme (discussed above). Second, under the Restart Scheme, people are called into the Job Centre after they have been unemployed one year, for an interview and advice on how to get a job. They will often be encouraged to take a low-paid job because under the Job Start Scheme they get a £20 a week for 6 months top-up to their pay if they take a job where the wage is under £80 a week. These two schemes do not create extra jobs and the government estimates that they only cut unemployment by 30,000.

By contrast the pressure group for the unemployed – the Charter for Jobs – and the House of Commons Employment Select Committee have both called for a year-long job guarantee with a million places to provide work for all the long-term unemployed who wish it. For example the Select Committee suggested the job guarantee might be built up over 3 years as follows:

	Places
Building improvement scheme	300,000
Social Services and NHS	100,000
Subsidy to private firms to recruit more labour	350,000
Community Programme	250,000
TOTAL	1 million

When on stream, the net Exchequer cost would be under £4 billion or some £4,000 per year per person.

There are problems with such a bold scheme. First, it would have to deal with both the existing stock of 1.3 million long-term unemployed and the half a million people who become long-term unemployed each year. Presumably priority would be given to those unemployed the longest. Second, such a large scheme is bound to involve some displacement of 'normal'

---

1   See Charter for Jobs, *We Can Cut Unemployment*, March 1985, and House of Commons Employment Committee, *Special Employment Measures and the Long Term Unemployed*, HC 199 (HMSO, January 1986).

work, for example in the building trades. But the MSC has long experience of dealing with this problem and would try to ensure that most projects were additional to existing work. Such problems must not deflect us from the central point. Without such a scheme more than a million of our fellow citizens will simply be left to rot.

III   INCOME AND EARNINGS

The distribution of income is described first. Pay is the most important income source, so we then turn to discuss the forces generating the distribution of earnings among individuals. Particular aspects of the pay structure – by occupation, industry, sex and race – and examined next. We conclude with an analysis of the twin problems of income support provided by social security and low pay.

III.1   Distribution of Income[1]

The *composition* of personal incomes in the UK in 1984 was:

Source	%
Pay	61
Income from self-employment	9
Rent, dividends and interest	7
Private pensions, annuities, etc.	7
Social security benefits	13
Other current transfers	3
	100

Pay accounts for a little over three-fifths of household income, some 8 percentage points lower than its 69% share in 1975. This partly reflects the growth of unemployment, which is also a major reason for the growing importance of social security benefits.

The distribution of *household* incomes in 1983 is given in table 5.3. The average original income per household was £7,760, ranging from £120 per average household in the bottom fifth of the distribution to £18,640 per average household in the top fifth. Those in the top 20% account for nearly half of original household income. Many such households will derive a part of their *income* flow from their *stock* of wealth (e.g. dwellings, shares). For example, the most wealthy 10% of the population owned 54% of marketable wealth in 1983 (when total marketable wealth was £745 bn).

---

1   Information in this section from *ST*, 1986, No. 16, chapter 5.

TABLE 5.3
Distribution and Redistribution of Household Income, 1983

	Original Income: Average		Final Income: Average	
	per household (£s)	% of total	per household (£s)	% of total
Bottom fifth	120	under 1	3,630	7
Next fifth	2,580	7	4,400	12
Middle fifth	6,880	18	6,190	18
Next fifth	10,570	27	8,160	24
Top fifth	18,640	48	12,920	39
Total all households	7,760	100	7,060	100

Source: *ST*, 1986, No. 16, tables 5.19, 5.21.
Note: Final income is original income *minus* income and other taxes *plus* social security cash benefits and benefits in kind such as education and health.

The average income of households in the top 20% is under £19,000. Many such households have more than one *person* receiving pay or other income. The fact that there are relatively few people and households with high incomes makes the redistribution of income and the greater provision of desirable health and education services difficult. While it may be possible to squeeze many thousands of pounds out of a rich individual, there are not many of them, so that the extra revenue raised by squeezing them harder is quite small. It should also be borne in mind that these figures refer to the distribution at one specific point in time – many of those in the bottom half of the distribution in 1983, like pensioners and students, will be in the top half at other points in their life. The inequality in lifetime incomes is less than the inequality of the income distribution observed at any particular point in time.

Some of the inequality is redressed via taxes on incomes and benefits in the form of cash and services. Income tax makes the distribution more equal because the percentage of income tax paid rises with income. Further, poorer families receive *proportionately* more (though *absolutely* less) than richer families from state spending on education and housing and transport subsidies. The extent of income redistribution from taxes and state spending can be seen from table 5.3. Final income is defined as original income *less* income and other taxes *plus* state spending on social security benefits and other things like education. The share of the top 20% of the income distribution fell from 48% of original income to 39% of final income, while the share of the bottom 20%, many of whom had no original income, rose from 1% to 7%. Nevertheless, the final income of the top fifth is still over five times greater than the final income of the bottom fifth.

III.2   Distribution of Earnings

The distribution of earnings, like the distribution of income, is positively skewed (median earnings are less than mean earnings). However, the earnings distribution is more equal than the distribution of income because the latter includes a return on wealth which is more concentrated.

The dispersion of earnings in April 1985 (full-time adult workers, whose pay for the survey week was not affected by absence) is set out in the following table.[1] Both men and women at the lowest 10% point earned under two-thirds of median pay, while the best-paid 10% earned over two-thirds more than the corresponding median.

| | Median earnings per week (£s) | Lowest decile | As a % of median | | |
			Lower quartile	Upper quartile	Highest decile
Men	173	61	77	131	172
Women	115	66	79	131	165

There are two particularly important and interesting facts concerning the distribution of gross weekly earnings of male *manual* workers. First, the dispersion of the distribution has been quite stable for almost a century:

Distribution of weekly earnings, manual men (% of median)		
	1886	1985
Lowest decile	69	66
Lower quartile	83	80
Median	100	100
Upper quartile	122	125
Highest decile	143	155

This stability suggests that we might seek to explain the distribution of earnings by factors such as differences in ability, motivation and luck, which might be expected to remain fairly stable from one generation to the next, rather than by appeal to institutional factors such as the growth of unions, or social forces such as the extension of public intervention, which have changed dramatically in the last century. However, we should note that the dispersion of the pay structure has increased somewhat in the 1980s, suggesting that unemployment and political factors have an impact.

Second, the position an individual occupies in the distribution changes

---

1   DE, *New Earnings Survey*, 1985, Part A, table 1. The data in this section refer to individuals, not families or Inland Revenue income units. Many people only work part-time or part of the year, and therefore the distribution of annual earnings of those who worked at any time during the year is different from the distribution above, because the annual earnings distribution has a concentration of people in the lower tail. A full discussion of the evidence on the distribution of earnings and evaluation of theories seeking to explain this distribution is contained in A.R. Thatcher, 'The New Earnings Survey and the Distribution of Earnings', in A. Atkinson (ed.), *The Personal Distribution of Incomes* (Allen and Unwin, 1975). E.H. Phelps Brown, *The Inequality of Pay* (OUP, 1977) also contains much evidence on the topic.

from year to year. Evidence on the gross weekly earnings of all full-time adults who were in the *New Earnings Surveys* in 1970 to 1974 (*DEG*, January 1977) indicates that the lowest-paid workers received by far the largest percentage increase in earnings between one survey and the next, while the higher-paid workers tended to experience much smaller percentage increases. Such movements are known as 'regression towards the mean'. Between 1970 and 1974, 21% of male manual workers were in the lowest-paid tenth in at least one of the five surveys, but only 3% were in this tenth in all of the surveys. These movements refer to weekly earnings of full-time workers and therefore reflect the variable nature of many components of manual workers' earnings (e.g. overtime, short-time, bonuses, piecework), the effects of job changes and the incidence of wage settlements. Movements in individuals' hourly earnings, which may more nearly reflect skill and motivation, or in annual earnings, which may reflect the incidence of unemployment, could be more or less pronounced than the fluctuation in weekly earnings.

One important explanation of the positive skew in the earnings distribution relates to the coupling of natural ability and training. In a smoothly functioning, competitive labour market, earnings will reflect productivity at the margin. Among all the determinants of marginal productivity we may concentrate here on a worker's 'natural ability' and training. If, for a given level of formal training, a man comes to the labour market with relatively great motivation, ability and drive he will tend to earn more than the average worker. Further, it is established that on average the more naturally gifted man tends to undertake more than average amounts of training. An unskewed distribution of ability combined with a skewed distribution of training produces a skewed distribution of productivity. The last, in an approximately competitive market, produces a skewed earnings distribution.

This simple picture is only a partial explanation of the actual earnings distribution. First, not everyone has equal access to the educational and training sectors, even where natural ability is the same for all. One implication is that relatively bright working-class children have difficulty in getting sufficient secondary and advanced education. This means that ability is not properly harnessed with education, thereby reducing the degree of earnings inequality.

Second, in some activities, including many of the profession, free entry of labour is restricted and earnings are pushed above the competitive level by union activity. The impact of such behaviour on the distribution of pay depends on (i) the numbers affected, and (ii) the size of the union mark-up. Union activity among male manual workers probably reduces inequality because even though a similar proportion of skilled and unskilled workers are covered by union agreements, the pay premium associated with union coverage is higher for unskilled workers than for the skilled.

Third, luck plays a significant part in determining earnings, particularly in any one year. The last qualification is important because the discounted sum of lifetime earnings is a more valid measure of material well-being than current earnings.

If a man is lucky one year but unlucky the next, we would have a misleading view of his well-being by looking at either year in isolation. Similarly, if a man is receiving a low wage currently because he is training, but expected to do well when he is trained, it would be mistaken to view him as a poverty case. The same may apply to people approaching retirement.

The *General Household Survey* (*GHS*) provides, each year, information on individual earnings and related individual characteristics such as age, schooling, work experience, race and family background. The 1975 *GHS* has been extensively analysed.[1] Let us consider the factors which generated the distribution of pay among the 5,000 or so full-time male employees in the sample.

Consider first the distribution of hourly earnings. Years of full-time education have a substantial effect on hourly earnings. Holding constant father's occupation, work experience, ethnic background, health and marital status, each additional year of education raises pay by between 5% and 10%. Does this mean education is a good weapon against poverty? The trouble with ordinary education is that while a person is being educated one does not know whether or not he is going to end up poor. In any case there is such a spread of earnings for people with a given level of education that even if all education disparities were eliminated the remaining inequality would be still over 93% of what it is now.

One could go further than eliminating educational disparity. Positive discrimination could be practised whereby those who had low earnings potential would be given *more* education than others. But this implies the ability to spot low earners while they are still being educated, and it is doubtful whether this is practicable. It could, however, be done for adult training – by then people have shown what they can and cannot earn – and there is evidence that short periods of vocational training can improve a person's position in the occupational hierarchy.

Pay is influenced by work experience. On average an individual with between 30–40 years of work experience earns, *ceteris paribus*, twice as much as a person with 5–10 years' experience. But the individual stuck in a particular manual job has little prospect of a real wage increase (other than from general economic growth) after the first 10 years.

Family background, measured by father's occupation, influences hourly earnings directly and also indirectly via education levels. An individual with a non-manual father had in 1975, *ceteris paribus*, hourly earnings 12% higher than those with unskilled fathers.

Marriage is also associated with higher pay. After controlling for other factors, married men had hourly pay 14% greater than single men. This may

1   R. Layard, D. Piachaud, M. Stewart, *The Causes of Poverty*, Royal Commission on Distribution of Income and Wealth (Diamond Commission), *Background Paper*, No. 5 (to *Report* No. 6, *lower Incomes*), HMSO, 1978, especially chapter 4. This is the best discussion on the factors generating the distribution of pay in Britain. The remainder of this section draws freely on this source.

be because marriage puts pressure on individuals to work harder or may simply reflect the fact that better-quality men are more likely to get married.

The factors above account for around a third of the variance of *annual* earnings. Another third is explained by differences in the number of weeks worked in the year by each individual. This is itself influenced by human capital factors. Individuals with relatively high hourly earnings work more weeks – it is the unskilled who bear the burden of unemployment and, to a lesser extent, sickness.

We now turn to examine some more narrowly defined aspects of the distribution of earnings. In the next section the pay structure by occupation and industry is examined. This is followed by a discussion of labour-market discrimination against women and non-whites. The lower tail of the distribution is studied in the final section on low pay.

III.3   Wage Structure by Occupation and Industry

Wage structure by occupation: The foundations of wage theory are contained in two famous principles. First, Adam Smith's principle of net advantage states that when competition exists in the labour market the 'whole of the advantages and disadvantages' of different occupations will continually tend towards equality. Note that this principle does not imply that wages will tend towards equality, but that (suitably discounted) lifetime returns to one occupation will tend to equal those in another occupation. The returns that make an occupation attractive or unattractive are both pecuniary and non-pecuniary. Second, we have the principle of non-competing groups, which evolved from the work of John Stuart Mill and Cairnes: this states (broadly) that certain non-competitive factors may inhibit the tendency towards equality in net advantages.

Linked to these two principles are two sets of reasons for the existence of occupational wage differentials: compensatory wage differentials and non-compensatory wage differentials.

Compensatory wage differentials are those which are consistent with competition in the labour market. If individuals were not compensated for the factors listed below (in the form of higher wages when at work), then the supply of labour to those occupations would tend to be deficient. All other things being equal, individuals will tend, for example, to be compensated in the form of higher wages for entering occupations that (1) require long periods of education and/or training, (2) are dangerous or dirty, (3) are subject to lay-offs or have a relatively short working life. (4) Also if they are risk-averters, they will desire to be compensated by higher mean earnings in the occupation if the dispersion of the earnings around the mean is very large. (5) Differentials will also accrue to wholly exceptional workers, such as professional sportsmen and entertainers, this being an example of economic rent applied to the labour market.

Non-compensating occupational wage differentials are different. They occur where economic or institutional reasons inhibit competition in the labour market. For example, closed-shop agreements protect union members from non-union competition. Legal restrictions boost solicitors' pay for conveyancing work. And minimum-wage legislation might raise the pay of those at the bottom of the earnings distribution above the competitive level.

Earnings by broad occupational groups are presented in table 5.4. It will be seen that earnings of non-manual workers are greater than those of manual workers. This reflects in some large part the relative education/ training intensities of the two groups. There is also evidence of other compensating differentials. Bricklayers (in group 16) earn 337p per hour, while general labourers (in group 10) earn 294p: the bricklayers are being compensated for their relatively low earnings while apprenticed. Within group 9, firemen earn 434p per hour while security guards earn 351p. The firemen are being compensated because their job is more dangerous and requires more training.

There is also evidence of individuals being compensated for being more

TABLE 5.4
Earnings by Occupation: Full-Time Adult Men, April 1985

	Average gross weekly earnings (£)	Average gross hourly earnings (p)
Non-manual		
2 Professional and related management and administration	270	—
3 Professional and related in education, welfare and health	223	—
4 Literary, artistic, sports	238	—
5 Professional and related in science, engineering and technology	230	—
6 Managerial	229	—
7 Clerical and related	159	390
8 Selling	174	419
9 Security and protective service	222	499
Manual		
10 Catering, cleaning, hairdressing	133	288
11 Farming, fishing and related	123	268
12 Materials processing (excluding metal)	164	357
13 Making and repairing (excluding metal and electrical)	168	376
14 Processing, making, repairing (metal and electrical)	179	391
15 Painting, repetitive assembling, product inspection	159	356
16 Construction, mining	161	362
17 Transport operating	163	341
18 Miscellaneous	150	328
Total: Manual	164	357
Total: Non-manual	225	573
Total: All occupations	192	450

Source: DE, *New Earnings Survey*, 1985, Part D, table 86.
Note: Both sets of figures exclude those whose pay was affected by absence. The gross hourly earnings figure excludes the effect of overtime.

able, or having more alternative job opportunities, or undertaking a more skilled task, even though the length of education and training is similar to that of their less-skilled colleagues. In group 3, for example, teachers in further education earn £42 a week more than secondary-school teachers. Within group 17, the earnings of a lorry driver are positively related to the size of vehicle: drivers of heavy-goods vehicles (over 3 tons) earn 31p per hour more than other goods drivers.

Wage structure by industry:[1]   There are a number of reasons for studying the industrial wage structure. First, it is important to know whether labour can be allocated among industries independently of wages, or whether expanding (contracting) industries must pay higher (lower) wages to get the labour they require. Such information is useful in designing a pay policy. Second, how are the gains in labour productivity distributed? They can go to labour in the form of higher wages, or firms in the form of higher profits or consumers in the form of lower prices. Analysis of the industrial wage structure provides evidence on the topic. Third, it is important to know whether, independent of the characteristics of the individuals working in the industry, highly concentrated industries or industries with large plants pay higher wages; such data would be useful in, for example, designing our monopoly legislation.

Price theory implies that in the long run, given competitive conditions, each industry will, *ceteris paribus*, pay for a given grade of labour a wage identical to that paid by other industries. The *ceteris paribus* assumption implies that there are no differences in the non-pecuniary attractions of different industries or location or in the cost of living by location. In the long run, therefore, the growth in industry wage levels should not be correlated with the growth in the amount of labour employed. In the short run, an industry which expands its demand for labour will tend to have to raise the wages it pays because of short-run inelasticities in labour supply. Therefore the theory predicts a positive association in the short run between changes in employment by industry and changes in wages by industry.

It is clear that in the long run there is no relationship between changes in pay and changes in employment. Wragg and Robertson studied 82 manufacturing industries over the period 1954–73. The pay changes in each industry were very similar but employment experience was very different. Indeed, the weaving industry suffered a loss of employment of 6.2% p.a. yet had a higher-than-average increase in earnings. In the long run, therefore, expanding industries do not have to increase their pay at a rate above the average to meet their labour requirements, and industries where employment is contracting still give around average pay rises. This reflects the

---

1   The most substantial recent work on this issue is R. Wragg and J. Robertson, *Post-War Trends in Employment, Output, Labour Costs and Prices by Industry in the UK*, Research Paper No. 3, DE, June 1978.

continual churning which goes on in the labour market – 8m job-changes a year, and around 0.75m new entrants to the labour force and individuals retiring from it – which allows the labour force to adjust to the changing requirements imposed by the economy.

But what of the short run? It appears that there is a positive association between earnings changes and employment changes. This upward-sloping short-run market-labour supply curve implies that, to avoid labour shortages developing, a pay policy might need to permit such shortage sectors to pay above the norm.

An industry may react to an increase in physical productivity by lowering its relative product price or raising the relative wages it pays. If wage changes among industries are significantly (positively) related to movements in value productivity (i.e. variations in physical productivity and product prices taken together), this implies that non-competitive forces, such as ability to pay, determine the wage structure. In contrast, if the differential wage changes are unrelated to changes in value productivity by industry, this implies that competitive forces dominate in the explanation of wages. We anticipate such forces will be important because there is no reason, on equity or efficiency grounds, to expect that sectors with high labour productivity or growth in labour productivity will, *ceteris paribus*, pay high wages; working with bigger machines, if the intensity of work is unchanged, is no reason for higher pay.

The statistical association found for 1954–73 for 82 manufacturing industries by Wragg and Robertson among the growth rates of output per head (i.e. labour productivity), earnings, unit labour costs and prices, were clear and unambiguous. Earnings changes were very similar across the 82 industries while labour productivity changes differed markedly. In turn, there was a negative association between labour productivity changes and movements in unit labour costs and, finally, a negative relation between labour productivity changes and price rises. This suggests that workers who cannot increase their productivity easily (such as musicians or nurses) do not find their relative position in the pay structure worsening persistently. Further, after allowing for general inflation, the gains from increased labour productivity flow mainly to consumers.

III.4   Wage Structure by Sex and Race

Evidence: Females account for 44% of employment in Britain, yet among full-time workers in 1985 men were 4 times more likely than women to be earning over £200 a week and 10 times more likely to be earning over £300 a week. Females earn less than males in each broad occupational and industrial group: the data in table 5.5 show that the hourly earnings of full-time female adult workers were, on average, 74% of male hourly earnings, and that the percentage differential between male and female pay is higher for non-manual workers than for manual workers.

There are two broad reasons why average male pay exceeds average female

TABLE 5.5
Male–Female Hourly Earnings, Full-Time Workers, April 1985

	Female (p)	Male (p)	Female/Male (%)
Total manual	253	357	71
Total non-manual	358	573	62
Total	332	450	74
Occupations: manual			
Catering, cleaning, hairdressing	243	288	84
Materials processing (excluding metals)	249	357	70
Making and repairing (excluding metal & electrical)	248	376	66
Processing, making, repairing (metal & electrical)	270	391	69
Repetitive assembling, etc.	262	356	74
Transport, etc.	276	341	81
Occupations: non-manual			
Clerical	316	390	81
Selling	254	419	61
Security	462	499	93

Source: DE, *New Earnings Survey*, 1985, Part D, tables 86, 87.
Note: Data refer to adult workers whose pay in the survey week was not affected by absence and excludes the effect of overtime.

pay. First, and most important, women are crowded into the low-paying occupations and industries. Second, within occupational groups women tend to be paid less than men. In education, for example, women are disproportionately represented in the relatively low-paying primary segment, and within primary-school teaching women earn 15% less than men. It must be noted, however, that even within primary teaching the main reason for the differential is not that women are paid less than men for doing the same job but rather that women are under-represented in the higher-paying headship and deputy headship jobs. This example could be repeated for other occupations and industries.

Reasons why women earn less than men: One reason why women earn less than men is that their attachment to the labour force is weaker than that of men. On average, each year of labour-force experience raises the pay of both men and women by around 3%. But, when women drop out of the labour force their pay potential *drops* 3% for each year of home time. So, essentially, if a man and woman enter the labour force with equal potential and the woman works for 10 years and then drops out of the labour force for 10 years, by the time she re-enters work she is 20 years 'behind' the man – it is as if she is entering the labour force 20 years later. This relatively weak female attachment is in large part because it is widely believed that it is the role of women rather than men to drop out of the labour force to care for young children.

Attitudes on the role of the two sexes can certainly be influenced by economic factors; for example the two world wars, which caused the demand for female labour to rise substantially, were particularly important in raising the labour-force status of women. This suggests that the respective roles of men and women are thus amenable to change via economic and other influences. The observed weaker labour-force attachment shows up in differences between men and women in turnover rates, qualifications, size of local labour markets and the industries worked in.

Labour turnover is a little higher for women than for men. Such turnover imposes costs on the employer; at a minimum these costs will be the costs incurred when replacing employees. For example, in manufacturing the separation rate of women is two-thirds higher than the male rate. It is often argued that these figures reflect a composition effect, i.e. that females are disproportionately represented in industries and occupations which themselves have high turnover. This appears not to be true: in almost every industry and every occupation, female turnover is greater than male turnover. An alternative possibility, however, concerns the age composition of the labour force. Young workers have dramatically higher turnover rates than prime-age and older workers. Therefore some of the observed higher female labour turnover may occur because younger workers account for a higher fraction of the female labour force than the male labour force.

Because women have higher turnover rates than men, employers have less incentive to pay for female training. A profit-maximizing employer will be willing to pay for his employees' training if he can get a return on his investment by paying the trainee less than the value of his services when the training is completed. Given that women are more likely to quit or to be absent from a firm than men, employers will prefer to train men. This is compounded by hours legislation prohibiting women from working over a certain number of hours per week or at certain times.

Similarly, girls have less incentive to finance their own education and training. Staying on at school or university or taking a computer-programming course entails costs, for example tuition costs or forgone earnings (i.e. earnings that would have been received if working). If a woman has children this will involve a period out of the labour force; further, women retire at a younger age than men. The time over which she will receive benefits in the form of higher earnings from the training is less than for a man. Thus, among those aged 16–29 in 1981, only 10% of females held a post-school qualification below degree standard (e.g. apprenticeship, teaching qualification, nursing qualification) but 30% of men held such qualifications. In contrast, women in this age-group are far more likely to hold CSE or O-Level qualifications, a preparation for their segmentation into clerical occupations. The contrast is also clear if we consider highly qualified people (i.e. those holding an academic or professional qualification of degree standard). In 1981 10% of men but only 4% of women in the working population held such qualifications.

Females will also tend to be paid less than men if the firm draws them from a limited geographical area: they will incur lower transport costs on average than men. Also, women may tend to work in more pleasant conditions. The structure of the industries in which females work is a further element in the explanation of the sex differential. Females are disproportionately represented in small plants and atomistic industries, which tend to pay less and offer poorer career prospects than larger plants and concentrated industries; also a relatively low proportion of the female labour force is unionized, which reflects in part the higher costs of organizing in industries consisting of small plants.

Equal Pay Act and Sex Discrimination Act:[1]   The Equal Pay Act requires that a woman is to receive equal treatment to a man within the same firm when she is employed (a) on work of the same or broadly similar nature to that of men; (b) in a job which, though different from those of men, is of equal value. It was passed in 1970 but its full application was delayed until the end of 1975 to allow employers time to adjust to the new set of conditions on pay. The end of 1975 was also the time when the Sex Discrimination Act, requiring equal opportunities for men and women, became law.

The course of movements in relative female/male pay and female/male employment is outlined in table 5.6. Among full-time workers the hourly minimum wage rates set out in collective agreements had reached equality by 1976, and the hourly earnings of females rose from 64% of the male figure in 1973 to 73% in 1976, an enormous increase in such a short period. Simultaneously the relative employment of females was rising.

TABLE 5.6
Relative Female/Male Pay and Employment Movements 1970–80 (%)

April	Full-time workers			Part-time females, full-time males	
	Hourly wage rates	Hourly earnings	Employment	Hourly earnings	Employment
	W_f/W_m	W_f/W_m	F/M	W_f/W_m	F/M
1970	83	64	40	—	—
1973	87	64	41	51	10
1976	100	73	42	59	11
1980	100	71	46	57	12

Source: Z. Tzannatos and A. Zabalza, 'The anatomy of the rise of British female relative wages in the 1970s: evidence from the New Earnings Survey', *BJIR*, 1984, tables 1, 2 and 7.

Note: W_f is wage or earnings of female: W_m is wage or earnings of male; F and M are, repectively, employment of females and males. The hourly wage rate data refer to the weighted average of minimum rates of manual workers laid down in collective agreements.

The changes in female relative pay 1973–6 are coincident with the imple-

---

1   This section draws on A. Zabalza and Z. Tzannatos, 'The effect of Britain's antidiscrimination legislation on relative pay and employment', *EJ*, Sept. 1985, and 'The anatomy of the rise of British female relative wages in the 1970s: evidence from the New Earnings Survey', *BJIR*, 1984.

mentation of the Equal Pay Act. It is sometimes held that the Equal Pay Act is likely to be ineffective in improving the relative pay of part-time female workers because many work in segregated jobs which do not afford easy comparison with similar tasks done by men. But note that the relative hourly earnings of part-time females to full-time males also rose substantially between 1973 and 1976, from 51% to 59%.

Before jumping to the conclusion that the Equal Pay Act was responsible for the large rise in female relative earnings in the mid-1970s, let us examine some possible alternative explanations. First, theory and evidence suggest that relative pay gets compressed during a cyclical upswing. This cannot account for the rise in female relative pay because real GDP *fell* between 1973 and 1975. Second, was there an autonomous decrease in the supply of female labour? On the contrary, we see from table 5.6 that female employment *rose* from 40% of the male figure in 1970 to 46% in 1980, a rise of 15% over the decade.

A third possibility concerns composition effects. Female relative pay can rise if females are now paid more in all sectors or (although pay in male and female jobs stays the same) because females have moved into higher-paying industries and occupations. It turns out that almost all the rise in the relative pay of females is because of the rise *within* occupations and industries. Such as uniformity in the behaviour of relative pay among quite different sectors must surely have been the consequence of a common cause – like the Equal Pay Act – and it is not attributable to the particular fortunes of each of the sectors. Indeed, the importance of the Equal Pay legislation is confirmed by Public Administration, the only sector where female relative pay did not rise during 1970–80. This is consistent with the fact that for the majority of workers in this sector – the non-manual employees – equal-pay principles were already in force before 1970.

Fourth, the letter of the Act, if not its aim, could be met by reducing men's pay. In sectors where there are many females employed, the equality of female and male pay might be achieved by lowering male pay in that sector relative to average male pay. This did not happen. For example, male pay (relative to average male pay) rose in both the Wage Board sector and among NHS Ancillaries, two sectors where female employment is substantial.

A final alternative explanation for the rise in female relative pay concerns the role of incomes policy. Many of the incomes policies of the 1970s were wholly or partially flat-rate (e.g. £1 + 4% or £6 a week) and a flat-rate rise gives equal cash amounts to all employees, so narrowing percentage differentials. In fact, there is strong evidence that the egalitarian aims of these incomes policies were not achieved and the pay structure among individuals or across industry and occupations did not narrow. Further, statistical estimates suggest that well under a fifth of the rise in female relative pay was due to the independent effect of incomes policy norms.

So we are left with one major explanation – the Equal Pay Act. There are two main channels through which the Equal Pay Act might have worked to raise female relative pay – collective agreements or the process of law. It seems clear that the major impact of the Act was via collective bargaining. The system of setting basic wage rates is centralized in Britain, and a small number of collective agreements determine the wage rates of a large number of workers. In the early 1970s, the 15 largest national agreements covered around 5.5 million workers, a quarter of all employees, and the number of workers covered by collective agreements or minimum Wage Orders was 14m, or nearly two-thirds of all employees. Over the period 1950–70 the weighted average of the minimum female hourly wage rate to the minimum male rate remained constant at around 82%. But, as the Equal Pay Act came gradually into force, it reached 87% by 1973 and then 100% by the time the Act was fully implemented in 1976 (table 5.6). Further, it is clear from the table that the rise in the female relative minimum wage rates was simultaneously translated into a rise in relative earnings, of workers both covered and uncovered by collective agreements.

The other channel through which the Equal Pay Act might have worked is via the legal machinery. If a woman (or man) believes she has been treated unfairly by her firm under the Act she can apply to an industrial tribunal (a court dealing with labour laws). There have been few such applications. In 1976, the first year of the operation of the Act, there were 1,742 applications but by 1984 the number had fallen to 70. Most applications are settled by conciliation and of those that reach the tribunal, only a small minority are decided in favour of the applicant. It is clear that, so far, the legal process has very much taken second place to collective bargaining as the vehicle for implementing the Act. However, an important change in the Act was implemented in 1984 to bring Britain into line with European practice. Previously, the 'work of equal value' dimension of the Act required a job-evaluation exercise. But from 1984 that is no longer so. It is to be expected that many individuals will feel that, inside a given firm, they do work of equal value to a colleague even though the job is not the same. Such individuals are now likely to apply to an industrial tribunal to get equal pay. Up to the time of writing (April 1986), there have been surprisingly few such cases, but important test cases are pending in the NHS.

Studies show that in 1970 the hourly earnings of men were around 30% higher than those of women with similar education, experience and father's occupation.[1] By 1975 the corresponding differential had fallen to between 12% and 15%. So the Equal Pay Act achieved over half of the total relative-pay gains needed to eliminate labour-market discrimination completely.

---

1   Calculated from A. Zabalza and J. Arrafut, 'Wage differentials between married men and women in Great Britain: the depreciation effect of non-participations, *RES*, 1984. See also R. Layard *et al.*, *The Causes of Poverty*, Background Paper No. 5, Royal Commission on the Distribution of Income and Wealth (HMSO, 1978), pp. 52–6, and Christine Greenhalgh, 'Male-Female Wage Differentials in Great Britain', *EJ*, December 1980. Broadly, these estimates are derived by computing separate earnings-functions for men and women. Then an estimated female wage is calculated by assuming that a female of particular characteristics is paid according to the male wage structure. The difference between the estimated female wage and the actual female wage is termed 'discrimination'. Such calculations are, as the authors recognize, very difficult to undertake accurately.

It is unlikely that there is now much unequal pay for identical work. For example in 1983 male sales assistants were paid 289p an hour while female sales assistants were paid 191p an hour. Obviously, if the men and women were perfect substitutes the females would soon replace the males. Rather, remaining labour-market discrimination mainly concerns access to the higher-paying occupations. It is here that the Sex Discrimination Act comes in as a potentially important channel in overcoming the current under-representation of women in high-paying sectors. It covers education and the supply of goods and services as well as employment. The Act states that women must be given equal treatment in the arrangements for selecting a candidate for a job, in the terms on which a job is offered, on access to promotion, transfer and training or any other aspects of the job and on dismissal. The Act established the Equal Opportunities Commission with fairly wide powers: it can help individuals to bring cases if it considers them of wider interest; it can conduct formal investigations compelling people to give evidence; it can serve non-discrimination notices and seek injunctions against persistent discriminators. Unfortunately the EOC has so far done little to raise the status of women.

In 1985 the hourly earnings of full-time women were 74% of those of full-time men. The evidence above suggests that approximately half of the difference is because men and women have on average different characteristics. Women have, for example, less labour-force experience and education than men. The other half is discrimination, not in the sense of unequal pay for equal work but because, for given characteristics, women do not rise so high in the hierarchy of occupations. Although a better use of the Sex Discrimination Act could help with both these factors, another way to eliminate the remaining pay differential, if it is held desirable to do so, would be to strengthen the attachment of women to the labour market.

The government could consider a number of alternative methods to improve the labour-force status of women. First, it might encourage them to join unions: the male-female wage differential is, *ceteris paribus*, smaller in those industries which are highly unionized. Second, more girls could be encouraged to take apprenticeship or college training by providing them with differentially large training grants. Third, female quotas, especially in the higher occupational grades, could be enforced. Finally, women's pay could be forced up relative to men's pay by subsidizing women's employment.

Race:[1]   There is clear evidence that non-whites suffer discrimination in employment. Other things being equal (i.e. holding constant age, experience, weeks worked, years of schooling, marital status etc.), non-white males

1   Evidence in this section is taken from R. Layard *et al.*, *The Causes of Poverty*, op. cit.; M. Stewart, 'Racial discrimination and occupational attainment in Britain', *EJ*, September 1983; DE *Gazette*, October 1983, pp. 424–30; J. Smith, *Labour Supply and Employment Duration at London Transport*, Greater London Paper, No. 15, 1976; DE *Gazette*, December 1985, pp. 467–77.

earn around 17% less than equivalent whites. The extent of this discrimination is greater for those of Asian ethnic origin than men of West Indian origin. The bulk of this discrimination is not attributable to unequal pay for equal work, rather the problem is that black and brown workers seem not to be able to gain access to the higher-paying occupations. Thus while 58% of Pakistani males and 32% of West Indian males working in Britain are unskilled or semi-skilled, the corresponding figure for whites is 18%. Further, almost no whites with degree-level qualifications do manual work but around one-fifth of such men from minorities do manual work and members of ethnic minorities are much less likely than whites to be in professional and management occupations.

Another way of describing this discrimination is to say that non-whites have, on average, flat experience-earnings profiles, while for whites the earnings profile rises with labour-market experience. This has a particularly important consequence for the returns to education for non-whites and whites. Non-whites born outside the UK do no worse in terms of occupational attainment than equivalent whites providing they left school at age 15 or below. But those non-whites who left full-time education at 16 or over suffer substantial discrimination: they simply do not rise up the hierarchy of occupations in the same way as white workers. Thus the returns to extra education are substantially lower for non-whites than for whites.

Although the majority of the non-white labour force was born outside the UK, there is evidence that the vicious circle of non-whites crowding into lower-level occupation – hence flat experience-earnings profiles and lower returns to extra education – is continuing among non-whites born in the UK. For such people in the age-group 16–29 in Great Britain in 1981, the percentages with post O-Level qualifications were:

	Male	Female
White	45	23
Non-white	25	13

These post O-Level qualifications include degrees, HNC/HND, teaching and nursing qualifications, apprenticeships, City and Guilds and A-Levels. It is rather worrying that whites are almost twice as likely to possess such a qualification as non-whites. Indeed, in the case of degree or equivalent qualifications, white men are six times more likely to possess the qualification than non-whites. A plausible explanation for the discrepancy is that British-born non-whites observe the relative occupational attainments of whites and non-whites in the labour force and conclude there is not much point in pursuing the extra education.

A further problem is that the occupational status of non-whites may lead employers to conclude that, in some cases, they have a more relaxed attitude to work than whites. In fact, a higher average turnover rate or absenteeism rate is likely to be a characteristic of their occupations and industries rather than an inherent racial characteristic. For example a study of labour turnover at London Transport showed that, other things being equal, blacks had a longer duration of employment than whites. Although non-white immigrants to Britain may have been content with lower average occupational status than the indigenous population, the same is unlikely of their sons and daughters. The relative educational and occupational achievements of young British-born whites and non-whites are a cause for concern.

III.5   Social Security

One aspect of income distribution which causes widespread concern is the problem of poverty. Low earnings from work are only part of the problem (and are discussed in the next section). Others at the lower end of the income distribution include old people, the sick and disabled, large families or families with lone parents, and the unemployed. In this section we discuss how to measure poverty, the current social security system and suggested reforms.[1]

Measurement: Poverty can be defined as an absolute or relative standard. Absolute standards are based on consumption of necessities. Relative standards are normally related to some measure of income in the general population. Thus, the amount of supplementary benefit (SB) payments, which is often taken as defining the level below which poverty may be said to exist, would reflect an absolute concept if, over a long period of time, it was geared exclusively to prices and it would reflect a relative concept if it were geared to average earnings. Over most of the postwar period the poverty line as defined by supplementary benefits was being determined by relative rather than absolute standards: the real value of benefits has more than doubled since 1948.

At the end of 1981 (the latest date for which published information is available!), the numbers of families and people living (a) below the poverty line or (b) on it were:

		Families	People
(a)	Numbers with incomes below SB level	1.8m	2.8m
(b)	Numbers receiving SB	3.0m	4.8m

Nearly 2m families and 3m people lived *below* the supplementary benefit level. Around half these people are unemployed or are in work. The other half are sick, disabled or pensioners. There has been a substantial rise in the

---

1   For more information see DHSS, *Reform of Social Security*, vols 1, 2, 3, Cmnd. 9517, 9518, 9519 (HMSO, June 1985); also Treasury and Civil Service Committee (Chairman: M. Meacher), *The Structure of Personal Income Taxation and Income Support*, HC 386 (HMSO, May 1983). This document is particularly clear on the vexed issues of the poverty trap and unemployment trap discussed in the next section. It also contains a concise description of the negative income tax scheme and social dividend scheme, and that description is replicated here. See also W. Beckerman, 'The impact of income maintenance payment on poverty in Britain', *EJ*, June 1979.

numbers living below the poverty line since 1977, when the corresponding number of people was 1.9m. Presumably the main reason why people live below the poverty line is that, although eligible for SB or Family Income Supplement (FIS, see below, the corresponding benefit for those in work), they do not claim it. The number of families (3.0m) and people (4.8m) in families in receipt of supplementary benefit have also risen in recent years. Two-fifths of these SB recipients are pensioners.

There are other ways of measuring poverty than counting heads. One way is to calculate a 'poverty gap' in money terms. The poverty gap is simply the amount by which income falls short of the official poverty line. In 1975, before social security benefits were paid, the gap was 6% of GDP, but after social security benefits were paid the gap was only 0.25% of GDP. When put like this, the performance of the social security system is impressive, though this is not to deny that families who are falling below the poverty line face real hardship or that the official poverty line itself may be inadequate.

Social security system: The social security system provides income in two main ways. First, contributory benefits are based on national insurance contributions and paid from the National Insurance Fund.[1] In 1985–6, retirement pensions accounted for £17bn out of the £22bn total spending on contributory benefits. Second, disability benefits, supplementary benefit, family benefits and housing benefits are paid direct from the Exchequer. Over half of the total non-contributory benefits of £16bn consists of means-tested supplementary benefit and housing benefit. The other major non-contributory item is child benefit. Total social security spending of £40bn represented 31% of public expenditure in 1985–6.

Social security has undergone important changes in the last decade. First, national insurance contributions are earnings-related and there is an earnings-related component to the state pension scheme. However, the reverse has happened with unemployment and sickness benefit, where the earnings-related component has been axed, causing many more among the sick and unemployed to need supplementary benefit. Second, unemployment benefit is now taxable. Third, child benefit (£7 a week for each child in 1986) is a cash benefit paid to the mother. Previously the main family support was given via the tax system to the father. Fourth, an array of new benefits for disabled people has been introduced. Fifth, the employer is now responsible for paying the first 26 weeks of statutory sick pay (SSP) in any one year. For

---

1 In 1986–7, national insurance contributions are as follows. The employer pays 5% of earnings of £38 a week, rising to 10.45% on earnings of £140 or more. The employee pays 5% on earnings of £38 a week, rising to 9% at earnings of £95 or more, up to a ceiling of £285. Both the employer and the employee pay a lower rate if the employee is contracted-out of the state earnings-related pension scheme. For full details, see leaflet NI 208.

those earning £75 a week or more, the SSP is £47 a week. The employer then claims the money back from the National Insurance Fund.

Despite these changes, there are real faults in the system. First, nearly 3m people are living below the poverty line, which shows that the benefits are simply not getting to people in need. Second, another 5m people have to rely on SB, which shows that other anti-poverty measures are not working properly. Third, the income-related nature of many benefits discourages full take-up and also results in high implicit marginal tax rates (this poverty-trap problem is discussed, together with the unemployment trap, in the next section). Fourth, certain groups – particularly the disabled and lone parents – fit uneasily into the current system and this makes it difficult to apply a coherent benefit structure to them. Finally, successive Governments have worried about the growing cost of social security benefits. This prompted a serious look at the system in 1985, which resulted in reforms to be introduced in 1987 and 1988.

Reform: A major review of the social security system was undertaken by the DHSS in 1984/5. Proposals were outlined in a Green Paper, published in June 1985, which attracted 7,000 responses, many critical. The ultimate proposals for reform steming from this exercise are quite modest. They repair the system rather than fundamentally altering it.

The major change concerns the State Earnings Related Pension Scheme (SERPS), paid for by national insurance contributions. There was a worry that this scheme would have become very expensive – i.e. required much higher rates of national insurance contributions – in the next century. The changes proposed have cut the estimated cost of the scheme in year 2033 from £26bn (1985 prices) to £13bn. The important modifications to SERPS include : (i) it will be based on lifetime average earnings, instead of an average of an employee's best 20 years' earnings, and (ii) the amount that will be inherited by a spouse will be one half rather than the full amount as at present. However, these modifications do not result in any savings in this century.

There are also proposed reforms in non-contributory benefits. Income support (IS) will replace supplementary benefit, which has become excessively complex. IS will pay a personal allowance (e.g. £48 a week for a couple) and various premiums (e.g. age-related child premiums). IS will be simpler to understand and calculate than the present SB system with its long list of small payments for additional requirements, down to 25p a week for baths. These will all be abolished. Once the reform is completed, 1.7m people will lose compared with the old system and 1.4m will gain.

A Social Fund is to be established to cope with the sort of emergencies covered at present by special payments such as the £30 death grant, extra heating allowances during cold weather, and single payments for clothing or furniture. The Fund is to be cash-limited and discretionary – there is no external appeals mechanism if the claimant disagrees with the local DHSS social fund officers' decision.

Many people believe that the social security system should be radically restructured rather than patched up. In particular, it is widely believed that the benefit system should be made more congruent with the tax system. There have been three main alternative sets of suggestions concerning such future directions of reform: a 'new Beveridge plan', a negative (or reverse) income tax, and a social dividend scheme. They have a superficial similarity – in that under each scheme individuals will be guaranteed a minimum income at around supplementary benefit (or income support) level, and the need for means-testing would be much reduced or abolished. In fact, however, these three schemes are very different from each other.

Under the original Beveridge proposals it was proposed that social *insurance* should guarantee everyone a minimum standard of living. This subsistence income was to be provided as a right, without a means test: the part played by SB was to be virtually phased out. In the postwar period, however, National Insurance benefits have usually been below the prescribed minima laid down by supplementary benefit. Under the 'new Beveridge Plan' it is therefore proposed to implement fully the original Beveridge proposals. One of the aims of the current pension scheme is to ensure pension benefits of sufficient size to virtually eliminate the need for pensioners to turn to supplementary benefits to augment their income. Higher child benefits are also important. Advocates of this universalistic approach to curing poverty generally qualify it by suggesting that the benefits from raising social security payments could be taxed and thereby directed towards those with lower incomes. This policy would obviously be successful in raising the incomes of non-employed disadvantaged individuals. It does not involve high marginal tax rates at low incomes and is therefore less likely to have disincentive effects on working harder. Moreover, it would not involve any major administrative headaches. But it does have two problems. First, it would cost an additional 4–7p on the basic rate of income tax (quite apart from the tax clawed-back from benefits). However, this is merely another way of stating the seriousness of the poverty problem. Second, the problem of the employed with low incomes remains.

The negative (or reverse) income tax (NIT) and social dividend (SD) schemes assume a minimum income guarantee (the poverty line), which is a cash benefit varying according to the circumstances of a family. This cash benefit is paid in full to those without any other income and so it supplants those social security benefits which are at present paid to those without any work.

It is for those in work that these NIT and SD schemes differ in their mode of operation. Under the NIT, the minimum income guarantee is withdrawn as quickly as possible as earnings rise, until a level of income is reached (the break-even point) where the guarantee payment disappears and tax starts to be paid. Typically the withdrawal rate below the break-even point might be 70% and the tax rate above around 30%. Unless the minimum income guarantee is kept very low – below present levels of social security – even a withdrawal rate of 70% puts the break-even point above the present tax thresholds. So a substantial minority of the population faces a 70% marginal rate and some of the characteristics of the present poverty trap are reproduced.

Under a social dividend scheme, the minimum income guarantee is paid to every individual either as a cash benefit or as a credit against tax. There is no withdrawal of benefit as such. Nevertheless, because tax is charged on all income other than guaranteed income, there comes a point at which tax liability equals benefit (or credit) received. This is the tax break-even point. So the high withdrawal rate on low incomes is avoided, but the tax above the break-even point is higher than under NIT. The break-even point is significantly higher than under NIT.

Assume the poverty line (guaranteed payment) for a married couple with two children is £70 a week. A typical NIT might have a withdrawal rate of 70%, giving a break-even gross income of £100 (£70/0.7), and a tax rate of 32% above £100. The typical social dividend scheme might have a constant tax rate of 43%, giving a break-even point at a gross income of £163 (£70/0.43). It is unlikely that the Chancellor of the Exchequer would be content with such high break-even income levels.

III.6   Low Pay[1]

Low pay is one part of the poverty problem. Industries which are at the bottom of the earnings structure tend to be characterized by high proportions of small plants, of women workers, of unskilled workers and of falling demand for labour. It is also clear that low-paid workers are disproportionately represented in the service sector.

Low pay is also related to age and skill. Teenagers, workers in their early twenties and workers over fifty are disproportionately represented. Older and unskilled workers not only tend to have relatively low earnings, but also to suffer higher rates of unemployment. Unemployment rates referring specifically to unskilled workers are at least three times the national average unemployment rate. The annual earnings differential between them and other workers is therefore greater than is apparent from a comparison of the earnings of those who are in work.

Two important features of the structure of the low-pay problem are worth noting. First, if the low-paid are described as those in the lowest tenth of the distribution of manual earnings, we observe considerable movement across the boundary of this lowest tenth. 21% of manual men were in the lowest tenth at least once in the five years 1970 to 1974, but only 3% were in this tenth in each of the years. Second, low pay must be seen as part of a general

---

1   For fuller discussion, see Chris Pond, 'Wage Councils, the Unorganized and the Low Paid', ch. 8 in G.S. Bain (ed.), *Industrial Relations in Britain* (Basil Blackwell, 1983); D. Metcalf, *Low Pay, Occupational Mobility and Minimum Wage Policy in Britain* (American Enterprise Institute, 1981); *Social Trends*, 1986, ch. 5; DE Consultative Paper on *Wage Councils*, March 1985.

problem of labour-market disadvantages in that it is associated with high incidence of job instability, ill-health and lack of fringe benefits. The low-paid worker is more vulnerable to the interruption of earnings power, cannot save for old age or emergencies, and can only borrow at very high interest rates such as through HP. Thus low pay is an important element in the cycle of poverty.

The interaction of low pay, social security benefits and income tax generates the poverty trap and the unemployment trap. The *poverty trap* results from increased reliance on income-related benefits and causes high marginal tax rates on additional earnings faced by people on such means-tested benefits. DHSS calculations suggest that it is low-income married couples with children that are caught in the poverty trap. For example, for a married couple living in local authority housing with 4 dependent children in April 1985, an increase in the husband's gross weekly earnings from £60 to £135 brought no improvement in living standards because net weekly spending power remained at £110, i.e. he suffered a marginal tax rate of 100%. There is no real evidence that the poverty trap has undermined work incentives. Some decisions – such as whether or not the wife works – are not subject to the same high tax rates. But, as the Meacher Report noted: 'It is impossible to believe that there is not widespread resentment, confusion, frustration and cynicism.'

The other incentive issue is the *unemployment trap* – the possibility that incomes out of work may be little different from those in work. Supplementary benefit is the relevant out-of-work income measure. Of 2.1m male unemployed claimants in November 1984 (the latest available data), only 21% were receiving unemployment benefits alone, 61% were receiving only supplementary benefit, 9% were having their unemployment benefit topped-up by supplementary benefit, and 10% were receiving no benefit.

Again, there is no strong evidence that the unemployment trap results in a disincentive to work. The DHSS calculate that in 1982 (the latest available data) only 3% of unemployed men would have had a higher income out of work than in work:

Ratio of income out of work to income in work	% of unemployed
Under 50%	39
50–79%	40
80–100%	18
Over 100%	3
Total	100

Thus two-fifths of unemployed men had incomes under half what they would have had if they were in work, and four-fifths had incomes below 80% of their in-work incomes.

The Meacher Committee concluded that the poverty trap and unemployment trap can be moderated by a rise in income-tax thresholds or a rise in child benefit. Since those with children are more at risk from the two traps than those without, they favoured increasing child benefit. One option considered superior to the present tax-benefit system was to raise child benefit to £15 a week for the first child and £10 for subsequent children. This permits abolition of FIS and the child needs allowance for rent and rate rebates. It would be paid for by reducing the income-tax allowance of a married man to that of a single person.

Family Income Supplement (FIS) was introduced in 1971 to help offset poverty caused by low pay. When family income falls short of a prescribed level (from November 1985 £86 per week for a one-child family, plus £11.50 per child aged under 11, £12.50 per child aged 11–15 and £13.50 per dependent child aged 16 plus), the family is paid a benefit equal to one half the difference between its total gross income and the prescribed level (with a maximum supplement of £22.50 for a one-child family and an average of £3 per additional child). This is a potentially powerful policy to raise the incomes of low-paid people, but it has two drawbacks. First, only around half those eligible for FIS actually claim it. Second, the withdrawal of benefit as earnings rise contributes to the poverty trap.

Therefore as part of the reform of social security, FIS is to be abolished in 1988 and replaced by Family Credit (FC). It is anticipated that the number of claimants will double to 440,000. FC is to be paid through the wage packet of the principal earner (usually the father) rather than claimed (usually by the mother) at the social security office. To qualify for FC, the family will have to have: at least one dependent child, at least one earner working 24 hours a week, low net income and capital of under £6,000. If it had been in operation in 1986 it would have worked as follows. There is an adult credit of £30 a week plus age-related child credits. If the family's net income is £48 a week or under, the credit is paid in full. If net income is above the £48 benchmark, the maximum credit will be reduced by 70p for each excess £1. FC is whatever is left and paid in full. For most families, FC will, in practice, work as an offset to income tax and national insurance (whereas now the family often pays income tax while simultaneously receiving FIS). This is a useful reform because it will increase take-up, stop the poverty-trap tax rates of greater than 100% and, most important, represents a modest attempt to integrate the tax and benefit system of some people. It can be thought of as a prototype negative income tax.

Elements of a minimum-wage policy exist via the wages councils, which set minimum rates in certain industries.[1] This direct state intervention in fixing minimum wages first occurred in 1909 with the Trade Boards Act. In 1945 trade boards were renamed wage councils. There are 27 wage councils covering 2.75m workers in around half a million establishments. Three councils cover over a million workers in hotels, clubs, pubs, cafes and

---

1   The impact of wage councils on employment is rather controversial. DE Research Papers report conflicting results, with no effect in the retail distribution sector and a modest adverse effect in clothing (papers 51 and 52 respectively, 1985). There was speculation that the Government might opt for abolition of the councils but, instead, it went for the more limited changes outlined in the text. For more details see DE *Gazette*, 1985, pp. 136, 211, 223–6 and 291.

restaurants, and two more cover a million shopworkers. There are also two wage boards covering 275,000 farm-workers. Wage councils are to be reformed from 1986. First, 500,000 young people aged under 21 are to be removed from any regulation by wage councils. This is because of the belief that teenage pay rates set by wage councils have an adverse effect on employment. Second, each wage council will be confined to setting only a single minimum hourly rate and a single overtime rate. By contrast, the 1985 wage order covering wages of employees in cafes ran to 34 pages and set 144 different rates of pay. Third, the procedure by which the Secretary of State for Employment can modify or abolish individual wage councils are to be simplified.

A national minimum wage is advocated by those who do not like FIS because it is an income-related benefit and who believe that wage councils have been ineffective. If the minimum wage was set at around two-thirds of median male earnings, its cost would be equivalent to around 5% of the total wage bill (1.5% for men and 15% for women). Although a national minimum wage is, at first sight, an attractive proposition, it is not without drawbacks. First, many low-paid people are single people and married women. They typically live in families with more than one earner. So a national minimum wage would leave much family poverty untouched: it would not help the family just above the minimum wage but with needs greater than income, perhaps because the family is large. Second, unless other workers are content to see their pay differentials eroded, a national minimum wage is simply inflationary – it pushes the whole distribution of money wages to the right, leaving the lowest-paid no better off, in either relative or real terms, than before. Third, the minimum wage implies an increase in unit labour costs and is likely to result in lower employment. Recall that the young and old and unskilled – those the minimum wage is designed to help most – already have the highest unemployment rates. It is sometimes said, however, that the minimum-wage legislation will have a 'shock effect' and thereby raise productivity without any loss in employment. This is unlikely to be widespread in that it implies that firms currently have a careless attitude towards profits. Further, many of the low-paying industries are competitive and are therefore unlikely to need a national minimum wage as a spur to efficiency.

This suggests that provision of more training facilities, better information about wages and opportunities both locally and nationally, inducement to labour mobility, wage subsidies, and running the economy with lower, more evenly distributed unemployment levels, are likely to be more effective solutions to the problem of low pay than is a national minimum wage.

IV   TRADE UNIONS, INDUSTRIAL RELATIONS AND WAGE INFLATION

IV.1   Trade Unions

Trade-union membership in the UK is continuing to fall, although more slowly than in the early 1980s. Between 1979 and 1984, the last year for which the Department of Employment has published estimates, membership fell by 17%, from 13.3m to 11.1m. This decline is in sharp contrast to the pattern of the 1970s, a period in which membership grew very quickly by historical standards. In the ten years to end-1979, union membership rose by 28%, more than three times faster than in the 1960s.[1]

The major immediate reason for the turn-around in union membership growth is the fall in the number of people in work. Employment in the heavily unionized manufacturing sector, for example, has been cut by nearly a quarter since 1979. Union membership, however, is now falling faster than employment, at least for the economy as a whole. Expressed as a percentage of all employees in employment, trade-union membership reached 58% in 1980; by 1984 it has fallen to 52%. Even though the number of employees in work is estimated to have risen in 1984, the number of union members fell, by 250,000.

Recent empirical work suggests that, over a fairly extended period, changes in trade-union membership in the economy as a whole have been systematically associated with certain economic developments. Membership has tended to fall when unemployment has grown, and to have increased when price inflation has risen, when average money wages have been rising fast and when the labour force has been expanding quickly. These associations are now reasonably well established, but their interpretation is not straightforward. It could be, for example, that more rapidly rising wages encourage workers to join trade unions; equally, however, more workers joining trade unions could lead to more rapidly rising wages. What does seem plausible is that, in addition to these aggregate associations, certain structural changes have influenced trade-union growth. The changing industrial and occupational composition of the labour force, the great rise in the number of women in work, and the changing boundaries between the public and private sectors are all likely to have had an effect on union membership. Union membership rates among women, for example, are still significantly below those for men, even though the gap is closing.[2]

It should be stressed that the direct impact of unions extends far beyond its members. The *New Earnings Survey* for 1973 and 1977 gave estimates of the number of workers whose pay was affected by various kinds of collective agreements, whether they were union members or not. Only 17% of full-time male workers and 28% of full-time female workers were found not to have had their pay covered by collective bargaining; i.e. the influence of unions was far more pervasive than their membership figures might imply.

---

1 *DEG*, January 1986, pp. 16–18.

2 G. Bain and F. Elsheikh, *Union Growth and the Business Cycle* (Basil Blackwell, 1976). See also the review by R. Richardson in *BJIR*, July 1977, and A. Booth, 'A Reconsideration of Trade Union Growth in the UK', *BJIR*, November 1983.

Union membership is particularly extensive among male workers, manual workers and workers in the manufacturing and public sectors. There are no absolutely reliable figures on union membership by industry, because even the unions involved do not always know how many of their members work in each industry. The most authoritative study, however, estimated that union density in 1979 ranged from 7% in the very large miscellaneous services industry, which includes accounting services, legal services, hotel and catering etc., to over 95% in such industries as cotton textiles, coal mining, the public utilities and much of the transport industry.[1]

There is a substantial body of empirical research seeking to explain the variations in trade-union membership between industries and occupations. Two broad classes of reasons have been suggested. The first refers to the workforce and suggests that some types of workers believe that unions offer little of value. A study of workers' voting behaviour in union representation elections in the US, for example, showed that workers were more likely to want a union if they earned relatively low wages within the firm, felt that they had a poor chance of promotion, felt that they suffered from arbitrary behaviour by their supervisors or had experienced racial discrimination. The higher wage earners, and those who were optimistic about promotion or had good relations with their supervisors, tended to see much less attraction in union representation and voted against it.[2]

The second set of reasons refers not so much to the workers as to the kind of situation they find themselves in at work. A recent survey of over 2,000 British establishments, covering all sectors of the economy, stressed the importance of the workplace context. It concluded that the chief reasons for the different patterns of union recognition and density were the type of ownership, the size of establishments, and the size and workforce composition of the enterprises. Unions were more likely to be found in the public sector, in large plants, in large organizations and in establishments where male workers predominated. Unions were also more likely to be found, other things being equal, in multi-establishment than in single establishment firms. Overall, the authors of the study concluded, their results were consistent with the view that union recognition and density patterns were mainly the result of government and management policies and practices, especially in relation to the implications of managing large numbers of people. The authors felt that the inclinations and wishes of individual workers were of relatively minor significance in determining union density.[3]

This conclusion ties in with some related work on the closed shop, i.e. on the arrangements that make union membership a condition of employment. There are both pre-entry shops, where membership is required before a

---

1   R. Price and G. Bain, 'Union Growth in Britain: Retrospect and Prospect', *BJIR*, March 1983.

2   H. Farber and D. Saks, 'Why Workers Want Unions', *JPE*, April 1980.

3   W. Daniel and N. Millward, *Workplace Industrial Relations in Britain* (1983), Chapter II.

worker can be hired, and post-entry shops, where a worker must join on being hired. Post-entry closed shops are the much more common form. The incidence of closed shops in Great Britain has grown strongly in the last 15–20 years and it may well not have fallen appreciably even in the last five. One estimate, for the late 1970s, was that they covered at least 5.2m workers, nearly 25% of all employees. They were estimated to be particularly common in mining, in gas, electricity and water, in printing, in transport and communications, and in shipbuilding. They were rare in agriculture, in professional and scientific services, and in insurance, banking and business finance.

Although closed shops quite properly arouse strong emotions, it should be recalled that in most cases their existence has been preceded by very high levels of union densities. A closed shop, or union-membership agreement, is nearly always a formal recognition of extensive unionization. On many occasions, managements appear to have seen them not so much as leading to a significant increase in union power but as a potential force for making industrial relations more orderly. Whether they were correct in taking this position remains an open question, but there can be little doubt that some of the surge in the extent of the closed shop during the 1970s was due to at least tacit management approval.[1]

Finally, something should be said about the number and size-distribution of trade unions. The number of unions has been tending to fall for many years, both as a result of trade-union mergers and because some unions simply cease to function. By the end of 1984, the Department of Employment estimated that there were 371 trade unions, down from 470 in 1975. The number of very small unions is still surprisingly large; in 1984, there were no less than 67 unions with fewer than 100 members. At the other end of the scale, the number of unions who reported having at least 100,000 members (the level which now gives automatic membership on the General Council of the TUC) fell from 27 in 1979 to 21 in 1984.

In addition to those in independent trade unions, many workers belong to other staff associations that engage in collective discussions or negotiations on terms and conditions of employment. Still other workers, numbering perhaps 2.75 million, are in industries or occupations that have wages councils, public bodies that are designed to reproduce some of the features of collective bargaining where trade-union growth is thought to be inherently difficult. The wages councils are now to be reformed. Under the Wages Bill, currently being considered by Parliament, wages councils orders will no longer apply to workers under the age of 21. This would remove perhaps ½ million workers from their coverage. In addition, wages councils will now be limited to setting one basic hourly rate of pay, an overtime rate and a limit to the charge for any accommodation the employer provides.

---

1   J. Gennard, S. Dunn and M. Wright, 'The Extent of Closed Shop Arrangements in British Industry', *DEG*, January 1980, pp. 16–22. See also Daniel and Millward, op.cit.

This will very significantly reduce the extent to which wages councils are a substitute for collective bargaining.

IV.2   Economic Analysis of Unions

The existence and activities of trade unions raise very large questions in the fields of politics, sociology and law. On a somewhat narrower and more practical front, trade unions have had a considerable influence on the operation of work rules, consultation procedures and worker representation. Economists, however, have tended to concentrate on the impact of trade unions on wages and resource allocation.

The theoretical analysis of union behaviour by economists is not very satisfactory. At its simplest, the union is often assumed to have organized all the relevant workers and to be facing a set of unorganized employers. In many respects, the analysis is analogous to the standard treatment of monopolies in product markets. In this context, the decision that the union has to make is to trade off jobs for higher wages.

The union is seen to face a given demand curve for its members' services. Higher wages mean fewer jobs (a) because they tend to raise product prices and reduce product demand, and (b) because they are liable to raise the price of labour relative to other factors of production and encourage factor substitution. In this model, therefore, it is the prospect of reduced employment possibilities that disciplines the union wage claims. In order to predict what a union will decide to press for, it is necessary to know both the elasticity of the demand facing it and the relative value placed by the union on job opportunities and wages. In order to know the latter it is necessary, in the spirit of this model, to know something about how decisions are arrived at within the union.

Economists frequently ignore some of these qualifications and simply predict that unions will secure a greater wage where they face relatively inelastic demand conditions. As a corollary of this prediction, it is also suggested that in situations where demand elasticities are high, a union may have nothing to offer its potential members and may therefore not exist. If we add to this some consideration of the costs of successful organization, we have at least an embryo theory of union-density patterns. It is usually said that such costs are low when the workforce in question is (a) stable and so not subject to high rates of quits or lay-offs, (b) concentrated among relatively few employers, (c) concentrated geographically, and (d) has certain attitudes, e.g. group loyalties.

The simple theory of union behaviour sketched above is greatly weakened by the assumption that employers are not organized but act atomistically. When they too are organized, as they usually are in the UK, we enter the world of bargaining and bilateral monopoly. The theories relating to such a world are often elegant and are sometimes entertaining but they are rarely fruitful. Certainly they have not yet produced operational models that have been widely accepted by those who wish to understand the real world. This failure is not confined to the analysis of union behaviour but appears throughout economics whenever strategic, or 'game', situations are central. We therefore have in this area a fragile theoretical platform from which to survey and analyse the real world.

Turning now to empirical work, it is possible to investigate the impact of unions on (a) relative average wages between trades, (b) the dispersion of wages within trades, and (c) average real wages. Most of the recent research has been concerned with the first of these three dimensions. The standard approach is to use multiple regression analysis to isolate and measure the impact of unions on relative wages once other possible influences have been taken into account. A great variety of 'other possible influences' have been considered and different authors have investigated different wage structures. Attention has most commonly been focused on average wages by manufacturing industry for manual male workers.

The early research in this area concluded that unions had a very powerful effect on relative wages. Estimates of the union mark-up – i.e. the difference in average wages, other things equal, between a wholly unionized industry and one where unions were completely absent – were of the order of 20–30%.[1] More recent estimates have been much lower. These have come from enquiries using the same general procedure but different kinds of data. In particular, the data have referred to individual workers or individual establishments rather than to broad industry averages. For various technical reasons these newer estimates are likely to be more accurate. For example, it is probable that they can more accurately take into account the fact that the unionized and non-unionized are dissimilar types of workers and should not be compared without careful qualification.

The newer studies suggest that the average union mark-up tends to be 10% or less.[2] This seems a much more plausible number than the earlier estimates. If unions really did raise relative wages by an average of 30%, it would be difficult to understand why the whole labour force was not unionized. Even the newer mark-up estimates are not beyond criticism, however, and future research might well reach significantly different conclusions. Thus, if the standard approach were applied to non-manual workers it might find that the mark-up was negative. The best interpretation of this finding would not be that unions reduced the earnings of their non-manual members, but that union membership tends to be high among low-wage non-manuals and low among those towards the top of hierarchies. In other words, union-density patterns may be both a consequence and a determinant of relative wages.

1   D. Metcalf, 'Unions, Incomes Policy and Relative Wages in G.B.', *BJIR*, July 1977.

2   M. Stewart, '*Relative Earnings and Individual Union Membership in the UK*', *EC*, May 1983. D. Blanchflower, 'What Effects Do Unions Have on Relative Wages in Great Britain?', *BJIR*, July 1986.

Apart from having a significant effect on relative average earnings between industries, unions also tend to compress the distribution of earnings within industries and occupations. An emphasis on 'the rate for the job' is a frequent and explicit union goal. It is seen to increase group cohesiveness, solidarity and determination, fundamental requisites of successful trade unions.

Finally, there is the impact of unions on real wages. The theoretical analysis on this question is complex, and the empirical work is very scanty. Real wages are a reflection of (a) labour productivity and (b) the bargaining power of labour over the division of total output. It is obviously likely that unions tend to increase labour's bargaining power, at least for a period. It may of course be the case that in the very long run most, or even all, groups of workers face highly elastic demand conditions for their services and enjoy no permanent bargaining power. Over a period of many decades, however, large numbers of workers can clearly gain significant bargaining power through collective action. The degree and duration will clearly vary from case to case. The impact of unions on labour productivity, however, is very much less clear.

The traditional view is that the impact of unions on their members' productivity should be broken down into a number of steps. First, any rise in wages that a union secures for its members is very likely to raise the capital/labour ratio, as factor substitution takes place. This will, in turn, raise labour productivity in the unionized sector (the capital/labour ratio, and hence labour productivity, in the non-unionized sector might fall or rise). A second consequence of the higher wage is that more productive workers might be encouraged to move to the unionized sector. This would also raise labour productivity there but would clearly reduce it in the sectors which the more productive workers left.

Over and above these effects, the standard analysis of union behaviour suggests that unions will tend to be responsible for a lowering of labour productivity. They are widely believed, and in some cases known, to institute and consolidate a large variety of restrictive labour practices, in the form of manning rules, job demarcation rules, etc. They are also believed to resist the rapid introduction of technological changes. In some cases this might be root-and-branch opposition, while more commonly it is associated with extensive and detailed consultation, as well as extra compensation. One study claimed that a very significant part of the difference in productivity between comparable British and foreign plants could be attributed to restrictive practices.[1]

There is, however, an alternative view that has begun to be investigated with some seriousness, so far exclusively in the US. This view does not deny that unions may be instrumental in promoting restrictive labour prac-

---

1   C.F. Pratten, *Labour Productivity Differentials within International Companies* (CUP, 1976).

tices, but it suggests that these should be set against a second set of factors. A non-unionized workforce, it is claimed, may have a range of discontents and grievances which are not being effectively communicated to management. As a result, it is argued, workers will have poor motivation, low performance levels, high absenteeism and high voluntary turnover, all of which raise costs and reduce productivity. Finally, it is claimed, unionization may ameliorate these problems by forcing management to consider and perhaps deal with the workers' discontents. This could raise performance, reduce absenteeism and turnover, make training more profitable than it would otherwise be and raise labour productivity. The empirical work explicitly considering these possibilities in the US has concluded that on balance unions raise labour productivity, i.e. that the advantages via better communications are greater than the disadvantages from restrictive practices.[1]

As might be expected, this recent work has generated substantial controversy and disagreement.[2] To some it seemed that the estimated increases in productivity were so large that we should expect to see managements encouraging unions to organize their workers. This does not, of course, follow. Any increase in productivity would have to be set against wage increases and there is no presumption that the net effect would be to lower costs. The other criticisms of the new work are fairly technical, some of them revolving around severe measurement problems. There is, however, another interpretation of the statistical findings. If labour productivity is relatively high in unionized firms, it does not follow that unions have been responsible for raising productivity over what it would otherwise have been. It may merely be that unions tend to be found in plants where labour productivity is high for other reasons, for example in large plants with high capital/labour ratios and a degree of monopoly power in the product market. It is perfectly possible that unions could be reducing labour productivity through restrictive practices but still leaving it higher than in non-unionized plants or industries.

The last point to be considered is at whose expense, if anybody's, these various union effects are made. If unions secure higher wages for their members, who loses? If unions really do raise labour productivity, it could be that no one loses, that the gain is an uncovenanted benefit. For the other effects, however, a loss could fall (a) on the employer, in the form of lower profits, (b) on consumers, in the form of higher prices, (c) on workers who are not union members, in the form of lower wages elsewhere and reduced job opportunities in the unionized sectors, or (d) on taxpayers, in the form of higher taxes to pay for larger industrial subsidies, e.g. to nationalized industries. Examples can be found of each of those

1   R. Freeman and J. Medoff, *What Do Unions Do?* (Basic Books, 1984).
2   J. Addison and A. Barnett, 'The Impact of Unions on Productivity', *BJIR*, July 1982.

groups having been adversely affected by particular union activities, but it is not possible to say where, on average, any burden does fall.

IV.3 Strikes

The significance of strikes can be measured by the number of stoppages that occur, by the number of workers involved in the stoppages and by the number of working days lost through stoppages. The official estimates of all of these measures are known to be something of an understatement because they exclude most of the stoppages which last for less than one day, as well as those which involve fewer than ten workers. Further, the official figures include only those stoppages deemed to result from industrial disputes over terms and conditions of employment. Those deemed to be 'political' are excluded. Finally, there is no obligation on the parties to report stoppages, and many that take place may not be picked up.

The most volatile of the three measures is the series on working days lost. In recent years it has ranged from a peak of nearly 29m in 1979 down to 3.8m in 1983. The number of stoppages has also fallen, down to about 1,200 in 1984, as against more than double that figure during most of the 1960s and 1970s. These figures put the strike problem into perspective. If the coalminers' strike is excluded, the number of working days lost through stoppages in 1984 is officially estimated at under 5 million. When this is divided by the number of employees, it can be seen that the average UK employee loses less than 2 hours a year by striking. For the economy as a whole, in contrast to particular industries, the economic significance of strikes can easily be exaggerated.[1]

Although the UK has a rather poor international reputation for strikes, its performance, as measured by working days lost per thousand employees, is not unusual for a developed economy. During the last decade the UK has usually lost many fewer days than Spain, Italy or Eire, and significantly fewer than Canada. Finland and Australia; however, the record is much poorer when compared with Holland, Japan, West Germany and France.

The incidence of strikes is very unevenly distributed across workers, firms, industries and occupations. Industries that typically lose a relatively high number of days per worker through strikes include drink, many of the engineering industries, especially motor vehicles, printing and some of the transport industries. Other industries, for example agriculture, clothing, textiles, gas, electricity and water, and most of the private-sector service industries, tend to lose very few days through strikes.

It is important to note that the very great majority of workplaces experi-

---

1 *DEG*, August 1985, pp. 295–306.

ence no strikes at all in any one year. This is clearly evident in the official figures and is confirmed in a number of large-scale surveys. The latest of these, relating to the year up to mid-1980, a year of relatively high strike incidence, produced some very interesting but complex results. First it confirmed that strikes are but one form of industrial action, and not necessarily the one to which workers usually have recourse. Thus, for manual workers as a whole, the strike was only marginally more frequent than were all other forms, including overtime bans, working-to-rule, go-slows or blacking of work. For non-manual workers, these other forms of industrial action were more common than strikes.

The study also sought to shed fresh light on what factors were associated with the taking of industrial action in one form or another. It concluded, first, that size of establishment was strongly associated with strike activity. More precisely, manuals (and non-manuals) were more likely to take industrial action in plants with large numbers of fellow manual (non-manual) workers. In addition to plant size, industrial action among manual workers was also found to be higher where union density was high, where the proportion of male workers was high, where there was collective bargaining at establishment level, and where there was extensive piece-rate bargaining. Many of these associations were also found for non-manuals.[1]

An important public policy issue of recent years concerns the payment of supplementary benefit (SB) to strikers' families. It is certainly true that state support to strikers' families increased in the 1970s compared with the earlier post-war period. This increase was associated, in part, with a change in the pattern of strikes, in particular with an increase in the number of longer, official strikes, particularly in the public sector (e.g. postmen 1971, miners 1974, firemen 1977, and steelworkers 1980). But the proportion of those eligible who actually received supplementary benefit was, at most, around one-third. Further, SB seems to have played only a minor role in the budgets of those on strike. Only 15% of the postmen's income while on strike came from the state. Strikers and their families relied far more on running down their savings, deferring HP and rent and mortgage payments, living off wives' pay and back-pay, and tax rebates. Gennard provided persuasive evidence that state income support did not cause or prolong strikes.[2] In spite of this, the present government decided to change the rules governing transfer payments to the families of strikers, and generally to reverse the trends of the 1970s. It is certainly true that the number of strikes has fallen substantially since these rules were modified. But such a fall is only to be expected in a period of high and rising unemployment, falling inflation and rising real earnings. Whether the reduction in state support to strikers' families has had

1 Daniel and Millward, *op.cit.*, Chapter IX.

2 J. Gennard, *Financing Strikes* (Macmillan, 1977); see also J. Gennard, 'The Effects of Strike Activity on Households,' *BJIR*, November 1981, and 'The Financial Costs and Returns of Strikes', *BJIR*, July 1982.

an impact after taking these other factors into consideration is by no means clearly established.

IV.4   Industrial Relations

Strike activity is the most heavily publicized aspect of industrial relations but is by no means the most important one. It arouses considerable public comment and often provides dramatic situations with great political significance but, in so doing, it tends to obscure other aspects of the relationships between employer and employee which make up industrial relations. For a number of reasons, the British 'system' of industrial relations has been the subject of much analysis and debate, particularly since the mid-1960s.

Initially many observers were disturbed by the UK's slow rate of growth in comparison to that of the rest of Europe. It was felt by many that our complex, old-fashioned and rather ramshackle industrial relations arrangements had a lot to do with this, It was also widely felt that unions or, more even-handedly, our particular system of collective bargaining, either caused or exacerbated inflation. To these largely economic issues were added related social, legal and political matters. There was, for example, a long-standing debate as to the tactics that were proper in the pursuit of wage claims. There was also a debate on the question of the closed shop, the circumstances in which it should be allowed, and the rights and position of individual workers who did not wish to be union members.

Most generally, there was a growing unease over the power that trade unions were thought to be acquiring. Whether they did grow in power and in what respects this might have happened, and in what ways any such changes might have affected behaviour or events, were all questions whose answers were not easy to establish. But if opinion polls were to be believed, there was a considerable body of opinion in the country which held that in a variety of ways unions were too powerful.

These and other questions prompted a spate of industrial relations legislation. Following the Donovan Commission Report of 1968, the then Labour government proposed reforms but withdrew them in the face of strong union and backbench opposition. It was left to the Conservatives to legislate substantial reform but their Industrial Relations Act (1971) had a stormy history, arousing bitter hostility in the trade-union leadership, before it was repealed in an early action by the Labour government of 1974. That action, the Trade Union and Labour Relations Act, together with the associated Trade Union and Labour Relations (Amendment) Act (1976), in many ways restored the pre-1971 situation, but in some respects the position of trade unions was further strengthened.

Additional industrial relations legislation was also introduced. The Employment Protection Act (1975) encouraged constructive union activity. Employers were, for example, required to disclose certain information judged to be relevant to collective bargaining, consult with unions on the handling of redundancies, and face more pressure to recognize independent trade unions when their employees wished to be represented. The legislation also gave powers to the Advisory, Conciliation and Arbitration Service and extended the legal rights of individual employees, for example in maternity pay and leave provision. The position of unions was also strengthened by the passing of the Health and Safety at Work Act (1975) and the Industry Act (1975).

After its return to power in 1979, the Conservative government adopted a new strategy. Instead of attempting root-and-branch structural reform, in the manner of the 1971 Act, the government introduced a series of relatively limited measures. They were designed, in the words of Sir Geoffrey Howe, 'to create a more reasonable balance of bargaining power between the partners in industry'. The principal measures in this step-by-step approach were the 1980 and 1982 Employment Acts and the 1984 Trade Union Act. Taken together, these Acts did a number of things. For example, they narrowed the limits of legal picketing, they reduced the scope of legal immunities applying to industrial action, they significantly regulated the closed shop and they required a great extension in the use of secret ballots, whether as a prelude to industrial action or for elections to union office. In addition to these three Acts, the government took a number of other steps. For example, in 1982 it announced the abolition of the Fair Wages Resolution, which had required employers with government contracts to pay wages and offer conditions in line with those in their industry locally. Again, in 1984 it declared that no worker employed at certain government establishments could henceforth be a union member; a sum of £1,000 per worker was paid to compensate for the loss of previous rights.

There is no doubt that the trade-union movement felt that it was being attacked by these measures, but their direct influence can easily be overstated. Thus, the new legislation effectively requires regular ballots in closed shop situations to ensure that a substantial majority of workers covered by any agreement supports its continuation. The great majority of such elections so far have supported the agreements and, arguably, have thereby increased their legitimacy. The new legislation, however, was not introduced in circumstances that were otherwise neutral for 'the partners in industry'. The huge loss of employment since 1979, and the sharply increased competitive pressures experienced by many employers, have themselves directly affected the conduct and form of industrial relations. Brown, for example, concludes that during the 1980s 'employment practices have altered at a rate that is probably unprecedented'.[1] By this he means such arrangements as the growth of part-time work, the use of unstandardized shift patterns, self-employment, homeworking, temporary

---

1   W. Brown, 'The Changing Role of Trade Unions in the Management of Labour', *BJIR*, July 1986.

employment, contracting-out, the decline in apprenticeships, the growth of company-specific training and changes in payment methods. All these changes are seen as stemming, in part, from the shock of recession on employers, forcing them to find new ways of raising labour productivity. They will also affect industrial relations, partly by changing the composition of the employed labour force and partly by changing the locus of collective bargaining. Thus, as Brown notes, old-style, multi-employer, industrywide agreements are continuing to give way to single-employer bargaining at company or establishment level. This implies a growing tendency for terms and conditions to be more company-specific, and for workers and trade-union structures to be more fragmented. There is also increased pressure in many firms for long-standing demarcation patterns to be scrapped and for greater labour flexibility to be encouraged. This again has an impact on the loyalties and orientations of workers and, to an extent, of the unions.

These and other pressures, for example falling union membership, have led to new styles of union leadership. This is most prominently associated with the electricians' union, which has been in the forefront of signing so-called 'no strike' agreements with new employers. In return for union recognition and for such concessions as extensive consultation and staff status for manual workers, these agreements usually specify procedural arrangements which are novel to the UK and which substantially reduce, but do not eliminate, the probability of strike action. Questions such as how far these agreements will spread, and how durable and influential they will be, are currently the focus of much research.

IV.5   Wage Inflation and Incomes Policies[1]

Of all the areas of controversy and disagreement in economics, the one that is most confused and least resolved is probably that of inflation, particularly its causes and cures. It is widely agreed that the most important immediate determinant of price inflation is changes in money wages. This is because wages are the major component of production costs and, as a matter of fact, the prices of finished goods usually change only after costs have changed. There are, of course, other components of costs, and changes in these may also affect prices. Thus, the rate of price inflation is additionally affected by changes in (a) non-wage labour costs, e.g. training costs or National Insurance costs, (b) productivity, (c) taxes or subsidies on goods and services, (d) the foreign currency price of imported goods, (e) the exchange rate, and (f) profit margins. In the recent past, each of these has had an influence on the price level for a time but changes in wages have been even more important.

---

1   See also Chapter 1, Section IV.

The determinants of at least some of these non-wage-cost components are not a matter of very great controversy, though they are often very difficult to forecast at any given time. However, there is very little agreement as to what determines the course of wage costs, and correspondingly little agreement on how that course might be changed by policy.

There are, however, many observers who believe that wage inflation is the result of the configuration of unions or of collective bargaining structures. Such analysts have also tended to believe that the course of wage inflation is largely uninfluenced by the unemployment rate, except for relatively brief periods, i.e. they tend to stress the importance of rates of change in unemployment rather than levels of unemployment.

A relatively early expression of this diverse group is to be found in the work of Hines, who attributed wage inflation to trade-union pushfulness. Hines set out an index of trade-union pushfulness $\Delta T = T_t - T_{t-1}$ (where T_t denotes the proportion of the workforce unionized, or union density, in year t). His thesis was that ΔT is a measure of union activity which manifests itself simultaneously both in increased union membership and density and in pressure on money wage rates. He tested this hypothesis with aggregate data from 1893 to 1961 and found, broadly, that through time excess demand for labour had become less important as a cause of inflation and that in the postwar period wage pushfulness was a key factor in the explanation of inflation.[1]

Given the controversial nature of this topic and the originality of Hines' contribution, it is not surprising that the latter has been subjected to careful scrutiny. The most wide-ranging critique was that of Purdy and Zis,[2] who examined Hines' theory, data, estimation technique and interpretation, and re-estimated his model to take account of their various criticisms. When this was done, the impact of ΔT on wage changes, although still positive, was much reduced. This was confirmed by Wilkinson and Burkitt, who used carefully constructed data on unionization by industry and found that ΔT was significantly associated with changes in only one industry, textiles, out of the eleven they studied.[3]

Statistical studies have neither confirmed nor rejected the central place of unions in the inflationary process and, in consequence, the debate concerning the underlying causes of inflation continues unabated. It is generally agreed that a correlation exists between the growth in the money supply and the rate of inflation, and that this correlation is stronger in the long run than in the short run. What is in dispute is whether inflation is caused by excessive growth in the money supply, or whether union power or some other social

1   A. Hines, 'Trade Unions and Wage Inflation in the UK 1893–1961', *RES*, 1964, and A. Hines, 'Wage Inflation in the UK 1948–62: A Disaggregated Study', *EJ*, 1969, pp. 66–89.

2   D. Purdy and G. Zis, 'Trade Unions and Wage Inflation in the UK', in D. Laidler and D. Purdy (eds), *Inflation and Labour Markets* (Manchester UP, 1974).

3   R. Wilkinson and B. Burkitt, 'Wage Determination and Trade Unions', *SJPE*, June 1973.

force causes money wages to rise which in turn induces the authorities to expand the money supply in order that unemployment does not result.

In response to the problem of wage inflation, there have been many attempts since the 1960s to run incomes policies. These have taken a very wide variety of forms. For example, they have differed as to whether they were voluntary or compulsory, as to whether they had a flat-rate norm (i.e. so many pounds per week) or a percentage norm, and as to whether they permitted exceptions or not. The key question for these experiments is whether they were effective. More precisely, any incomes policy is likely to lead to some loss of allocative efficiency in the economy, by inhibiting changes in relative wages. Does it provide some compensating benefits by slowing down the rates of wage and price inflation below what they would otherwise have been?

The accumulated evidence on the effect on wage inflation of incomes policies as they have been applied in the UK suggests very strongly that they have generally been ineffective. Earnings increases are usually reduced below what they would otherwise have been in the early stages of the policy; but increasingly, and most notably when a government is compelled to dismantle the policy, earnings rise again to reach a level very close to that which they would have reached had no such policy ever existed.

For example, a Department of Employment Working Party estimated that over the years 1965, 1966 and 1967 earnings rose about 4% less than they otherwise would have done without a policy, whilst in 1968 and 1969 earnings rose 4% more than they would have done had there never been a policy. The total impact of the policy was nil.[1] This raises the question, why are incomes policies taken off? Presumably the answer is that, at least as they have been applied in the UK, they become politically or economically unsustainable after a while.

This is also the conclusion reached by two extremely thorough studies of the effect of incomes policies over the whole postwar period. In one study the authors summarize all the recent literature and conclude 'incomes policy apparently has little effect either on the wage determination process or on the average rate of wage inflation'.[2]

In the other study, a careful and subtle statistical analysis, the conclusion was that wage increases in the period immediately following the ending of the various policy experiments matched any reductions gained during their operation.[3]

One reason for these findings is that incomes policies have often been introduced while the economy was being expanded. This was notably the

1 DE, *Prices and Earnings in 1951–69*, (HMSO, 1971), para. 57.

2 M. Parkin *et al.*, 'The Impact of Incomes Policy on the Rate of Wage Change', in M. Parkin and M. Sumner (eds), *Incomes Policy and Inflation* (Manchester UP, 1972).

3 S. Henry and P. Ormerod, 'Incomes Policy and Wage Inflation', *NIER*, August 1978, pp. 31–9.

case with the policies of the Conservative government in 1972 and 1973. It is precisely in such circumstances that one might expect least success because tight labour markets lead both workers and employers to try to circumvent the policy, the former because they want higher wages and the latter because they want more labour. Arguably one of the few incomes policy successes was with Stage 1 of the Labour government's policy in 1975. At the time, unemployment was rising rapidly and output was stagnant or falling, so that macroeconomic policy and the incomes policy were working in harmony against inflation. It could be argued that in these circumstances the incomes policy contributed nothing, that the success in reducing inflation should be ascribed to macroeconomic or monetary policy alone. However, most observers agree that the incomes policy at least caused the reduction in wage inflation to come earlier than it would otherwise have done.

Another strand of thinking on incomes policies is that in some circumstances they might raise the rate of wage inflation. This view is based on the proposition that the policy norm might become a floor rather than a ceiling – the norm might be seen as a minimum entitlement. This view probably influenced the Labour government in 1978 when it pitched the norm quite low, at 5%, and hoped that any excess, or drift, would still keep wage inflation in bounds. In the event, the tactic was transparent and the experiment backfired. 5% was judged to be far too low in comparison with most workers' expectations and any small chance that the continuation of the policy might secure official union support disappeared.

In spite of the fact that they are widely judged to have had only a temporary success in reducing the rate of wage inflation, while at the same time frequently giving rise to political embarrassments, incomes policies have always retained their advocates. These usually become more numerous with the passage of time after any previous incomes policy experiment has been scrapped, because the costs of alternative policies then become more clearly revealed. The principal anti-inflation alternative to incomes policy has been economic contraction, either passively tolerated or actively engineered. The deeper that alternative has bitten and the higher the unemployment rate has climbed, the more people have tended to turn back to incomes policies in the hope that they might offer a more sensible and rational way of conducting our economic affairs. In such a context, the failures of previous incomes policies are attributed to errors in their form or design rather than to generic defects.

The most recent revival of interest in incomes policies appeared after about 3 years of seeking to manage the economy without one. During that time, unemployment soared to another postwar record but wage inflation came down only to around 10%. Their advocates began to stress the possibility that incomes policies can increase employment without raising inflation. It was admitted that all incomes policies are likely to generate economic costs; for example, they might make the structure of wages more rigid than it would otherwise be, thereby adversely affecting the efficiency with which labour and other resources are allocated. It was claimed, however, that the size of any such costs was likely to be greatly exceeded by the benefits of a successful incomes policy, in particular by the increase in employment which it would bring about. If there were true, the only problem would be to design a successful policy. In attempting this, some economists began to advocate a form of incomes policy that was originally designed some years ago but never put into practice. Its principal mechanism was a tax levied on employers who grant wage increases in excess of the government's norm.[1]

The main reason for reviving this particular incomes policy variant was the belief that previous policies in the UK did not provide sufficient incentives for wage bargainers to comply with their terms. Even when incomes policies have been statutory in form, their penalties for non-compliance have not usually been clear or believable, particularly to those engaged in wage negotiations. A tax on excess settlements, however, is likely to be clear to everyone, even if some of its implications are in doubt.[2]

Whatever its particular form, the tax is held to give an important additional incentive to employers to resist above-norm settlements; further, any net tax payments would increase total costs of production and thereby threaten employment, so that it might also give trade unions an additional reason not to push as hard for 'excessive' wage increases. Both sides of the labour market are said to be given a clear reason to moderate their wage settlements.

The discussion surrounding this device was necessarily speculative, because it has not so far been tried in practice. However, many observers doubted that it would work effectively for more than a relatively brief period. They looked at the developments in labour markets after 1970 and noted that many firms were under immense and sustained economic pressures. During that time, wage settlements nearly always greatly outstripped productivity increases, even when firms generally faced profits difficulties, liquidity crises, loss of markets and problems of mass redundancies. The picture was similar on the workers' side. The rapid rise in unemployment since 1979 has certainly attenuated wage inflation, but it has not eliminated it. At the beginning of 1986, average money earnings were officially estimated to be still growing at an underlying rate of $7\frac{1}{2}\%$ p.a. This was in spite of an unemployment rate of 14% and an inflation rate of roughly 5%. In these circumstances, the behaviour of money wages is so puzzling that few observers are confident that any mechanism will be a reliable control.

---

1 The idea seems originally to have been proposed by H. Wallich and S. Weintraub, 'A Tax-based Incomes Policy', *Journal of Economic Issues*, June 1971. It has been revived more recently by R. Jackman and R. Layard; see, for example, R. Layard, 'Is Incomes Policy the Answer to Unemployment?', *EC*, August 1982.

2 It should be stressed that different writers favour different taxes, even when they are all sympathetic to the same broad ideas; thus, for example, some would advocate seeking to tax all excess settlements while others, for reasons of administration, would confine the tax to large employers. A complete discussion of the available permutations would take many pages and would be out of place here.

REFERENCES AND FURTHER READING

A.B. Atkinson, *Economics of Inequality* (second edition, Clarendon Press, 1983).

G. Bain (ed.), *Industrial Relations in Britain* (Blackwell, 1983).

Department of Employment, *British Labour Statistics: Historical Abstract 1886–1968* (HMSO, 191).

C. Greenhalgh, R. Layard and A. Oswald (ed.), *The Causes of Unemployment* (Clarendon Press, 1983).

E. Hobsbawm, *Labouring Men* (Weidenfeld and Nicolson, 1968, reissued 1986).

W.J. McCarthy (ed.), *Trade Unions* (second edition, Penguin, 1985).

E.H. Phelps Brown, *The Inequality of Pay* OUP, 1977).

Royal Commission on the Distribution of Income and Wealth, *An A to Z of Income and Wealth* (HMSO, 1980).

Statistical Appendix

TABLE A-1
UK Gross Domestic Product, Expenditure (at 1980 prices), 1973–85 (£m)

Year	Consumers' Expenditure		General Government Final Consumption	Gross Domestic Capital Formation		Value of Physical Increase in Stocks and Work in Progress	Exports of Goods and Services	Total Final Expenditure at Market Prices[2]	Imports of Goods and Services	Adjustment to Factor Cost[1]	Gross Domestic Product at Factor Cost[2]
	Durable Goods	Non-Durable Goods and Services		Excluding Dwellings	Dwellings						
1973	12,644	115,034	43,119	33,882	9,472	5,025	49,149	268,195	−52,544	−28,013	187,122
1974	11,074	114,754	43,926	33,356	8,922	2,278	52,755	266,980	−53,223	−27,080	185,834
1975	11,263	113,655	46,377	32,400	9,140	−2,644	51,315	261,320	−49,469	−26,999	184,499
1976	11,818	113,485	46,951	32,786	9,431	1,235	55,919	271,493	−51,539	−28,120	191,466
1977	10,993	113,638	46,175	32,465	8,976	2,602	59,611	274,426	−52,177	−28,242	193,576
1978	12,690	118,931	47,220	33,678	9,048	2,208	60,735	284,510	−54,203	−31,048	199,259
1979	14,411	123,141	48,257	34,658	9,197	2,534	63,129	295,327	−59,891	−31,890	203,546
1980	13,673	123,322	48,906	33,132	8,456	−2,875	63,115	287,729	−57,718	−30,765	199,246
1981	13,789	122,722	48,943	30,692	7,222	−2,484	62,042	282,926	−55,918	−30,021	196,987
1982	14,475	123,117	49,360	32,207	7,892	−1,121	62,790	288,720	−58,744	−30,562	199,414
1983	16,629	126,287	50,240	33,247	8,931	673	64,401	300,408	−62,123	−31,537	206,748
1984	16,800	128,751	50,919	36,598	8,932	−142	69,062	310,920	−68,015	−32,700	210,205
1985	17,383	132,273	51,175	37,376	8,589	878	73,239	320,913	−70,069	−33,627	217,217

Sources: National Accounts 1985: *ET*, April 1986; *ET(AS)*, 1986.
Notes: 1 This represents taxes on expenditure, less subsidies valued at constant prices.
2 For the years before 1978, totals differ from the sum of their components.

National Insurance and Health Contribu- tions	Total Personal Dispo- sable Income[2]	CONSUMERS' EXPENDITURE				PERSONAL SAVINGS		
		Durable Goods		Other				
		Amount (£m)	As % of PDI	Amount (£m)	Total	Amount (£m)[2]	As % of PDI	Year
9	10	11	12	13	14	15	16	
3,937	52,235	4,538	8.7	41,466	46,004	6,231	11.9	1973
5,000	60,240	4,658	7.7	48,411	53,069	7,171	11.9	1974
6,848	74,805	5,872	7.8	59,339	65,211	9,594	12.8	1975
8,426	86,058	6,986	8.1	68,689	75,675	10,383	12.1	1976
9,508	97,781	7,754	7.9	78,724	86,478	11,303	11.6	1977
10,107	114,089	10,228	9.0	89,420	99,648	14,441	12.7	1978
11,531	136,648	13,138	9.6	105,018	118,156	18,492	13.5	1979
13,944	161,182	13,673	8.5	123,322	136,995	24,187	15.0	1980
15,923	175,547	14,226	8.1	138,019	152,245	23,302	13.3	1981
18,106	191,113	15,452	8.1	151,112	166,564	24,549	12.8	1982
20,749	205,830	18,243	8.9	163,808	182,051	23,779	11.6	1983
22,220	220,913	19,251	8.7	174,630	193,881	27,032	12.2	1984
23,974	237,868	21,002	8.8	189,096	210,098	27,770	11.7	1985

TABLE A-4
UK Population, Working Population, Unemployment and Vacancies, 1973–85 (thousands)

Year	Total Population (Mid-year estimate) [1]	Working Population [1,2] [2]	Unemployed including school-leavers[1] (Monthly average) [3]	Unemployed excluding school-leavers[3] (Monthly average) [4]	Unemployment Rate (%)[4] [5]	Vacancies (Monthly average)[5,6] [6]
1973	56,210	25,613	557	744	2.4	307
1974	56,224	25,658	528	826	2.4	297
1975	56,215	25,877	838	591	3.7	154
1976	56,206	26,094	1,265	902	5.0	122
1977	56,179	26,209	1,359	1,313	5.3	155
1978	56,167	26,342	1,343	1,299	5.1	210
1979	56,227	26,609	1,235	1,227	4.8	241
1980	56,314	26,819	1,513	1,561	6.1	143
1981	56,379	26,718	2,395	2,420	9.5	91
1982	56,335	26,663	2,770	2,793	11.0	114
1983	56,277	26,575	2,984	2,970	12.1	137
1984	56,488	27,014	3,030	3,047	12.6	150
1985[7]	n.a.	27,418	3,179	3,163	13.1	162

Sources: Column 1: *MDS* March 1986; Columns 2 and 3: *ET(AS)*, 1986, and *MDS*, March 1986; Columns 4 and 5: *MDS*, March 1986; Column 6: *ET*, April 1986, *ET(AS)*, 1986; *DEG* May 1986 and previous issues; Column 6: *ET*, April 1986, *ET(AS)*, 1986.

Notes:
1 Estimates are for June of each year.
2 The Working Population includes employees in employment, self-employed persons, HM Forces and the unemployed (including school-leavers).
3 From April 1, 1983 figures are affected by the 1983 Budget provision for some men aged 60 and over, who no longer have to sign on at an unemployment benefit office.
4 The unemployment rate is obtained by dividing the monthly average unemployment figure by the relevant figure for total employees (including unemployed) for June of that year; self-employed and HM Forces are excluded from the figure for total employees.
5 Figures for 1974, 1975, 1976 and 1977 are based on estimates for some of the months.
6 The method of compiling vacancy statistics was changed in October 1985. Data back to 1980 have been revised.
7 The estimate for Column 1 for 1985 is not available.

TABLE A-5
UK General Government: Current Account, 1972–84 (£m)

	1972	1973	1974	1975	1976	1977	1978	1979	1980	1981	1982	1983	1984
RECEIPTS													
Taxes on income	8,116	9,257	12,716	16,758	18,969	20,476	22,617	25,242	30,875	36,023	40,545	43,182	46,635
Taxes on expenditure	9,191	10,050	11,374	14,036	16,284	19,836	22,752	29,710	36,355	42,389	46,529	49,176	52,578
National Insurance, etc. contributions	3,337	3,937	5,000	6,848	8,426	9,508	10,107	11,531	13,944	15,923	18,106	20,688	22,484
Gross Trading Surplus	162	150	132	115	131	160	185	149	132	155	113	−76	−250
Rent, etc.[1]	782	943	1,276	1,524	1,942	2,256	2,517	3,173	4,251	4,713	4,858	4,824	5,355
Interest and dividends, etc.	1,171	1,374	1,722	1,996	2,354	2,534	2,721	3,235	3,767	4,280	5,333	4,977	5,028
Miscellaneous current transfers	46	55	57	73	118	136	151	136	164	164	184	214	223
Imputed charge for consumption of non-trading capital	402	444	584	766	907	1,032	1,173	1,394	1,744	1,961	2,034	2,111	2,190
Total[2]	23,209	26,184	32,861	42,134	49,131	55,938	62,223	74,570	91,232	105,608	117,702	125,096	134,243
EXPENDITURE													
Current expenditure on goods and services	11,740	13,396	16,130	22,353	26,133	28,441	32,223	37,458	47,162	53,396	58,346	63,587	67,465
Non-trading capital consumption			584	766	907	1,032	1,173	1,394	1,744	1,961	2,034	2,111	2,190
Subsidies	1,154	1,480	3,056	3,675	3,421	3,194	3,615	4,485	5,590	6,355	5,903	6,474	7,797
Grants to personal sector	5,837	6,411	7,863	10,263	12,731	15,054	17,924	20,957	25,533	31,122	36,298	39,419	42,703
Current grants abroad (net)	220	344	302	337	776	1,083	1,664	2,018	1,782	1,634	1,798	1,954	2,090
Debt interest	2,276	2,669	3,491	4,121	5,290	6,287	7,097	8,685	10,896	12,706	13,988	14,208	15,659
Total current expenditure	21,227	24,300	31,426	41,515	49,258	55,091	63,696	74,997	92,707	107,174	118,367	127,753	137,904
Balance: current surplus[3]	1,982	1,884	1,435	619	−127	847	−1,473	−427	−1,475	−1,566	−665	−2,657	−3,661
Total	23,209	26,184	32,861	42,134	49,131	55,938	62,223	74,570	91,232	105,608	117,702	125,096	134,243

Sources: *NIE*, 1983, 1984, 1985.
Notes: 1 Includes royalties and licence fees on oil and gas production.
2 For the years before 1974, totals differ from the sum of their components.
3 Before providing for depreciation and stock appreciation.

TABLE A-6
UK Money Stock, Domestic Credit Expansion, Public Sector Borrowing Requirement (£m), Interest Rates and Exchange Rate, 1973–85

Year	Money Stock[1,4] (M_1)	Money Stock[2,4] (Sterling M_3)	Money Stock[3,4] (M_3)	Change in Money Stock[5] (Sterling M_3)	Public Sector Borrowing Requirement[6]	Yield on UK Treasury bills (%)	Yield on 2½% Consols (%)	Sterling Effective Exchange Rate[7]
	1	2	3	4	5	6	7	8
1973	13,303	31,321	32,753	6,602	4,100	12.82	10.85	116.3
1974	14,739	34,644	37,042	3,324	6,439	11.30	14.95	112.7
1975	17,387	36,574	39,513	2,083	10,211	10.93	14.66	104.1
1976	19,335	40,107	44,003	3,533	8,957	13.98	14.25	89.2
1977	23,523	43,876	48,027	3,769	5,475	6.39	12.31	84.5
1978	27,364	50,579	55,378	6,703	8,416	11.91	11.93	84.8
1979	29,856	57,230	62,432	6,651	12,679	16.49	11.39	90.8
1980	31,044	67,810	73,999	10,595	11,822	13.58	11.88	100.0
	34,452	77,155	87,027					
1981	36,533	84,592	94,441	9,295	10,590	15.39	12.99	99.2
1982	40,657	92,113	104,869	7,515	4,954	9.96	11.90	94.4
1983	45,190	102,309	118,736	9,480	11,609	9.04	10.24	86.7
1984	52,164	112,561	133,512	9,847	10,213	9.33	10.15	82.0
1985	61,606	127,662	148,015	15,081	7,628	11.48	10.11	81.9

Sources: Columns 1–3: *AAS*, 1985, 1986 and *FS*, April 1986; Column 4: *ET(AS)*, 1986 and *FS*, April 1986; Column 5: *AAS*, 1985, 1986 and *FS*, April 1986; Column 6: *ET(AS)*, 1986 and *ET*, April 1986; Column 7: *AAS*, 1985, 1986 and *FS*, April 1986; Column 8: *ET(AS)*, 1986, *ET*, April 1986, *FS*, April 1986.

Notes :

1   M_1 consists of notes and coins in circulation plus sterling deposits held by the private sector.

2   Sterling M_3 is a wide definition of the money stock. It includes notes and coins, together with all sterling deposits (including certificates of deposit) held by residents in the private and public sectors.

3   This is column 2, plus all deposits held by UK residents in other countries.

4   The money stock series contains a number of breaks caused by changes in the method of compilation of the series and, in particular, a major break at the end of 1980, for which two figures are shown above. The figures given here should be used with caution and reference should be made to the listed official publications for details of the statistical changes and the quantitative significance of the breaks.

5   For various reasons partly covered in Note 4, the annual change given in column 4 is not necessarily equal to the first difference of column 2.

6   The public sector includes the central government, the local authorities and public corporations. The borrowing requirement is discussed in Chapter 2.

7   This is a trade-weighted index of the foreign-exchange value of sterling. The official index is based on 1975 = 100 but for this table, the figures have been recalculated to give 1980 = 100. A decline in the index indicates an overall depreciation of sterling.

TABLE A-7
UK Balance of Payments, 1973–85(£m)

	CURRENT ACCOUNT[1]						
	Visible Trade			Invisibles			
Year	Exports (f.o.b.)	Imports (f.o.b.)	Visible Balance	Government Services and Transfers (net)	Private Services and Transfers (net)	Interest, Profits and Dividends (net)	Invisible Balance
	1	2	3	4	5	6	7
1973	11,937	14,523	−2,586	−753	994	1,327	1,568
1974	16,394	21,745	−5,351	−821	1,348	1,507	2,034
1975	19,330	22,663	−3,333	−906	1,767	890	1,751
1976	25,191	29,120	−3,929	−1,428	2,887	1,557	3,016
1977	31,728	34,012	−2,284	−1,783	3,693	246	2,156
1978	35,063	36,605	−1,542	−2,397	4,084	827	2,514
1979	40,687	44,136	−3,449	−2,824	4,349	1,188	2,713
1980	47,422	46,061	1,361	−2,481	4,439	−219	1,739
1981	50,977	47,617	3,360	−2,493	4,411	948	2,866
1982	55,565	53,234	2,331	−3,150	3,794	1,058	1,702
1983	60,776	61,611	−835	−3,006	4,537	2,468	3,999
1984	70,367	74,758	−4,391	−3,253	5,181	3,342	5,270
1985	78,072	80,140	−2,068	−4,612	7,338	2,294	5,020

Sources: *ET(AS)*, 1986, *ET*, March 1986.
Notes: 1 All items listed represent a positive flow if unsigned. Negative flows are indicated by a − sign preceding the figure. For capital-account items, a positive flow represents an increase in assets or a reduction in liabilities.
      2 Includes Capital Transfers for 1973 (−£59m) and 1974 (−£75m).
      3 The sum of columns 8, 13 and 14 is defined in official sources as 'Balance for Official Financing'. The balance is normally the negative of the items, shown in Column 15. For certain years this relationship is disturbed by special items which should be added to the sum of Columns 8, 13 and 14 in order to get the appropriate figure for Column 15. The special items during the period covered by this Table relate to various allocations of SDRs as follows: 1979, +195; 1980, +180; 1981, +158.

INVESTMENT AND OTHER CAPITAL TRANSACTIONS[1]

Current Balance	Official Long-term Capital	Overseas Long-term Investment in UK Private and Public Sectors	UK Private Long-term Investment Overseas	Other Capital Flows Mainly Short-term	Total Investment and Other Capital Trans-actions[2]	Balancing Item	Total Official Financing[3]
8	9	10	11	12	13	14	15
−1,018	−255	1,497	−1,760	696	119	128	771
−3,317	−287	2,204	−1,148	833	1,527	144	1,646
−1,582	−291	1,514	−1,367	298	154	−37	1,465
−913	−161	2,091	−2,269	−2,638	−2,977	261	3,629
−128	−303	4,399	−2,334	2,407	4,169	3,320	−7,361
972	−336	1,877	−4,604	−1,194	−4,257	2,159	1,126
−736	−401	4,282	−6,802	4,757	1,836	610	−1,905
3,100	−91	5,206	−8,150	1,488	−1,547	−361	−1,372
6,226	−336	3,447	−10,389	97	−7,184	−110	687
4,033	−337	3,487	−10,910	4,107	−3,654	−1,663	1,284
3,164	−380	5,083	−11,596	1,640	−5,254	1,270	820
879	−327	3,594	−15,377	6,397	−5,713	3,518	1,316
2,952	−310	7,480	−22,247	12,217	−2,860	835	−927

TABLE A-8
Production in Industry, 1973–85 (index numbers, 1980 = 100)

	1973	1974	1975	1976	1977	1978	1979	1980	1981	1982	1983	1984	1985
Energy	55.8	52.1	54.5	60.8	74.8	85.0	100.5	100.0	103.9	110.0	115.8	110.1	120.0
Manufacturing													
Food, drink, tobacco	96.0	95.4	92.8	95.6	97.0	99.4	100.9	100.0	98.2	99.8	101.0	102.1	102.2
Chemicals	98.7	103.1	92.3	104.2	107.1	108.5	111.2	100.0	99.6	99.7	107.5	113.9	118.0
Metals	155.1	142.3	123.0	131.4	129.4	126.8	132.1	100.0	106.1	103.2	104.5	108.4	112.9
Engineering & Allied inds.	114.2	116.1	110.0	107.8	110.0	109.6	107.2	100.0	91.8	92.9	94.9	99.2	104.4
Building materials	128.6	122.3	112.7	112.8	111.9	114.2	111.8	100.0	89.1	90.9	93.9	95.1	93.9
Textiles, clothing	128.7	121.6	116.7	117.1	120.6	119.4	117.9	100.0	92.7	91.2	94.6	97.9	101.7
Other manufacturing	114.6	109.7	98.5	103.4	106.5	109.2	111.7	100.0	93.2	90.8	93.6	97.7	99.0
Total Manufacturing	114.1	112.7	104.9	106.9	108.9	109.6	109.4	100.0	94.0	94.2	96.9	100.7	103.9
Production Industries	99.4	97.4	92.2	95.2	100.1	103.1	107.0	100.0	96.6	98.4	101.9	103.2	108.2
Construction	122.4	109.7	103.9	102.5	102.1	105.0	105.6	100.0	89.9	91.6	95.3	98.6	99.9[1]
Production and Construction	102.5	98.8	93.5	95.8	99.8	103.4	106.8	100.0	95.6	97.4	100.9	102.5	106.7[1]

Source: *NIER, MDS*. The headings are those of the 1980 Standard Industrial Classification (SIC).
Note: 1 Estimate based on figures for the first three quarters of 1985 and 1984.

TABLE A-9
GDP by Industry[1]

	1960		1973		1984	
	£m	(%)	£m	(%)	£m	(%)
Agriculture, forestry and fishing	913	(4.0)	2,006	(3.0)	5,966	(2.1)
Energy and water supply	1,297	(5.7)	3,018	(4.6)	31,541	(11.3)
Manufacturing	8,244	(36.5)	20,919	(31.7)	68,375	(24.4)
Construction	1,363	(6.0)	4,995	(7.6)	15,838	(5.7)
Distribution, hotels and catering; repairs	2,756	(12.2)	8,982	(13.6)	37,048	(13.2)
Transport	1,532	(6.8)	3,248	(4.9)	12,204	(4.4)
Communication	421	(1.9)	1,608	(2.4)	7,609	(2.7)
Banking, finance, insurance, business services and leasing	681	(3.0)	4,709[2]	(7.1)	21,916[2]	(7.8)
Ownership of dwellings	901	(4.0)	3,525	(5.3)	16,695	(6.0)
Public administration, national defence and compulsory social security	1,323	(5.9)	4,220	(6.4)	18,864	(6.7)
Education and health services	906	(4.0)	5,276	(8.0)	25,652	(9.2)
Other services	2,545	(11.3)	3,507	(5.3)	18,201	(6.5)
GDP at factor cost	22,583	(100.0)	66,013	(100.0)	279,909	(100.0)

Notes: 1 The contribution of each industry to GDP before providing for depreciation but after providing for stock appreciation. Comparisons across years may be affected by revisions in SIC definitions of industries or sectors.
2 After deducting financial companies' net receipts of interest.

TABLE A-10
Regional Unemployment Rates (%), 1966 and 1975-85[1]

	1966	1975	1976	1977	1978	1979	1980	1981	1982	1983	1984	1985
Northern Ireland	5.3	7.4	9.5	10.5	11.0	10.7	12.8	16.8	18.7	20.2	20.9	21.0
Scotland	2.7	5.0	6.7	7.7	7.7	7.4	9.1	12.4	14.0	14.9	15.1	15.7
North	2.5	5.8	7.2	8.0	8.6	8.3	10.4	14.7	16.6	17.9	18.3	18.8
North West	1.4	5.2	6.7	7.0	6.9	6.5	8.5	12.7	14.7	15.8	15.9	16.3
Wales	2.8	5.5	7.1	7.6	7.7	7.3	9.4	13.5	15.4	16.0	16.3	17.0
West Midlands	0.8	3.9	5.5	5.5	5.3	5.2	7.3	12.5	14.7	15.7	15.3	15.5
Yorkshire and Humberside	1.1	3.8	5.3	5.5	5.7	5.4	7.3	11.4	13.2	14.1	14.4	15.0
East Anglia	1.4	3.3	4.7	5.1	4.9	4.2	5.3	8.3	9.7	10.3	10.1	10.6
South West	1.7	4.6	6.2	6.5	6.2	5.4	6.4	9.2	10.6	11.2	11.4	12.0
East Midlands	1.0	3.5	4.5	4.8	4.7	4.4	6.1	9.6	11.0	11.8	12.2	12.7
South East	0.9	2.6	4.0	4.3	3.9	3.4	4.2	7.0	8.5	9.3	9.5	9.9
UK	1.4	4.0	5.5	5.8	5.7	5.3	6.8	10.4	12.1	12.9	13.1	13.5

Source: AAS, MDS.

Note: 1 Number of unemployed claimants expressed as a percentage of the estimated total number of employees (employed and unemployed). Figures for 1966 are included for comparison, and because of a significant policy change in that year (see Chapter 4, section V.2).

Index